SIR HUDSON LOWE

MEMOIRS

OF THE

LIFE, EXILE, AND CONVERSATIONS

OF THE

EMPEROR NAPOLEON

BY

THE COUNT DE LAS CASES

WITH PORTRAITS AND OTHER ILLUSTRATIONS

A NEW EDITION IN FOUR VOLUMES

VOL. III.

NEW YORK
WORTHINGTON CO.
747 BROADWAY
1890

on our coasts to the violence of tempests, to the danger
of rocks, to all the hazards of disaster, while we, on the
contrary, had every chance of success, should any unforeseen catastrophe occur from natural events, or the faults
of their admirals, which could not fail to happen in the
course of time. What advantages should we not have
derived from the event ? We, fresh and in excellent condition ; we, waiting only for the opportunity, always ready
to set sail and engage ! Should the English be tired out?
Our vessels would immediately put to sea for the purpose of exercising and training their crews.

On the completion of our armaments and at the approach of the decisive moment, were the English alarmed
for the safety of their island, to collect their strength in
front of their principal arsenals, Plymouth, Portsmouth,
and the Thames, our three divisions of Brest, Cherbourg,
and Antwerp, would attack them, and our wings would
turn then upon Ireland and Scotland. Were they,
relying upon their skill and bravery, resolved to oppose
us in one great body, then the struggle would be reduced
to a decisive issue, of which we should have been at
liberty to choose the *time*, the *place*, and the *opportunity* ;
—and this is what the Emperor called the battle of
Actium, in which, if we were defeated, we should experience but simple losses, while, if we proved victorious,
the enemy would cease to exist. But our triumph, he
maintained, was certain, for the two nations would have
to contend man to man, and we were upwards of forty
millions against fifteen. This was the favourite position
on which he uniformly dwelt. Such was one of his
grand ideas, his gigantic conceptions.

Napoleon has been the founder of so many establishments, that his works and monuments are injurious to
each other by their number, variety, and importance. It
was my earnest wish to have given a full relation of his
works, which were executed at Cherbourg, as well as of
those which he had projected. A person precisely of
the profession best qualified to appreciate the subject, and
one of its brightest ornaments, has promised me a description of them Should he keep his word, it shall be
given hereafter

MEMOIRS

OF

THE EMPEROR NAPOLEON.

THE BILL RESPECTING OUR EXILE.—BEAUMARCHAIS.—
THE WORKS OF CHERBOURG.

JULY 15, 1816. About ten o'clock, the Emperor entered my apartment: he came unawares, as he wished to take a walk. I followed him, and he walked for some time towards the wood, where we were taken up by the calash. A considerable interval had elapsed since he made use of it. I was the only person with him, and the Bill, which related to him, and with the nature of which we were unacquainted, was, during the whole time, the subject of our conversation.

Upon our return, the Emperor, after some hesitation whether he should breakfast under the trees, determined to go in, and remained at home the whole of the day. He dined alone.

He sent for me after dinner: I found him engaged in reading some *Mercures* or old newspapers. He found in them various anecdotes and circumstances respecting Beaumarchais, whom the Emperor, during his Consulate, had, notwithstanding all his wit, uniformly discountenanced, on account of his bad character and his gross immorality. The difference of manners imparted a poignancy to the anecdotes, although the difference of times was so trifling. He found an account of Louis the Sixteenth's visit to Cherbourg, on which he dwelt for some time. He next adverted to the works of Cher-

bourg, and took a rapid review of them, with the clearness, precision, and lively manner that characterized
every thing he said.

Cherbourg is situated at the bottom of a semicircular
bay, the two extremities of which are the Pelée Island
on the right, and Point Querqueville on the left. The
line, by which these two points are connected, forms the
chord or the diameter, and runs East and West.

Opposite to the North, and at a very small distance,
about 20 leagues, is the famous Portsmouth, the grand
arsenal of the English. The remainder of their coast
runs nearly parallel opposite to ours. Nature has done
every thing for our rivals; nothing for us. Their shores
are safe and clear themselves daily from obstructions.
They abound in deep soundings, in the means of shelter,
in harbours and excellent ports; ours are, on the contrary, full of rocks, the water is shallow, and they are
every day choking up. We have not in these parts a single
real port of large dimensions, and it might be said that
the English are, at the same moment, both at home and
on our coast, since it is not requisite for their squadrons,
at anchor in Portsmouth, to put to sea to molest us. A
few light vessels are sufficient to convey intelligence of
our movements, and, in an instant, without trouble or
danger, they are ready to pounce upon their prey.

If, on the contrary, our squadrons are daring enough
to appear in the British Channel, which ought, in reality,
to be called the French Sea, they are exposed to perpetual danger; their total destruction may be effected by
the hurricane or the superiority of the enemy, because in
both these cases there is no shelter for them. This is
what happened at the famous battle of La Hogue, where
Tourville might have united the glory of a skilful retreat
with that of a hard fought and unequal contest, had
there been a port for him to take shelter in.

In this state of things, men of great sagacity and anxious for the welfare of their country, prevailed upon
government, by dint of projects and memorials, to seek,
by the assistance of art, those resources of which we had
been deprived by nature; and, after a great deal of hesitation, the bay of Cherbourg was selected. and it wa.

determined to protect it by an immense dike, projecting into the sea. In that way we were to acquire, even close to the enemy, an artificial road, whence our ships might be able, in all times and in all weathers, to attack his, or to escape his pursuit.

"It was," said the Emperor, "a magnificent and glorious undertaking, very difficult with respect to the execution and to the finances of that period. The dike was to be formed by immense cones constructed empty in the port and towed afterwards to the spot, where they were sunk by the weight of the stones with which they were filled.* There certainly was great ingenuity in the invention. Louis XVI. honoured these operations with his presence. His departure from Versailles was a great event. In those times, a king never left his residence, his excursions did not extend beyond the limits of a hunting party; they did not hurry about as at present, and I really believe that I contributed not a little to the rapidity of their movements.

"However, as it was absolutely necessary that things should be impressed with the character of the age, the eternal rivalry between the land and sea, that question which can never be decided, continued to be carried on. It might have been said in that respect, that there were two kings in France, or that he who reigned had two interests, and ought to have two wills, which proved rather that he had none at all. Here the sea was the only subject for consideration, yet the question was decided in favour of the land, not by superiority of argument, but by priority of right. Where the fate of the empire was at stake, a point of precedence was substituted, and thus the grand object, the magnificent enterprise, failed of success. The land-party established itself at Pelée Island and at fort Querqueville; it was employed there merely to lend an auxiliary hand to the construction of the dike, which was itself the chief object; but instead of that, it began by establishing its own predominance, and afterwards compelled the dike to become

---

* The diameter of these cones, which were 60 feet high, was 104 feet at the base, and 60 at the top.

the instrument of its convenience, and subservient to its plans and discretion. What was the result? The harbour, which was forming and which was intended to contain the mass of our navy, whether designed to strike at the heart of the enemy's power, or to take occasional shelter, could only accommodate fifteen sail at most, while we wanted anchorage for more than a hundred, which might have been effected without more labour and with little more expense, had the works been carried more forward into the sea, merely beyond the limits which the land-party had appropriated to itself.

" Another blunder highly characteristic, and scarcely conceivable, took place. All the principal measures for completing the harbour were fixed upon; the dike commenced; one of the channels, that to the eastward, finished, and the other to the westward was on the point of being formed, without an exact and precise knowledge of all the soundings. This oversight was so great that the channel already formed, that to the eastward, five hundred fathoms broad, having been carried too close to the fort, did not, without inconvenience, admit vessels at low water, and that the other, which was about to be constructed to the westward, would have been impracticable, or at least very dangerous, but for the individual zeal of one officer (M. de Chavagnac), who made that important discovery in time, and caused the works on the left extremity of the dike to be stopped at the distance of twelve hundred fathoms from fort Querqueville, by which it was to be defended. This seems to me, and is, in fact, too great a distance.*

" The system adopted in the works of the dike, which is more than a league from the shore, and more than 1900 fathoms long by 90 feet broad, was also subjected to numerous changes, suggested, however, by experience.

---

* It was not until 1789, five years after the commencement of these works, that orders were given by government for taking the soundings of the harbour and ascertaining the state of the bottom. Up to that time, the works had been carried on solely on vague and imperfect notions!! (Mémoire du Baron Cachin, Inspecteur Général des ponts et chaussées.)

The cones, which, according to the established principle, ought to have touched each other at their bases, were, in that respect, either separated by accident or with a view to economy. They were damaged by storms, eaten by worms, or rotted with age. They were at length altogether neglected, with the exception of stones thrown at random into the sea; and when it was observed that these were scattered by the rolling of the waves, recourse was had to enormous blocks, which finally answered every expectation.

"The works were continued, without interruption, under Louis XVI. An encreased degree of activity was imparted to them by our legislative assemblies; but in consequence of the commotions which soon followed, they were completely abandoned, and at the time of the Consulate, not a trace of that famous dike was to be seen. Every thing had been destroyed for several feet under low water level, by the original imperfection of the plan, by the length of time, and the violence of the waves.

" The moment, however, I took the helm of affairs, one of the first things I did was to turn my attention to so important a point. I ordered commissions of inquiry; I had the subject discussed in my presence; I made myself acquainted with the local circumstances; and I decided that the dike should be run up with all possible expedition, and that two solid fortifications should, in the course of time, be constructed at the two extremities; but that measures should be immediately taken for the establishment of a considerable provisional battery. I had then to encounter, on all sides, the inconveniencies, the objections, the particular views, the fondness which attaches itself to individual opinions, &c. Several maintained that the thing certainly could not be done; I continued steady, I insisted, I commanded, and the thing was done. In less than two years, a real island was seen rising as it were, by magic, from the sea, on which was erected a battery of large calibre. Until that moment, our labours had almost constantly been the sport of the English; they had, they said, been convinced, from their origin, that they would prove fruitless;

they had foretold that the cones would destroy themselves, that the small stones would be swept away by the waves, and above all, they relied upon our lassitude and our inconstancy. But here things were completely altered, and they made a shew of molesting our operations; they were, however, too late; I was already prepared for them. The western channel naturally continued very wide, and the two extreme fortifications, which defended, each its peculiar passage, being incapable of maintaining a cross-fire, it was probable that an enterprising enemy might be enabled to force the western channel, come to an anchor within the dike, and there renew the disaster of Aboukir. But I had already guarded against this with my central provisional battery. However, as I am for permanent establishments, I ordered within the dike, in the centre, by way of support, and which in its turn might serve as an envelope, an enormous elliptical paté to be constructed, commanding the central battery, and mounted itself in two casemated stories, bomb-proof, with 50 pieces of large calibre and 20 mortars of an extensive range, as well as barracks, powder-magazine, cistern, &c.

" I have the satisfaction of having left this noble work in a finished state.

" Having provided for the defensive, my only business was to prepare offensive measures, which consisted in the means of collecting the mass of our fleets at Cherbourg. The harbour, however, could contain but fifteen sail. For the purpose of increasing the number, I caused a new port to be dug; the Romans never undertook a more important, a more difficult task, or one which promised a more lasting duration! It was sunk into the granite to the depth of 50 feet, and I caused the opening of it to be celebrated by the presence of Maria Louisa, while I myself was on the fields of battle in Saxony. By this means I procured anchorage for 25 sail more. Still that number was not sufficient, and I therefore relied upon very different means of augmenting my naval strength. I was resolved to renew the wonders of Egypt at Cherbourg. I had already erected my pyramid in the sea; I would also have my lake Mœris.

period. He, therefore, retained the whole of his shipping in port, and confined himself to the gradual augmentation of our naval resources, without exposing them to any further risk. Every thing was calculated on the basis of a remote result.

Our navy had lost a great number of vessels, the greatest part of our good seamen were prisoners in England, and all our ports were blockaded by the English, who obstructed their communications. The Emperor ordered canals in Britanny, by means of which, and in spite of the enemy, points of communication for providing Brest with all kinds of supplies were established between Bordeaux, Rochefort, Nantes, Holland, Antwerp, Cherbourg, and that port. He was desirous of having wet docks at Flushing or in its neighbourhood, for the purpose of containing the Antwerp squadron, completely equipped and ready to put to sea in four-and-twenty hours, which was necessarily confined in the Scheldt four or five months of the year. Finally, he projected near Boulogne, or on some spot along that coast, the construction of a dike similar to that of Cherbourg, and between Cherbourg and Brest, a suitable harbour at the Ile-à-Bois. All this was planned, for the purpose of securing, at all times and without danger, a full and free communication to our large ships between Antwerp and Brest. To obviate the want of seamen, and the great difficulty of forming them, it was ordered that the young conscripts should be, every day, trained in all our ports. They were, at first, to be put on board small light vessels, and a flotilla of that kind was even to navigate the Zuiderzee; they were afterwards to be turned over to large ships and immediately replaced by others of the same class. The vessels were ordered to get under sail every day, to go through every possible manœuvre and evolution, and even to exchange shots with the enemy, without exposing themselves to the chance of an engagement.

The last point was the force and number of our vessels; they were considerable, notwithstanding all our losses, and the Emperor calculated on being enabled to build 20 or 25 yearly. The crews would be ready as fast as they were wanted, and thus, at the expiration of four or six years, he could have relied upon having 200 sail of the line, and perhaps 300, had that number been necessary, in less than 10 years. And what was that period in comparison with the perpetual war, or the war for life, which was declared against us? The affairs of the continent would, in the mean time, be brought to a termination; the whole of it would have embraced our system; the Emperor would have marched back the greatest part of his troops to our coast, and it was in that situation that he looked with confidence to a decisive issue of the contest. All the respective resources of the two nations would have been called into action, and we should then, in his opinion, subdue our enemies by moral energy, or strangle them by our material strength.

The Emperor entertained several projects for the improvement of the navy, and adapted to that end part of his military tactics. He intended to establish his offensive and defensive line from Cape Finisterre to the mouth of the Elbe. He was to have had three squadrons with admirals commanding in chief, as he had corps d'armée with their generals in chief. The Admiral of the centre was to establish his head quarters at Cherbourg; of the left, at Brest; and of the right, at Antwerp. Smaller divisions were to be stationed at the extremities, at Rochefort, and at Ferrol, in the Texel, and at the mouth of the Elbe, for the purpose of turning and outflanking the enemy. All these points were to be connected by numerous intermediate stations, and their respective commanders in chief were to be considered as constantly present, by the assistance of telegraphs, which, lining the coast, were to preserve an uninterrupted communication between the parts of the grand system.

Let us consider, however, what would have been the conduct of the English during our preparations and the progressive increase of our naval power. Would they have continued the blockade of our ports? We should have had the satisfaction of witnessing the wear and tear of their cruising squadrons; we should have compelled them to maintain 100 or 150 vessels constantly exposed

16th.—About nine o'clock, the Emperor took an
airing in the calash. There was a vessel in sight, at
which he looked through the glass. He invited the
Doctor, whom he found employed in the same way, to
accompany him. On our return, we breakfasted under
the trees. He conversed at great length with the Doctor respecting the Governor's conduct to us, his endless
vexations, &c.

About two o'clock, a person came to enquire if the
Emperor would receive the Governor. He gave him
an audience that lasted nearly two hours, and ran over,
without falling into a passion, he said, all the objects
under discussion. He recapitulated all our grievances;
enumerated all his wrongs; addressed himself, he observed, by turns to his understanding, his imagination
his feelings, and his heart. He put it in his power to
repair all the mischief he had done, to recommence upon ·
a plan altogether new, but in vain, for that man, he
declared, was without fibres; nothing was to be expected
from him.

This Governor, said the Emperor, assured him that,
when the detention of M. de Montholon's servant took
place, he did not know he was in our service, and he
added that he had not read Madame Bertrand's sealed
letter. The Emperor observed to him that his letter to
Count Bertrand was altogether repugnant to our manners
and in direct opposition to our prejudices; that if he,
the Emperor, were but a mere general and a private
individual, and had received such a letter from him, the
Governor, he would have called him out; that a man so
well known and respected in Europe, as the Grand
Marshal, was not to be insulted, under the penalty of
social reprobation; that he did not take a correct view
of his situation with regard to us; that all his actions
here came within the province of history, and that even
the conversation which was passing at that moment
belonged to history; that he injured every day, by his
conduct, his own government and his own nation, and

ON THE BEAUTIFUL WOMEN OF ITALY.—MADAME GRAS-SINI—MADAME V . . . . AND BERTHIER.

17th.—The Emperor sent for me about two o'clock he dressed himself and went out in the calash. Madame de Montholon was of the party. It was her first appear-ance since her accouchement. The conversation turned particularly on the Italian ladies, their character and beauty.

The young General, who effected the conquest of Italy, excited in that country, from the first moment, every feeling of enthusiasm and ambition. This the Emperor was delighted to hear and to repeat. Above all, there was not a beauty who did not aspire to please and touch his heart, but in vain. " My mind," he said, " was too strong to be caught in the snare; I fancied that there was a precipice under the flowers. My situation was singularly delicate; I had the command of veteran generals; the task I had to execute was immense; all my motions were watched by jealous eyes; my circum-spection was extreme. My good fortune consisted in my prudence; I might have forgotten myself for an hour, and how many of my victories," said he, " de-pended on no greater length of time !"

Several years afterwards, at the time of his coronation at Milan, his attention was attracted by *Grassini*, the celebrated singer. Circumstances were then more aus-picious. He desired to see her, and immediately after her introduction, she reminded him that she had made her début precisely during the early achievements of the General of the army of Italy. " I was then," said she, " in the full lustre of my beauty and my talent. My performance in the Virgins of the Sun was the topic of universal conversation. I fascinated every eye and in-flamed every heart. The young General alone was insensible to my charms, and yet he was the only object of my wishes! What caprice, what singularity! When I possessed some value, when all Italy was at my feet, and I heroically disdained its admiration for a single glance from you, I was unable to obtain it; and now, how strange an alteration! you condescend to notice me

—now, when I am not worth the trouble and am nc
longer worthy of you!"

The celebrated Madame V . . . . . . was also among
the crowd of Armidas; but, tried with losing her time,
she lowered her pretensions to Berthier, who, from
the first instant, lived but for her. The Commander-in-
Chief made him a present one day of a magnificent
diamond worth more than 100,000 francs. "Here,'
said he, "take that; we often play high, lay it up
against a rainy day."—Scarcely had four-and-twenty
hours elapsed, before Madame Bonaparte came to tell
her husband of a diamond which was the subject of her
admiration. It was the present that was to have been
laid up against a rainy day, which had already found its
way from Berthier's hand to Madame V . . . . . 's head.
He has since, in all the circumstances of his life, been
uniformly governed by her.

The Emperor, having gradually heaped riches and honours upon Berthier, pressed him often to marry, but he
as constantly refused, declaring, that Madame V . . .
could alone make him happy. The son, however, of
Madame V . . . . . . having got acquainted with
a duchess of Bavaria, who had come to Paris, with
the hope of obtaining a husband, through the Emperor's
favour, Madame V . . . . thought she was doing
wonders and advancing her son's fortune by the marriage
of her lover; and, with this impression, she prevailed
upon Berthier to espouse the Bavarian princess. But,
said the Emperor, there is no project, however excel
lent, which does not become the sport of fortune; for
scarcely was the marriage concluded, when Madame
V . . . . . . 's husband died and left his wife at liberty.
That event proved to her and to Berthier the source of
real despair; they were inconsolable. Berthier came with
tears in his eyes to communicate his wretched fate to the
Emperor, who laughed at his misfortune. To what a
miserable condition, he exclaimed, was he reduced; with
a little more constancy, Madame V . . . . might
have been his wife!

FAUBOURG SAINT GERMAIN.—ARISTOCRACY; DEMOCRACY.
—THE EMPEROR'S INTENTION TO MARRY A FRENCH
WOMAN.

18th.—About four o'clock, I was sent for by the
Emperor, who was in a very weak state. He had, by
an absence of mind, remained three hours in a very hot
bath and scalded his right thigh with the boiling water.
He had read two volumes in the bath. He shaved, but
would not dress himself.

At half-past seven, the Emperor ordered two covers
to be laid in his cabinet, and was very much out of temper, because his papers were thrown into confusion by
being removed for the purpose of using the table on
which they lay. They were replaced by his direction,
and the covers laid upon another small table.

We conversed for a long time; he brought me back
to topics which often suggested themselves to him when
we were together, and upon which I must endeavour
not to be guilty of repetitions, the more so, as they possess attractions, which to me are peculiarly interesting.
We talked a great deal about our youthful years and the
time we passed at the military school. This subject led
him again to notice the new schools which he had established at St. Cyr and at St. Germain, and he finally
recurred to the emigrants and those he called *nos en-
croûtés*. He became gay and lively in consequence of
some anecdotes of the Faubourg St. Germain, respecting his person, which I related, and as the slightest
things grew into importance the moment he touched
upon them, he said—"I see plainly that my plan with
respect to your Faubourg St. Germain was ill-managed.
I did too much or too little. I did enough to dissatisfy
the opposite party, and not enough to attach it to me
altogether. Although some of them were fond of money,
the multitude would have been content with the rattles
and sound, with which I could have crammed them, without any injury, in the main, to our new principles. My
dear Las Cases, I did too much and not enough, and yet
I was earnestly occupied with the business. Unfortunately, I was the only one seriously engaged in the un-

dertaking. All who were about me thwarted, instead of
promoting it, and yet there were but two grand measures
to be taken with regard to you;—that of annihilating, or
that of melting you down into the great mass of society.
The former could not enter my head, and the latter was
not an easy task, but I did not consider it beyond my
strength. And, in fact, although I had no support, and
was even counteracted in my views, I nearly realized
them at length. Had I remained, the thing would have
been accomplished. This will appear astonishing to him
who knows how to appreciate the heart of man and the
state of society. I do not think that history can furnish
any case of a similar kind, or that so important a result,
obtained in so short a space of time, can be found. I
should have carried that fusion into effect, and cemented
that union by every sacrifice ; it would have rendered us
invincible. The opposite conduct has ruined us, and
may for a long time protract the misfortunes, perhaps
the last gasps of unhappy France. I once more repeat,
that I did too much or too little. I ought to have attached the emigrants to me upon their return ; I might have
easily become an object of adoration with the aristocracy. An establishment of that nature was necessary
for me. It is the real, the only, support of monarchy—
its guide—its lever—its point of resistance. Without
it, the state is but a vessel without a rudder, a real balloon in the air. But, the essence of aristocracy, its
talismanic charm, consists in antiquity, in age ; and
these were the only things I could not create. The intermediate means were wanting. M. de Breteuil, who
had insinuated himself into my favour, encouraged me.
On the contrary, M. de T. . . . . . , who certainly
was not a favourite with the emigrants, discouraged me
by every possible means. Reasonable democracy contents itself with husbanding equality for all, as a fair
ground of pretension and possession. The real line of
conduct would have been to employ the remains of aristocracy, with the forms and intention of democracy.
Above all, it was necessary to collect the ancient names,
those celebrated in our history. This is the only mode
of giving an instantaneous air of antiquity to the most
modern institutions.

" I entertained, upon that subject, ideas which were
altogether peculiar to myself. Had any difficulties been
started by Austria and Russia, I would have married a
French woman. I would have selected one of the most
illustrious names of the monarchy. That was even my
original thought, my real inclination. If my ministers
prevented me, it was only by their earnest appeals to
political views. Had I been surrounded by the Mont-
morencies, the Nesles, and the Clissons, I should, by
adopting their daughters, have united them with foreign
sovereigns. My pride and my delight would have been
to extend these noble French stocks, had they taken part
with us, or given themselves up to us altogether. They
and those belonging to me thought that I was influenced
by prejudice alone, when I was acting in conformity with
the most profound combinations. Be that as it will, your
friends have lost more in me than they are aware of!
. . . . . They are destitute of soul, of the feeling of
true glory. By what unhappy propensity have they preferred wallowing in the mire of the allies to following
me to the top of mount Simplon, and commanding, from
its summit, the respect and admiration of the rest of
Europe. Senseless men !—I had, however," he continued, " a project in my portfolio ; time alone was wanting to mature it, which would have rallied round me a
great number of that class of persons, and which, after
all, would have been but just. It was that every des-
cendent of ancient marshals, ministers, &c., should be
considered at all times capable of getting himself declared a duke, by presenting the requisite endowment.
All the sons of generals and governors of provinces were
upon the same principle, to be qualified to assume the
title of count, and so on in gradation. This would have
advanced some, raised the hopes of others, excited the
emulation of all, and hurt the pride of none ; grand, but
altogether harmless rattles, and belonging, besides, to my
system and my combinations.

" Old and corrupt are not governed like ancient and
virtuous nations. For one individual, at present, who
would sacrifice himself for the public good, there are
thousands and millions who are insensible to every thing

but their own interests, enjoyments and vanity. To
pretend, therefore, to regenerate a people in an instant,
or as if one were travelling post, would be an act of
madness.   The genius of the workman ought to consist
in knowing how to employ the materials he has at hand,
and that is one of the causes of the resumption of all the
monarchical forms, of the re-establishment of titles, of
classes, and of the insignia of orders.   The secret of
the legislator should consist in knowing how to derive
advantage even from the caprice and irregularities of those
whom he pretends to rule ; and, after all, these gewgaws
were attended with few inconveniences, and not destitute
of benefit.   At the point of civilization to which we have
now attained, they are calculated to attract the respect
of the multitude, provided always that the person de-
corated with them preserves respect for himself.   They
may satisfy the vanity of the weak, without scaring, in
the slightest degree, strong and powerful minds.''   It
was very late, and the Emperor said, at parting, ''There
is another pleasant evening spent.''

OUR HOUSE ON FIRE.—ETIQUETTE AT LONGWOOD.

19th.—The chimney of the saloon took fire in the
night, but the flames did not break out until day-light.
Two hours sooner, and the building would have been a
heap of ashes.

The Emperor took a walk ; he was attended by several
of us, and we went round the park on foot.

One of his shoe-buckles fell out, and we all eagerly
strove to put it in again ; he, who succeeded, considered
himself the most fortunate.   The Emperor, who would
not have permitted this at the Tuileries, seemed here to
feel a kind of satisfaction at our conduct ; he let us do
as we liked, and we were thankful to him for indulging us in an act, that did honour to us, in our own
opinion.

This leads me to observe that I have not yet spoken
of our customary manners when about his person, and I
am more peculiarly induced to notice them because we
have received several London newspapers, which circu-
late a thousand idle stories on this subject, and assert

20th.—The Emperor sent for —
found him reading an English work on the poor's rate.

the immense sums raised, and the vast number of individuals maintained at the expense of their parishes ; the
account embraced millions of men and hundreds of
millions of money.

The Emperor was apprehensive that he had not read
the work correctly, or that he had mistaken the meaning.
The thing, he said, seemed altogether impossible. He
could not conceive by what vices and defects so many
poor could be found in a country so opulent, so indus-
trious, and so abundant in resources for labour as
England. He was still less capable of comprehending,
by what prodigy the proprietors, overloaded with an
oppressive ordinary and extraordinary taxation, were
also enabled to provide for the wants of such a multitude.
" But we have nothing," he observed, " in France to be
compared to it in the proportion of a hundredth or a
thousandth part. Have you not told me that I sent you
into the departments on a particular mission with regard
to mendicity ? Let us see, what is the number of our beggars ? What did they cost ? How many poor-houses did
I establish ? What was the number they held ? What
effect had they in removing mendicity ?"

To this crowd of questions I was compelled to answer
that a considerable period of time had since elapsed, that
my mind had been occupied with several other objects,
and that it was impossible for me to enter into correct
statements from mere recollection ; but that I had the
official report itself among the few papers I had preserved,
and that, the first time he might be pleased to send for
me, I should be enabled to satisfy him. " But," said he,
" go instantly and look for it, things are not profitable
unless seasonably applied, and I shall soon run it over
with my thumb, as Abbé de Pradt ingeniously said ;
although, to tell the truth, I don't much like to think of
such subjects ; they remind me of mustard after dinner."

In two minutes the report was in his hand. " Well !"
said the Emperor to me, also, in a very few minutes, for
it might be really said that he had not turned over the
leaves ; " well, this, in fact, is not at all like England.
Our organization, however, had failed ; I suspected as
much, and it was on that account I entrusted you with

the mission. Your report would have been in perfect conformity with my views You took up the consideration frankly and like an honest man, without fear of exciting the displeasure of the minister, by depriving him of a great many appointments.

" I am pleased with a great number of your details. Why did you not come and converse with me about them yourself ? You would have satisfied me, and I should have known how to value your services."—" Sire, as things were then situated, it would have been impossible for me to do so; we were then involved in the confusion and embarrassment caused by our misfortunes."—" Your observation is perfectly correct; you establish an unquestionable position. The fact is that, in the flourishing state to which I had raised the empire, no hands could any where be found destitute of employment. It was idleness and vice alone that could produce mendicants.

" You think that their complete annihilation was possible ; and, for my part, I am of the same opinion.

" Your levy *en masse*, to build a vast and single prison in each department, was equally adapted to the tranquillity of society and to the well-being of those confined in it ; —your idea of making them monuments for ages would have attracted my attention. That gigantic undertaking, its utility, its importance, the permanence of its results, were all in my way.

" With respect to your university for the people, I am very apprehensive that it would have been but a beautiful chimera of philanthropy, worthy of the unsophisticated Abbé de Saint Pierre. There is, however, some merit in the aggregate of those conceptions ; but energy of character, and an unbending perseverance, for which we are not generally distinguished, would be requisite to produce any good result.

" For the rest, I every day collect ideas from you in this place, of which I did not imagine you capable ; but it was not at all my fault. You were near me ; why did you not open your mind to me ? I did not possess the gift of divination. Had you been minister, those ideas, however fantastical they might at first have appeared to

me, would not have been the less attended to, because
there is, in my opinion, no conception altogether unsusceptible of some positive good, and a wrong notion,
when properly controlled and regulated, often leads to a
right conclusion. I should have handed you over to
commissioners, who would have analyzed your plans ;
you would have defended them by your arguments, and,
after taking cognizance of the subject, I alone should
have finally decided according to my own judgment.
Such was my way of acting, and my intention ; I gave an
impulse to industry ; I put it into a state of complete
activity throughout Europe ; I was desirous of doing as
much for all the faculties of the mind, but time was not
allowed me. I could not bring my plans to maturity at
full gallop; and, unfortunately, I but too often wasted
them upon a sandy foundation, and consigned them to
unproductive hands.

" What were the other missions with which I entrusted
you ?"—" One in Holland, another in Illyria."—" Have
you the reports ?"—" Yes, Sire."—" Go for them." But
. had not got to the door, when he said, " Never mind,
come back, spare me the trouble of reading such matters !—They are henceforth, in reality, altogether useless."
—What did not these words unfold to me !

The Emperor resumed the subject of Illyria. " In ob-
taing possession of Illyria, it was never my intention to
retain it; I never entertained the idea of destroying Austria. Her existence was, on the contrary, indispensably
requisite for the execution of my plans. But Illyria was,
in our hands, a vanguard to the heart of Austria, calculated to keep a check upon her; a sentinel at the gates
of Vienna, to keep her steady to our interests. Besides,
I was desirous of introducing and establishing in that
country our doctrines, our system of government, and
our codes. It was an additional step to the regeneration
of Europe. I had merely taken it as a pledge, and intended, at a later period, to exchange it for Gallicia, at
the restoration of Poland, which I hurried on against my
own opinion. I had, however, more than one project
with regard to Illyria ; for I frequently fluctuated in my
designs, and had few ideas that were fixed on solid

grounds. This arose rather from adapting myself to circumstances than from giving an impulse and direction to
them, and I was every instant compelled to shift about.
The consequence was that, for the greater part of the
time, I came to no absolute decision, and was occupied
merely with projects. My predominant idea, however,
particularly after my marriage, was to give it up to Austria as an indemnity for Gallicia, on the re-establishment
of Poland, at any rate, as a separate and independent
kingdom. Not that I cared upon whose head, whether
on that of a friend, an enemy, or an ally, the crown was
placed, provided the thing was effected. The results were
indifferent to me. I have, my dear Las Cases, formed
vast and numerous projects, all unquestionably for the advancement of reason and the welfare of the human race.
I was dreaded as a thunderbolt; I was accused of having
a hand of iron; but the moment that hand had struck the
last blow, every thing would have been softened down for
the happiness of all. How many millions would have
poured their benedictions on me, both then and in future
times! But how numerous, it must be confessed, the
fatal misfortunes which were accumulated and combined
to effect my overthrow, at the end of my career! My unhappy marriage; the perfidies which resulted from it;
that villainous affair of Spain; that fatal war with Russia, which occurred through a misunderstanding; that horrible rigour of
the elements, which devoured a whole army; . . . .
and then, the whole universe against me! . . . . Is it not
wonderful that I was still able to make so long a resistance, and that I was more than once on the point of sur-
mounting every danger and emerging from that chaos
more powerful than ever! . . . . . O destiny of man!—
What is human wisdom, human foresight!"—And then
abruptly adverting to my report, he said, " I observed,
that you travelled over a great number of departments.
Did your mission last long? Was your journey agreeable?
Was it of real benefit to you? Did you collect much
information? Were you enabled to form a correct
judgment on the state of the country, on that of public
opinion?

Vol. III.—2

"I now recollect that I selected you precisely because you had just returned from your mission to Illyria, and I found in your report several things which made a strong impression upon me; for it is surprising how many things at present are every day brought back to my memory, which, at the time, struck me in you, and which, by a singular fatality, were immediately afterwards completely forgotten. When any appointments were about to take place to those special and confidential missions, the decree, with blanks for the names, was laid before me, and I filled them up with persons of my own selection—I must have written your name with my own hand."

"Sire," I replied, "there never was, perhaps, a mission more agreeable and satisfactory in every point of view. I commenced it early in the spring, and proceeded from Paris to Toulon, and from Toulon to Antibes, following the line of coast and occasionally diverging into the interior. I travelled nearly thirteen hundred leagues, but unfortunately the time was short. The minister, in his instructions, had strictly limited the period to three, or at most, to four months. It would be difficult for me to give an adequate description of all the delight, enjoyments, and advantages which I derived from the journey. I was a member of your Council, an officer of your household. I was every where considered as one of your *missi dominici*, and was received with suitable respect. The more I behaved with discretion, moderation, and simplicity, visiting myself the high functionaries, whose attendance I was authorized to require, the more I was treated with deference and complaisance. For one, who shewed any distrust, or betrayed any symptom of ill-humour or envy; (for I afterwards learnt from themselves, that my character, as a nobleman, emigrant, and chamberlain, formed three certain grounds for reprobation;) for one, I repeat, who looked upon me with a jealous eye, I found many whose communications were altogether unreserved, even upon subjects, respecting which I should not have presumed to make inquiry. They assured me that they took pleasure in unbosoming themselves to me with perfect openness, that they viewed my situation, near the person of the sovereign, as a favourable medium; and considered me as the confessor upon whom they relied for transmitting their most secret thoughts to the *Most High*. The more I endeavoured to convince them that they were mistaken with regard to my situation and the nature of my mission, the more they were confirmed in the contrary opinion. In so short a period, what a lesson for me on mankind! There were none of these high functionaries who did not differ from each other with regard to the views, means, and designs of all the objects under consideration; and yet they were all men selected with care, of tried ability, and generally of great merit. Persons in private life also looked up to me as to a ray of Providence, and applied to me either publicly or in secret. How many things did I not learn! How numerous the denunciations and accusations communicated to me! What a multitude of local abuses, of petty intrigues, were disclosed to me!

"Altogether unacquainted with affairs, and until then absolutely ignorant of official proceedings, I made use of that peculiar opportunity to obtain information. I did not fail to make myself acquainted with all the objects and particular circumstances of every party. I was not apprehensive of shewing my ignorance to the first who presented themselves, for I was thus enabled to qualify myself for discussing business with the others.

"It is true, Sire, that my special mission was restricted to the mendicity establishments and the houses of correction: but feeling, as I did, all the want of a stock of knowledge, fit to render myself useful to the Council of State, and taking advantage of my appointment, I connected with it, of my own accord, the minute inspection of prisons, hospitals, and beneficent institutions, and I also took a survey of all our ports and squadrons.

"How magnificent the combination which thus presented itself to my view! I every where beheld the most perfect tranquillity and complete confidence in the government; every hand, every faculty, every branch of industry, was employed; the soil was embellished by the flourishing state of agriculture, it was the finest time of the year; the roads were excellent; public works were

in progress in almost in every quarter;—the canal of
Arles, the noble bridge of Bordeaux, the works of Rochefort, the canals from Nantes to Brest, to Rennes, to
Saint Malo; the foundation of Napoleonville, intended
to be the key of the whole peninsula of Britanny; the
magnificent works of Cherbourg, those of Antwerp, sluices,
moles, or other improvements in most of the towns of
the Channel——such is the sketch of what I saw.

" On the other hand, the ports of Toulon, Rochefort,
L'Orient, Brest, Saint Malo, Havre, and Antwerp, displayed an extraordinary degree of activity; our roads
were filled with vessels, and the numbers increased daily:
our crews were training in spite of every obstacle, and
our young conscripts were becoming good seamen, fit for
future service. I, who belonged to the old naval establishment, was astonished at every thing I saw on board,
so very great were the improvements made in the art,
and so far did they exceed, in every point of view, all
that I had witnessed.

" The squadrons belonging to the different ports got
under sail every day, and executed their regular manœuvres, like the parades of garrisons, and all this took
place within sight of the English, who thought it a ridiculous farce, without foreseeing the danger with which
they were threatened; for, never at any period was our
navy more formidable, or our ships more numerous. We
already had upwards of 100 afloat or on the stocks, and
we were making daily additions to the number. The
officers were excellent, and animated with zeal and
ardour. I had no idea whatever of the forward state of
our preparations, before I witnessed it in person, and
should not have believed it, had I been told of it.

" With respect to the mendicity establishments, the
special object of my mission, your intentions, Sire, had
been ill understood, and the plan was altogether unsuccessful. In most of the departments, mendicity not
only remained with all its defects, but no steps whatever
had been taken for its annihilation. The fact was that
several prefects, so far from making the establishments a
terror to the *mendicants*, had merely considered them as
a refuge for the *poor*. Instead of holding out confine-

ment as a punishment, they caused it to be sought after as an asylum ; and thus the lot of the prisoners might be envied by the hard-working peasantry of the neighbourhood. France might, in that way, have been covered with similar establishments, which might have been filled without diminishing the number of mendicants, who commonly make a trade of begging, and follow it in preference. I was, however, enabled to judge that the extirpation of the evil was possible, and the example of some departments, in which the prefects had taken a better view of the subject was sufficient to produce that conviction. There were a few in which it had entirely disappeared.

" It is an observation which makes an immediate and striking impression, that, all other things fairly averaged, mendicity is much more rare in those parts which are poor and barren, and much more common in those which are fruitful and abundant. It is also infinitely more difficult to effect its destruction in the places where the clergy have enjoyed superior wealth and power. In Belgium, for instance, mendicants were seen to derive honour from their trade, and boast of having followed it for several generations. These claims belonged peculiarly to them, and that country was accordingly the rendezvous of mendicity." " But I am not surprised at it," resumed the Emperor, " the difficulty of this important consideration consists entirely in discriminating accurately between the *poor* man who commands our respect, and the *mendicant* who ought to excite our indignation ; besides, our religious absurdities confound these two classes so completely that they seem to make a merit, a kind of virtue, of mendicity, and to encourage it by the promise of heavenly rewards. The mendicants are, in reality, neither more nor less than monks *au petit pied ;* so that in the list of them we even find the mendicant monks. How was it possible for such ideas not to produce confusion in the mind, and disorder in society ? A great number of saints have been canonized, whose only apparent merit was mendicity. They seem to have been transplanted to Heaven for that, which, considered as a matter of sound policy, ought to have subjected them to

castigation and confinement in this world. This would
not, however, have prevented them from being worthy of
Heaven. But go on."—

"It was not, Sire, without emotion that I observed
the details of the charitable establishments. In contem-
plating the anxiety, the cares, the ardent charity, of so
many sympathetic hearts, I was enabled to ascertain that
we were far from yielding the palm, whatever might be
the consideration, to any other people, and that we
merely had less ostentation and made less use of artificial
means to enhance our merits. The South, above all, and
Languedoc, in particular, displayed a zeal and animation of
which it would be difficult to form an adequate conception. The hospitals and alms-houses were every where
numerous and well attended to. The foundlings had
increased tenfold since the revolution, and I instantly
ascribed it to the corruption of the times; but I was
desired to remark, and constant reflection convinced me
of the truth, that the result was, on the contrary, to be
attributed to very satisfactory causes. I was assured
that formerly the foundlings were so wretchedly taken
care of, and so badly fed, that the whole of them were
diminutive, sickly, and short-lived, and that from seven
to nine perished out of ten; while at present their food,
cleanliness, and the care taken of them, in every respect
are such that nearly all of them are preserved, and constitute a fine race of children. They are thus indebted
for their numbers solely to their preservation. Vaccina-
tion has also contributed, in an immense proportion, to
their increase. These children are now treated with such
attention as to give rise to a singular abuse. Mothers,
even in easy circumstances, are tempted to expose their
infants; they afterwards apply at the hospital, and,
under a charitable pretence, offer to bring up one them
selves; it is their own which is restored to them with
the benefit of a small allowance. All this is carried on
through the favour of the agents themselves, and often
for the purpose of obtaining a trifling pension for one of
their relations. Another abuse of this kind, and not less
extraordinary, was that which I observed in Belgium, of
persons getting their names entered a long time before,

for the purpose of entitling them to send their children
to the hospital. Any young couple, on their marriage,
strove to get their names entered for vacancies, which
fell to them some years afterwards, as a matter of right ;
it was a part of the marriage settlement."—" O Jesus !
Jesus !" exclaimed the Emperor, shrugging up his
shoulders and laughing, " and after this make laws and
regulations !"—

"But with regard to the prisons, Sire, they were
almost uniformly the scenes of horror and real misery,
the shame and disgrace of our provinces, absolute sinks
of corruption and infection, which I was obliged to pass
through with the utmost haste, or from which I was
driven back in spite of all my efforts. I had formerly
visited certain prisons in England, and indulged in a
smile at the kind of luxury which I observed in them ;
but it was quite a different thing with respect to ours,
and my indignation was excited by the contrary extreme.
There are no offences, I might even say crimes, that are
not sufficiently punished by such habitations, and those
who leave them should not, in strict justice, have any
further expiation to make. Yet after all those confined
in them were merely under a simple accusation, while
those who had been found guilty, the real criminals, and
hardened villains, had their special prisons, their houses
of correction, where they were, perhaps, too well taken
care of ; and even, in the latter case, the honest day-
labourer might have reason to envy their lot, and make
comparisons injurious to Providence and society. Another
striking inconsistency was observable in these houses
of correction ; it was the amalgamation, the habitual
mixture of all the classes upon whom sentence had been
passed. Some being imprisoned for small offences only
for a year, and others for fifteen, twenty years, or for
life, on account of the dreadful crimes they had perpetrated, it necessarily followed that they would be all
reduced to one moral level, not by the amelioration
of the latter, but rather by the corruption of the
former.

"What struck me also very forcibly in La Vendée
and the adjacent country was that maniacs had in-

creased there, perhaps, tenfold more than in any other
part of the empire, and that persons were detained in
the mendicity establishments and other places of confinement, who were treated as vagabonds, or likely to become so, and who having been taken up in their childhood, had no knowledge of their parents or origin. Some
of them had marks of wounds on their persons, but were
ignorant how they had been inflicted. They had, no
doubt, been made in their infancy. The opportunity of
employing these persons, who had not acquired a single
social idea, has been suffered to pass by ; they are now
unfit for any purpose."—"Ah!" exclaimed the Emperor,
"this is civil war and its hideous train; its inevitable
consequences and its certain fruits ! If some leaders
make fortunes, and extricate themselves from danger, the
dregs of the population are always trodden under foot,
and become the victims of every calamity !"

"With respect to other matters, I found in the aggregate of these establishments a considerable number of
persons who, I was told, whether right or wrong, were
prisoners of state, and were kept in custody by order of
the high, the intermediate, or the low, police.

"I listened to all those prisoners, I heard their complaints, and received their petitions, certainly, without
any engagement on my part; for I had no right to
contract any ; and besides, I was perfectly aware that,
having heard their testimony only, I could not attach
guilt to any person. With the exception, however, of
some notorious villains, they did not really, in general,
deserve more at farthest than the common punishments
of the correctional police.

"I found among them, in the prisons of Rennes, a
boy between twelve and fourteen, who had, when only
a few months old, been taken with a band of *Chauffeurs.*
They had been all executed, and the boy had remained
there ever since, without any decision on his case. His
moral capabilities may be easily appreciated. He never
saw, knew, or heard any but villains; they were the
only kind of people of whose existence he was able to
form an idea.

"At Mont Saint-Michel, a woman, whose name I

have forgotten, particularly attracted my attention. She had rather a pretty face, pleasing manners, and a modest deportment. She had been imprisoned fourteen years, having taken a very active part in the troubles of La Vendée, and constantly accompanied her husband, who was the chief of a battalion of insurgents, and whom she succeeded, after his death, in the command. The wretchedness she suffered, and the tears she shed, had sensibly impaired her charms. I assumed a severe air during the recital of her misfortunes, but it was put on for the purpose of concealing the emotions which she excited. She had, by the kindness of her manners and her other qualifications, acquired a kind of empire over the vulgar and depraved women that were about her. She had devoted herself to the care of the sick; the prison infirmary was entrusted to her, and she was beloved by every one.

" With the exception of that woman, a few priests, and two or three old Chouan spies, the rest exhibited but a filthy compound of disgusting or extravagant depravity.

" I met with a married man, possessing an annual income of 15,000 livres, evidently confined in consequence of his wife's intrigues, after the manner of the ancient *lettres de cachet*; and with prostitutes, who assured me they were detained, not as a punishment for the indiscriminate profusion of their favours, but out of spite at their want of complaisance for a single person. They told me lies, or they did not; but in either case ought they to be honoured with the title of prisoners of state, to be maintained at the expense of two francs a day, and contribute to render the government odious and ridiculous? Finally, I met with an unhappy man in a town of Belgium, who had married one of those girls for whom the municipalities provide marriage portions on great occasions. He was imprisoned on a charge of having stolen the portion, because he had neglected to earn it. He was positively required to discharge that important debt, and he as positively refused. He was, perhaps, required to do what was absolutely impossible for him.

2*

"Immediately upon my return to Paris, I called on M. Réal, prefect of police of the district I had just visited. I considered it my duty, I said, to communicate to him, in a *friendly* manner, the result of my observations. I must do him justice; for whether he was far from having a bad heart, whether he was impressed with my plain dealing, or affected perhaps, Sire, by the magic influence of your uniform, he thanked me, observed that I was doing him a real service, and assured me that he would take immediate steps for *relieving* and *redressing*, such were his words, the cases I had laid before him. Meeting him, however, a few days afterwards at an assembly, he said, with apparent grief, 'That is an unfortunate business, and very unfavourable to your Amazon (he alluded to General Mallet's rash enterprise), which I thought myself capable of doing a few days ago of my own accord. I cannot now pretend to undertake it without an order from a superior quarter.'—I do not know how the thing ended."

The Emperor dwelt some time on the abuses I had pointed out, and then concluded: "In the first place, in order to proceed regularly, it was incumbent upon you to ascertain whether your information was well founded, and to hear the evidence against the persons accused; and then it must be frankly admitted that abuses are inherent in every human establishment. You see that almost every thing, of which you complain, is done by the very persons who were expressly entrusted with the means of prevention. Can a remedy be provided, when it is impossible to see what passes every where? There is, as it were, a net spread over the low places, which envelops the lower classes. A mesh must be broken and discovered by a fortunate observer like you, before any thing of the matter is known in the upper regions. Accordingly, one of my dreams would have been, when the grand events of war were completely terminated, and I returned to the interior in tranquillity and at ease, to look out for half a dozen, or a dozen, of real philanthropists, of those worthy men who live but to do good. I should have distributed them through the empire, which they should have secretly inspected for the purpose of making their report to me. They would have been *spies of virtue !* They should have addressed themselves directly to me, and should have been my confessors, my spiritual guides, and my decisions with them should have been my good works done in secret. My grand occupation, when at full leisure, and at the height of my power, would have been the amelioration of every class of society. I should have descended to the details of individual comfort; and, had I found no motive for that conduct in my natural disposition, I should have been actuated by the spirit of calculation; for, after the acquisition of so much glory, what other means would have been left me to make any addition to it? It was because I was well aware that that swarm of abuses necessarily existed, because I wished for the preservation of my subjects, and was desirous of throwing every impediment in the way of subordinate and intermediate tyranny, that I conceived my system of state prisons, adapted to any crisis that might occur."—" Yes, Sire, out it was far from being well received in our saloons, and contributed not a little to make you unpopular. An outcry was every where raised against the *new bastiles,* against the renewal of *lettres de cachet."*—" I know it very well." said the Emperor, " the outcry was echoed by all Europe, and rendered me odious. And yet, observe how powerful was the influence of words, envenomed by perfidy! The whole of the discontent was principally occasioned by the preposterous title of my decree, which escaped me from distraction, or some other cause; for, in the main, I contend that the law itself was an eminent service, and rendered individual liberty more complete and certain in France than in any other country of Europe.

" Considering the crisis from which we had emerged, the factions by which we had been divided, and the plots which had been laid, and were still contriving, imprisonment became indispensable. It was, in fact, a benefit; for it superseded the scaffold. But I was desirous of sanctioning it by legal enactments, and of placing it beyond the reach of caprice, of arbitrary power, of hatred, and of vengeance. Nobody, according to my law, could be imprisoned and detained as a prisoner of state, without the decision of my privy council, which consisted of sixteen persons; the first, the most independent and most distinguished characters of the state What unworthy feeling would have dared to expose itself to the detection of such a tribunal? Had I not voluntarily deprived myself of the power of consigning individuals to prison? No man could be detained beyond a year, without a fresh decision of the Privy-Counc'l, and four votes out of sixteen were sufficient to effect his release. Two councillors of state were bound to attend to the statements of the prisoners, and became from that moment their zealous advocates with the Privy Council. These prisoners were also under the protection of the Committee of individual liberty, appointed by the Senate, which was the object of public derision, merely because it made no parade of its labours and their results. Its services, however, were great; for it would argue a defective knowledge of mankind to suppose that Senators, who had nothing to expect from ministers, and who were their equals in rank, would not make use of their prerogative to oppose and attack them, whenever the importance of the case called for their interference. It must also be considered that I had assigned the superintendence of the prisoners, and of the police of the prisons, to the tribunals, which, from that instant, paralyzed the exercise of every kind of arbitrary authority by the other branches of administration and their numerous subordinate agents. After such precautions, I do not hesitate to maintain that civil liberty was as effectually secured by that law in France as it could possibly be. The public misconceived, or pretended to misconceive, that truth, for we Frenchmen must murmur at every thing and on every occasion.

" The fact is, that at the time of my downfal the state prisons scarcely contained 250 persons, and I found 9000 in them, when I became Consul. It will appear, from the list of those who were imprisoned, and upon an examination into the causes and motives of their confinement, that almost every one of them deserved death, and would have been sentenced to it by regular process of law; and it consequently follows that their imprisonment was, on my part, a benefit conferred upon them. Why is there nothing published against me on this subject at present? Where are the serious grievances to be found with which I am reproached? There are none in reality. If some of the prisoners afterwards made a merit of their sufferings with the King, on account of their exertions in his favour, did they not by that proceeding pronounce their own sentence and attest my justice? For what may seem a virtuous action in the King's eye was incontestably a crime under me; and it was only because I was repugnant to the shedding of blood on account of political crimes, and because such trials would have but tended to the continuance of commotion and perplexity in the heart of the country, that I commuted the punishment to mere imprisonment.

"I repeat it, the French were, at my era, the freest people of all Europe, without even excepting the English; for, in England, if any extreme danger causes the suspension of the *Habeas Corpus* act, every individual may be sent to prison at the mere will of ministers, who are not called upon to justify their motives, or to account for their conduct. My law had very different limits." He concluded with saying;—"And then, at last, if, in spite of my good intention, and notwithstanding my utmost care, all that you have just said, and no doubt, many other things, were well founded, it must not still be considered so easy a task as it is thought to create a beneficial establishment for a nation. It is a remarkable circumstance that the countries which have been separated from us have regretted the laws with which I governed them. This is an homage paid to their superiority. The real, the only, mode of passing a decisive sentence upon me, with regard to their defects, would be to shew the existence of a better code in any other country. New times are drawing near, it will be seen," &c.

About five o'clock, I was told by the Grand Marshal, who had just left the Emperor, that he wished to see me. He had staid at home the whole of the day. I found him engaged in examining the new billiard-table. He was apprehensive that the weather was too damp for walking, and he played at chess until dinner. In the evening, he read us Crebillon's *Atrée et Thyeste*. That piece seemed horrible to us; we found it disgusting, and by no means of a tragic cast. The Emperor could not finish it.

EGYPT.—ST. JEAN D'ACRE.—THE DESERT.—ANECDOTES

21st. About three o'clock, the Emperor called for his calash. He sent for me, and we walked together to the bottom of the wood where he had ordered the carriage to take him up. I had some particulars of no great moment to communicate, which personally concerned him. We observed, in the course of our ride, two vessels under sail for the island.

At dinner, the Emperor was very talkative. He had been just employed on his campaign in Egypt, which he had, for some time, neglected, and which, he said, would be as interesting as an episode of romance. In speaking of his position at St. Jean d'Acre, he observed :—It was certainly a daring thing to post myself thus in the heart of Syria, with only 12,000 men. I was 500 leagues from Desaix, who formed the other extremity of my army. It has been related, by Sydney Smith, that I lost 18,000 men before Acre, although my army consisted but of 12,000. An obscure person, M. . . . . , who had just left college, as it seemed, who knows nothing of what he describes, and whose only talent is that of tacking some sentences together, with a view, no doubt, of converting them to his emolument, the brother, however, of one whom I have loaded with favours, and who was one of my Council of State, has recently published something on that subject, on which I have cast a glance, and which vexes me on account of its silliness and the unfavourable colouring which he endeavours to throw over the glory and exploits of that army.

" Had I been master of the sea, I should have been master of the East, and the thing was so practicable that it failed only through the stupidity or bad conduct of some seamen.

" Volney, who travelled in Egypt before the revolu

tion, had stated his opinion that that country could not be occupied without three great wars, against England, the Grand Signor, and the inhabitants. The latter, in particular, seemed difficult and terrible to him. He was altogether mistaken in that respect, for it gave us no trouble. We had even succeeded in making friends of the inhabitants, in the course of a short time, and of uniting their cause with ours. A handful of Frenchmen had thus been sufficient to conquer that fine country, which they ought never to have lost. We had actually accomplished prodigies in war and in politics. Our undertaking was altogether different from the crusades ; the crusaders were innumerable and hurried on by fanaticism. My army, on the contrary, was very small, and the soldiers were so far from being prepossessed in favour of the enterprise that, at first, they were frequently tempted to carry off the colours and return. I had, however, succeeded in familiarizing them with the country, which supplied every thing in abundance, and at so cheap a rate that I was one time on the point of placing them on half-pay for the purpose of laying by the other half for them. I had acquired such an ascendancy over them, that I should have been able, by a mere order of the day, to make them Mahometan. They would have treated it as a joke, the population would have been gratified, and the very Christians of the East would have considered themselves gainers, and approved it, knowing that we could do nothing better for them and for ourselves.

"The English were struck with consternation at seeing us in possession of Egypt. We exposed to Europe the certain means of wresting India from them. They have not yet dismissed their apprehensions, and they are in the right. If 40 or 50,000 European families ever succeed in establishing their industry, laws, and government in Egypt, India will be more effectually lost to the English by the commanding influence of circumstances than by the force of arms."

In the course of the evening, the Grand Marshal put the Emperor in mind of one of his conversations with Monge, the mathematician, at Cutakié, in the midst of the desert. "What do you think of all this, citizen

Monge?" said Napoleon.—"Why, citizen general,"
answered Monge, "I think, if there are ever seen in this
place as many equipages as at the Opera house, there
must first be some wonderful revolutions on the globe."
The Emperor laughed very heartily at the recollection.
He had, however, he observed, a carriage with six horses
on the spot. It was unquestionably the first of the kind
that travelled over the desert, and accordingly it very
much surprised the Arabs.

The Emperor remarked that the desert always had a
peculiar influence on his feelings. He had never crossed
it without being subject to a certain emotion. To him,
he said, it was an image of immensity: it seemed to
have no bounds, neither beginning nor end; it was an
ocean on terra firma. His imagination was delighted
with the sight, and he took pleasure in drawing our
attention to the observation that Napoleon meant *Lion
of the Desert!* . . . . .

The Emperor also told us that, when he was in Syria,
it was a settled opinion at Cairo that he never would be
seen there again, and he noticed the thievery and impu-
dence of a little Chinese, who was one of his servants.
"It was," said he, "a little deformed dwarf, whom
Josephine once took a fancy to at Paris. He was the
only Chinese in France; thenceforth she would always
have him behind her carriage. She took him to Italy,
but as he was in the constant habit of pilfering, she
wished to get rid of him. With that view, I took him
with me on my Egyptian expedition. Egypt was a lift
to him half-way on his journey. This little monster was
entrusted with the care of my cellar, and I had no sooner
crossed the desert than he sold, at a very low price,
2000 bottles of capital claret. His only object was to
make money, convinced that I should never come back.
He was not at all disconcerted at my return, but came
eagerly to meet me, and acquainted me, as he said, like
a faithful servant, with the loss of my wine. The rob-
bery was so glaring that he was himself compelled to
confess it. I was much urged to have him hanged, but
I refused, because, in strict justice, I ought to have done
as much to those in embroidered clothes, who had know-

ingly bought and drunk the wine. I contented myself with discharging and sending him to Suez, where he was at liberty to do what he pleased."

On this subject I must observe that we were induced, in this place, to give momentary credit to a very singular coincidence. We were informed a few months ago, that on board one of the Chinese traders, which were then off the island, on their return to Europe, there was a Chinese, who said he had been in the Emperor's service in Egypt. The Emperor instantly exclaimed, that it must be his little thief, whose story I have just told; but it was, in fact, a cook of Kleber's.

The Emperor put a sudden stop to the conversation, and, with more gaiety than usual, turning to Madame Bertrand, said with a smile, "When shall you be at your apartments in the Tuileries? When will you give your splendid dinners to the ambassadors? But you will be obliged, at least, I am told so, to have new furniture, for it is reported that the fashions have entirely changed." The conversation then naturally turned on the magnificence and luxury which we had witnessed under the Emperor.

PATERNAL ADVICE—REMARKABLE CONVERSATION—CAG-
LIOSTRO; MESMER, GALL, LAVATER, &C.

22nd.—The Emperor came to my apartment about 10 o'clock, and took me out to walk. We all breakfasted under the trees. The weather was delightful, and the heat, though great, was not unwholesome. The Emperor ordered his calash; two of us were with him, and the third accompanied us on horseback. The Grand Marshal could not attend. The Emperor recurred to some misunderstanding which had taken place among us a few days before. He took a view of our situation and our natural wants;—"You are bound," said he, "when you are one day restored to the world, to consider yourselves as *brothers*, on my account. My memory will dictate this conduct to you. Be so, then, from this moment!" He next described how we might be of mutual advantage to each other, the sufferings we had it in our power to alleviate, &c. It was, at once, a family and moral lesson, a lesson of feeling and conduct.

It ought to have been written in letters of gold. It lasted nearly an hour and a quarter, and will, I think, never be forgotten by any of us. For myself, not only the principles and the words, but the tone, the expression, the action, and above all, the heart with which he delivered them, will never be forgotten by me.

About five o'clock, the Emperor entered my apartment where I was employed with my son, on the chapter of the battle of Arcole. He had something to say to me, and I followed him to the garden, where he resumed, at great length, the conversation that had taken place in the calash . . . .

We now dined in the old topographical cabinet, adjoining to that of the Emperor, and the apartment formerly occupied by Montholon's family, which, with the help of the books and shelves lately received from England, was converted into a tolerable library.

As the damage done by the fire in the saloon was long in repairing, we were obliged to continue at table in our new dining-room until the Emperor withdrew. This circumstance, however, gave additional interest to the conversation.

The Emperor was very communicative to-day. The conversation turned on dreams, presentiments, and foresights, which the English call *second sight*. We exhausted every common-place topic, ordinarily connected with these objects, and came at last to speak of sorcerers and ghosts. The Emperor concluded with observing, " All these quackeries, and many others, such as those of Cagliostro, Mesmer, Gall, Lavater, &c. are destroyed by this sole and simple argument: *All that may exist, but it does not exist.*

" Man is fond of the marvellous; it has for him irresistible fascinations; he is ever ready to abandon what is near at hand, to run after what is fabricated for him. He voluntarily gives way to delusion. The truth is, that every thing about us is a wonder. There is nothing which can be properly called a phenomenon. Every thing in nature is a phenomenon. My existence is a phenomenon. The wood that is put on the fire and warms me, is a phenomenon; that candle yonder which gives me light, is a phenomenon. All the first causes, my understanding, my faculties, are phenomena; for they all exist and we cannot define them. I take leave of you here," said he, "and lo! I am at Paris, entering my box at the Opera. I bow to the audience; I hear their acclamations; I see the performers; I listen to the music. But if I can bound over the distance from Saint Helena, why should I not bound over the distance of centuries? Why should I not see the future as well as the past? Why should the one be more extraordinary, more wonderful, than the other? The only reason is, that it does not exist. This is the argument which will always annihilate, without the possibility of reply, all visionary wonders. All these quacks deal in very ingenious speculations; their reasoning may be just and seductive, but their conclusions are false, because they are unsupported by facts.

"Mesmer and Mesmerism have never recovered from the blow dealt at them by the report of Bailly on behalf of the Academy of Sciences. Mesmer produced effects upon a person by magnetizing him to his face, yet the same person, magnetized behind, without his knowing it, experienced no effect whatever. It was therefore, on his part, an error of the imagination, a debility of the senses; it was the act of the somnabule, who, at night runs along the roof without danger, because he is not afraid; but who would break his neck in the day, because his senses would confound him.

"I once attacked the quack Puységur, on his somnabulism, at one of my public audiences. He would have assumed a very lofty tone: I brought him down to his proper level with only these words: If your doctrine is so instructive, let it tell us something new! Mankind will, no doubt, make very great progress in the next two hundred years; let it specify any single improvement which is to take place within that period! Let it tell me what I shall do within the follow ng week! Let 't declare the numbers of the lottery, which will be drawn to-morrow!

"I behaved in the same manner to Gall, and contributed very much to the discredit of his theory. Corvisart

was his principal follower. He and his colleagues have
a great propensity to materialism, which is calculated to
strengthen their theory and influence. But nature is not
so poor. Were she so clumsy as to make herself known
by external forms, we should do our business more
promptly and know a great deal more. Her secrets are
more subtle, more delicate, more evanescent, and have
hitherto escaped the most minute researches. We find a
great genius in a little huuchback; and a man, with a
fine commanding person, turns out to be a stupid
fellow. A big head, with a large brain, is sometimes
destitute of a single idea; while a small brain is found
to possess a vast understanding. And observe the
imbecility of *Gall*. He attributes to cerʉain protube-
rances propensities and crimes, which are not in nature,
but arise solely from society and the conventional usages
of mankind. What would become of the protuberance
of theft, if there were no property; of drunkenness, if
there were no fermented liquors; and of ambition, if
there were no society?

"The same remarks apply to that egregious charlatan
Lavater, with his physical and moral relations. Our
credulity lies in the defect of our nature. It is inherent
in us to wish for the acquisition of positive ideas, when
we ought, on the contrary, to be carefully on our guard
against them. We scarcely look at a man's features,
before we pretend to know his character. We should
be wise enough to repel the idea and to neutralize those
deceitful appearances. I was robbed by a person who
had grey eyes, and from that moment am I never to look
at grey eyes without the idea, the fear, of being robbed?
A weapon wounded me, and I am afraid of it wherever I
see it; but was it the grey eyes that robbed me? Reason
and experience, and I have been enabled to derive great
benefit from both, prove that all those external signs
are so many lies; that we cannot be too strictly on our
guard against them, and that the only true way of appreciating and gaining a thorough knowledge of mankind is by trying and associating with them. After all,
we meet with countenances so hideous, it must be
allowed," (and as an instance he described one; it was

that of the governor,) "that the most powerful understanding is confounded, and condemns them in spite of
itself."

SINGULAR SERIES OF VEXATIONS, &C.

23d. — The Emperor called upon me about three
o'clock. He wished to take a walk. He had a gloomy
look, and had suffered much since yesterday. He was
seriously affected by the intense heat during his ride in
the calash. He had observed a new outer door which
was making, and which would have altered the whole
interior of the topographical cabinet and of Madame
Montholon's former apartment. He had not been consulted on the occasion, and was sensibly affected at it.
He sent instantly for the person who had given the
directions, and the wretched reasons he assigned served
only to vex him still more. We had come out to walk ;
but it seemed decided that every thing was to irritate
and put him in ill humour that evening. He saw some
English officers on his way, and turned aside from them
almost in anger, observing that shortly it would be impossible for him to put his foot out of doors. A few
paces off he was joined by the Doctor, who came to tell
him, unseasonably enough, of some arrangements that
were making for him, (the Emperor) and to ask his
opinion on the subject. It was one of the topics which,
perhaps, hurt his feelings most. He made no answer,
his ordinary resource against disappointment ; but this
time' he kept silence with a fretfulness which he could
not conceal. He came up with the carriage, and got in;
but on our way we met some more English officers, and
then he suddenly ordered the coachman to drive off, at a
gallop, in another direction.

The new door-way, however, which had been made in
the house without his knowledge, and which he found
so inconvenient, still lay heavy on his heart. He was
about to lighten the load by a lively playfulness with
the wife of the person who had ordered it, and who
happened to be in the calash. "Ah," said he, "are
you there ? You are in my power ; you shall pay the
penalty. The husband is the guilty person ; it is the

wife that shall answer for him." But instead of accom-
modating herself to the sense in which the words were
uttered, which she might have done without the least
inconvenience, and with the certainty of a satisfactory
result, she persisted in making lame excuses for her
husband, and repeating reasons, which served but to
revive his dissatisfaction. Finally, to fill up the chapter
of cross-purposes, one of us, on discovering the tents
of the camp, informed him that the evolutions and
manœuvres of the preceding day were in celebration of
one of the great victories gained by the English in
Spain, and that the regiment which executed them had
been very nearly destroyed in that battle. "A regiment, Sir, is never destroyed by the enemy; it is im-
mortalized," was his only answer. It is true, that it
was delivered very dryly.

For myself, I meditated in silence on this accumulation of contrarieties, which struck such repeated blows
in so short a time. It was a precious moment for an
observer. I estimated the mortification which they
were calculated to produce, and I remarked with admiration, how little he betrayed. I said to myself:
This is the *intractable man*, this the *tyrant !* One would
have supposed that he knew what was passing in my
mind, for, when we left the calash, and were a few paces
before the others, he said to me in a low tone, "If you
like to study mankind, learn how far patience can go,
and all that one can put up with," &c.

On his return, he called for tea; I had never seen him
take any. Madame de Montholon was, for the first
time, in possession of her new saloon. He wished to
see it, and observed that she would be much better accommodated than any of us. He called for fire, and
played at chess with several of us successively. He
gradually recovered his natural temper and ate a little at
dinner, which completely restored him. He indulged
in conversation, and again reverted to his early years,
which always possessed fresh charms for him. He
spoke a great deal of his early acquaintances, and of the
difficulties which some of them experienced in obtaining
admission to him after his elevation, and observed that.

"·if the threshold of his palace was impassable, it ·as in spite of himself.   What then," said he, " must be the situation of other sovereigns in that respect!"

We continued the conversation until eleven without noticing the lateness of the hour

MADAME DE B. . . . .—ANECDOTES RESPECTING THE EMIGRANTS.

24th.—To-day the Emperor tried the billiard-table which had just been placed, and went out, but the weather being very damp, he returned almost immediately.

He conversed with me in his apartment, before dinner, on the emigrants, and the name of Madame de B . . ., who had been *dame d'atours* to Madame, and was very conspicuous in the commencement of our affairs, was mentioned.   The Emperor observed, "But is not this Madame de B . . . . a very dangerous woman?"— " Certainly not," I replied; " she is, on the contrary, one of the best women in the world, with a great deal of wit, and an excellent judgment."   " If that is the case," said the Emperor, " she must have much cause to complain of me.   This is the painful consequence of false representations ; she was pointed out as a very dangerous character."—" Yes, Sire, you made her very unhappy. Madame de B . . . . placed all her happiness in the charms of society, and you banished her from Paris.   I met with her in one of my missions, confined within her province. and pining away with vexation, yet she expressed no resentment against your Majesty, and spoke of you with great moderation."   " Well, then! why did you not come to me, and set me right?"—" Ah, Sire, your character was then so little known to us, compared with what I know it to be at present, that I should not have dared to do so.   But I will mention an anecdote of Madame de B . . . . when in London, during the high tide of our emigration, which will make you better acquainted with her than any thing I could say.   At the time of your accession to the Consulate, a person, just arrived from Paris. was invited to a small party at her house.   He engrossed the attention of the company, in consequence of all the particulars that he had to communicate respecting a place, which interested us so very materially. He was asked several questions respecting the Consul. He cannot, said he, live long, he is most delightfully *sallow*. These were his words. He grew more animated by degrees, and gave as a toast —The death of the First Consul! Oh horrible! was the instantaneous exclamation of Madame de B . . . What, drink to the death of a fellow creature! For shame! I will give a much better one : The King's health!"

" Well," said the Emperor, " I repeat that she was very ill used by me, in consequence of the representations which were made to me. She had been described to me as a person fond of political intrigues, and remarkable for the bitterness of her sarcasms. And this puts me in mind of an expression which is perhaps wrongly attributed to her, but which struck me, however, solely on account of its wit. I was assured that a distinguished personage, who was very much attached to her, was seized with a fit of jealousy, for which she clearly proved that she had given no cause. He persisted however, and observed that she ought to know that the wife of Cæsar should be free from suspicion. Madame de B . . . . replied that the remark contained two important mistakes ; for it was known to all the world that she was not his wife, and that he was not Cæsar."

After dinner, the Emperor read to us parts of the comedies of the Dissipateur and the Glorieux, but he was so little pleased with them that he left off ; they did not possess a sufficient degree of interest. He had a severe pain in his right side. It was the effect of the damp to which he had been exposed during his morning walk, and we were not without apprehensions of its being a symptom of the ordinary malady of this scorching climate.

On my return home, I found a letter from England, with a parcel, containing some articles for my toilet. The Griffin ship of war had just arrived from England.

THE EMPEROR RECEIVES LETTERS FROM HIS FAMILY.
CONVERSATION WITH THE ADMIRAL.—THE COMMIS
SIONERS OF THE ALLIED POWERS.

25th.—About nine o'clock, I received from the Grand
Marshal three letters for the Emperor. They were from
Madame Mère, the Princess Pauline, and Prince Lucien.
The latter was enclosed in one addressed to me, from
Rome, by Prince Lucien, dated the 6th of March. I
also received two from my agent in London.

The Emperor passed the whole of the morning in
reading the papers from the 25th of April to the 13th of
May. They contained accounts of the death of the Empress of Austria, the prorogation of the French Chambers,
Cambrone's acquittal, the condemnation of General
Bertrand, &c. He made many remarks upon all these
subjects.

About three, Admiral Malcolm requested to be presented to the Emperor. He brought him a series of the
Journal des Debats to the 13th of May. The Emperor
desired me to introduce him, and he conversed with him
nearly three hours. He gave great pleasure to the Emperor, who treated him, from the first moment, with a
great deal of freedom and good nature, as if he had been
an old acquaintance. The Admiral was entirely of his
opinion with respect to a great number of subjects. He
admitted that it was extremely difficult to escape from
St. Helena, and he could see no inconvenience in allowing him to be at large in the island. He considered it
absurd that Plantation-house had not been given up to
the Emperor, and felt, but only since his arrival, he confessed, that the title of General might be offensive. It
struck him that Lady Loudon's conduct had been ridiculous here, and would be laughed at in London. He
thought that the Governor had good intentions, but did
not know how to act. Ministers had, in his opinion,
been embarrassed with respect to the Emperor, but
entertained no hatred against him ; they did not know
how to dispose of him. Had he remained in England,
he would have been, and was still, a terror to the Conti-

nent; he would have been too dangerous and efficient an
instrument in the hands of Opposition, &c. He was
apprehensive, however, that all these circumstances put
together would detain us here a long time; and he expressed his confidence that it was the intention of
Ministers, with the exception of the necessary precautions to prevent his escape, that Napoleon should be
treated with every possible indulgence at St. Helena, &c.
He delivered himself upon all these points in so satisfactory a manner that the Emperor discussed the business with him, with as little warmth as if he had not
been concerned in the matter.

At one moment, the Emperor produced a sensible
effect upon him; it was when, alluding to the Commissioners, he pointed out the impossibility of receiving
them. " After all, Sir," said he, "you and I are men.
I appeal to you, is it possible that the Emperor of
Austria, whose daughter I married, who implored that
union on his knees, who keeps back my wife and my
son, should send me his Commissioner, without a line
for myself, without the smallest scrap of a bulletin with
respect to my son's health? Can I receive him with
consistency? Can I have any thing to communicate to
him? I may say the same thing of the Commissioner
sent by Alexander, who gloried in calling himself my
friend, with whom, indeed, I carried on political wars,
but had no personal quarrel. It is a fine thing to be a
Sovereign, but we are not on that account the less entitled to be treated as men; I lay claim to no other character at present! Can they all be destitute of feeling?
Be assured, Sir, that when I object to the title of
General, I am not offended. I decline it merely because
it would be an acknowledgment that I have not been
Emperor; and, in this respect, I advocate the honour of
others more than my own. I advocate the honour of
those with whom I have been, in that rank, connected
by treaties, by family and political alliances. The only
one of those Commissioners, whom I might perhaps receive, would be that of Louis XVIII., who owes me
nothing. That Commissioner was a long time my subject, he acts merely in conformity to circumstances, in-

dependent of his option; and I should accordingly receive him to-morrow, were I not apprehensive of the misrepresentations that would take place, and of the false colouring that would be given to the circumstance."

After dinner, the Emperor again alluded to the time of his Consulate, to the numerous conspiracies which had been formed against him, to the celebrated persons of that period, &c. I have already noticed these topics at considerable length. The conversation lasted until one o'clock in the morning — a very extraordinary hour for us.

THE EMPEROR'S COURT.—EXPENSES, SAVINGS, HUNTING AND SHOOTING ESTABLISHMENT, MEWS, PAGES, SERVICE OF HONOUR, &c.

26th—28th. Our usual mode of living, an airing in the carriage in the middle of the day; conversation at night.

On the 27th the Emperor received, for a moment, a colonel, a relation of the family of Walsh Serrant, who was on his return from the Cape in the Haycomb, and was to sail next day for Europe. He had been Governor of Bourbon, and entertained us with many agreeable particulars respecting that island.

After dinner, the conversation turned on the old and new Court, with their arrangements, expenses, etiquette, &c. I have already mentioned most of these points in another place, and many of them were repeated on the present occasion. I pass over what would seem but a literal repetition.

The Emperor's Court was, in every respect, much more magnificent than any thing seen up to that period, and yet, said he, the expense was infinitely less. That vast difference was caused by the suppression of abuses, and by the introduction of order and regularity into the accounts. His hunting and shooting establishment, with the exception of some useless and ridiculous particulars, he observed, as that of falconry and some others, was as splendid, as numerous, and as striking, as that of Louis XVI., and the annual disbursement, he assured us, was but 400,000 francs, while the King's amounted to

seven millions. His table was regulated according to
the same system. Duroc had, by his regularity and
strictness, done wonders in that respect. Under the
kings, the palaces were not kept furnished, and the same
articles were transferred from one palace to another; the
people belonging to the Court had no furniture allowed
them, and every one was obliged to look out for himself.
Under him, on the contrary, there was not a person in
attendance who did not find himself provided as comfortably, or even more so, with every thing that was
necessary or suitable, in the apartment assigned to him,
than in his own house.

The Emperor's stud cost three millions, the expense
of the horses was averaged at 3000 francs a horse yearly.
A page cost from 6 to 8000 francs. That establishment,
he observed, was perhaps the most expensive belonging
to the palace, and accordingly the education of the pages
and the care taken of them, were the subjects of just
encomium. The first families of the empire were solici-
tous to place their children in it, and they had good
reason, said the Emperor.

With respect to the etiquette of the Court, the Emperor said he was the first who had separated the *service
of honour* (an expression invented under him) from
that which was absolutely necessary. He had dismissed
every thing that was laborious and substantial, and substituted what was nominal and ornamental only. "A
king," he said, "is not to be found in nature, he is the
mere creature of civilization. There are no naked kings;
they must all be dressed," &c.

The Emperor remaked that it was impossible for any
one to be better informed of the nature and relation of
all these matters than himself; because they had been
all regulated by him, according to the precedents of past
times, from which he had lopped off whatever was ridiculous, and preserved every thing that appeared suitable.

The conversation lasted until after eleven o'clock. It
had been kept up with tolerable spirit; and the Emperor
again observed, on leaving us, that, after all, we must be
a good-natured kind of people to be able to lead so contented a life at St. Helena.

FRESH INSTANCE OF THE GOVERNOR'S MALIGNITY, &c
—DESPERATE PROJECT OF SANTINI, THE CORSICAN.

29th.—The weather had been bad for some days; the
Emperor took advantage of a fine interval to examine a
tent, which the admiral had, in a very handsome manner,
ordered to be erected for his accommodation by his ship's
crew, having heard him complain, in the course of conversation, of the want of shade, and of the impossibility
of enjoying himself in the air out of his apartment. The
Emperor conversed with the officer and men who were
putting the last hand to the work, and ordered a napoleon
to be given to each of the seamen.

We learnt to-day that the last vessel had brought a
book on the state of public affairs for the Emperor,
written, as it was said, by a Member of Parliament. It
had been sent by the author himself, and the following
words were inscribed in letters of gold on the outside,—
To Napoleon the Great. This circumstance induced the
Governor to keep back the work, a rigour, on his part,
which formed a singular contrast with his eagerness to
supply us with libels, that treated the Emperor so dis-
respectfully.

During dinner, the Emperor, turning, with a stern
look, to one of the servants in waiting, exclaimed, to
our utter consternation: "So then, assassin, you intended to kill the Governor!—Wretch!—If such a
thought ever again enters your head, you will have to do
with me; you will see how I shall behave to you." And
then, addressing himself to us, he said, "Gentlemen, it
is Santini, there, who determined to kill the Governor.
That rascal was about to involve us in a sad embarrassment. I found it necessary to exert all my authority,
all my indignation to restrain him."

In order to explain this extraordinary transaction, it
is necessary for me to observe that Santini, who was
formerly usher of the Emperor's cabinet, and whose
extreme devotion had prompted him to follow his master
and serve him, no matter, he said, in what capacity,
was a Corsican, of deep feeling and a warm imagination.
Enraged at the Governor's ill usage, no longer able to

bear with patience the affronts which he saw heaped
upon the Emperor, exasperated at the decline of his
health, and affected himself with a distracting melancholy,
he had, for some time, done no work in the house, and,
under pretence of procuring some game for the Emperor's table, his employment seemed to be that of
shooting in the neighbourhood.   In a moment of confidence, he told his countryman Cypriani that he had
formed the project, by the means of his double barrelled
piece, of killing the Governor, and then putting an
end to himself.   And all, said he, to rid the world of a
monster.

Cypriani, who knew his countryman's character, was
shocked at his determination, and communicated it to
several other servants.   They all united in entreating
him to lay aside his design, but their efforts, instead of
mitigating, seemed but to inflame his irritation.   They
resolved then to disclose the project to the Emperor,
who had him instantly brought before him : " And it
was only," he told me some time afterwards, " by
imperial, by *pontifical* authority, that I finally succeeded
in making the scoundrel desist altogether from his project.   Observe for a moment the fatal consequences
which he was about to produce.   I should have also
passed for the murderer, the assassin, of the Governor,
and in reality it would have been very difficult to destroy
such an impression in the mind of a great number of
people."

The Emperor read to us La Mort de Pompée, which
was stated in the journals to be the subject of general
interest at Paris, on account of its political allusions.
And this gave rise to the remark that government had
been obliged to forbid the representation of Richard, and
that, certainly on the fifth and sixth of October, Louis
XVI. little thought of its ever being prohibited for its
allusions to another.   " The fact is that times are
wonderfully changed," said the Emperor.

30th.—The Emperor, after a few turns in the garden,
went to General Gourgaud's apartment, where he was a
long time employed, with his compasses and pencil, in
laying down the coast of Syria, and the plan of Saint

Jean d'Acre, which the general was to execute. In marking some points about Acre, he said:—" I passed many unpleasant moments there."

In the evening we had Le Mariage de Figaro, which entertained and interested us much more than we had been led to expect. " It was," observed the Emperor, in shutting the book, " the Revolution already put into action."

LA HARPE'S MÉLANIE. — NUNS. — CONVENTS. — MONKS OF LA TRAPPE.—THE FRENCH CLERGY.

31st.—The weather was horrible about three o'clock, and the Emperor could scarcely reach Madame de Montholon's saloon. He amused himself for some time there in reading the Thousand and One Nights, and afterwards, perceiving a volume of the Moniteur on which M. de Montholon was then employed, and which lay open in the part relative to the negotiations for a maritime armistice in 1800, his whole attention was absorbed by them for upwards of an hour.

After dinner, the Emperor read first La Mère Coupable, in which we felt interested, and next the Mélanie of La Harpe, which he thought wretchedly conceived and very badly executed. " It was," he said, " a turgid declamation, in perfect conformity with the taste of the times, founded in fashionable calumnies and absurd falsehoods. When La Harpe wrote that piece, a father certainly had not the power of forcing his daughter to take the veil; the laws would never have allowed it. This play, which was performed at the beginning of the Revolution, was indebted for its success solely to the extravagance of public opinion. Now, that the passion is over, it must be deemed a wretched performance ! La Harpe's characters are all unnatural. He should not have attacked defective institutions with defective weapons."

The Emperor said that La Harpe had so completely failed in his object, with regard to his own impressions, that all his feelings were in favour of the father, while he was shocked at the daughter's conduct. He had never seen the performance, without being tempted to

start from his seat, and call out to the daughter : " You
have but to say, No, and we will all take your part ;
you will find a protector in every citizen."

He observed that, when he was on service with his
regiment, he had often witnessed the ceremony of taking
the veil.   " It was a ceremony very much attended by
the officers, and which raised our indignation, particularly when the victims were handsome.   We ran in
crowds to it, and our attention was alive to the slightest
incident. Had they but said, *No,* we should have carried
them off sword in hand. It is consequently false that
violence was employed : seductive means only were
resorted to. Those, upon whom they were practised,
were kept secluded perhaps, like recruits. The fact is
that, before they had done, they had to pass the ordeal
of the nuns, the abbess, the spiritual director, the
bishop, the civil officer, and finally the public spectators.
Can it be supposed that all these had agreed to concur
in the commission of a crime ?"

The Emperor declared that he was an enemy to
convents in general, as useless, and productive of degrading inactivity. He allowed, however, in another
point of view, that certain reasons might be pleaded in
their favour. The best *mezzo termine,* and he had
adopted it, was, in his opinion, that of tolerating them,
of obliging the members to become useful, and of allowing annual vows only.

The Emperor complained that he had not had time
enough to complete his institutions. It had been his
intention to enlarge the establishments of Saint Denis
and Ecouen, for the purpose of affording an asylum to
the widows of soldiers, or women advanced in years.
" And then," he added, " it must also be admitted that
there were characters and imaginations of all kinds; that
compulsion ought not to be used with regard to persons
of an eccentric turn, provided their oddities are harmless, and that an empire, like France, might and ought
to have houses for madmen, called *Trappistes.* With
respect to the latter," he observed, " that if any one
ever thought of inflicting upon others the discipline
which they practised, it would be justly considered a

most abominable tyranny, and that it might, notwithstanding, constitute the delight of him who voluntarily exercised it on himself. Such is man, such his whims, or his follies ! . . . He had tolerated the monks ot Mount Cenis, but these, at least," he added, "were useful, very useful, and might be even called heroic."

The Emperor expressed himself in his Council of State in the following words, when the organization of the University was about to take place : " It is my opinion that the monks would be far the best body for communicating instruction, were it possible to keep them under proper control, and to withdraw them from their dependence upon a foreign master. I am disposed to be favourable to them. I should, perhaps, have had the power to reinstate them in their establishments, but they have made the thing impossible. The moment I do any thing for the clergy, they give me cause to repent it. I do not complain of the old established clergy, for with them I am sufficiently satisfied ; but the young priests are brought up in a gloomy fanatical doctrine ; there is nothing Gallican in the young clergy.

" I have nothing to say against the old bishops. They have shewn themselves grateful for what I did for religion : they have realized my expectations.

" Cardinal de Boisgelin was a man of sense, a virtuous character, who had faithfully adopted me.

"The Archbishop of Tours, Barral, a man of great acquirements, and who was of essential service to us in our differences with the Pope, was always very much attached to me.

" The worthy Cardinal du Belloy, and the virtuous Bishop Roquelaure, had a sincere affection for me.

" I made no difficulty whatever in placing Bishop Beausset among the Dignitaries of the University, and I am convinced that he was one of those who, in that capacity, most sincerely conducted themselves in conformity with my views.

"All these old bishops possessed my confidence, and none of them deceived me. It is not a little singular that those whom I had the greatest cause to complain of were precisely those whom I had chosen myself; so

3*

very true is it that the holy unction, though it attaches us to the kingdom of Heaven, does not deliver us from the infirmities of the earth, from its irregularities, its obscenities, its turpitudes."

The conversation next turned upon the want of priests in France, the obligation of engaging them at the age of sixteen, and the difficulty, even the impossibility, of finding any at twenty-one.

It was the Emperor's wish that they should be ordained at a more advanced age. The answer of the bishops and the Pope himself was, " It is very well : your reasons are very just; but if you wait for that period you will find none to ordain, and yet you admit that you are in want of them."

" I have no doubt," observed the Emperor, " that, after me, other principles will be adopted. A conscription of priests and nuns will, perhaps, be seen in France, as a military conscription was seen in my time. My barracks will, perhaps, be turned into convents and seminaries. Thus goes the world. Poor nations! In spite of all your knowledge, all your wisdom, you continue, like individuals, the slaves of fashionable caprice."

It was nearly one o'clock in the morning before the Emperor retired. It was, he said, a real victory over *ennui,* and a great relief for the want of sleep.

MARIA ANTOINETTE.—THE MANNERS OF VERSAILLES.—ANECDOTE.—BEVERLEY.—DIDEROT'S PÉRE DE FAMILLE.

AUGUST 1.—The weather was dreadful. About three o'clock, the Grand Marshal came to look for me; but as I had at that moment ventured out, I was not to be found. It was on account of some English, whom he had to present to the Emperor.

The Emperor sent for me at five ; he was in a bad humour, and not a little so, he said, on my account. The visit of the English, the bad weather, the want of the saloon and an interpreter, had all combined to vex him.

He was reading the Veillées du Château, which, he observed, were tiresome, and he left them for the Tales of Margaret, Queen of Navarre.

He afterwards adverted to Versailles; the Court, the Queen, Madame Campan, and the King, were the principal subjects of his remarks, and he said many things, some of which I have already noticed. He concluded with observing that Louis XVI. would have been a perfect pattern in private life, but that he had been a sorry King; and that the Queen would no doubt have been, at all times, the ornament of every circle, but that her levity, her inconsistencies, and her want of capacity, had not a little contributed to promote and accelerate the catastrophe. She had, he remarked, deranged the manners of Versailles; its ancient gravity and strict etiquette were transformed into the free and easy manners and absolute tittle-tattle of a private party. No man of sense and importance could avoid the jests of the young courtiers, whose natural disposition for raillery was sharpened by the applauses of a young and beautiful Sovereign.

One of the most characteristic anecdotes of that day was told. A gallant and worthy German general arrived at Paris, with a special recommendation to the Queen, from the Emperor Joseph, her brother. The Queen thought she could not do him a greater favour than to invite him to one of her private parties. He found himself, it may be easily imagined, a little out of his element in such company, but it was every one's wish to treat him with marked respect, and he was obliged to take a leading part in the conversation. He was unfortunate in the selection of his topics, and in his manner of introducing them. He talked a great deal about *his white mare, and his grey mare*, which he valued above all things. The subject gave rise to a number of arch inquiries on the part of the young courtiers, respecting a thousand frivolous points, which he had the good-nature to answer, as if they were matters of importance. In conclusion, one of them asked to which of the two he gave the decided preference: "Really," answered the general, with peculiar significance, "I must confess, that, if I were in the day of battle on my white mare, I do not believe I should dismount to get on my grey one." At length he made his bow, and the bursts of

laughter that followed may be easily conceived. The conversation took another turn after his departure; the
attractions of white and brown beauties were long and
ingeniously canvassed, and. the Queen having asked one
of the party which he preferred, he instantly assumed a
grave air, and imitating the solemn tone of the Austrian,
answered, "Really, Madam, I must confess, that if I
were in the day of battle on . . . . . ." "Enough,"
interposed the Queen, "spare us the remainder."

After dinner he read Beverley and the Père de Famille
to us. The latter, in particular, excited his animadver-
sion. To us it seemed a paltry production. What
most amused the Emperor, as he said, was that it was
Diderot's, that Coryphœus of philosophers and of the
Encyclopedia. All it contained was, he said, false and
ridiculous. The Emperor entered into a long examination of the details, and concluded with saying, "Why
reason with a madman in the height of a raging fever?
It is remedies and a decisive mode of treatment that he
needs. Who does not know that the only safeguard
against love is flight? When Mentor wishes to secure
Telemachus, he plunges him into the sea. When Ulysses
endeavours to preserve himself from the Syrens, he
causes himself to be bound fast, after having stopped the
ears of his companions with wax."

HISTORICAL SKETCH OF THE EMIGRATION TO COBLENTZ.— ANECDOTES, &c.

2nd.—Uninterrupted bad weather, with heavy rains·
The Emperor was not well; he felt his nerves very
much irritated.

He sent for me to breakfast with him. During the
whole of breakfast, and a long time afterwards, the conversation again turned on the emigration. I have
already remarked that he often brought me back to the
subject. His enquiries to-day were directed to the particulars of what had passed at Coblentz, our situation,
our disposition, our organization, our views, and our resources, and at the end of all my answers, he concluded,
observing: "You have already several times acquainted
me with a considerable part of those things, and yet I

do not retain them, because you communicate them
without regularity. Reduce them to a consistent historical summary. How could you be better employed in
this place? And then, my dear Las Cases, you will have
a piece ready at hand for your journal." This demand
was like that addressed by Dido to Æneas, and I to*
might have exclaimed, *Infandum regina, jubes.* . . .
however, I executed the sketch as completely as my
memory and judgment enabled me, for the subject began
to grow old, and I was, at that time, very young. I
give it as I read it, a short time afterwards, to Napoleon.

" Sire, after the famous events which overthrew the
Bastile, and set all France in agitation, most of our
Princes, who found themselves implicated in the consequences, fled from the country, with the sole view, at
that period, of securing their personal safety. They
were soon after joined by persons of considerable rank,
and by a number of young men; the former, induced by
the connection which they had with them, and the latter
by a persuasion that the measure of itself indicated, in
some degree, a striking, generous, and decided devoted-
ness. When a certain number were collected, the idea
suggested itself of converting to a political end that
which, until then, had been produced by zeal and chance
alone. It was thought that if, with the assistance of
these assemblages, a kind of small power could be created,
it might be enabled to re-act, with advantage, or. the
interior, become a lever to insurrection there, make an
impression on the public mind, and restrain popular commotion; while it would be, abroad, a title or pretext
for applying to foreign Powers and claiming their attention. This was the origin of the emigration; and it is
confidently stated that this grand idea was conceived by
M. de Calonne,* as he passed through Switzerland, in
the suite of one of our Princes, who was on his way
from Turin to Germany.

---

* Some one who considers himself well informed has assured
me that this is erroneous, as M. de Calonne did not reach Germany
till the measure of emigration had been already decided upon;
adding that, so far from having contrived or instigated it, he had
actually censured it.

" The first assemblage took place at Worms, under
the Prince de Condé. The most celebrated was that at
Coblentz, under the King's two brothers, one of whom
came from Italy, where he had at first found an asylum
in the Court of the King of Sardinia, his father-in-law,
and the other arrived by way of Brussels, after escaping
the crisis, which had made a captive of Louis XVI. at
Varennes.

" I was one of the first of those who assembled at
Worms. The number about the Prince was scarcely
fifty when I arrived. In the entire effervescence of
youth, and with the first inspiration of what was noble,
I hastened to Worms with the most innocent simplicity
of heart. My reading and my prayer each morning
consisted of a chapter of Bayard. I expected, on
reaching Worms, to be, at the very least, seized and
embraced by so many brothers in arms; but, to my
great surprise (and it was my first lesson on mankind),
instead of this affectionate reception, I and a companion
were, all at once, examined and watched, for the purpose of ascertaining that we were not spies. We were
afterwards carefully sounded with regard to our interests,
our views, and the pretensions by which we might have
been actuated, and, finally, great pains were taken to
prove to us, and to make the Prince perceive (and this
plan was renewed on every fresh arrival), that our
numbers increased greatly, and exceeded, no doubt,
already, the places and favours which he had to confer.
My companion was so shocked that he proposed to me
to return instantly to Paris.

" We, who composed the assemblage, in order to
make ourselves useful or to acquire importance, undertook, three or four of us by turns, to form a kind of
regular guard about the Prince's person night and day ;
for we dreamt already of nothing but conspiracies and
assassination, so very powerful and redoubtable did we
think ourselves, and when relieved, whilst on this kind
of voluntary guard, we had the honour of being admitted to the Prince's table. Three generations of
Condé constituted its ornament, a singular circumstance,
which was renewed with more striking effect in the army

of Condé, in which the grandfather fought in the centre, while the son and grandson commanded the right and left, where they were, I believe, both wounded, and on the same day.

" The Princess of Monaco had followed the Prince of Condé ; he married her afterwards, but she then governed and did the honours of his establishment. We had the opportunity of hearing at that table some of the guests assert and re-assert to the Prince that we were already more than enough to enter France ; that his name and a white handkerchief were sufficient ; that the star of Condé was about to shine forth once more ; that the occasion was singularly happy, and that it was necessary to seize it ; and I would not pledge myself, that adulation wsa not pushed so far as to suggest very interested personal views to the Prince.

" Worms, from the nature of its meeting, and the character of its chief, always evinced more regularity, more austerity of discipline, than Coblentz, where there was a display of more agitation, luxury, and pleasure. Worms was accordingly called the *camp*, and Coblentz the *City* or the *Court*.

" The importance of the leader was in proportion to the force under his command, and of this the Prince of Condé was so sensible that he never saw any one leave him without regret, and remembered it a long time. I was not, on that account, the less eager to go to Coblentz, the moment it acquired a certain degree of splendour. I had relations and friends there, and it was, besides, more attractive, from superior magnificence, activity, and grandeur. Coblentz became in a short time a focus of foreign and domestic intrigues. Two distinct parties might be observed there ; Messrs. d'Avaray, de Jaucourt, and some others, were the confidential friends, the advisers, or the ministers, of Monsieur, now Louis XVIII. The Bishop of Arras, the Count de Vaudreuil, and others, were those of Monseigneur, the Count d'Artois ; and it was confidently stated that, even then, these Princes manifested distinctly enough the same political differences which, it is pretended, have since characterized them. M. de Breteuil, resident at Brussels,

and charged, according to his own declaration, with unlimited powers by Louis XVI., had formed a third party
and added to the complication of our affairs.

"M. de Calonne was relied on for our financial department, and the old Marshal de Broglie and the
Marshal de Castries were at the head of our military
establishment. The brave and able M. de Bouilly, who
had left France after the affair of Varennes, found
it impossible to remain with us, and followed King
Gustavus III. to Sweden.

"The emigration had, however, assumed a grand character, thanks to the care employed for its propagation.
Agents had traversed the provinces, circulars had been
distributed in the mansions and country-seats, summoning every gentleman to join the Princes, and act in co-
operation with them for the security of the altar and the
throne, the revenge of their honour, and the recovery of
their rights. An absolute crusade had been preached,
and with so much more effect, as it made an impression
on minds disposed to attend to it. Among the whole of
the nobility and privileged classes there was not a single
person who did not feel himself cut to the quick by the
decrees of the Assembly. All, from him who filled the
highest rank to the lowest country squire, had been deprived of what they held most dear; for the former had
lost his title and his vassals, and the latter had seen his
turret and his pigeon-house invaded, and his hares shot.
Accordingly, the movement to begin the journey was
immediate and universal; it could not be abandoned,
under the penalty of dishonour, and the women were
directed to send spindles to those who hesitated, or were
too tardy. Whether then from passion, pusillanimity,
or a point of honour, the emigration became a real infection; multitudes rushed furiously beyond the frontiers;
and what contributed not a little to increase the evil was
the means employed by the leaders of the Revolution to
promote it in secret, while they affected to oppose it in
public. They declaimed, in vague terms, against it from
the tribune, it is true; but they took great care that all
the passages should be left open. Did the zeal of the
emigrants slacken?—the declaimers became more violent,

and it was decided that the barriers should be strictly
guarded. Then those who had been left behind were reduced to despair, because they had not taken advantage
of the favourable moment. But, accidentally, or from
inattention, the barriers were again opened, and they
were passed with eagerness by those who were determined not to expose themselves to another disappointment.
It was by this dextrous management that the Assembly
assisted its enemies in plunging themselves into the
abyss.

" The able men of the faction had, from the beginning,
conceived that such a measure would deliver them from
the heterogeneous parts that checked their progress, and
that the property of all these voluntary exiles would secure to them incalculable resources. The officers thought
they did wonders in stealing away from their regiments,
while the leaders of the Revolution, on their part, excited
the soldiers to revolt, in order to force them to it. They
got rid, by these means, of enemies who were highly
dangerous, and obtained, on the contrary, in the non-
commissioned officers, zealous co-operators, who became
heroes in the national cause ; it was they who furnished
great captains, and who beat all the veteran troops of
foreign powers.

" The consequence was that Coblentz collected all
that was illustrious belonging to the Court in France, and
all that was opulent and distinguished belonging to the
provinces. We were thousands, consisting of every
branch, uniform, and rank of the army ; we peopled the
town and overran the palace. Our daily assemblages
about the persons of the Princes seemed like so many
splendid festivals. The Court was most brilliant, and
our Princes were so effectually its Sovereigns that the
poor Elector was eclipsed and lost in the midst of us,
which induced a person to observe to him, very pleasantly, one day, whether from perfect simplicity or keen
raillery, that, among all those who thronged his palace,
he was the only stranger.

" During the grand solemnities, we occasionally had
public galas ; and the respectable inhabitants were permitted to take a view of the tables. We then exulted at

witnessing the admiration expressed by the people of the
country for the pleasing countenance and chivalrous appearance of Monseigneur the Count d'Artois, and we
were proud of the homage paid by them to the acquirements and talents of Monsieur. It was worth while to
see with what arrogance we paraded with us, as it were,
the whole dignity, the lustre of our monarchy, and,
above all, the superiority of our Sovereign and the elevation of our Princes. *His Majesty the King*, was the expression which we pompously used in the German circles
to designate the King of France; for that was, or ought
to be, in our opinion, his title in point of pre-eminence
with respect to all Europe. The Abbé Maury, whom we
had at first received with acclamation, but who, by the
by, lost much of our esteem in a very short time, had
discovered, he assured us, that such was his right and
his prerogative. Shall I give another instance of over-
weening pride and conceit?

" At a later period, during our greatest disasters, and
when our cause was completely ruined, an Austrian
officer, of superior rank, charged with despatches for the
Court of London, invited to dinner several of our officers
with whom he had formerly been acquainted on the
Continent. After dinner, and very near the time when
every truth comes out, the company began to talk politics, and he happened to say that, on his departure from
Vienna, one of the principal subjects of conversation was
the marriage of Madame Royale (now Duchess d'An-
gouleme) with the Archduke Charles, who at that moment enjoyed great celebrity. ' But it is impossible !'
observed one of his French guests. ' And why ?' ' Because it is not a suitable marriage for Madame.'—' How !'
exclaimed the Austrian, seriously offended, and almost
breathless, ' His Royal Highness Monseigneur, the
Archduke Charles ! not a suitable match for your Princess.
' Oh ! no, Sir, it would be but a garrison match for her !'

" Besides, these lofty pretensions were instilled into us
with our education; they belonged to us as national
sentiments, and our Princes were not exempt from them.
With us the King's brothers disdained the title of Royal
Highness, they had the pretension of addressing all the

sovereigns by the title of brother; the rest of the system
was carried on in a proportionate way, and there was
accordingly but one feeling in Europe against our Versailles, manners and the presumption of our Princes.

"Gustavus III. said, at Aix-la-Chapelle—'Your Court
of Versailles was not accessible; it indulged too much in
haughtiness and ridicule. When I was there, there was
scarcely any attention paid to me, and, when I left it, I
brought away the titles of *booby* and *blockhead*.'

"The Duchess of Cumberland, who was married to the
King of England's brother, had to complain, at the same
time and in the same city, that the Princess de Lamballe
did not grant her the honours of the folding-doors.

"The old Duke of Gloucester complained, on his own
account, at a later period in London, of one of our
Princes of the blood, and added that the Prince of Wales
laughed heartily, because he, the Prince of Wales, addressing the same Prince by the title of Monseigneur,
the latter studiously endeavoured to model his language
so as not to return the compliment.

"At Coblentz, however, when our circumstances were
altered, our Princes condescended to change their manners in that respect, and to let themselves down to the
level of the foreign Princes. They were then with the
Elector of Treves, a Prince of Saxony, their mother's
brother, whom, by way of parenthesis, we were at that
time eating up, and who was afterwards deprived of his
possessions on our account. They condescended to call
him their *uncle*, and he was allowed to call them his
nephews. It is confidently stated that he said to them
one day, 'It is to your misfortunes that I am indebted
for such affectionate expressions; at Versailles you
would have treated me as plain M. l'Abbé, and it is not
certain that you would have received my visits every
day.' It was added that he spoke the truth, and that
they had given melancholy proofs of it to his brother,
the Count of Lusatia, who was present.

"The Princes generally passed their evenings in the
company of their intimate friends. One of them was,
most of the time, at the house of Madame de Polastron,
to whom he paid attentions that were justified by her

constancy and her behaviour. Frequent attempts were
made to destroy the intimacy, but in vain, for Madame
de Polastron was above all the cabals employed for the
purpose ; and, in addition to her amiable manners and
excellent conduct, was completely disinterested, and
carefully avoided all interference in political affairs. She
saw but very little company. I was indebted to a
female relative for the pleasure of being admitted to it ;
but, as it was necessary to withdraw before the Prince's
arrival, I never had the honour of seeing him there.

" Monsieur passed his evenings at Madame de Balby's,
Dame d'Atours to Madame. Madame de Balby, who
was lively, witty, a warm friend and a determined enemy,
attracted all the most distinguished characters. It was
an honour to be admitted to her house, which was the
centre of taste and fashion. Monsieur sometimes remained there until a late hour ; and when, after the
crowd had slipped away and the circle was contracted,
he happened to be communicative, it must be confessed
that he was as superior to us by the charms of his conversation as by his rank and dignity.

" So much for our manner of living and our outward
appearance at Coblentz ; this was the fair side of our
situation ; but we were less happy in a political point of
view—that was the degrading side."

" Good !" said the Emperor, " I begin to find your
drawing-room details too long. This is, however, excusable in you. The subject is a pleasing one to you. You
were then young ; but go on."

" Sire, the whole of our number was but a noble and
brilliant mob, and presented the image of complete confusion. It was anarchy striving without, to establish, it
was said, order within—a real democracy struggling for
the re-establishment of its aristocracy. We presented,
on a small scale, and merely with a few shades of difference, a copy of every thing that was passing in France.
We had among us zealous adherents to our ancient
forms, and ardent admirers of novelty ; we had our con-
stitutionalists, our intolerants, and our moderates. We
had our empirics, who sincerely regretted that they had
not made themselves masters of the King's person, for

the purpose of acting with violence in his name, or who frankly avowed that they entertained the design of declaring his incapability. Finally, we had also our Jacobins, who wished, on their return, to kill, to burn, to destroy every thing.

" No direct authority was exercised over the multitude by our Princes.—They were our Sovereigns, it was true, but we were very unruly subjects, and very easily irritated. We murmured on every occasion, and it was particularly against those who joined us last that our common fury was directed. It was, we declared, so much glory and good fortune of which they deprived our exploits and our hopes. Those who were once admitted considered every subsequent arrival too late. It was maintained that all merit on that score was at an end. If all continued to be received in the same way, the whole of France would soon be on our side, and there would no longer be any person to punish.

" Denunciations of every kind, and from every quarter, were then showered down upon those who joined us. A Prince de Saint-Maurice, son of the Prince de Montbarey, found it impossible to resist the storm, although he had the formal support of every distinguished character, and that of the Prince himself, who deigned to employ supplication in his favour, and said, 'Alas! gentlemen, who is there that has not faults to reproach himself with in the Revolution? I have been guilty of several, and, by your oblivion of them, you have given me the right of interceding for others.' This did not spare M. de Saint-Maurice the necessity of making his escape as soon as possible. His crime was that of having belonged to the Society of the Friends of the Negroes, and of having been violently attacked in the midst of us by a gentleman of Franche Comté, who denounced M. de Saint-Maurice for having caused his mansions to be burnt. It was, however, discovered, a few days afterwards, that the brawling assailant had no mansion, and was neither from Franche Comté, nor a gentleman : he was a mere adventurer.

" M. de Cazalès, who had filled France and Europe with the celebrity of his eloquence and courage in the

National Assembly, had, notwithstanding, lost the popular favour at Coblentz.   When he arrived at Paris, a
report was spread among us that the Princes would not
see him, or would give him an ungracious reception.
We collected eighty natives of Languedoc to form, in
opposition to his own wishes, a kind of escort for him.
M. de Cazalès was the honour of our province; we conducted him to the Princes, by whom he was well received.

   " A deputy of the third estate, who had highly distinguished himself in the Constituent Assembly by his
attachment to royalty, was among us.   One of our
Princes, addressing him one day in the crowd, said,
' But, Sir, explain to me then.—You are so worthy a
man, how could you, at the time, take the oath of the
jeu de paume ? '   The deputy, struck dumb by the attack,
at first stammered out that he had been taken unawares
—that he did not foresee the fatal consequences—but
promptly recovering himself, he replied with vivacity :
' I shall, however, observe to Monseigneur that it was
not that which led to the ruin of the French monarchy,
but in fact the assemblage of the nobility, which joined
us in consequence of the very persuasive letter written
by Monseigneur.'—' Stop there,' exclaimed the Prince,
patting him on the stomach, ' be cool, my dear Sir ; I
did not intend to vex you by that question.'

   " Something like a system of regularity, whether good
or bad, was, however, adopted in the course of time.
We were classed by corps and by provinces; we had
cantonments assigned to us, and were supplied with
arms.   The King's body - guards were again formed,
clothed, equipped, and paid, and soon became a superb
corps in appearance and discipline.   The coalition of
Auvergne and the marine corps, part on foot and part on
horseback, attracted peculiar notice by its discipline,
knowledge, and union.   Our resignation and self-denial
could not be too much admired.   Each officer was
henceforth but a private soldier, subject to exercises and
fatigues, very contrary to his former manner of life, and
exposed to the greatest privations, for there was no pay,
and many of that number had soon no resource to de-

pend on but the contributions of their more fortunate comrades. We deserved a better fate, or, to speak more correctly, we were worthy of a better enterprize. All the officers belonging to the same regiments had been collected together in separate bodies, in order that they might be ready to take the command of their soldiers, who would not fail to join them, as we thought, on their first seeing them. Such was our delusion! It was from a similar motive that the gentlemen were classed according to their respective provinces, no doubt being entertained of their efficient influence over the mass of the population. Our weakness consisted in the conviction that we continued to be wished for, respected, adored.

"All these bodies were publicly exercised and manœuvred, and the diplomatic remonstrances which were made on the subject were answered with a confident assurance that no such thing existed, or that it certainly should be prevented. We had generals appointed, a staff formed, and every thing which distinguishes headquarters, even to the office of grand-provost, arranged. Our Princes were gradually surrounded with all that constitutes a real government. They had Ministers for the affairs of the moment, and even for France, when we should return, so certain and near at hand did that time appear.

"M. de Lavilleurnois, who was afterwards so much talked of, on account of the share which he had in a royalist conspiracy, and who died at Sinnamary, in consequence of the events of Fructidor, was intrusted with the Administration of the Police. He set off at an early period to perform its duties clandestinely at Paris. He had conceived a sincere affection for me, and was determined to make me his son-in-law. He made use of the most urgent arguments to induce me to follow him; but I refused: I disliked the nature of his office. Otherwise, what different combinations in my destiny!

"We had also direct relations with almost every Court. The Princes had envoys at them, and received theirs at Coblentz. Monseigneur, the Count d'Artois, visited Vienna, I believe, but I can state with certainty

that he was at Pilnitz. The nobility, in a body, ad
dressed a letter to Catherine, from whom we received
M. de Romansoff as Ambassador. That Empress saw,
with pleasure, the storm that was rising in the south o
Europe; she cheerfully fanned a flame, which might
prove very favourable to her views, without putting her
to any expense, and she accordingly shewed herself
ardent in her sentiments, and enthusiastic in her promises.
She did not despair, in that crisis, of making a dupe of
Gustavus III., whose contiguous activity was troublesome
to her; she had prevailed upon him, it is said, to undertake the crusade, by flattering him with the rank of
Generalissimo. I do not know if this Prince, who
certainly was a very superior character for his time, and
possessed a great share of understanding and talent,
suffered himself to be deluded by her. It is, however,
undeniable that he displayed great attachment to our
cause, and announced his wish to fight for it in person.
When he left Aix la Chapelle to arrange his ultimate
measures for that purpose in Sweden, I heard him say,
on taking leave of the Princess de Lamballe : " You
will see me again shortly, but I am, nevertheless, obliged,
on my own account, to adhere to certain proceedings, to
certain measures of caution; for the part I have to play
is of a very delicate nature. Know that I, who am desirous of returning to fight at the head of your aristocrats
in France, am, at home, the first democrat of the
country.'

" We also received envoys from Louis XVI., who
presented public messages in reprobation of our conduct,
and had confidential conferences, perhaps totally different. At least, we acted as if that had been the case;
openly declaring that he was a captive, and that we
ought to take no notice of any of his orders; that we
were bound to take every thing he was compelled to say
in a contrary sense, and that, when he exhorted us to
peace, he was, in reality, calling upon us to go to war.
It is accordingly my opinion that we were very detrimental to the tranquillity of the unfortunate Monarch,
and that we had our special share in the pardon which
he bequeathed by his will to his friends, who, by an
indiscreet zeal, as he observes, did him so much injury.

" Our emigration, however, was prolonged in spite of
all the promises which were made to us, and of all the
hopes with which our fancy was flattered. With what
illusions, what idle tales, what absurdities, was our impatience mocked! whether those who invented them
anticipated our disappointment, or were themselves deceived. It was pleasantly calculated that, according to
our letters and gazettes, we had, in less than eighteen months, set in motion nearly two millions of men,
although we ourselves had seen none of them. But
those initiated in the mystery assured us, in special
confidence, that these troops marched only by night, for
the purpose of more effectually surprising the democrats,
or that they passed in the day-time only by platoons and
without uniform ; or told us some other story of a similar
kind. On the other hand, we shewed each other a heap
of letters from all countries and the best sources, written
in an enigmatical style, and which were thought to be
intelligible to us alone. One was acquainted that fifty
thousand Bohemian glasses had been just sent off for his
country ; another was informed that ten thousand pieces
of Saxon porcelain would soon be sent off; and a third
received intelligence that twenty-five bales of cocoa
would be addressed to him, with other fooleries of the
same kind.

" How was it possible, I now ask myself, that men of
understanding, for there certainly were a great many
among the number, that Ministers, who had formerly
governed us, and others who were destined to succeed
them, should be gulled by such wretched stuff, or that
the plain good sense, which we possessed as a multitude,
did not make us laugh in their faces? But no ; we were
not the less convinced that we were near the accom-
plishment of our hopes ; that the moment was at hand ;
that it would infallibly happen ; that we had only to show
ourselves ; that we were eagerly expected, and that all
would fall prostrate at our feet."

Here the Emperor, who had often interrupted me with
laughter and raillery, said, in a very serious tone, " How
very faithful is the picture you have drawn ! I recognise
a crowd of your friends in it. Truly, my dear Las Cases,

and I say it without meaning any offence to you, vapour-
ing, credulity, inconsistency, stupidity itself, might be
said, in spite of all their wit, to be specially their lot.
When I occasionally wished to be amused, and divested
myself of all reserve, for the purpose of giving them full
scope, and encouraging their confidence in me, I have
heard, in the Tuileries, under the Consulate and the
Empire, things not less ridiculous than those which you
now relate. None of them ever entertained a doubt of
any thing. The love of the French for their Kings was
centered, they assured me, in my person. I could henceforth do what I pleased ; I had a right to use my power ;
I should never meet with any other obstacle but a handful of incorrigible persons who were the detestation of
all. That counter-revolution so much dreaded, observed
another, was but child's play to me ; I had effected it with
the utmost ease. And (will this be believed ?) ' the only
thing wanting to it,' said he, in an insinuating tone, ' is
the substitution of the ancient white colour for those
which have done us so much injury in all countries.'
The idiot ! That was the only blot which he could find
in our escutcheon. I laughed out of sheer pity, although
I felt some difficulty in restraining my feelings ; but for
his part, his sincerity was unquestionable ; he was fully
persuaded that he spoke as I thought ; and still more
so that the generality thought as he did.* But go on.''

---

* It is certainly an inherent weakness in our nature to deceive
ourselves with respect to the sentiments that are entertained of us
by others. At Coblentz, where we threw away so much money,
where so many amiable and brilliant young men, more to be
dreaded, no doubt, from an excess than a want of education, filled
every house and visited every family, it was natural to believe that
we should be beloved, and accordingly we thought ourselves
adored. Well ! at the time of my exile at the Cape of Good Hope,
I was placed by a singular chance under the guard of an inhabitant of Coblentz, who had witnessed the brilliant moments of our
emigration. I felt great pleasure in renewing the subject with him.
We could not have any secrets on that head to conceal from one
another ; twenty-five years had elapsed. Well, then, " you were
not absolutely hated," said he, " but our real affection was reserved
for your adversaries, for their cause was ours. Liberty had slipped
in among us through you. There, in the midst of you, even
before your eyes, we had formed clubs, and God knows how often

"The appearance of the Duke of Brunswick at Coblentz, and the arrival of the King of Prussia at the head of his troops, were subjects of great joy and expectation to the whole of the emigrants. Heaven opens at length before us! was our exclamation, and we are about to return to the land of promise. It was, however, the opinion of persons of judgment and experience, from the beginning, that our struggle would have the same result as all those that resembled it in history, and that we should be but instruments and pretexts for foreigners, who only pursued their private interest, and entertained no feeling for us.

"M. de Cazalès, whom a short time much improved, expressed himself to that effect with much energy. We beheld, with delight, the Prussians, as they filed off through the streets of Coblentz, on their march to our frontiers. 'Foolish boys,' he exclaimed, 'you admire, with enthusiasm, those troops and all their train. You rejoice at their march; you ought rather to shudder at it. For my own part, I should wish to see these soldiers, to the last man of them, plunged in the Rhine. Wo be to them who incite foreigners to invade their country! O my friends, the French nobility will not survive this atrocity! They will have the affliction of expiring far from the places of their birth. I am more guilty than any other, for I see it, and yet I act like all the rest; but my only excuse is that I cannot prevent the catastrophe. I repeat, wo to them who call in foreigners against their country, and trust in them.'

"How oracular these last words! Facts would have speedily convinced us of their truth, had we been less

we laughed in them at your expense, &c." And it happened to him more than once, he assured me, when mingled with the crowd, which resounded with acclamations as we passed, to shout with a considerable number of his comrades, "Long live the French Princes, and may they drink a little in the Rhine! You spoke of the reception we gave you," said he, "it was that which we gave to Custine, which you should have seen! There you would have had an opportunity of appreciating our real sentiments. We ran with enthusiasm to meet him : we crowned his soldiers ; a great number of us enlisted in his army, and several of them became generals. As for me, I missed the opportunity of making my fortune.'

infatuated, or had the multitude been capable of reasoning and acting with propriety; but we were destined to
enrich history with one of those lessons that are most
entitled to the meditation of mankind. We might be
estimated at 20 or 25,000 men under arms; and certainly, such a force, filled with ardour and devotion,
fighting for its own interests, maintaining an understanding with the sympathetic elements of the interior,
acting against a nation, shaken to its foundation and
convulsed by the agitation of new rights, not yet established and but imperfectly understood, might be capable
of striking decisive blows. But it was not upon our
strength, our success, our activity, that the foreigners
relied for the attainment of their views. Accordingly,
under the pretence of employing that influence and of
directing its operation, as they said, against several
points at once, they annihilated us by parcelling out our
numbers, and by making, as it were, prisoners of us in
the middle of their different corps. In this way, 6000
of us, under the Prince of Condé, were marched against
Alsace; 4000, under the Duke of Bourbon were to act
in Flanders, and from 12 to 15,000 continued in the
centre, under command of the King's two brothers, to
co-operate in the invasion of Champagne.

  " It had been the plan and wish of our Princes, that
Monsieur, as heir to the crown and the natural repre-
sentative of Louis XVI., should, on account of his
captivity, proclaim himself Regent of the kingdom, the
moment he set foot on the French territory; that he
should march with his emigrants at the head of the
expedition, and that the allies, in his rear, should be
considered only as auxiliaries. But the allies treated
the plan with derision, and confined us to a station at
their tail, under the orders and at the will and pleasure
of the Generalissimo, Brunswick, who caused us to be
preceded by the most absurd of manifestoes; from the
ridicule and odium of which, however, he at least saved
us.

  " It is but just, however, to acknowledge that this
treatment had not escaped the foresight of some experienced and better advised heads among us. They had

accordingly suggested, it was said, in the Council of the
Princes, that we should throw ourselves, before the
arrival of the allies, on some point of France, and maintain a civil war there by ourselves.   Others more
desperate, or more ardent, were of opinion that we
should nobly seize upon the states of the Elector of
Treves, our benefactor; occupy the town and fortress of
Coblentz, and establish there a central rallying point, or
point of support, independent of the Germanic body;
and when we exclaimed against such perfidy and ingratitude, their answer was :—' Desperate evils called for
desperate remedies.'   It is impossible to say what
might have been the result of such resolutions, which
were, however, more consistent with the bold spirit of
enterprize, that characterizes the present times, than
with the state of manners as they then existed.   They
were, therefore, unattended to, and besides, the opportunity had slipped by; we were too closely involved in
the midst of foreigners; we were already in their power,
and our destiny was to be fulfilled ! . . .

   " As for us who formed the multitude, we were far
from foreseeing the calamities that were to attend us.
We began our march in high spirits. There was not one
of us who did not expect to be, in a fortnight from that
moment, at home, triumphant in the midst of his sub-
missive, humiliated, and increased vassals.   Our confidence would not have endured a single observation or
doubt upon that head.   Of this I am about to give an
instance, which though personal and very trifling in
itself, will not be the less characteristic with respect to
us all.   We were marching through the city of Treves;
one of my granduncles had, during the war of the succession, been Governor for Louis XIV. while were tained
possession of it.   I went to see his tomb, which is in a
chapel, belonging to the Carthusians of that town.   The
ardour of my youth and the emotion of the moment
determined me to erect a small monument to his memory, with a superb inscription, suitable to the circumstances.   I entertained no doubt of executing my wish.
The good friars were of a different way of thinking; the
prior wished me to arrange the matter with the Abbé, a

kind of bishop, and of German bishop. His reserve
and coldness, in spite of his numerous coats of arms,
prepossessed me very much against him, when I communicated my chivalrous project; but when, after some
circumlocution, he declared that under the present circumstances . . . prudence,—discretion,—if the French
were to enter the place—At these last words, my
indignation was extreme; it was such that I did not
wait to utter a single word in reply. I instantly hurried
away, with a mingled laugh of contempt and anger,
convinced that I had left the most horrible Jacobin in
existence behind me ; and nothing but my natural
generosity and respect for my own character could have
prevented me calling in my comrades, who would have
certainly pulled down the chapel.   But alas ! the abbot
saw farther than I did ! Three weeks had not elapsed
before the republicans were in Treves, the poor abbé put
to flight, and the ashes of my good uncle profaned by
the infidels.

" But no sooner were we in full operation, no sooner
had we set foot on French ground, than it became no
difficult matter, except in cases of downright stupidity
and blindness, to comprehend that it actually might be
just possible that we had been the dupes of our own
folly. We found ourselves in the midst of the Prussians,
who fettered all our movements ; we could not take a
step in advance, to the right or to the left, without their
permission, and they never granted it.   Our subsistence,
all our resources, depended solely upon their will; we
had the shame of appearing as slaves on the soil where
we aspired to reign.

" As for our countrymen, instead of receiving us as
their deliverers, as we had been convinced they would,
they only gave us proofs of dislike and aversion.   With
the exception of a few country gentlemen or others who
joined us, the whole mass of the population fled at our
approach ; we were treated as enemies, with the look or
reproach and the stern silence of reprobation.   They
seemed to say to us : ' Do you not shudder then at thus
staining your country's soil ? Are you not Frenchmen
by birth ? Do your hearts then make no appeal to you

in favour of your native land ? You say you are wrong-
ed; but what wrong, what injury ever gave to a son
the right or the wish to tear open the bosom of his
mother ? . . . We are told that in ancient times a fiery
patrician, Coriolanus, was infamous enough to fight
against his country, but he had at least the merit of
uniting elevated sentiments with his furious passion; he
came forward with a victorious arm; he imposed his
own conditions; *he* was not dragged along at the tail of
barbarous foreigners; he commanded them, and he also
suffered himself to be moved to compassion. Can you
be unsusceptible of that tenderness, and do you not
tremble at our maledictions, which will be perpetuated
on you by our children ? At any rate, whatever may be
your success, it will not equal your mortifications! You
pretend to come for the purpose of governing, and you
will have brought your masters with you.'

" At Verdun and at Estain, we were quartered in the
town. Some of my comrades and myself were lodged
in a handsome house, but all the furniture and all the
proprietors had disappeared, with the exception of two
very pretty young ladies, who put us in possession of it.
This last circumstance seemed a favourable omen, we
took the opportunity of remarking it to them, and were
desirous of ingratiating ourselves by our politeness and
attentions. 'Gentlemen,' said one of the two amazons in
rather a sharp tone, ' we have remained, because we
have felt that we had the courage to tell you, face to
face, that our lovers are in arms against you, and that
they have our prayers at least as much as our hearts.'
This was intelligible language ; we wished for no
more of it, and even shifted our quarters to another
house.

" Be it as it may, we were at length in France, and
in the rear of that Prussian army, which pushed forward
its brilliant successes, leaving us three or four marches
behind. And, whether their object was to turn us into
ridicule, because we had assured them that all the towns
would throw open their gates on our appearance, or to
rid themselves of our importunities, they charged us
with the siege of Thionville. We made our approaches

and, by a fantastical singularity, the marine corps found
itself precisely opposed to the national volunteers of
Brest. When they recognised each other, it is impossible to describe the volley of invectives and insults that
was instantly exchanged.

"Thionville is, however, as it is known, one of the
strongest places, and we found the reduction of it impossible with our limited means, for we were in want of
every thing; and it absolutely required an important
negociation to obtain two 24-pounders from the Austrians at Luxembourg. After a great deal of solicitation
and hesitation, the two pieces were at length brought in
triumph, and it was with this formidable train, that we
summoned the place, and fired at night, in pure waste of
powder, some hundreds of cannon shot. On my return
from emigration, having fallen by chance into company
with General de Wimphen, who commanded the fortress,
he asked me, ' what could have been our intention, or
the meaning of the jest we had thus attempted to play
off?' ' It was done, I believe,' said I, ' because reliance
was placed upon you.' ' But even had that been the
case,' said he, ' you still ought to have furnished me
with an excuse for surrendering; you could not expect
that I should solicit you to attack me.' Every thing
was on a proportionate scale : the slightest sally spread
confusion through all our forces; the most trifling circumstance was an event with us; the cause was obvious;
we were unacquainted with every thing, and accordingly,
setting courage aside, I do not scruple to believe that a
hundred picked men of the Imperial guard would have
routed the whole of our army. Happily, our adversaries
were as ignorant as ourselves, all were pigmies then,
although in a very short time giants were found every
where.

" Meanwhile we were extremely discontented with all
this, under our tents, and on our wretched straw; but à
la Française, we found relief in our gaiety; our ill humour evaporated in puns and jests. All our principal
officers had nicknames, there was not one, even to our
Commander in Chief, the venerable Marshal de Broglie,
who escaped us, and this puts me in mind of a circum-

stance, which gave rise to a nickname for one of his lieutenants, which he never got rid of. Should any of my comrades in the field ever read this, it may even now excite a laugh.

"At a moment of a sally, which, as usual, made us very uneasy, every one pressed forward. We had two small pieces of cannon, which we had bought, and which, for want of horses, were drawn by the officers of artillery themselves." "Well!" observed the Emperor, "I might myself have been attached to these very pieces, and yet what different combinations in our destinies and in those of the world! For it is incontestable that I have given an impulse and direction to it, emanating solely from myself. But go on."

"Sire, our two small pieces were rolling along the highway, when the general officer of the day arrived at full gallop, and stopped with indignation at the sight of our little cannon, as they were drawn towards the fortress, breech foremost.—'How,' exclaimed he, 'are these really gentlemen, who draw their cannon in this manner against the enemy? And, if he were actually to present himself, how could you contrive to fire upon him?' He persisted in his blunder, refusing to comprehend what the officers of artillery strove by every possible means to explain; that such was the mode of proceeding every where, and that, unless he had some new invention to communicate, there was no other mode to be adopted. From that moment we dubbed him by a nickname, by which he soon became universally known.

"But all this burlesque was soon exchanged for what was serious in the extreme; the scene shifted, as it were by magic, and our misfortunes burst upon us in an instant. Whether from treachery, weakness, political interest, or sickness in his army, from the real superiority of force, or the mere dexterity of the French general, the King of Prussia entered into secret negotiation with him, suddenly faced about, and marching to the frontier, evacuated the French territory. A most dreadful storm now burst over our heads; words are inadequate to express the scandalous treatment we experienced, as well as the just indignation, which could not fail to animate

4*

every generous heart against our allies, the Prussians
Our Princes degraded, disavowed, insulted, by them;
our equipages, our most necessary effects, even our linen,
plundered; our persons ill-used: and thus we were
basely driven and thrust beyond the frontiers by our
friends, our allies!!!

"For my part, sinking under the fatigue of too long
marches in the mud, and under torrents of rain; bend-
ing under a musquet and a load of accoutrements, which
did harm to no one but to myself, I took advantage of
my privilege as a volunteer, to leave the ranks, and effect
my retreat as well as I could. I proceeded as occasion
served; I never sought the common halting place; I
took refuge in the nearest farm-yard, and whether it was
my own peculiar good fortune, or because the peasants
were in reality kind and not exasperated against us, I
passed the frontier without any unlucky accident. It
was not until some time afterwards that I was enabled
to form a correct estimate of the whole extent of the
danger to which I had exposed myself, when I read, in
the papers, that from fifteen to eighteen of us, stragglers
like myself, and some of whom stood near me in the
ranks, had been seized, dragged to Paris, and executed
in public, in a kind of auto-da-fé, and, as it were, by
way of expiation.

"As soon as we were out of France, we received
notice to disband, but the intimation was superfluous,
for that measure was rendered absolutely indispensable
by our wants, and the privation of every necessary.
We dispersed, each taking his own way at random,
with despair and rage for our companions. We travelled
as fugitives, the greater part of the time on foot, and
some almost naked, over the scenes of our past splendour and luxury; happy when the doors were not shut
in our faces, when we did not receive a brutal repulse!
In a moment, we were officially driven from every quarter; we were prohibited from residing in, or from entering, all the neighbouring states; we were compelled to
take refuge in distant countries, and to exhibit, throughout Europe, the spectacle of our miseries, which ought
to have been a grand moral and political lesson to the
people, to the great, and to Kings.

"The exploits of the French exacted, however, from foreigners, a cruel expiation of the indignities with which they overwhelmed us; whilst, on our part, we experienced a kind of consolation in seeing the honour of the emigration take refuge in the army of Condé, which displayed itself to public view, and inscribed itself in history, as a model of loyalty, valour, and constancy.

"Such, Sire, is that too celebrated era, that fatal determination, which, with respect to a great number, can be considered only as the delusion of youth and inexperience. None, however, but themselves, possess the right of reproaching them with the error. The sentiments by which they were actuated were so pure, so natural, so generous, that they might even, were it necessary, derive honour from them; and these dispositions, I must say, belonged to the mass of which we consisted, and more particularly to that crowd of country gentlemen, who, sacrificing all and expecting nothing, without fortune as well as without hope, displayed a devotion truly heroic, because its only aim was the performance of duties which they held to be sacred. In other respects, our defect lay in our political education, which did not teach us to distinguish our duties, and made us dedicate to the Prince alone what belonged to the country at large. Accordingly, in future times, when hostile passions shall be extinct, when no traces shall be left of jarring interests or of party infatuation and fury, what was doubtful with us will be positive and clear to others; what was excusable or even allowable in us, who were situated between an ancient order of things that was on the point of terminating, and a new one that was about to commence, will be considered highly culpable in those possessing established doctrines. Among them, the following will be held as articles of faith:—1st. That the greatest of all crimes is the introduction of a foreign power into the heart of one's country. 2ndly. That the sovereignty cannot be erratic, but that it is inseparable from the territory, and remains attached to the mass of the citizens. 3rdly. That the country cannot be transported abroad; but that it is immutable and entire on the sacred soil which has given us birth, and which con-

tains the bones of our ancestors. Such are the grand
maxims, and many others besides, which will remain the
offspring of our emigration; such the great truths, which
will be collected from our calamities !"

" Very well !" exclaimed the Emperor, " very well !
This is what is called being free from prejudices ! These
are really philosophical views ! And it will be said of
you, that you were enabled to convert to your advantage
the lessons of time and adversity."

" Sire, during our stay on board the Northumberland,
and the leisure hours of our passage, the English alluded
more than once to this delicate topic. Misled by the
war, which they had carried on with fury against us, as
well as by the maxims with which the interest of the
moment filled their journals, even in opposition to their
national doctrines, they conversed about the merits of
the emigration, and the virtues they had witnessed : and
condemned the nation for having resisted it. But when
the arguments became too complicated, or we were desirous of putting a sudden stop to them, we gained our
point with a single word. We merely said to them :—
' Go back to the period of your own Revolution ; imagine
James II. threatening you from the opposite shore and
under French banners : although surrounded by faithful
subjects, what would you have done ? And if Louis XIV.
had brought him back to London at the head of 50,000
French, who should have afterwards maintained garrisons
in your country, what would have been your feelings ?'—
' Ah ! . . . But . . . . . Ah ! . . . .' they exclaimed,
endeavouring to find out some difference, but not being
able to discover it, they laughed, and were silent." " And
in fact," said the Emperor, " there was not a word to be
said in reply."

He then began to review, with his accustomed rapidity
and talent, the different subjects I had noticed, and stopped to reflect on the absurdity, the inconsistency, the
great mistake of our emigration, and the real injuries
that it had done to France, to the King, and to ourselves.
' You have established, and consecrated in political
France," he observed, " a separation similar to that which
the Catholics and Protestants introduced into religious

Europe; and to what calamities has it not given rise! I
had succeeded in destroying its results, but are they not
on the point of being revived?" He next developed the
means which he had employed to annihilate that plague,
the precautions he had been forced to adopt, and the
effects which he had in view. How every thing that fell
from his tongue was changed in appearance!—how every
thing seemed magnified in my eyes in proportion as he
discussed the subject! "And," he remarked, " a peculiar singularity in my situation was that in the whole of
those transactions I held the helm myself constantly in
the midst of rocks. Every one, judging according to his
own standard, attributed to passion, to simple prejudice,
or to littleness, what in me, however, was but the consequence of profound views, of grand conceptions, and
the most elevated state maxims. It might have been
said that I reigned only over pigmies with respect to
intellectual talent. I was comprehended by none. The
national party felt only jealousy and resentment at what
they saw me do in favour of the emigrants, and the latter,
on their part, were persuaded that I sought only to gain
lustre by their assistance. Poor creatures! . . .

"I obtained, however, my object, in spite of reciprocal
infatuation and prejudice, and I had the satisfaction of
leaving every thing quiet in port, when I launched out to
sea in prosecution of my grand enterprises."

Having mentioned, since my return to Europe, these
expressions of Napoleon's to a great Officer of the Crown,
who had often the honour of conversing with him in
private (1e Comte de S . . .), he related to me, in his
turn, a conversation precisely on the same subject. Its
coincidence with what has been just read is so very
striking as to induce me to insert it here. The Emperor
said to him one day : "What, think you, is my reason
for endeavouring to have about me the great names of
the ancient monarchy?"—"Perhaps, Sire, for the splendour of your throne, and for the purpose of keeping up
certain appearances in the eyes of Europe."—"Ah!
That is just like you, with your pride and your prejudices of rank! Well then, learn, that my victories and
my power are much better recommendations for me in

Europe than all your great names, and that my apparent
predilection for them does me a great deal of injury, and
renders me very unpopular at home.   You attribute to
narrow views what arise from most extensive ones.   I
am engaged in renovating a society, a nation, and the
elements that I am obliged to employ are hostile to each
other.   The nobility and the emigrants are but a point in
the mass, and that mass is inimical to them, and continues very much exasperated against them; it hardly for-
gives me for having recalled them.   For my own part, I
considered it as a duty: but if I suffer them to continue
as a body, they may one day be serviceable to foreign
powers, prove injurious to us, and subject themselves to
great dangers.   My object, then, is to dissolve their
union, and to render them independent of each other.
If I place some of them about my person, in the different
branches of administration, and in the army, it is for the
purpose of consolidating them with the mass, and of
managing so as to reduce all classes into a whole; for I
am mortal, and if I should happen to leave you before
that fusion is accomplished, you would soon see what
disasters would arise from these heterogeneous parts, and
the dreadful dangers of which certain persons might
become the victims! Thus, then, Sir, my views are all
connected with humanity and elevated political considerations, and, in no respect, with vain and silly prejudices."

When I observed to the person who related this anecdote, how little we were acquainted at the Tuileries with
Napoleon's real character, and the great and excellent
qualities of his soul and heart, he answered that, for his
own part, he had been personally more fortunate, and
that he would give me a proof of it, which he selected
out of ten : " The Emperor shewed himself, one day, in
his Privy Council, very much incensed against General
La F . . . ., whom he attacked with great severity, and
whose opinions and principles, he said, were capable of
effecting the complete dissolution of a state : becoming
animated by degrees, he at length put himself into a
real passion. I was present as a member of the Council;
I had been recently admitted, and was little accustomed

to the Emperor's manners, and, although stopped by the
two members placed next to me, I undertook to speak in
defence of the accused, asserting that he had been ca-
lumniated to the Sovereign, and that he lived quietly on
his estate, with personal opinions which were productive
of no ill effect whatever. The Emperor, still in a passion,
resumed the charge for the purpose of pressing it with
vehemence; but after five or six words, he stopped short,
and addressing himself to me, said: 'But he is your
friend, Sir, and you are right. I had forgotten that.—
Let us speak of something else.' 'And why,' I asked,
'did you not make us acquainted with all this at the
time?'—By a fatality which would seem to belong to
Napoleon's atmosphere, whether from prejudice or otherwise, the impression on our minds was that it could only
be told to his intimate friends; for whoever had said
much about it would only have passed for a clumsy
romancer of a courtier, who told not what he believed to
be true, but what he conceived best suited to obtain
favour and rewards."

Since I have mentioned this great Officer of the Crown,
who is no less distinguished by the graces of his mind
and the amenity of his manners than by his exalted character, I shall notice one of his answers to Napoleon, remarkable for its ingenious and delicate flattery. The
Emperor, at one of his levees, having been obliged to
wait some time for his appearance, attacked him on his
arrival, openly, in the presence of all. It happened to
be precisely at the time when five or six Kings (and
among others, those of Bavaria, Saxony, and Wurtemberg), were at Paris. "Sire," replied the culprit, "I
have, no doubt, a million of excuses to make to your
Majesty, but at this time, one is not at perfect liberty to
go through the streets as one pleases. I just now had
the misfortune to get into a *crowd of kings*, from which
I found it impossible to extricate myself sooner. This,
Sire, was the cause of my delay." Every one smiled,
and the Emperor contented himself with saying, in a
softened tone of voice: "Whatever, Sir, may be the
cause, take proper precautions for the future, and above
all, never make me wait again."

NAPOLEON'S SENTIMENTAL JOURNEY.—PUBLIC SPIR·
OF THE TIME.—EVENTS OF THE 10TH OF AUGUST.

3rd.—The weather is somewhat improved; the Em
peror attempted to take a walk in the garden.   Genera
Bingham and the Colonel of the 53d requested to see the
Emperor, who kept them rather long.   The appearance
of the Governor put us all to flight.   General Bingham
disappeared, and, for our part, we went to the wood, for
the purpose of keeping away from the spot.

The Emperor, during his walk, conversed a great deal
about a journey which he took to Burgundy in the beginning of the Revolution.   This he calls his *Sentimental
Journey* to Nuitz.   He supped there with his comrade
Gassendi, at that time captain in the same regiment, and
who was advantageously married to the daughter of a
physician of the place.   The young traveller soon remarked the difference of political opinion between the
father and son-in-law; Gassendi, the gentleman, was,
of course, an aristocrat, and the physician a flaming
patriot.   The latter found in the strange guest a powerful auxiliary, and was so delighted with him that the
following day at dawn he paid him a visit of acknowledgment and sympathy.   The appearance of a young
officer of artillery, with good logical reasoning and a
ready tongue, was, observed the Emperor, a valuable
and rare accession to the place.   It was easy for the
traveller to perceive that he made a favourable impression.   It was Sunday, and hats were taken off to him
from one end of the street to the other.   His triumph,
however, was not without a check.   He went to sup at
the house of a Madame Maret or Muret, where another of
his comrades, V . . . ., seemed to be comfortably
established.   Here the aristocracy of the canton were
accustomed to meet, although the mistress was but the
wife of a wine-merchant, but she had great property and
the most polished manners; she was, said the Emperor,
the duchess of the place.   All the gentlefolks of the
vicinity were to be found there.   The young officer was
caught, as he remarked, in a real wasp-nest, and it was

necessary for him to fight his way out again. The con
test was unequal. In the very heat of the action, the
mayor was announced. "I believed him to be an assis-
tant sent to me by Heaven in the critical moment, but
he was the worst of all my opponents. I see this vil-
ianous fellow now before me in his fine Sunday clothes,
fat and bloated, in an ample scarlet coat; he was a miserable animal. I was happily extricated by the generosity of the mistress of the house, perhaps from a secret
sympathy of opinion. She unceasingly parried with her
wit the blows which were dealt at me; and was a protecting shield on which the enemy's weapons struck in
vain. She guarded me from every kind of wound, and
I have always retained a pleasing recollection of the
services I received from her in that sort of skirmish.

"The same diversity of opinions," said the Emperor,
"was then to be met with in every part of France. In
the saloons, in the streets, on the highways, in the
taverns, every one was ready to take part in the contest,
and nothing was easier than for a person to form an
erroneous estimate of the influence of parties and opinions,
according to the local situation in which he was placed.
Thus a patriot might easily be deceived, when in the
saloons, or among an assembly of officers, where the
majority was decidedly against him; but, the instant he
was in the street, or among the soldiers, he found himself in the midst of the entire nation. The sentiments
of the day succeeded even in making proselytes among
the officers themselves, particularly after the celebrated
oath to the Nation, the Law, and the King. Until that
time," continued the Emperor, "had I received an order
to point my cannon against the people, I have no doubt,
that custom, prejudice, education, and the name of the
King, would have induced me to obey; but, the national
oath once taken, this would have ceased, and I should
have acknowledged the nation only. My natural propensities thenceforth harmonized with my duties, and
happily accorded with all the metaphysics of the Assembly. The patriotic officers, however, it must be
allowed, constituted but the smaller number; but with
the soldiers, as a lever, they led the regiment and m-

posed the law. The comrades of the opposite party and
the officers themselves, had recourse to us in every critical moment. I remember, for instance, having rescued
from the fury of the populace a brother officer, whose
crime consisted in singing from the windows of our
dining-room the celebrated ballad *O Richard ! O mon
Roi !* I had little notion then that that air would one
day be proscribed in the same manner on my account.
Just so, on the 10th of August, when I saw the palace
of the Tuileries stormed and the person of the King
seized, I was certainly very far from thinking that I
should replace him, and that that palace would be my
place of residence."

In dwelling upon the events of the 10th of August, he
said : " I was, during that horrible epoch, at Paris, in
lodgings in the Rue du Mail, Place des Victoires. On
hearing the sound of the tocsin, and the news of the
assault upon the Tuileries, I ran to the Carousel, to the
house of Fauvelet, the brother of Bourrienne, who kept
an upholsterer's shop. He had been my comrade at the
military school of Brienne. It was from that house,
which, by the by, I was never afterwards able to find, in
consequence of the great alterations made there, that I
had a good view of all the circumstances of the attack.
Before I reached the Carousel, I had been met by a
group of hideous-looking men, carrying a head at the
end of a pike. Seeing me decently dressed, with the
look of a gentleman, they called upon me to shout *Vive
la Nation !* which, as it may be easily believed, I did
without hesitation.

" The palace was attacked by the vilest rabble. The
King had unquestionably for his defence as many troops
as the Convention afterwards had on the 13th Vende-
miaire, and the enemies of the latter were much better
disciplined and more formidable. The greater part of the
national guard shewed themselves favourable to the
King ; this justice is due to them."

Here the Grand Marshal observed " that he actually
belonged to one of the battalions which manifested the
most determined devotion. He was several times on the
point of being massacred as he returned alone to his

residence." We remarked, on our part, that in general
the national guard of Paris had constantly displayed the
virtues of its class; the love of order, attachment to
authority, the dread of plunder, and the detestation of
anarchy; and that also was the Emperor's opinion.

"The palace being forced, and the King having repaired to the Assembly," continued he, "I ventured to
penetrate into the garden. Never since has any of my
fields of battle given me the idea of so many dead bodies,
as I was impressed with by the heaps of the Swiss;
whether the smallness of the place seemed to increase
the number, or because it was the result of the first impression I ever received of that kind. I saw well dressed
women commit the grossest indecencies on the dead
bodies of the Swiss. I went through all the coffee-
houses in the neighbourhood of the Assembly; the
irritation was every where extreme; fury was in every
heart and shewed itself in every countenance, although
the persons thus enflamed were far from belonging to
the class of the populace; and all these places must necessarily have been frequented daily by the same visitors:
for, although I had nothing particular in my dress, or
perhaps it was because my countenance was more calm,
it was easy for me to perceive that I excited many hostile and distrustful looks, as some one who was unknown
or suspected."

MASKED BALLS.—MADAME DE MÉGRIGNY.—PIEDMONT
AND THE PIEDMONTESE. — CANALS OF FRANCE.—
PLANS RESPECTING PARIS.—VERSAILLES.—FONTAINE-
BLEAU, &c.

4th.—The weather was much improved. The Emperor ordered his calash, and walked a good way until it
took him up.

The conversation turned upon masked balls, which
the Emperor was peculiarly fond of and frequently
ordered. He was then always sure of a certain meeting
which never failed to take place. He was, he said, regularly accosted every year by the same mask, who
reminded him of old intimacies, and ardently entreated
to be received and admitted at Court. The mask was a

most amiable, kind, and beautiful woman, to whm
many persons were certainly much indebted. The Emperor, who continued to love her, always answered ;—
" I do not deny that you are charming, but reflect a little
upon your situation; be your own judge and decide.
You have two or three husbands, and children by several
of your lovers. It would have been thought a happiness
to have shared in the first fault; the second would have
caused pain, but still it might be pardoned; but the
sequel—and then, and then! . . . Fancy yourself the
Emperor and judge; what would you do in my place, I
who am bound to revive and maintain a certain decorum."
The beautiful suitor either did not reply, or said :—" At
least do not deprive me of hope;" and deferred her
claims of happiness to the following year. And each of
us," said the Emperor, "was punctual at the new
meeting."

The Emperor took great pleasure in getting himself
insulted at these balls. He laughed heartily at the house
of Cambacérès, one day, on being told by a Madame de
St. D . . . ., " that there were people at the ball who
ought to be turned out, and that they certainly could not
have got admittance without stolen tickets."

Another time, he forced the tender and timid Madame
de Mégrigny to rise and retire in anger, and with tears
in her eyes, complaining that the freedom, allowed at a
masked ball, had, in her case, been sadly abused. The
Emperor had just put her in mind of a very remarkable
favour, which he had formerly granted to her, and added
that every one supposed she had paid for it by granting
him the lord's right. " But there was," said the Emperor, " nobody but myself who could say so, without
insulting her; because, although such was the report, I
was certain of its falsehood." The following is an
account of the circumstance.

When the Emperor was on his way to be crowned at
Milan, he slept at Troyes. The authorities were presented to him; and with them was a young lady, on the
point of being married, with a petition, intreating his
protection and assistance. As the Emperor was, besides,
desirous of doing something which might produce a

good effect, and prove agreeable to the country, the circumstance appeared favourable, and he took advantage of it with all imaginable grace. The young lady (Madame de Mégrigny) belonged to the first families of this province, but had been completely ruined by the emigration. She had scarcely returned to the miserable abode of her parents, when a page arrived with the Emperor's decree, which put them in possession of an income of 30,000 francs or more. The effect of such a proceeding may be well imagined. However, as the young lady was very charming and perfectly handsome, it was decided that her fascinations had some share in his gallantry, although he left the town a few hours afterwards, and never thought more of the thing; but the general opinion was not a jot altered on that account. It is well known how stories are formed; and as she married one of his equerries, and had consequently come to Court, all this had been so well mingled together that, when she was afterwards appointed sub-governess to the King of Rome, the choice shocked, for a moment, the austere Madame de Montesquiou, who suspected, said the Emperor, that it was but a mere arrangement.

The Emperor said that he renewed at Turin, in the person of Madame de Lascaris, the gracious gallantry exercised at Troyes; and that, in both instances, he had reason to be gratified with the results of his liberality. The two families gave proofs of attachment and gratitude.

We enquired what might have been the sentiments of Piedmont with regard to himself. He had, he said, a particular affection for that province. M. de Saint-Marsan, on whose fidelity he relied to the end, had assured him, at the period of our reverses, that the country would shew itself one of his best provinces.

"In fact," continued the Emperor, "the Piedmontese do not like to be a small state; their King was a real feudal lord, whom it was necessary to court, or to dread. He had more power and authority than I, who, as Emperor of the French, was but a supreme magistrate, bound to see the laws executed, and unable to dispense with them Had I it in my power to prevent the arrest

of a courtier for debt? Could I have put a stop to the
regular action of the laws, no matter upon whom they
operated?"

During the conversation at dinner, the Emperor inquired whether the quantity of river water flowing into the
Mediterranean and the Black Sea had been calculated.
This led him to express a wish that a calculation of the
fluvial water of Europe should be made, and that the
proportion contributed by each valley and each stream,
should be ascertained. He regretted much that he had
not proposed this series of scientific questions. This
was, he observed, his grand system. Did any useful,
curious or interesting idea suggest itself to him: "I
proposed, at my levees, or in my familiar communications, analogous questions to my Members of the Institute,
with orders to resolve them. The solution became the
subject of public inquiry; it was analyzed, contested,
adopted or rejected; and there is nothing which cannot
be accomplished in this way. It is the grand lever of
improvement for a great nation, possessing a great deal
of intelligence, and a great deal of knowledge."

The Emperor also observed on this subject, that
geography had never been so successfully cultivated as
at present, and that his expeditions had contributed
somewhat to its improvement. He afterwards noticed
the canals, which he had caused to be made in France,
and particularly mentioned that from Strasburg to Lyons,
in which, he hoped sufficient progress had been made to
induce others to complete it. He thought that, out of
thirty millions, twenty - four must have been already
expended.

"Communications are now established in the interior
from Bordeaux to Lyons and Paris. I had constructed a
great number of canals, and projected a great many
more." One of us having observed that a proposal for
the construction of a very useful canal had been submitted to the Emperor, but that measures had been taken
to deceive him, for the purpose of preventing his acceptance of the offer: "Without doubt," said the Emperor,
"the plan must have appeared advantageous only on
paper; but I suppose it would have been necessary to

advance money, which was drawn from me with difficulty."—No, Sire, the refusal was but the effect of an
intrigue. Your Majesty was deceived."—"It was impossible with respect to such a subject. You speak
without sufficient information."—"But I am confident
of it. I was acquainted with the plan, the offers and the
subscribers; my relations had put down their names for
considerable sums. The object was the union of the
Meuse with the Marne. The length of the canal would
have been less than seven leagues."—"But you do not
tell us all; it was, perhaps, required that I should grant
immense national forests in the environs, which I should
not have agreed to."—"No, Sire, the whole was an
intrigue of your Board of Bridges and Roads."—"But
even then, it was necessary for them to allege some reasons, some appearance of public interest. What reasons
did they assign ?"—"Sire, that the profits would have
been too considerable."—"But in that case the plan
ought to have been submitted to me in person, and I
would have carried it into execution. I repeat, that you
are not justified by the facts; you are speaking now to a
man upon the very subject which constantly engaged his
attention. The Board of Bridges and Roads were, on
their part, never better pleased than when they were
employed. There never was an individual who proposed
the construction of a bridge that was not taken at his
word. If he asked for a toll for twenty-five years, I was
disposed to grant him one for thirty. If it cost me
nothing, it was a matter of indifference whether it would
prove useful. It was still a capital with which I enriched the soil. Instead of rejecting proposals for canals,
I eagerly courted them. But, my dear Sir, there are no
two things that resemble each other so little as the conversation of a saloon, and the consideration of an Administrative Council. The projector is always right in a
saloon; his projects would be magnificent and infallible,
if he were listened to, and if he can, by some little
contrivance, but connect the refusal under which he
suffers with some bottles of wine, with some intrigue
carried on by a wife or a mistress, the romance is complete, and that is what you probably heard. But an

Administrative Council is not to be managed so, because it comes to no decision but on facts and accurate measurement. What is the canal you mentioned? I cannot be unacquainted with it."—"Sire, from the Meuse to the Marne, a distance of seven leagues only."—"Very well! my dear Sir, it is from the Meuse to the Aisne you mean, and it would have been less than seven leagues. I shall soon recollect all about it; there is, however, but one little difficulty to overcome, and that is that at this very instant it is doubtful whether the project be practicable. There, as in other places, Hippocrates says *yes*, and Galen says *no*. Tarbé maintained that it was impossible, and denied that there was a sufficiency of water at the point where it was to commence. I repeat, that you are speaking to him, who, of all others was the most attentive to these objects, more especially in the environs of Paris. It was the constant subject of my thoughts to render Paris the real capital of Europe. I sometimes wished it, for instance, to become a city with a population of two, three, or four millions, in short, something fabulous, colossal, unexampled until our days, and with public establishments suitable to its population."

Some one having then observed that, if Heaven had allowed the Emperor to reign sixty years, as it had Louis XIV., he would have left many grand monuments: "Had Heaven but granted me twenty years, and a little more leisure," resumed the Emperor with vivacity, "ancient Paris would have been sought for in vain; not a trace of it would have been left, and I should have changed the face of France. Archimedes promised to do any thing, provided he had a resting place for his lever; I should have done as much, wherever I could have found a point of support for my energy, my perseverance, and my budgets; a world might be created with budgets. I should have displayed the difference between a constitutional Emperor and a King of France. The Kings of France have never possessed any administrative or municipal institution. They have merely shown themselves great Lords who were ruined by their men of business.

"The nation itself has nothing in its character and its tastes but what is transitory and perishable. Every thing is done for the gratification of the moment and of caprice, nothing for duration. . . . . . That is our motto, and it is exemplified by our manners in France. Every one passes his life in doing and undoing; nothing is ever left behind. Is it not unbecoming that Paris should not possess even a French theatre, or an Opera house, in any respect worthy of its high claims?

" I have often set myself against the feasts which the city of Paris wished to give me. They consisted of dinners, balls, artificial fire-works, at an expense of four, six, or eight hundred thousand francs; the preparations for which obstructed the public for several days, and which afterwards cost as much for their removal as they had for their construction. I proved that, with these idle expenses, they might have erected lasting and magnificent monuments.

" One must have gone through as much as I have, in order to be acquainted with all the difficulty of doing good. If the business related to chimneys, partitions, and furniture for some individuals in the imperial palaces, the work was quickly accomplished; but if it was necessary to lengthen the garden of the Tuileries, to render some quarters wholesome, to cleanse some sewers, and to perform a task beneficial to the public, in which particular persons had no direct interest, I found it requisite to exert all the energy of my character, to write six, ten letters a day, and to get into a downright passion. It was in this way that I laid out as much as thirty millions in sewers, for which no body will ever thank me. I pulled down a property worth seventeen millions in houses in front of the Tuileries, for the purpose of forming the Carousel, and throwing open the Louvre. What I did is immense; what I had resolved to do and what I had projected was much more so."

A person then remarked that the Emperor's labours had not been limited either to Paris or to France, but that almost every city in Italy exhibited traces of his creative powers. Wherever one travelled, at the foot as well as on the top of the Alps, in the sands of Holland. on the banks of the Rhine, Napoleon, always Napoleon, was to be seen.

In consequence of this remark, he observed that he had determined on draining the Pontine marshes. "Cæsar," he said, "was about to undertake it, when he perished." Then reverting to France; "The kings, he said, had too many country-houses and useless objects. Any impartial historian will be justified in blaming Louis XIV. for his excessive and idle expenditure at Versailles, involved as he was in wars, taxes, and calamities. He exhausted himself for the purpose of forming after al but a bastard town." The Emperor then analyzed the advantages of an administrative city, that is to say, calculated for the union of the different branches of administration, and they seemed to him truly problematical.

The Emperor did not conceal his opinion that the capital was not, at times, a fit residence for the sovereign; but, in another point of view, Versailles was not suitable to the great, the ministers, and the courtiers. Louis XIV. therefore committed a blunder, if he undertook to build Versailles solely for the residence of the kings, when Saint Germain was, in every respect, ready for the purpose; Nature seemed to have made it expressly for the real residence of the kings of France. Napoleon himself had committed faults in that respect: for it was not right he said to praise himself for all that had been done in this way   He ought, for instance, to have given up Compiegne, and he regretted having celebrated his marriage there instead of selecting Fontainebleau. "That," said he, referring to Fontainebleau, "is the real abode of kings, the house of ages; it is not, perhaps, strictly speaking, an architectural palace; but it is, unquestionably, well calculated and perfectly suitable. It was certainly the most commodious and the most happily situated in Europe for a sovereign."

He then took a review of the capitals he had visited, of the palaces he had seen, and claimed a decided superiority in our favour. Fontainebleau, he further added, was also, at the same time, the most suitable political and military situation. The Emperor reproached himself with the sums he had expended on Versailles, but yet it was, he said, necessary to prevent it from falling into ruin. The demolition of a considerable part of that palace was a subject of consideration, during the Revolution; it was proposed to take away the centre, and thus to separate the two wings. "It would have been of essential service to me," he observed; "for nothing is so expensive or so truly useless as this multitude of palaces: and if, nevertheless, I undertook that of the King of Rome, it was because I had views peculiar to myself; and besides, in reality, I never thought of doing more than preparing the ground. There I should have stopped.*

"My errors, in disbursements of this kind, could not, after all, be very great. They were, thanks to my budgets, observed and necessarily corrected every year, and could never exceed a small part of the expense occasioned by the original fault."

The Emperor assured us that he experienced every possible difficulty in making his system of budgets intelligible, and in carrying it into execution. Whenever a plan to the amount of thirty millions, which suited me, was proposed; Granted, was my answer, but to be completed in twenty years, that is to say, at a million and a half francs a-year. So far, all went on very smoothly; but what am I to get, I added, for my first year? For if my expenditure is to be divided into parts, it is, however, my determination to have the result, the work, as far as it goes, entire and complete. In this manner, I wished at first for a recess, an apartment, no matter what, but something perfect, for my million and a half of francs.

---

* All the world knows, or ought to have known (if, by a fatality, altogether peculiar to Napoleon, the greater part of his most commendable actions had not been, at the time, stifled under the weight of malignity and libels), the history of that miserable hut, enclosed within the circuit of the palace of the King of Rome; the proprietor of which demanded successively ten, twenty, fifty, and one hundred times its real value. When he had reached that ridiculous price, the Emperor, whose directions on that point were taken, suddenly commanded a stop to be put to the bargain, exclaiming that that wretched stall, amidst all the magnificence of the palace of the King of Rome, would be, after all, the vineyard of Naboth, the most decisive testimony of his justice, the noblest trophy of his reign.

The architects seemed resolved not to comprehend my
meaning; it narrowed their expansive views and their
grand effects.   They would, at once, have willingly
erected a whole façade, which must have remained for a
long time useless, and thus involved me in immense dis
bursements, which, if interrupted, would have swallowed
up every thing.

" It was in this manner, which was peculiar to myself,
and in spite of so many political and military obstacles
that I executed so many undertakings.   I had collected
furniture belonging to the Crown, to the amount of forty
millions, and plate worth at least, four millions.   How
many palaces have I not repaired ? Perhaps, too many
I return to that subject.   Thanks to my mode of acting,
I was enabled to inhabit Fontainebleau within one year
after the repairs were begun, and it cost me no more
than 5 or 600,000 francs.   If I have since expended six
millions on it, that was done in six years.   It would have
cost me much more in the course of time.   My principal
object was to make the expense light and imperceptible,
and to give durability to the work.

" During my visits to Fontainebleau," said the Emperor, " from 12 to 1500 persons were invited and lodged,
with every convenience; upwards of 3000 might be
entertained at dinner, and this cost the Sovereign very
little, in consequence of the admirable order and regu-
'arity established by Duroc.   More than twenty or five-
and - twenty Princes, Dignitaries, or Ministers, were
obliged to keep their households there.

" I disapproved the building of Versailles; but in my
ideas respecting Paris, and they were occasionally gigantic, I thought of making it useful and of converting it,
in the course of time, into a kind of fauxbourg, an adjacent site, a point of view from the grand capital; and,
for the purpose of more effectually appropriating it to
that end, I had conceived a plan, of which I had a description sketched out.

" It was my intention to expel from its beautiful groves
those nymphs, the productions of a wretched taste, and
those ornaments *à la Turcaret*, and to replace them by
panoramas, in masonry, of all the capitals into which we

had entered victorious, and of all the celebrated battles, which had shed lustre on our arms.   It would have been a collection of so many eternal monuments of our triumphs and our national glory, placed at the gate of the capital of Europe, which necessarily could not fail of being visited by the rest of the world." Here he suddenly left off, and began reading Le Distrait, but he almost instantly laid it aside, whether from the agitation of his own thoughts, or from a nervous cough, with which he had, for a short time, been often affected after dinner.   He certainly gets considerably worse, and his health is altogether declining.

PLAN OF A HISTORY OF EUROPE.—SELIM III.—FORCES OF A TURKISH SULTAN.—THE MAMELUKES.—ON THE REGENCY

5th.—The Emperor did not go out until after five o'clock.   He was in pain, and had taken a bath, where he remained too long, in consequence of the arrival of Sir H. Lowe, as he would not leave it until the Governor was gone.

The Emperor had been reading, while in the bath, the Ottoman History, in two volumes.   He had conceived the idea, and regretted that he had been unable to execute it, of having all the histories of Europe, from the time of Louis XIV., composed from the documents belonging to our office for Foreign Affairs, where the regular official reports of all the ambassadors are deposited.

"My reign," he observed, "would have been a perfect epoch for that object.   The superiority of France, its independence, and regeneration, enabled the then government to publish such matters without inconvenience.   It would have been like publishing ancient history.   Nothing could have been more valuable."

He next adverted to Sultan Selim III., to whom, he said, he once wrote: "Sultan, come forth from thy seraglio; place thyself at the head of thy troops, and renew the glorious days of thy monarchy."

"Selim, the Louis XVI. of the Turks," said the Emperor, "who was very much attached and very favour-

able to us, contented himself with answering, that the
advice would have been excellent for the first Princes of
his dynasty; but that the manners of those times were
very different; and that such a conduct would, at present,
be unseasonable, and altogether useless.

The Emperor added, however, that nobody knew how
to calculate, with certainty, the energy of the sudden
burst, which might be produced by a Sultan of Constantinople, who was capable of placing himself at the
head of his people, of infusing new spirit into them, and
of exciting that fanatical multitude to action. At a later
period, he observed, that, for his own part, if he had
been able to unite the Mamelukes with his French, he
should have considered himself the master of the world.
" With that chosen handful, and the rabble," he added,
with a smile," recruited on the spot, to be expended in
the hour of need, I know nothing that could have resisted
me. Algiers trembled at it.

" 'But should your Sultan,' said, one day, the Dey
of Algiers to the French Consul, ' ever take it into his
head to pay us a visit, what safety could we hope for?
For he has defeated the Mamelukes.' The Mamelukes,"
observed the Emperor, " were, in fact, objects of veneration and terror throughout the East; they were looked
upon as invincible until our time."

The Emperor, while waiting for dinner in the midst of
us, opened a book, which lay at his side on the couch; it
was the Regency. He stigmatized it as one of the most
abominable eras of our annals: and was vexed that it
had been described with the levity of the age, and not
with the severity of history. It had been strewed with
the flowers of fashionable life, and set off with the
colouring of the Graces, instead of having been treated
with rigorous justice. The Regency, he observed, had
been, in reality, the reign of the depravity of the heart,
of the libertinism of the mind, and of the most radical
immorality of every species. It was such, he said, that
he believed all the horrors and abominations with which
the manners of the Regent were reproached in the bosom
of his own family; while he did not give credit to the
stories told of Louis XV., who, although plunged in the

'culest and most frightful debauchery, afforded, however
no grounds to justify his belief in such shocking and
monstrous indulgencies; and he vindicated him very
satisfactorily from certain imputations, which would have
seriously affected the person of one of his (Napoleon's)
former aides-de-camp. He considered the epoch of the
Regent to have been the overthrow of every kind of property, the destruction of public morals. Nothing had
been held sacred either in manners or in principles. The
Regent was personally overwhelmed with infamy. In
the affair of the legitimate Princes, he had exhibited the
most abject baseness, and committed a great abuse of
authority. The King alone could authorize such a decision, and he, the Regent, had felt pleasure in gratuitously
dishonouring himself in the person of his wife, the
natural daughter of Louis XIV., whom he had found it
his interest, however, to marry, while that King was on
the throne.

6th.—As we wished to try the tent, which was just
finished, the table was laid there, and we invited the
English officers, who had superintended the work, to
breakfast with us.

The Emperor sent for me to his apartment; he
dressed himself, and, when he went out, I accompanied
him to the bottom of the wood, where we walked for
some time. He entered into the discussion of some
important subjects.

The Emperor returned to the calash for the purpose
of ordering it to be in readiness, and we resumed our
walk, until it took us up. On our return, the Emperor
visited the tent, and said a few words, expressive of his
satisfaction to the officer and seamen who were employed
in putting the last hand to it.

CAMPAIGNS OF ITALY, &c. — EPOCH OF 1815, &c.—
GUSTAVUS III.—GUSTAVUS IV.—BERNADOTTE.—PAUL I.

7th.—After breakfasting in the tent, the Emperor
took a fancy to review some chapters of the Campaigns
in Italy: he sent for my son, whose foot was at length
mending, and whose eyes were much better. He finished
the chapters of Pavia and Leghorn. He afterwards

walked towards the bottom of the wood, having ordered
the carriage to follow.   On the way, the Emperor said
that he considered the Campaigns of Italy and Egypt as
completely finished, and in a fit state to be given to the
public, and it would, no doubt, he remarked, be a very
agreeable present to the French and Italians; it was the
record of their glory and their rights.   He did not think,
however, that he ought to put his name to it; and he
repeated that the different epochs of his memoirs would
perpetuate those of his faithful companions.

On the arrival of the calash, the conversation, continuing on the same subject, he was earnestly pressed to
finish 1815; and its importance, interest, and results,
were warmly canvassed.   " Very well !" said he, with a
smile, " I must give myself up to it entirely; it is a
pleasure to be encouraged ; but it is also requisite to go
to work with a proper temper.   We are surfeited here
with disgust and trickery; we seem to be envied the air
we breathe."

He returned to his apartment, and I followed him,
when a conversation peculiarly interesting and remarkable took place.   It related to Gustavus III., to Sweden,
to Russia, to Gustavus IV., to Bernadotte, to Paul I., &c.

I have said that, at Aix-la-Chapelle, Gustavus III.
ived among us as a private individual under the name of
Count de Haga.   He constituted the charm of society,
by the vivacity of his wit and the interest he imparted
to his conversation.   I had heard from his own mouth
his famous Revolution of 1772, and I was in the happiest
situation to obtain a thorough knowledge of that epoch
of the history of Sweden.   I was, at the same time, very
well acquainted with a Baron de Sprengporten, who,
after having displayed great zeal for Gustavus, had the
misfortune to remove to Russia, and to return at the
head of foreigners to fight against his country.   The
consequence was that sentence of death had been passed
upon him in Sweden.   He was also at Aix-la-Chapelle
at the moment, and had banished himself from it, out
of courtesy, he said, on the arrival of Gustavus.   He
had not, however, removed farther off than half a league,
so that all I heard the King say in the evening was

controverted, modified, or confirmed for me the next
morning at breakfast by the Baron. He had enjoyed a
very considerable share of that Prince's confidence, and
he communicated the most numerous and minute particulars, as positive facts, respecting the romance of the
birth of Gustavus IV., who had been represented as
altogether unconnected by blood with Gustavus III.,
according to his full knowledge and his own desire.

The Emperor observed that this same Sprengporten
had been actually sent to him as envoy by Paul, at the
time of his Consulate. With respect to Gustavus IV.,
he said that that Prince had, on his appearance in the
world, announced himself as a hero, and had terminated
his career merely as a madman, and that he had distinguished himself in his early days by some very remarkable traits. While yet a boy, he had insulted Catharine
by the refusal of her grand - daughter, at the moment
even when that great Express seated on her throne,
and surrounded by her Court, waited only for him to
celebrate the marriage ceremony.

At a later period, he had insulted Alexander, in no
less marked a manner, by refusing, after Paul's catastrophe, to suffer one of the new Emperor's officers to
enter his dominions, and by answering, to the official
complaints addressed to him on this subject, that Alexander ought not to be displeased that he, Gustavus,
who still mourned the assassination of his father, should
shut the entrance of his States against one of those,
accused by the public voice of having immolated his
(Alexander's).

"On my accession to the sovereignty," said the Emperor, "he declared himself my great antagonist; it
might have been supposed that nothing short of renewing
the exploits of the great Gustavus Adolphus would have
satisfied him. He ran over the whole of Germany, for
the purpose of stirring up enemies against me. At the
time of the catastrophe of the Duke d'Enghien, he swore
to avenge it in person; and at a later period, he inso-
lently sent back the black eagle to the King of Prussia,
because the latter had accepted my legion of honour.

"His fatal moment at length arrived; a conspiracy,
5*

of no common kind, tore him from the throne and
banished him from his country. The unanimity evinced
against him is, no doubt, a proof of the blunders which
he had committed. I am ready to admit that he was
inexcusable and even mad, but it is, notwithstanding,
extraordinary and unexampled that, in that crisis, not a
single sword was drawn in his defence, whether from
affection, from gratitude, from virtuous feeling, or even
from stupidity, if you please; and truly, it is a circumstance which does little honour to the atmosphere of
Kings."

This Prince, tossed about and deceived by the English,
who wished to make him their instrument, and repulsed
by his relatives, seemed determined to renounce the world,
and, as if he had felt his existence disgraced by his contempt of mankind and his disgust at things, he voluntarily lost himself altogether in the crowd.

The Emperor said that, after the battle of Leipsic, he
had been informed on the part of Gustavus, that he had
no doubt been his enemy a long time; but that, for a
long time, he (Napoleon) was of all others the sovereign
of whom he had the least to complain, and that, for a long
time also, his only sentiments with regard to him were
those of admiration and sympathy; that his actual misfortunes permitted him to express his feelings without
restraint; that he offered to be his Aide-de-camp, and requested an asylum in France.* "I was affected," observed the Emperor; "but I soon reflected that if I
received him, my dignity would be pledged to make
exertions in his favour. Besides, I no longer ruled the
world, and then common minds would not fail to discover

* It is right to remark that Colonel Gustafson (Gustavus IV.)
has declared this statement to be erroneous. But, from his letter
itself, one would be induced to think that the error proceeds solely
from misinterpretation of his real words: now every one knows how
easy, how common such inaccuracies are in regard to circumstances
transmitted through several intermediate persons. Fearful that the
misunderstanding might originate with myself, which is possible
enough, I should not have hesitated a moment to charge myself
with the error; but every reader must judge that the length of
Napoleon's conversation and the development of his ideas on this
subject, could not leave ne in any doubt.

n the interest I took for him, an impotent hatred against
Bernadotte; finally, Gustavus had been dethroned by the
voice of the people, and it was the voice of the people
by which I had been elevated. In taking up his cause,
I should have been guilty of inconsistency in my own
conduct, and have acted upon discordant principles. In
short, I dreaded lest I should render affairs more complicated than they were, and silenced my feelings of generosity. I caused him to be answered that I appreciated
what he offered me, and that I was sensible of it, but
that the political interest of France did not allow me
to indulge in my private feelings, and that it even imposed upon me the painful task of refusing, for the moment,
the asylum which he asked; that he would, however,
greatly deceive himself, if he supposed me to entertain
any other sentiments than those of extreme good will and
sincere wishes for his happiness, &c.

"Some time after the expulsion of Gustavus, while
the succession to the Crown was vacant, the Swedes, desirous of recommending themselves to me and securing
the protection of France, asked me to give them a King.
My attention was, for an instant, turned to the Viceroy;
but it would have been necessary for him to change his
religion, which I deemed beneath my dignity and that of
all those who belonged to me. Besides, I did not think
the political result sufficiently important to excuse an
action so contrary to our manners. I attached,
too much value to the idea of seeing the throne of
Sweden in possession of a Frenchman. It was, in my
situation, a puerile sentiment. The real King. according
to my political system and the true interests of France,
would have been the King of Denmark, because I should
then have governed Sweden by the influence of my simple contact with the Danish provinces. Bernadotte was
elected, and he was indebted for his elevation to his wife,
the sister-in-law of my brother Joseph, who then reigned
at Madrid.

"Bernadotte, affecting great dependence on me, came
to ask my approbation, protesting, with too visible an
anxiety, that he would not accept the Crown, unless it
was agreeable to me,

"I, the elected Monarch of the people, had to answer

that I could not set myself against the elections of other
nations. It was what I told Bernadotte, whose whole
attitude betrayed the anxiety excited by the expectation
of my answer. I added that he had only to take advantage of the good-will of which he had been the object;
that I wished to be considered as having had no weight
in his election, but that it had my approbation and my
best wishes. I felt, however, shall I say it, a secret instinct, which made the thing disagreeable and painful.
Bernadotte was, in fact, the serpent which I nourished
in my bosom; he had scarcely left us before he attached
himself to the system of our enemies, and we were
obliged to watch and dread him. At a later period, he
was one of the great active causes of our calamities; it
was he who gave to our enemies the key of our political
system and communicated the tactics of our armies; it
was he who pointed out to them the way to the sacred
soil! In vain would he excuse himself by saying that,
in accepting the Crown of Sweden, he was thenceforth
bound to be a Swede only; pitiful excuse, valid only with
those of the populace and the vulgar that are ambitious!
In taking a wife, a man does not renounce his mother,
still less is he bound to transfix her bosom and tear out
her entrails. It is said that he afterwards repented, that
is to say, when it was no longer time, and when the
mischief was done. The fact is that, in finding himself
once more among us, he perceived that opinion exacted
justice of him; he felt himself struck with death. Then
the film fell from his eyes; for it is not known to what
dreams his presumption and his vanity might have incited
him in his blindness.

"At the end of this and many other things besides, I
presumed to observe to him, as a very fantastical and
extraordinary matter of chance, that Bernadotte, the
soldier, elevated to a Crown, for which Protestantism was
a necessary qualification, was actually born a Protestant,
and that his son, destined, on that account, to reign over
the Scandinavians, presented himself in the midst of
them precisely with the national name of *Oscar*. "My
dear Las Cases" replied the Emperor, "it is because
that chance, so often cited, of which the ancients made a

deity, which astonishes us every day and strikes us every
instant, does not, after all, appear so singular, so capricious, so extraordinary, but in consequence of our ignorance of the secret and altogether natural causes, by which
it is produced; and yet this single combination is sufficient to create the marvellous and give birth to mysteries.
Here, for instance, with respect to the first point, that of
having been born a Protestant, let not the honour of that
circumstance be assigned to chance; blot that out. With
regard to the second, the name of Oscar; I was his
godfather, and, when I gave him the name, I doted upon
Ossian; it presented itself, of course, very naturally.
You now see how simple that is which so greatly
astonished you."

At the end of this conversation, the Emperor returned
to Paul; he talked of the passionate fits brought upon
him by the perfidy of the English ministry. He had been
promised Malta, the moment it was taken possession of,
and accordingly, he was in great haste to get himself
nominated Grand Master. Malta reduced, the English
ministers denied that they had promised it to him. It is
confidently stated that, on the reading of this shameful
falsehood, Paul felt so indignant that, seizing the dispatch
in full Council, he ran his sword through it, and ordered
it to be sent back in that condition, by way of answer.
" If it be a folly," said the Emperor, " it must be allowed
that it is the folly of a noble soul; it is the indignation
of virtue, which was incapable, until then, of suspecting
such baseness."

At the same time, the English ministers, treating with
us for the exchange of prisoners, refused to include, on
the same scale, the Russian prisoners taken in Holland,
who were in the actual service and fought for the sole
cause of the English. " I had," said the Emperor, " hit
upon the bent of Paul's character. I seized time by the
forelock; I collected these Russians; I clothed them and
sent them back to him without any expense. From that
instant, his generous heart was altogether devoted to
me; and, as I had no interest in opposition to Russia,
and should never have spoken or acted but with justice,
there was no doubt that I should be able, for the future,

THE HOUSE IN WHICH NAPOLEON WAS BORN,

AT AJACCIO, IN CORSICA.

foreign productions. This state of things is such that it
is impossible for me to decide whether French commerce
would gain much by peace with England.

"The maintenance, observance, or adoption of the
decree of Berlin is, therefore, I venture to say, more for
the interest of Sweden and of Europe, than for the
particular interest of France.

"Such are the reasons which my ostensible policy
may set up against the ostensible policy of England.
The secret reasons that influence England are the following: She does not desire peace; she has rejected all the
overtures which I have caused to be made to her; her
commerce and her territory are enlarged by war; she is
apprehensive of restitutions; she will not consolidate the
new system by a treaty; she does not wish that France
should be powerful. I wish for peace, I wish for it in
its perfect state, because peace alone can give solidity to
new interests, and States created by conquest. I think,
that on this point, your Royal Highness ought not to
differ in opinion from me.

"I have a great number of ships; I have no seamen:
I cannot carry on the contest with England for the purpose of compelling her to make peace; nothing but the
continental system can prove successful. In this respect,
I experience no obstacle on the part of Russia and
Prussia; their commerce can only be a gainer by the
prohibitive system.

"Your cabinet is composed of enlightened men. There
is dignity and patriotism in the Swedish nation. The
influence of your Royal Highness in the Government is
generally approved: you will experience few impedi-
ments in withdrawing your people from a mercantile
submission to a foreign nation. Do not suffer yourself
to be caught by the too tempting baits which England
may hold out to you. The future will prove to you that,
whatever may be the revolutions which time must produce, the Sovereigns of Europe will establish prohibitive
laws, which will leave them masters in their own
dominions.

"The third article of the treaty of the 21st of February, 1802, corrects the incomplete stipulations of the

reaty of Fredericsham. It must be rigorously observed in every point which relates to colonial commodities. You tell me that you cannot do without these commodities, and that, from the want of their introduction, the produce of your customs is diminished. I will give you twenty millions worth of colonial produce, which I have at Hamburgh; you will give me twenty millions worth of iron. You will have no specie to export from Sweden. Give up these productions to merchants; they will pay the import duties; you will get rid of your iron; this will answer my purpose. I am in want of iron at Antwerp, and I know not what to do with the English commodities.

" Be faithful to the treaty of the 24th of February: drive the English smugglers from the roads of Gottenburg; drive them from the coasts, where they carry on an open trade: I give you my word that I will, on my part, scrupulously observe the conditions of that treaty. I shall oppose the attempts of your neighbours to appropriate to themselves your continental possessions. If you fail in your engagements, I shall consider myself released from mine.

" It is my wish to be always on an amicable understanding with your Royal Highness; I shall hear with pleasure your communication of this answer to his Swedish Majesty, whose good intentions I have constantly appreciated.

" My Minister for Foreign Affairs will return an official answer to the last note, which the Comte d'Essen has submitted for my perusal.

"This letter having no other end, &c.
NAPOLEON."

NAPOLEON'S PATRIMONIAL VINEYARD, &c.—HIS NURSE —HIS PATERNAL HOME.—TEARS OF JOSEPHINE DURING WURMSER'S SKIRMISHES IN THE ENVIRONS OF MANTUA.

8th.—I went to the Emperor's apartment about eleven o'clock. He was dressing himself, and looking over with his valet, some samples of perfumery and scents, received from England. He enquired about them all,

however, extremely devout. Her husband was a coasting
trader of the island. She gave great pleasure at the
Tuileries, and enchanted the family by the vivacity of her
language and her gestures. The empress Josephine
made her a present of some diamonds."

After breakfast, the Emperor, adhering to his resolution of yesterday, proceeded with his work. He finished
the chapter of Castiglione, and then went to the wood,
with the intention of waiting for the calash. In continuance of the conversation, which had been brought on by
the chapter, he related that Josephine had left Brescia
with him, and had thus commenced the campaign
against Wurmser. Arrived at Verona, she had witnessed the first shots that were fired. When she returned
to Castel-Nuovo, and saw the wounded as they passed,
she was desirous of reaching Brescia; but she found
herself stopped by the enemy, who was already at Ponte-
Marco. In the anxiety and agitation of the moment,
she was seized with fear, and wept a great deal, on
quitting her husband, who exclaimed, when embracing
her, and with a kind of inspiration: "Wurmser shall
pay dearly for those tears which he causes thee!"
She was obliged to pass in her carriage very close to
the fortifications of Mantua. She was fired upon from
the place, and one of her suite was even wounded.
She traversed the Po, Bologna, Ferrara, and stopped at
Lucca, attended by dread and the unfavourable reports,
which were usually spread around our patriotic armies;
but she was internally supported by her extreme confidence in her husband's good fortune.

Such was, however, already the opinion of Italy, observed the Emperor, and the sentiments impressed by
the French General, that, in spite of the crisis of the
moment, and of all the false reports which accompanied
him, his wife was received at Lucca by the Senate, and
treated with the same respect as the greatest princess.
It came to compliment her, and presented her with the
oils of honour. It had reason to applaud itself for that
conduct. A short time afterwards the couriers brought
intelligence of the prodigious achievements of her husband, and the annihilation of Wurmser.

The Emperor returned to the saloon for the first time since the fire. It is gradually furnished with articles sent expressly from London, which make it a little more tolerable. After dinner, the Emperor began with reading Turcaret, with which, he said, notwithstanding all its wit, he felt himself disgusted, in consequence of its vulgarity; but it bore, he remarked, the impression of Le Sage. He then took up l'Avocat Patelin, and was much amused with its genuine humour.

9th.—The Emperor breakfasted in the tent, and revised the chapter of the Brenta. At three o'clock, he took an airing in the calash. The Governor called during our ride. It was understood that he wished to speak to the Emperor on the celebration of the Prince Regent's birthday, which is to take place next Monday, the 12th inst., and to give him notice of the salutes and volleys that are to be fired on the occasion at the camp, situated so closely to us. It is said, on the other hand, that he has given directions for supplying the Emperor's table only, and that each of us is to be put upon a particular allowance, as he finds the expense very much beyond his credit. At any rate, we shall see.

CATHERINE II.—IMPERIAL GUARDS.—PAUL I. &c.— PROJECTS ON INDIA, &c.

10th.—The Emperor was indisposed and took a bath. At three he walked out and called for the carriage. He had just read the history of Catherine. "She was," he said, "a commanding woman; she was worthy of having a beard upon her chin. The catastrophe of Peter and that of Paul were seraglio revolutions, the work of janissaries. These palace-soldiers are terrible, and dangerous in proportion as the Sovereign is absolute. My imperial guard might also have become fatal under any other but myself."

The Emperor said that he and Paul had been on the best terms together. At the time of his murder, in which the public spared neither his relations nor his allies, he had concerted a plan with him, at that very moment, for an expedition to India, and he would have certainly prevailed upon him to carry it into execution.

Paul wrote to him very often, and at great length. His first communication was curious and original. " Citizen First Consul," (he had written to him with his own hand,) ' I do not discuss the merits of the rights of man ; but, when a nation places at its head a man of distinguished merit and worthy of esteem, it has a government, and France has, henceforth, one in my eyes."

On our return, we found the Admiral and his lady; the Emperor took them in the calash and made another tour. He afterwards walked for some time with Lady Malcolm, to whom he behaved in a most gracious manner.

After dinner, the Emperor turned over the leaves of two volumes of the Théâtre Français, without being able to find any thing capable of fixing his attention.

THE EMPEROR BISHOP &c.

11th.—After our breakfast in the tent and a few turns in the garden, the Emperor read, for the last time, the chapter of Arcole.

During our ride in the calash, somebody observed that it was Sunday. " We should have mass," said the Emperor, " if we were in a Christian country, if we had a priest ; and that would have been a pastime for us during the day. I have been always fond of the sound of the bells in the country. We should," he added in a gay tone, " resolve upon choosing a priest among us ;—the curate of St. Helena."—But how ordain him, it was said, without a bishop ?—" And am I not one," replied the Emperor, " have I not been anointed with the same oil, consecrated in the same manner ? Were not Clovis and his successors anointed, at the time, with the formula of *Rex Christique sacerdos* ? Were they not, in fact, real bishops ? Was not the subsequent suppression of that formula caused by the jealousy and policy of the bishops and popes ?"

I did not eat at dinner, the Emperor wished to know the cause. I had a violent pain in my stomach, a complaint to which I said I was very subject. " I am more fortunate than you," he observed. " In all my life, I never had either the head-ache or a pain in my stomach.'

The Emperor often repeated what he had said, and he has pronounced these same words perhaps ten, twenty, or thirty times, in the midst of us at different moments.*

CAMPAIGN OF 1809, &c.

12th.—The Emperor passed the morning in his bath, reading the Journals des Debats of March and April, received yesterday by way of the Cape. The Emperor was very much occupied with them; they produced a great degree of agitation in his system.

In general, since the Emperor had received books, and particularly the Moniteur, he continued much more at home; he scarcely ever went abroad; he no longer used a horse, nor even the calash; he hardly took the air for a few moments in the garden; he was not the better for it, his features and his health underwent a visible alteration.

I found him to-day reading Les Croisades by Michaud, which he left to run over Les Memoires de Bezenval. He stopped at the duel between the Comte d'Artois and the Duc de Bourbon. He found the details curious, but they seemed to be very remote from us. "It is difficult," he observed, "to reconcile times so close to us with manners so different."

In the course of this day's conversations, the Emperor happened to repeat, what I have mentioned elsewhere, that his finest manœuvre had been at Eckmuhl, without, however, specifying it any further.

---

* I commonly pass over all details of this kind as trivial, unless an occasion for their utility presents itself, and unfortunately I have not time to look for, or to give rise to, such occasions. The trifling circumstance, however, which I relate here acquires but too great a value by the nature of the death and the protracted and terrible agonies of the immortal victim, who expired under the triple tortures of body, mind, and heart. He would have had much less to endure from the hands of cannibals! . . . . And these sufferings and these torments were coldly reserved for him by a barbarous administration, which, by that proceeding, has stained the annals of a people so justly renowned for the elevation of their sentiments and their sympathy with misfortune! . . . . But a sad and painful celebrity will attach to the names of the executioners of Napoleon. The indignation of the generous hearts of every age and of every country strikes them for ever with eternal reprobation'

ON THE WAR WITH RUSSIA. — FATALITIES, &c. — M. DE
TALLEYRAND, &c.— MADAME DE STAEL'S CORINNE —
M. NECKER, &c.

13th. At an early hour in the morning, I accompanied
the Emperor very far into the wood; he conversed for upwards of an hour, on the situation of France, and then
reverted to the persons who had betrayed him, and the
numerous fatalities which had hurried him along; to the
perfidious security caused by his marriage with Austria;
to the infatuation of the Turks, who made peace precisely
when they ought to have made war; to that of Bernadotte, who was actuated by his self-love and his resentment, rather than by his real grandeur and stability; to
a season severe beyond measure, and even to the superiority of talent, evinced by M. de Narbonne, who, discovering the designs of Austria, compelled her to take
active measures. Finally, he reverted to the successes of
Lutzen and Bautzen, which, by bringing back the king
of Saxony to Dresden, put him, Napoleon, in possession
of the hostile signatures of Austria, and deprived her of
all further subterfuge. "What an unhappy concurrence!"
he exclaimed in a most expressive tone, "and yet," he
continued, "the day after the battle of Dresden, Francis
had already sent a person to treat. It was necessary,
that Vandamme's disaster should happen at a given
moment, to second, as it were, the decree of fate."

M. de Talleyrand, to whose conduct the Emperor frequently alluded, for the purpose of discovering, he said,
when he had really begun to betray him, had strongly
urged him to make peace, on his return from Leipsic.
"I must," he observed, "do him that justice. He found
fault with my speech to the Senate, but warmly approved
of that which I made to the Legislative Body. He uniformly maintained, that I deceived myself with respect to
the energy of the nation; that it would not second
mine, and that it was requisite for me to arrange my
affairs by every possible sacrifice. It appears that he
was then sincere. I never, from my own experience,
found Talleyrand eloquent or persuasive. He dwelt a
great deal, and a long time, on the same idea. Perhaps

also, as our acquaintance was of old date, he behaved in a peculiar manner to me. He was, however, so skilful in his evasions and ramblings that, after conversations which lasted several hours, he has gone away, frequently avoiding the explanations and objects I expected to obtain from him on his coming."

With regard to the affairs of the moment and to the contents of the last journals which described France in a constantly increasing agitation, the result was that the chances of the future seemed indefinite, multiplied, and inexhaustible for all Europe, and that there existed, at that instant, an incontrovertible fact, communicated to us from all quarters, that nobody in Europe considered himself in a permanent situation. Every one seemed to apprehend or to foresee new events.

The Emperor kept me to breakfast with him in the tent. He afterwards sent for Madame de Staël's Corinne, and read some chapters of it. He said that he could not get through it. Madame de Staël had drawn so complete a likeness of herself in her heroine, that she had succeeded in convincing him that it was herself. "I see her," said he, "I hear her, I feel her, I wish to avoid her, and I throw away the book. I had a better impression of this work on my memory, than what I feel at present. Perhaps it is because, at the time, I read it with my thumb, as M. l'Abbé de Pradt ingeniously says, and not without some truth. I shall, however, persevere; I am determined to see the end of it; I still think that it was not destitute of some interest. Yet I cannot forgive Madame de Staël for having undervalued the French in her romance. The family of Madame de Staël is unquestionably a very singular one—her father, her mother and herself, all three on their knees, in constant adoration of each other, regaling one another with reciprocal incense, for the better edification and mystification of the public. Madame de Staël may, nevertheless, exult in surpassing her noble parents, when she presumed to write, that her sentiments for her father were such that she detected herself in being jealous of her mother.

"Madame de Staël," he continued, "was ardent in her passions, vehement and extravagant in her expres sions. This is what was discovered by the police, while she was under its superintendence. ' I am far from you;' (she was probably writing to her husband,) ' come instantly ;—I command ;—I insist upon it; I am on my knees; I beseech you, come. —My hand grasps a dagger. If you hesitate, I shall kill myself; and you alone will be guilty of my destruction.'' This was Corinne.

She had, said the Emperor, combined all her efforts and all her means to make an impression on the General of the army of Italy ; without any knowledge of him, she wrote to him, when far off; she tormented him when present. If she was to be believed, the union of genius with a little insignificant Creole, incapable of appreciating or comprehending him, was a monstrosity. Unfortunately the General's only answer was an indifference which women never forgive, and which, indeed, he remarked with a smile, is hardly to be forgiven.

On his arrival at Paris, he was followed with the same eagerness, but he maintained, on his part, the same reserve, the same silence. Madame de Staël resolved, however, to extract some words from him and to struggle with the conqueror of Italy, attacked him face to face, at the grand entertainment given by M. de Talleyrand, Minister for Foreign Affairs, to the victorious General. She challenged him in the middle of a numerous circle, to tell her who was the greatest woman in the world, whether dead or living. '' She, who has had most children,'' answered Napoleon, with great simplicity. Madame de Staël was, at first, a little disconcerted, and endeavoured to recover herself by observing that it was reported that he was not very fond of women. '' Pardon me, Madam,'' again replied Napoleon, '' I am very fond of my wife.''

The General of the army of Italy, said the Emperor, might, no doubt, have excited the enthusiasm of the Genevese Corinna to its highest pitch ; but he dreaded her political perfidy and her thirst of celebrity ; he was, perhaps, in the wrong. The heroine had, however, been too eager in her pursuit and too often discouraged, not to become a violent enemy. '' She instigated the person, who was then under her influence, and he,'' observed the Emperor, '' did not enter upon the business in a very

honouiable manner. On the appointment of the Tribu-
nate, he employed the most pressing solicitations with
the First Consul to be nominated a member. At eleven
o'clock at night, he was supplicating with all his might;
but at twelve, when the favour was granted, he was already erect and almost in an insulting attitude. The
first meeting of the Tribunes was a splendid occasion
for his invectives against me. At night, Madame de
Staël's hotel was illuminated. She crowned her Benja-
min amidst a brilliant assembly, and proclaimed him a
second Mirabeau. This farce, which was ridiculous
enough, was followed by more dangerous plans. At the
time of the Concordat, against which Madame de Staël
was quite furious, she united at once against me the
aristocrats and the republicans. 'You have,' she exclaimed, but a single moment left; to-morrow the tyrant
will have forty thousand priests at his disposal.'"

"Madame de Staël," said Napoleon, "having at
length tired out my patience was sent into exile. Her
father had seriously offended me before, at the time of
the campaign of Marengo. I wished to see him on my
way, and he struck me merely as a dull bloated college
tutor. Shortly afterwards, and with the hope, no doubt,
of again appearing, by my help, in public life, he published a pamphet, in which he proved that France could
neither be a republic nor a monarchy. What it might
be," remarked the Emperor, "was not sufficiently
evident. In that work, he called the First Consul,
the necessary man, &c. Lebrun replied to him, in a
letter of four pages, in his admirable style, and with all
his powers of sarcasm; he asked him whether he had
not done sufficient mischief to France, and whether his
pretensions to govern her again were not exhausted by
his experiment of the Constituent Assembly.

"Madame de Stael, in her disgrace, carried on hostilities with the one hand, and supplicated with the other.
She was informed, on the part of the First Consul, that
he left her the universe for the theatre of her achievements; that he resigned the rest of the world to her,
and only reserved Paris for himself, which he forbade
her to approach. But Paris was precisely the object of

Madame de Staël's wishes.   No matter, the Consul was
inflexible.   Madame de Staël, however, occasionally renewed her attempts.   Under the empire, she wished to
be a lady of the palace.   Yes or no might certainly be
pronounced ; but by what means could Madame de Staël
be kept quiet in a palace?" &c.

After dinner, the Emperor read the Horatii, and was
frequently interrupted by our bursts of admiration.   Never
did Corneille appear to us grander, more noble, more
nervous, than on our rock.

SHOOTING PARTY AT ST. HELENA, &C.—EVE OF THE 15TH OF AUGUST, &c.

14th. The Emperor went out early.   He sent for me
before nine o'clock.   His intention was to mount his
horse, and endeavour to get a shot at some partridges,
which we saw every time we were in the carriage ; but
which never let any one with a fowling-piece come near
them. The Emperor walked on for the purpose of placing
himself in a convenient situation, but the partridges were
no longer to be found.   He was soon fatigued, and got
on horseback, observing that our shooting party was not
exactly after the fashion of those of Rambouillet and
Fontainebleau.   We breakfasted, on our return, in the
tent.   The Emperor placed little Tristan, whom he saw
crossing the meadow, at table, and was much amused
with him during the whole of the repast.

After breakfast, the Emperor had the chapter of
Rivoli read over again to him, and finished it.   We had
gone through three-fourths of it, when the Governor
being announced, we made a precipitate retreat from the
tent, and each of us took refuge in his den.   The Emperor was less inclined than any other person to let himself be seen : his conversations with the Governor are by
far too disagreeable and painful to him.   " I am determined," he said, " to have no more to do with him.
Harsh remarks escape me, which affect my character and
my dignity ; nothing should fall from my lips but what
is kind and complimentary."   He found himself fatigued
with his exercise in the morning, and took a bath.

About five o'clock, he took a turn in the calash, the
weather was delicious.

The Governor had expressed an earnest desire to see the Emperor; he wished, he said, to speak with him on business. It is suspected that it was to tell him that he had no more money, that he had exhausted all, and that he no longer knew how to act; a matter of perfect indifference to the Emperor, who would not have failed, once more, to entreat to be let alone.

The Emperor played at chess, before dinner, in the saloon; he had taken some punch. It was late when I arrived; he told me, on entering, to take my share of the punch; but it was observed that there were no more glasses. "O yes," said he, handing me his, "and he will drink out of it, I am sure." He then added, "This is the English fashion; is it not? In our country one seldom drinks after any one but one's mistress."

It was remarked, during dinner, that it was the eve of the 15th of August; the Emperor then observed; "Many healths will be drunk to-morrow, in Europe, to St. Helena. There are certainly some sentiments, some wishes, that will traverse the ocean." He had entertained the same thought in the morning when on horseback, and had said the same things to me.

After dinner, Cinna;— Corneille appears to us divine.

THE EMPEROR'S BIRTH-DAY.

15th.—This day, the 15th of August, was the Emperor's birthday. We had determined to wait upon him, in a body, about eleven o'clock. He disappointed us by appearing gaily at our doors at nine. The weather was mild, he went to the garden, and we all assembled there in succession. The Grand Marshal, with his wife and children, joined us. The Emperor, surrounded by his faithful servants, breakfasted in the large and beautiful tent, which is a really fortunate acquisition. The temperature was fine, and he himself cheerful and talkative. He seemed, for some instants, to participate in our sentiments and wishes. He desired, he said, to pass the whole day in the midst of us. Accordingly, we continued together, and spent the time in conversation, in different pursuits, in walking, and in riding in the carriage.

16th.—My son and I went, at a very early hour, to the
tent, where the Emperor continued employed on different
chapters of the Campaign of Italy until two o'clock, when
the Governor being announced, he retired, muttering
" The wretch, I believe, envies me the air I breathe."

During breakfast, he had called for the Journal des
Débats, which contained the organization of the acade-
mies; he wished to see the names of the members, who
had been expelled from the Institute. This led him to
revert to the suppression of the Polytechnic School,
which was said to be useless and dangerous. The English
Journal, which we had received, was not of that opinion.
It maintained that the suppression alone was more valuable to the enemies of France than a signal victory, and
that nothing could more decidedly prove the real pacific
sentiments and the extreme moderation of the dynasty,
which then governed France, &c.   It also stated several
other things.

Somebody remarked, upon this subject, that the English
papers shewed a malevolence against the French Government, which extended to coarseness and indecency.

Lord or Lady Holland had, with a peculiar degree of
attention, sent to Longwood, for the Emperor's use, a
newly invented machine, adapted to the formation of ice.
It was delivered to us to-day, through the intervention of
Admiral Malcolm. The Emperor went out about five
o'clock, and was desirous of witnessing the experiment;
the Admiral was present, but the experiment proved very
imperfect.

The Emperor, after some time, took a walk, accompanied by the Admiral, and the conversation turned
upon a variety of subjects; it was maintained in the
most affable and friendly manner on the part of the
Emperor.

RELIGIOUS IDEAS OF NAPOLEON.—BISHOP OF NANTES
(DE VOISINS).—THE POPE.—LIBERTIES OF THE GAL-
LICAN CHURCH.—ANECDOTES.—CONCORDAT OF FON-
TAINEBLEAU.

17th.— While the Emperor was at breakfast in the
tent, two persons described the excesses which they had
witnessed in the army, and which had not come to his
knowledge.   They noticed the numerous violations of his
orders, the violent abuses of authority, and other outrages.   The Emperor listened ; but some were so shocking that he could not, he said, give credit to them, and
observed : " Come, gentlemen, these are libels."

The wind was very violent ; it blew a storm, with occasional showers.   The wet obliged the Emperor to go
in again.

After dinner Zaire and the beautiful scenes of Œdipe
were read, among which he particularly pointed out that
of the discovery, which he pronounced the finest and the
most finished of the drama.

In speaking of priests and religion, the conversation
led the Emperor to say : " Man, entering into life, asks
himself : Whence do I come ? What am I ? Whither am
I to go ? These are so many mysterious questions, which
urge us on to religion.   We eagerly embrace it ; we are
attracted by our natural propensity ; but as we advance
in knowledge our course is stopped.   Instruction and
history are the great enemies of religion, deformed by
human imperfection.   Why, we ask ourselves, is the
religion of Paris neither that of London nor of Berlin ?
Why is that of Petersburgh different from that of Constantinople ?   Why is the latter different from that of
Persia, of the Ganges, and of China ? Why is the religion of ancient times different from that of our days ?
Then reason is sadly staggered ; it exclaims, O religions,
religions ! the children of man ! . . . . We very properly believe in God, because every thing around us
proclaims him, and the most enlightened minds have
believed in him ; not only Bossuet, whose profession it
was, but also Newton and Leibnitz, who had nothing to
do with it.   But we know not what to think of the

doctrine that is taught us, and we find ourselves like the
watch which goes, without knowing the watchmaker that
made it. And observe a little the stupidity of those who
educate us; they should keep away from us the idea of
paganism and idolatry; because their absurdity excites
the first exercise of our reason, and prepares us for a
resistance to passive belief; and they bring us up, nevertheless, in the midst of the Greeks and Romans, with
their myriads of divinities. Such, for my own part, has
literally been the progress of my understanding. I felt
the necessity of belief; I did believe, but my belief was
shocked and undecided, the moment I acquired knowledge and began to reason; and that happened to me at
so early an age as thirteen. Perhaps, I shall again believe implicitly; God grant I may! I shall certainly
make no resistance, and I do not ask a greater blessing;
it must, in my mind, be a great and real happiness.

"In violent agitations, however, and in the casual
suggestions of immorality itself, the absence of that religious faith has never, I assert, influenced me in any
respect, and I never doubted the existence of God; for,
if my reason was inadequate to comprehend it, my mind
was not the less disposed to adopt it. My nerves were
in sympathy with that sentiment.

"When I seized on the helm of affairs, I had already
fixed ideas of all the primary elements by which society
is bound together; I had weighed all the importance of
religion; I was convinced, and I determined to re-establish it. But the resistance I had to overcome in
restoring Catholicism would scarcely be credited. I
should have been more willingly followed had I hoisted
the standard of Protestantism. This reluctance was carried so far that in the Council of State, where I found
great difficulty in getting the Concordat adopted, several
yielded only by forming a plan to extricate themselves
from it. 'Well!' they said to one another, 'let us turn
Protestants, and that will not affect us.' It is unquestionable that, in the disorder which I succeeded, upon
which I found myself I was at liberty to choose
between Catholicism and Protestantism; and it may also
be said, with truth, that the general disposition, at the

moment, was quite in favour of the latter: but, besides my real adherence to the religion in which I was born, I had the most important motives to influence my decision. What should I have gained by proclaiming Protestantism? I should have created two great parties, very nearly equal, in France, when I wished for the existence of none at all; I should have revived the fury of religious disputes, when their total annihilation was called for by the light of the age and my own feelings. These two parties would, by their mutual distractions, have destroyed France, and rendered her the slave of Europe, when I had the ambition to make her the mistress of it. By the help of Catholicism I attained much more effectually all the grand results that I had in view. In the interior, at home, the smaller number was swallowed up by the greater, and I relied upon my treating the former with such an equality that there would be shortly no motive for marking the difference. Abroad, the Pope was bound to me by Catholicism; and, with my influence, and our forces in Italy, I did not despair, sooner or later, by some means or other, of obtaining for myself the direction of that Pope, and from that time, what an influence! What a lever of opinion on the rest of the world!" &c. He concluded with saying: "Francis I. was really in a state to adopt Protestantism, at its birth, and to declare himself the head of it in Europe. Charles V., his rival, was the zealous champion of Rome, because he considered that measure as an additional means to assist him in his project of enslaving Europe. Was not that circumstance alone sufficient to point out to Francis the necessity of taking care of his independence; but he abandoned the greater to run after the lesser advantage. He persevered in pursuing his imprudent designs on Italy, and, with the intention of paying court to the Pope, he burnt Protestants at Paris.

"Had Francis I. embraced Lutheranism, which is favourable to royal supremacy, he would have preserved France from the dreadful religious convulsions brought on, at later periods, by the Calvinists, whose efforts, altogether republican, were on the point of subverting the throne and dissolving our noble monarchy. Unfortunately, Francis I. was ignorant of all that; for he could not allege his scruples for an excuse, he, who entered into an alliance with the Turks, and brought them into the midst of us. It was precisely because he was incapable of extending his views so far. The folly of the time! The extent of feudal intellect! Francis I. was, after all, but a hero for tilts and tournaments, and a gallant for the drawing-room, one of those pigmy great men.

"The Bishop of Nantes (De Voisins), said the Emperor, made me a real Catholic by the efficacy of his arguments, by the excellence of his morals, and by his enlightened toleration. Marie Louise, whose confessor he was, consulted him once on the obligation of abstaining from meat on Fridays.—'At what table do you dine?' asked the Bishop.—'At the Emperor's.' 'Do you give all the orders there?'—'No.' 'You cannot, then make any alteration in it; would he do it himself?'—'I am inclined to think not.' 'Be obedient then, and do not provoke a subject for scandal. Your first duty is to obey, and make him respected; you will not be in want of other means to amend your life, and to suffer privations in the eyes of God.'

"He also behaved in the same way with respect to a public communion, which some persons put into Marie Louise's head to celebrate on Easter-day. She would not, however, consent, without the advice of her prudent confessor, who dissuaded her from it by similar arguments. What a difference, said the Emperor, had she been worked upon by a fanatic! What quarrels, what disagreements might he not have caused between us! What mischief might he not have done, in the circumstances in which I was placed!"

The Emperor remarked to us, "that the bishop of Nantes had lived with Diderot, in the midst of unbelievers, and had uniformly conducted himself with consistency; he was ready with an answer to every one; and, above all, he had the good sense to abandon every thing that was not maintainable, and to strip religion of every thing which he was not capable of defending.— He was asked, 'has not an animal, which moves, con-

bines, and thinks, a soul ?' 'Why not,' was his answer.
'But whither does it go ? For it is not equal to ours.'
'What is that to you ? It dwells, perhaps, in limbo.'
He used to retreat within the last intrenchments, even
within the fortress itself, and there he reserved excellent
means for defending himself. He argued better than
the Pope, whom he often confounded. He was the
firmest pillar, among our bishops, of the Gallican
liberties. He was my oracle, my luminary ; in religious
matters, he possessed my unbounded confidence. For,
in my quarrels with the Pope, it was my first care,
whatever intriguers and marplots in cassocs may say, not
to touch upon any dogmatic point : I was so steady in
this conduct, that the instant this good and venerable
bishop of Nantes said to me, 'Take care, there you are
grappling with a dogma,' I immediately turned off from
the course I was pursuing, to return to it by other ways,
without amusing myself by entering into dissertations
with him, or by seeking even to comprehend his mean
ing ; and, as I had not let him into my secret, how
amazed must he not have been at the circuits I made !
How whimsical, obstinate, capricious, and incoherent,
must I not have appeared to him ! It was because
I had an object in view, and he was unacquainted
with it.

"The Popes could not forgive us our liberties of the
Gallican church. The four famous propositions of
Bossuet, in particular, provoked their resentment. It
was, in their opinion, a real hostile manifesto, and they
accordingly considered us at least as much out of the
pale of the church as the Protestants. They thought us
as guilty as they, perhaps more so, and if they did not
overwhelm us with their ostensible thunderbolts, it was
because they dreaded the consequences—our separation.
The example of England was before them. They did
not wish to cut off their right arm with their own hand,
but they were constantly on the watch for a favourable
opportunity ; they trusted to time for it. They are, no
doubt, ready to believe, that it has now arrived. They
will, however, be again disappointed by the light of the
age and the manners of the times.

6*

" Some time before my coronation," said the Emperor, ' the Pope wished to see me, and made it a point to visit me himself. He had made many concessions. He had come to Paris for the purpose of crowning me; he consented not to place the crown on my head himself; he dispensed with the ceremony of the public communion; he had, therefore, in his opinion, many compensations to expect in return. He had accordingly at first dreamt of Romagna and the Legations, and he began to suspect that he should be obliged to give up all that. He then lowered his pretensions to a very trifling favour, as he called it, my signature to an ancient document, a worn-out rag, which he held from Louis XIV. ' Do me that favour, said he, in fact, it signifies nothing.' ' Cheerfully, most holy father, and the thing is done, if it be feasible.' It was, however, a declaration, in which Louis XIV. at the close of his life, seduced by Madame de Maintenon, or prevailed upon by his confessors, expressed his disapprobation of the celebrated articles of 1682, the foundations of the liberties of the Gallican church. The Emperor shrewdly replied, that he had not, for his own part, any personal objection, but that it was requisite for him, as a matter of form, to speak to the bishops about it; on which the Pope repeatedly observed, that such a communication was by no means necessary, and that the thing did not deserve to make so much noise. ' I shall never,' he remarked, ' shew the signature, it shall be kept as secret as that of Louis XIV.' ' But, if it signifies nothing,' said Napoleon, ' what use is there for my signature? And if any signification can be drawn from it, I am bound by a sense of propriety to consult my doctors.' "

With the view, however, of avoiding the imputation of a constant refusal of every request, the Emperor wished to seem rather inclined to grant the favour. " The Bishop of Nantes and the other bishops, who were really French, came to me in great haste. They were furious, and watched me," said the Emperor, " as they would have watched Louis XIV. on his death-bed, to prevent him from turning Protestant. The Sulpicians were called in; they were Jesuits *au petit pied*, they strove to find out my intention, and were ready to do whatever I wished. The Emperor concluded with observing ;—"The Pope had dispensed with the public communion in my favour, and it is from his determination in that respect that I form my opinion of the sincerity of his religious belief. He had held a congregation of cardinals for the purpose of settling the ceremonial. The greater number warmly insisted upon my taking the communion in public, asserting the great influence of the example on the people, and the necessity of my holding it out. The Pope, on the contrary, fearful lest I should fulfil that duty as if I were going through one of the articles of M. de Ségur's programme, looked upon it as a sacrilege, and was inflexible in opposing it. 'Napoleon,' he observed, 'is not perhaps a believer; the time will, no doubt, come, in which his faith will be established, and in the mean time, let us not burthen his conscience or our own.'

" In his Christian charity, for he really is a worthy, mild, and excellent man, he never once despaired of seeing me a penitent, at his tribunal; he has often let his hopes and thoughts on that subject escape him. We sometimes conversed about it in a pleasant and friendly manner. 'It will happen to you, sooner or later,' said he, with an innocent tenderness of expression ; 'you will be converted by me or by others, and you will then feel how great the content, the satisfaction of your own heart,' &c. In the mean time, my influence over him was such, that I drew from him, by the mere power of my conversation, that famous Concordat of Fontainebleau, in which he renounced the temporal sovereignty, an act on account of which he has since shown that he dreaded the judgment of posterity, or rather the reprobation of his successors. No sooner had he signed than he felt the stings of repentance. He was to have dined the following day with me in public; but at night, he was, or pretended to be ill. The truth is that, immediately after I left him, he again fell into the hands of his habitual advisers, who drew a terrible picture of the error which he had committed. Had we been left by ourselves, I might have done what I pleased with him;

should have governed the religious with the same
facility that I did the political world.   He was, in truth,
a lamb, a good man in every respect, a man of real
worth, whom I esteem and love greatly, and who, on his
part, is, I am convinced, not altogether destitute of
interest with regard to me.   You will not see him make
any severe complaints against me, nor prefer, in particular, any direct and personal accusation against me,
any more than the other sovereigns.   There may, perhaps, be some vague and vulgar declamations against
ambition and bad faith, but nothing positive and direct;
because statesmen are well aware, that when the hour of
libels is past, no one would be allowed to prefer a public
accusation without corroborative proofs, and they have
none of these to produce : such will be the province of
history.   On the other hand, there will be at most but
some wretched chroniclers, shallow enough to take the
ravings of clubs, or intrigues, for authentic facts, or
some writers of memoirs, who, deceived by the errors of
the moment, will be dead before they are enabled to
correct their mistakes.

   " When the real particulars of my disputes with the
Pope shall be made public, the world will be surprised at
the extent of my patience, for it is known that I could not
put up with a great deal.   When he left me, after my
coronation, he felt a secret spite at not having obtained
the compensations which he thought he had deserved.
But, however grateful I might have been in other respects, I could not, after all, make a traffic of the
interests of the empire by way of paying my own
obligations, and, I was, besides, too proud to seem to have
purchased his kindnesses.   He had hardly set his foot
on the soil of Italy, when the intriguers and mischief-
makers, the enemies of France, took advantage of the
disposition he was in, to govern his conduct, and from
that instant every thing was hostile on his part.   He no
longer was the gentle, the peaceable Chiaramonti, that
worthy bishop of Imola, who had at so early a period
shown himself worthy of the enlightened state of the
age.   His signature was thenceforth affixed to acts only
which characterised the Gregories and Bonifaces more

than him. Rome became the focus of all the plots
hatched against us. I strove in vain to bring him back
by the force of reason, but I found it impossible to ascertain his sentiments. The wrongs became so serious,
and the insults offered to us so flagrant, that I was im-
peratively called upon to act, in my turn. I, therefore,
seized his fortresses; I took possession of some provinces; and I finished by occupying Rome itself, at the same
time declaring and strictly observing that I held him
sacred in his spiritual capacity, which was far from being
satisfactory to him. A crisis, however, presented itself;
it was believed, that fortune had abandoned me at
Essling, and measures were in immediate readiness for
exciting the population of that great capital to insurrection. The officer, who commanded there, thought that
he could escape the danger only by getting rid of the
Pope, whom he sent off to France. That measure was
carried into effect without my orders, and was even in
direct opposition to my views. I despatched instant orders for stopping the Pope, wherever he might be met
with, and he was kept at Savona, where he was treated
with every possible care and attention; for I wished to
make myself feared, but not to ill-treat him; to bend him
to my views, not to degrade him;—I entertained very
different projects! This removal served only to inflame
the spirit of resentment and intrigue. Until then, the
quarrel had been but temporal; the Pope's advisers, in
the hope of re-establishing their affairs, involved it in
all the jumble of spirituality. I then found it necessary
to carry on the contest with him on that head; I had my
council of conscience, my ecclesiastical councils, and I
invested my imperial courts with the power of deciding
in cases of appeal from abuses; for my soldiers could be
of no further use in all this: I felt it necessary to fight
the Pope with his own weapons. To his men of erudi-
tion, to his sophists, his civilians, and his scribes, it was
incumbent upon me to oppose mine.

"An English plot was laid to carry him off from
Savona; it was of service to me; I caused him to be
removed to Fontainebleau; but that was to be the period
of his sufferings, and the regeneration of his splendour.

All my grand views were accomplished in disguise and
mystery. I had brought things to such a point, as to
render the development infallible, without any exertion,
and in a way altogether natural. It was accordingly
consecrated by the Pope in the famous Concordat of
Fontainebleau, in spite even of my disasters at Moscow.
What then would have been the result, had I returned
victorious and triumphant? I had consequently obtained
the separation, which was so desirable, of the spiritual
from the temporal, which is so injurious to his Holiness,
and the commixture of which produces disorder in
society, in the name and by the hands of him who ought
himself to be the centre of harmony : and from that time
I intended to exalt the Pope beyond measure, to surround
him with grandeur and honours. I should have succeeded in suppressing all his anxiety for the loss of his
temporal power ; I should have made an idol of him ;
he would have remained near my person. Paris would
have become the capital of the Christian world, and I
should have governed the religious as well as the political world. It was an additional means of binding
tighter all the federative parts of the empire, and of preserving the tranquillity of every thing placed without it.
I should have had my religious as well as my legislative
sessions ; my councils would have constituted the representation of Christendom, and the Popes would have
been only the presidents. I should have called together
and dissolved those assemblies, approved and published
their discussions, as Constantine and Charlemagne had
done; and if that supremacy had escaped the Emperors,
it was because they had committed the blunder of letting
the spiritual heads reside at a distance from them ; and
the latter took advantage of the weakness of the princes,
or of critical events, to shake off their dependence and to
enslave them in their turn.

"But," resumed the Emperor, " to accomplish that
object, I had found it requisite to manœuvre with a
great deal of dexterity; above all, to conceal my real way
of thinking, to give a direction, altogether different to
general opinion, and to feed the public with vulgar trifles,
for the purpose of more effectually concealing the impor-

tance and depth of my secret design. I accordingly experienced a kind of satisfaction in finding myself accused of barbarity towards the Pope, and of tyranny in religious matters. Foreigners, in particular, promoted my wishes in this respect, by filling their wretched libels with invectives against my pitiful ambition, which, according to them, had driven me to devour the miserable patrimony of Saint Peter. But I was perfectly aware, that public opinion would again declare itself in my favour at home, and that no means could exist abroad for disconcerting my plan. What measures would not have been employed for its prevention, had it been anticipated at a seasonable period; for how vast its future ascendency over all the Catholic countries, and how great its influence even upon those that are not so, by the co-operation of the members of that religion who are spread throughout these countries!"

The Emperor said, that this deliverance from the Court of Rome, this legal union, the control of religion in the hands of the sovereign, had been, for a long time, the constant object of his meditations and his wishes. England, Russia, the northern crowns, and part of Germany, are, he said, in possession of it. Venice and Naples had enjoyed it. No government can be carried on without it; a nation is otherwise, every instant, affected in its tranquillity, its dignity, its independence. But the task, " he added, " was very difficult; at every step I was alive to the danger. I was induced to think, that, once engaged in it, I should be abandoned by the nation. I more than once sounded and strove to elicit public opinion, but in vain, and I have been enabled to convince myself that I never should have had the national co-operation. And this explains a sally, which I had witnessed."

The Emperor perceiving, at one of those grand Sunday audiences, which were very numerously attended, the Archbishop of Tours (de Barral) addressed him in a very elevated tone: " Well! Monsieur l'Archevêque, how do our affairs with the Pope go on ?—' Sire, the deputation of your bishops is about to set out for Savona.' Very well! endeavour to make the Pope listen to reason prevail upon him to conduct himself with prudence; otherwise the consequences will be unpleasant. Tell him plainly, that he is no longer in the times of the Gregories, and that I am not a Débonnaire. He has the example of Henry the VIIIth., and, without his wickedness, I possess more strength and power than he had. Let him know, that whatever part I may take, I have 600,000 Frenchmen in arms, who, in every contingency will march with me, for me, and as myself. The peasantry and mechanics look to me alone, and repose unlimited confidence in me. The prudent and enlightened part of the intermediate class, those who take care of their interest, and wish for tranquillity, will follow me; the only class favourable to him will be the meddling and talkative, who, will forget him at the end of ten days, to chat upon some fresh subject."

And as the archbishop, who betrayed his embarrassment by his countenance, was about to stammer out some words, the Emperor added in a greatly softened tone: "You are out of all this; I participate in your doctrines; I honour your piety; I respect your character!"

The Emperor, I now understand him perfectly, had, no doubt, merely thrown out those observations, in order that we might give effect to them in other places; but he deceived himself with respect to our dispositions, or at least to those of the palace. Some, the least reflecting part, were decided and loud in censuring his conduct on these occasions; others, with the best intentions, were extremely cautious not to let a word transpire, lest it should prove injurious to him in the public opinion; for, such was, in general, our misconception, our singular manner of understanding and explaining the Emperor's meaning, that, although without any bad design, and solely through levity, incoherency, or for fashion's sake, instead of making him popular, we were perhaps the very persons who did him most injury. I very well remember that, on the morning when that famous concordat of Fontainebleau unexpectedly appeared in the Moniteur, some persons confidentially assured each other in the saloons of St. Cloud, that nothing was less authentic than that document, and that it was a base fabrication. Others whispered, that it was, no doubt, genuine in the main points, but that it had been extracted from the Pope by the Emperor's anger and violence. To that I should not be surprised, if the piquant dramatic episode of Napoleon, at Fontainebleau, *dragging the father of the faithful by his white hair*, was not precisely the invention of the political proser who wrote it, but caught up from the mouths of the courtiers and even of the Emperor's servants themselves; and this is the way in which history is written!

WARM CONVERSATION WITH THE GOVERNOR, IN THE ADMIRAL'S PRESENCE.

18th. The weather was most dreadful during the whole of the night and day. About three o'clock, the Emperor took advantage of its clearing up a little and went out. He came to my apartment, and we called on General Gourgaud, who was indisposed. We then visited Madame de Montholon, who accompanied us to the garden. The Emperor was in excellent spirits, which enlivened the conversation. He undertook to persuade Madame de Montholon to make a general confession, particularly insisting upon her setting out with her first sin. "Come," said he, "speak out without apprehension, do not let our neighbour constrain you; consider him merely as your confessor; we shall forget it all in a quarter of an hour."

And I really believe he would have succeeded in persuading her, when the Governor unfortunately came to interrupt so pleasant a scene; he made his appearance, and the Emperor to avoid receiving him, hastily took shelter in the bottom of the wood. We were joined in a few moments by M. de Montholon, who acquainted the Emperor that the Governor and the Admiral earnestly requested the honour of speaking with him. He thought that some communication was to be made on their part, and returned to the garden, where he received them.

We remained behind, with the Governor's officers. The conversation soon became animated on the part of the Emperor, who, as he walked between the Governor and the Admiral, almost uniformly addressed himself to the latter, even when he spoke to the former. We continued

at too great a distance to hear any thing distinctly; but
I have since learned, that he again repeated, and with,
perhaps, more energy and warmth, all that he said to
him in the preceding conversations.

In consequence of the favourable explanations, which
the Admiral, who acted the part of mediator, laboured to
give of the Governor's intentions, the Emperor observed;
"The faults of M. Lowe proceed from his habits of
life. He has never had the command of any but foreign
deserters, of Piedmontese, Corsicans, and Sicilians, all re-
negadoes, and traitors to their country; the dregs and
scum of Europe. If he had commanded Englishmen;
if he were one himself, he would shew respect to those
who have a right to be honoured." At another time,
the Emperor declared, that there was a moral courage,
as necessary as courage on the field of battle; that M.
Lowe did not exercise it here with regard to us, in dream-
ing only of our escape, instead of employing the only
real, prudent, reasonable, and sensible means for preventing it. The Emperor also told him that, although his
body was in the hands of evil-minded men, his soul was
as lofty and independent as when at the head of
400,000 men, or on the throne, when he disposed of
kingdoms.

To the article respecting the reduction of our expenses
and the money which was required of the Emperor, he
answered: "All those details are very painful to me;
they are mean. You might place me on the burning
pile of Montezuma or Guatimozin without extracting from
me gold, which I do not possess. Besides, who asks you
for any thing? Who entreats you to feed me? When
you discontinue your supply of provisions, those brave
soldiers, whom you see there," pointing, with his hand,
to the camp of the 53d, "will take pity on me; I shall
place myself at the grenadiers' table, and they will not,
I am confident, drive away the first, the oldest soldier
of Europe."

The Emperor having reproached the Governor with
having kept some books. which were addressed to him,
he answered, that he had done so in consequence of their
having been sent under the address of *Emperor*. "And

who," replied the Emperor, with emotion, " gave you
the right of disputing that title? In a few years, your
Lord Castlereagh, your Lord Bathurst, and all the others
—you, who speak to me—will be buried in the dust of
oblivion, or if your names be remembered, it will be only
on account of the indignity with which you have treated
me, while the Emperor Napoleon shall, doubtless, continue for ever the subject, the ornament of history, and
the star of civilized nations. Your libels are of no avail
against me; you have expended millions on them; what
have they produced? Truth pierces through the clouds,
it shines like the sun, and like it, is imperishable."

The Emperor admitted that he had, during this conversation, seriously and repeatedly offended Sir Hudson
Lowe; and he also did him the justice to acknowledge,
that Sir Hudson Lowe had not precisely shewn, in a single
instance, any want of respect; he had contented himself
with muttering, between his teeth, sentences which were
not audible. He once said that he had solicited his
recal, and the Emperor observed, that that was the most
agreeable word he could possibly have said. He also
said, that we endeavoured to blacken his character in
Europe, but that our conduct, in that respect, was a
matter of indifference to him. The only disrespect, perhaps, said the Emperor, on the part of the Governor, and
which was trifling, compared with the treatment he had
received, was the abrupt way in which he retired, while
the Admiral withdrew slowly, and with numerous salutes.
" The Admiral was precisely then," observed the Emperor, in a gay tone of voice, " what the Marquis de
Gallo was at the time of my rupture of Passeriano."—
An allusion to one of the chapters of the Campaign in
Italy, which he had dictated to me.

The Emperor remarked that, after all, he had to reproach himself with that scene. " I must see this officer
no more; he makes me fly into a violent passion; it is
beneath my dignity; expressions escape me which would
have been unpardonable at the Tuileries; if they can at
all be excused here, it is because I am in his hands and
subject to his power."

After dinner, the Emperor caused a letter to be read

.n answer to the Governor, who had officially sent the
treaty of the 2nd of August, by which the allied Sovereigns stipulated for the imprisonment of Napoleon. Sir
Hudson Lowe, by the same conveyance, asked to introduce the foreign Commissioners to Longwood. The
Emperor had, in the course of the day, dictated the letter
to M. de Montholon. It was his wish, that every one
of us should make his objections, and state his opinions.
It seemed to us a master-piece of dignity, energy, and
sound reasoning.

THE CONVERSATION WITH THE GOVERNOR AGAIN NOTI-
    CED, &C.—EFFECT OF THE LIBELS AGAINST NAPOLEON.
    - TREATY OF FONTAINEBLEAU.— THE WORK OF
    GENERAL S——N.

19th.—The weather continued as dreadful as we had
ever seen it. It has been, for several days, like one of
our equinoctial storms in Europe. The Emperor exposed himself to it, to come to my apartment about ten
o'clock; in going out, he struck one of his legs against
a nail near the door; his stocking was torn halfway down
the leg; luckily the skin was only scratched. He was
obliged to return to change. " You owe me a pair of
stockings," he said, while his valet de chambre was
putting on another pair; " a polite man does not expose
his visitors to such dangers in his apartments. You are
lodged too much like a seaman; it is true, that is not
your fault. I thought myself careless about these matters, but you actually surpass me."—Sire," I answered,
" my merit is not great, no choice is left me. I am
truly a hog in its mire, I must confess; but as your
Majesty says, it is not altogether my fault."

We went into the garden, when it had cleared up for
a moment. The Emperor reverted to the conversation
which he had yesterday with the Governor, in the Admiral's presence, and again reproached himself with the
violence of his expressions. " It would have been more
worthy of me, more consistent and more dignified, to
have expressed all these things with perfect composure;
they would, besides, have been more impressive." He
recollected, in particular, a name which had escaped him

as applied to Sir H. Lowe (*scribe d'etat-major,*) which must have shocked him, and the more so because it expressed the truth, and that, we know, is always offensive. " I have myself," said the Emperor, " experienced that feeling in the island of Elba. When I ran over the most infamous libels, they did not affect me even in the slightest manner. When I was told or read, that I had *strangled, poisoned, ravished ;* that I had massacred my sick ; that my carriage had been driven over my wounded ; I laughed out of commiseration. How often did I not then say to Madame : ' Make haste, mother, come and see the *savage,* the *man-tiger, the devourer of the human race ;* come and admire your child !' But when there was a slight approach to truth, the effect was no longer the same ; I felt the necessity of defending myself ; I accumulated reasons for my justification, and even then, it never happened, that I was left without some traces of a secret torment. My dear Las Cases, such is man !"

The Emperor passed from this subject to his protest against the treaty of the 2nd of August, which had been read to us after dinner. I presumed to ask him, whether after noticing in a conspicuous manner the acknowledgment of his title of Emperor by the English, during their negotiations at Paris and Chatillon, he had not forgotten that, which they must have made on occasion of the treaty of Fontainebleau, and which, it struck me, was omitted. " It was," he quickly replied, " done on purpose ; I have nothing to do with that treaty ; I disclaim it, I am far from boasting of it, I am rather ashamed of it. It was discussed for me. I was betrayed by N . . ., who brought it to me. That epoch belongs to my history, but to my history on a large scale. If I had then determined to treat in a sensible manner, I should have obtained the kingdom of Italy, Tuscany, or Corsica,— all that I could have desired. My decision was the result of a fault inherent in my character, a caprice on my part, a real constitutional excess. I was seized with a dislike and contempt of every thing around me ; I was affected with the same feeling for fortune, which I took delight in defying. I cast my eye on a spot of land, where I might be uncomfortable and take advantage of the mistakes that might be made. I fixed upon the island of Elba. It was the act of a soul of rock. I am, no doubt, my dear Las Cases, of a very singular disposition but we should not be extraordinary, were we not of a peculiar mould; I am a piece of rock, launched into space! You will not, perhaps, easily believe me, but I do not regret my grandeur, you see me slightly affected by what I have lost."

"And why, Sire," I observed, "should I not believe you? What have you to regret? . . . . The life of man is but an atom in the duration of history, but with regard to your majesty, the one is already so full, that you scarcely ought to take any interest but in the other; if your body suffers here, your memory is enriched a hundred-fold. Had it been your lot to end your days in the bosom of uninterrupted prosperity, how many grand and striking circumstances would have passed away unknown! You yourself, Sire, have assured me of this, and I have remained impressed with the force of that truth. Not a day, in fact, passes in which those, who were your enemies, do not repeat with us, who are your faithful servants, that you are unquestionably greater here than in the Tuileries. And even on this rock, to which you have been transferred by violence and perfidy, do you not still command? Your jailors, your masters, are at your feet; your soul captivates every one that comes near you, you shew yourself what history represents St. Louis in the chains of the Saracens, the real master of his conquerors. Your irresistible ascendancy accompanies you here. We, who are all about you, Sire, entertain this opinion of you; the Russian commissioner expressed the same sentiment, we are assured, the other day, and it is felt by those who guard you. What have you to regret?"

On our return the Emperor, in spite of the storm, ordered his breakfast in the tent, and kept me with him. The rain did not penetrate; the only inconvenience was a considerable degree of damp; but the squalls of wind and rain whirled round us, and vented themselves far before us, towards the bottom of the valley; the spectacle was not destitute of beauty

The Emperor retired about two o'clock; he sent for me some time afterwards to his cabinet. "I have," said he, laying down the book, just read General S———n; he is a madman, a hair-brained fellow, he writes nonsense. He is, however, after all, readable and amusing, he cuts up, dissects, judges, and pronounces sentence upon men and things. He does not hesitate to give advice, in several instances, to Wellington, and asserts, that he ought to have made some campaigns under Kleber, &c. Kleber was no doubt a great general, but the notice taken of Soult is not precisely the best part of the book; he is an excellent director, a good minister at war.

"This S———n," he continued, "deserted from the camp at Boulogne, carrying all my secrets to the English; that might have been attended with serious consequences. S———n was a general officer; his conduct was dreadful and unpardonable. But observe how a man, in the moment of revolution, may be a bad character, impudent, and shameless. I found him, on my return from the island of Elba; he waited for me with confidence, and wrote a long letter in which he attempted to make me his dupe. The English, he said, were miserable creatures; he had been a long time among them; he was acquainted with their means and resources, and could be very useful to me. He knew that I was too magnanimous, too great, to remember the wrongs I had suffered from him. I ordered him to be arrested, and as he had been already tried and condemned, I am at a loss to know why he was not shot. Either there was not time to carry his sentence into effect, or he was forgotten. There can be no forbearance, no indulgence for the general, who has the infamy to prostitute himself to a foreign power."

The Grand Marshal came in; the Emperor, after continuing the conversation for some time, took him away to play at chess. He suffered much from the badness of the weather.

After dinner, he read Le Tartuffe; but he was so fatigued, that he could not get through it. He laid down the book, and, after paying a just tribute of eulogy

to Moliere, he concluded in a manner which we little
expected. " The whole of the Tartuffe," he remarked, " is
unquestionably, finished with the hand of a master, it
's one of the best pieces of an inimitable writer.   It is.
however, marked with such a character, that I am not at
all surprised, that its appearance should have been the
subject of interesting negotiations at Versailles, and of a
great deal of hesitation on the part of Louis XIV.   If I
have a right to be astonished at any thing, it is at his
allowing it to be performed.   In my opinion, it holds
out devotion under such odious colours ; a certain scene
presents so decisive a situation, so completely indecent,
that, for my own part, I do not hesitate to say, if the
comedy had been written in my time, I would not have
allowed it to be represented."

THE BARONESS DE S . . . ., &c.

20th.—About four o'clock, I attended the Emperor,
according to his orders, in the billiard-room.   The weather still ...tinued dreadful ; it did not allow him to set
his foot out of doors, and he was, he said, nevertheless,
driven from his apartment and the saloon by the smoke.
My looks told him, he said, that I was quite flustered ;
it was with the most lively indignation, and he wished to
know the cause of it.

" Two or three years ago," said I, " a clerk in the war
office, a very worthy man, as far as I know, used to come
to my house to give my son lessons in writing and in
Latin.   He had a daughter, whom he wished to make a
governess, and begged us to recommend her, should an
occasion present itself.   Madame Las Cases sent for her ;
she was charming, and in every respect highly attractive.
From that moment, Madame Las Cases invited her occasionally to her house, with the view of introducing her
into the world, and obtaining some acquaintances for her
who might prove useful.   But, how strange ! this young
person, our acquaintance, our obliged friend, is actually
at this moment the Baroness de S . . . . , the wife of
one of the Commissioners of the allied powers, who
arrived nearly a month since, in the island.

" Your Majesty may judge of my surprise and of all
my joy at this singular freak of fortune.   I am then

about to have, I said to myself, positive, particular, and even secret information respecting every thing that interests me. Several days passed without any communication, but without any anxiety, and even with some satisfaction on my part. For, I thought, the greater the caution, the more I had to expect. At length, hurried on by my impatience, I sent three or four days ago my servant to Madame de S . . . . ; I had described her very properly, and, as an inhabitant of the island, he found no difficulty in gaining admittance. He returned soon with an answer from Madame de S . . . . , that she did not know the person who had sent him. I might, under every circumstance, be still induced to think, that this was an excess of prudence, and that she was unwilling to place confidence in one unknown to her. But this very day, I received notice from the governor, not to attempt to form any secret connexion in the island ; that I ought to be aware of the danger to which I exposed myself; and that the attempt with which he reproached me was not a matter of doubt; for he was put in possession of it by the very person to whom I had addressed myself. Your Majesty now knows what has confounded me. To find that so villainous a charge should come from a quarter where I had a right to expect some interest in my affairs, and even gratitude, has irritated me beyond measure; I am no longer the same person."

The Emperor laughed in my face: "How little do you know of the human heart! What! her father was your son's tutor, or something of that kind; she enjoyed your wife's protection when she was in want of it, and she is become a German baroness! But, my dear Las Cases, you are the person whom she dreads most here, who lay her most under constraint; she will allege that she never saw your wife at Paris, and besides, this mischievous Sir Hudson Lowe may have been delighted with giving an odious turn to the thing; he is so artful, so malignant." And he then began to laugh at me and my anger.

After dinner, the Emperor resumed his reading of the Tartuffe, which he had not finished yesterday, and there

was enough left for to-day. The Emperor was quite
dejected; the bad weather has a visible effect upon him.

CORVISART.—ANECDOTES OF THE SALOONS OF PARIS.

21st.—The weather as horrible as ever.—We are
seriously incommoded with the wet in our apartments;
the rain penetrates every where.

The governor's secretary brought me a letter from
Europe; it afforded a few moments of real happiness;
it contained the recollections and good wishes of my
dearest friends. I went and read it to the Emperor.

The Emperor suffered seriously from the badness of
the weather. He went to his saloon about four o'clock;
he thought that he was feverish, and found himself
much depressed; he called for some punch, and played
a few games at chess with the grand marshal. The
doctor is come from the town. The two vessels just
arrived are from the Cape; one of them is the Podargus,
which left Europe ten days after the Griffin; the other,
a small frigate, on her way from India to Europe. There
was, it was said, a letter for the *Emperor Napoleon*, but
it was not delivered, and we did not know from whom
it came.

After dinner it was said that the medicines in the
island were exhausted, and it was remarked, that the
Emperor could not be accused of having contributed to
it. This led him to observe, that he did not recollect
having ever taken any medicine. At the Tuileries, he
had had three blisters at once, and even then he had not
taken any. He received a serious wound at Toulon; it
was, he said, like that of Ulysses, by which his old nurse
knew him again; he had recovered altogether, without
taking physic. One of us taking the liberty to say; "If
your majesty had the dysentery to-morrow, would you
still reject all kind of medicine?" The Emperor answered; " Now that I am tolerably well, I answer, yes,
without hesitation; but if I were to be very ill, I should,
perhaps, alter my mind, and should then feel that kind of
conversion, which is produced on a dying man through
the fear of the devil." He again mentioned his in-
credulity in physic, but he did not think so, he said, of

surgery. He had three times commenced a course of anatomy, but they had always been broken off by business and disgust. "On a certain occasion, and at the end of a long discussion, Corvisart, desirous of speaking to me, with his proofs in hand, was so abominably filthy as to bring a stomach, wrapped up in his pocket-handkerchief, to St. Cloud, and I was instantly compelled, at that horrible sight, to cast up all that I had in mine."

The Emperor attempted, after dinner, to read a comedy, but he was so fatigued, and suffered so much, that he was forced to stop and retire about nine o'clock. He made me follow him, and as he felt no inclination to sleep, he said; "Come, my dear Las Cases, let us see; let us have a story about your fauxbourg Saint Germain, and let us endeavour to laugh at it, as if we were listening to the Thousand and One Nights'!"—"Very well, Sire; there was, formerly, one of your Majesty's chamberlains, who had a grand-uncle, who was very old, very old indeed, ... and I remember your Majesty telling us the story of a heavy German officer, who, taken prisoner at the opening of the campaign in Italy, complained that a young conceited fellow had been sent to command against them, who spoiled the profession, and made it intolerable. Well! we had precisely his likeness among us; it was the old grand-uncle, who was still dressed nearly in the costume of Louis XIV. He showed off, whenever you sent accounts of any extraordinary achievements on the other side of the Rhine; your bulletins of Ulm and Jena operated upon him like so many revulsions of bile. He was far from admiring you. You also spoiled the profession, in his opinion. He had, he frequently said, made the campaigns under Marshal de Saxe, which indeed were prodigies in war, and had not been sufficiently appreciated. 'War was, no doubt, then an art; but now!!!' he remarked, shrugging up his shoulders . . . . 'In our time we carried on war with great decorum; we had our mules; we were followed by our canteens; we had our tents; we lived well; we had even plays performed at headquarters, the armies approached each other; admirable

positions were occupied; a battle took place; a siege
was occasionally carried on, and afterwards we went into
winter-quarters, to renew our operations in the spring.
That is,' he exclaimed, with exultation, 'what may be
called making war! But now, a whole army disappears
before another in a single battle, and a monarchy is over-
turned; a hundred leagues are run over in ten days; as
for sleeping and eating, they are out of the question.
Truly, if you call that genius, I am, for my own part,
obliged to acknowledge, that I know nothing about it;
and, accordingly, you excite my pity, when I hear you
call him a great man.' "

The Emperor burst into fits of laughter, particularly
when the mules and canteens were mentioned. He then
added; "You were of course accustomed to say a great
many foolish things about me."—"O yes, Sire, and in
vast abundance." "Very well! We are alone; nobody
will intrude; tell me some more of them." "A fine
gentleman, who had formerly been a captain of cavalry,
and who seemed perfectly satisfied with his own person
and accomplishments, was introduced to a select society
where I was present. 'I come,' he said, 'from the
Plain of Sablons. I have just seen *our Ostrogoth* manœuvre.' That, Sire, was your Majesty. 'He had two
or three regiments, which he threw into confusion upon
each other, and they were all lost in some bushes. I
would have taken him and all his men prisoners with
fifty maitres (formerly troopers) only. An usurped
reputation!' he exclaimed. 'Accordingly, Moreau was
always of opinion, that he would fail in Germany. A
war with Germany is talked of; if it takes place, we
shall see how he will get out of it. He will have justice
done to him.'

"The war took place, and your Majesty sent us, in
a very few days, the bulletin of Ulm, and that of Austerlitz; our fine gentleman again made his appearance in
the same company, and for the moment, in spite of our
malevolence, we could not help crying out all at once:
'And your fifty maitres!' 'Oh! truly,' said he, 'it is
impossible to comprehend the thing; this man triumphs
over every obstacle: Fortune leads him by the hand,

and, besides, the Austrians are so awkward; such fools !' " ....

The Emperor laughed heartily, and wished for some anecdote still more absurd. "That would indeed, Sire, be very difficult to find. I recollect, however, an old dowager, who, to the day of her death, obstinately refused to give credit to any of your successes in Germany. When Ulm, Austerlitz, and your entrance into Vienna were mentioned in her presence :—' So, you believe all that,' said she, shrugging up her shoulders. ' It is all his fabrication. He would not presume to set a foot in Germany ; be assured, that he is still behind the Rhine, where he is perishing from fear, and sends us those silly stories : you will learn, in time, that I am not to be imposed upon.' "

And these stories being over, the Emperor sent me away, saying : " What are they doing, what must they say, at present ? I am certainly now giving them a fine opportunity."

22nd.—This was a day of real mourning for me : it was the first, since our departure from France, in which I did not see the Emperor. I was the only one, in consequence of fortunate circumstances, who, until now, had enjoyed that happiness. His sufferings were great, and his seclusion complete. He did not ask to see a single person.

THE EMPEROR CONTINUES ILL.—REMARKABLE OFFICIAL
DOCUMENT, ADDRESSED TO SIR HUDSON LOWE.

23d.—The weather has continued wet and rainy. About half-past three, the Emperor sent for me to his chamber. He was dressing himself; he had been very seriously indisposed, but, thanks to his mode of treating himself, he said, and to his hermetical seclusion of the preceding day, his complaint was over. He was again well.

I dared to express my sincere grief; I had inscribed, I said, an unhappy day in my journal; I should have marked it in red ink. And when he learned what it was : " What indeed," he said, " is it the only day, since we left France, in which you have not seen me ?. . .

And you are the only one ! . . . ." And after a silence
of some seconds, he added, in a tone peculiarly adapted
to make me amends, if that were possible ; " But, my
dear Las Cases, if you set such a value on it, if you consider it of so much moment, why did you not come and
knock at my door ? I am not inaccessible to you."

The Doctor was introduced ; he assured us that the
Governor had promised never again to set foot at Longwood. It was ironically observed by one of us that he
began to make himself agreeable.

The Emperor then went to his library, where a long
letter which I had written to Rome,* was read to him
by my son. He was driven out by the wet, and, on his
way to the saloon and billiard-room, he was tempted by
the sight of the steps to walk a little. " I know," he
said, " I am doing what is not prudent." Luckily, the
wet weather forced him to return almost instantly. He
took a seat in the saloon, where there was a good fire,
called for infusion of orange-leaves, and played some
games of chess.

After dinner, the Emperor read Marmontel's Tales,
and stopped at that of the self-styled philosopher. He
still coughed a great deal, and again called for some of
the same drink. He entered into a long and most interesting review of Jean Jacques, of his talents, his influence,
his eccentricities, his private vices. He retired at ten
o'clock. I regret very much, that I cannot now recollect
the particulars relative to all these subjects.

In the course of the day M. de Montholon addressed
the following official answer to the Governor, who had
sent a letter, respecting the commissioners of the allied
powers, and the embarrassed state of his finances. It is
the letter, which I have already noticed on the 18th of
this month.

* It was my letter to Prince Lucien, since so celebrated in the
history of my persecutions, and which will be found in its proper
place.

OFFICIAL DOCUMENT.

" General,—I have received the treaty of the 2d of August, 1815, concluded between his Britannic Majesty, the Emperor of Austria, the Emperor of Russia, and the King of Prussia, which was annexed to your letter of the 23d of July.

" The Emperor Napoleon protests against the purport of that treaty ; he is not the prisoner of England. After having placed his abdication in the hands of the representatives of the nation, for the benefit of the constitution adopted by the French people, and in favour of his son, he proceeded voluntarily and freely to England, for the purpose of residing there, as a private person, in retirement, under the protection of the British laws. The violation of all laws cannot constitute a right in fact. The person of the Emperor Napoleon is in the power of England ; but neither, as a matter of fact, nor of right, has it been, nor is it, at present, in the power of Austria, Russia, and Prussia ; even according to the laws and customs of England, which has never included, in its exchange of prisoners, Russians, Austrians, Prussians, Spaniards, or Portuguese, although united to these powers by treaties of alliance, and making war conjointly with them. The Convention of the 2d of August, made fifteen days after the Emperor Napoleon had arrived in England, cannot, as a matter of right have any effect ; it merely presents the spectacle of the coalition of the four principal powers of Europe, for the oppression of a single man ; a coalition which the opinion of all nations disavows, as do all the principles of sound, morality. The Emperors of Austria and Russia, and the King of Prussia, not possessing, either in fact or by right any power over the person of the Emperor Napoleon, were incapable of enacting any thing with regard to him. If the Emperor Napoleon had been in the power of the Emperor of Austria, that prince would have remembered the relations formed by religion and nature between a father and a son, relations which are never violated with impunity. He would have remembered that four times Napoleon re-established him on his throne ; at Leoben, in 1797, and at Luneville in 1801, when his armies were under the walls of Vienna; at Presburgh in 1806, and at Vienna in 1809, when his armies were in possession of the capitel and of three-fourths of the monarchy. That prince would have remembered the protestations which he made to him at the bivouac in Moravia in 1806, and at the interview at Dresden in 1812. If the person of the Emperor Napoleon had been in the power of the Emperor Alexander, he would have remembered the ties of friendship, contracted at Tilsit, at Erfurth, and during twelve years of daily intercourse; he would have remembered the conduct of the Emperor Napoleon the day after the battle of Austerlitz, when, having it in his power to take him prisoner with the remains of his army, he contented himself with his word, and suffered him to effect his retreat; he would have remembered the dangers to which the Emperor Napoleon personally exposed himself to extinguish the fire of Moscow and preserve that capital for him : unquestionably that prince would not have violated the duties of friendship and gratitude towards a friend in distress. If the person of the Emperor Napoleon had been even in power of the King of Prussia, that sovereign would not have forgotten that it was optional with the Emperor, after the battle of Friedland, to place another prince on the throne of Berlin; he would not have forgotten, in the presence of a disarmed enemy, the protestations of attachment and the sentiments which he expressed to him in 1812, at the interviews at Dresden. It is, accordingly, evident from the 2d and 5th articles of the said treaty, that, being incapable of any influence whatever over the fate, and the person of the Emperor Napoleon, who is not in their power, these princes refer themselves in that respect to the future conduct of his Britannic Majesty, who undertakes to fulfil all obligations.

" These princes have reproached the Emperor Napoleon with preferring the protection of the English laws to theirs. The false ideas which the Emperor Napoleon entertained of the liberality of the English laws, and of the influence of a great, generous, and free people on its government, decided him in preferring the protection of these laws to that of his father-in-law, or of his old friend. The Emperor Napoleon always would have been able to obtain the security of what related personally to himself, whether by placing himself again at the head of the army of the Loire, or by putting himself at the head of the army of the Gironde, commanded by General Clausel; but, looking for the future only to retirement and to the protection of the laws of a free nation, either English or American, all stipulations appeared useless to him. He thought that the English people would have been more bound by his frank conduct, which was noble and full of confidence, than it could have been by the most solemn treaties. He has been mistaken, but this error will for ever excite the indignation of real Britons, and, with the present as well as future generations, it will be a proof of the perfidy of the English administration. Austrian and Russian commissioners are arrived at St. Helena; if the object of their mission be to fulfil part of the duties, which the Emperors of Austria and Russia have contracted by the treaty of the 2d of August, and to take care, that the English agents, in a small colony, in the midst of the Ocean, do not fail in the attentions due to a prince connected with them by the ties of affinity, and by so many relations, the characteristics of these two sovereigns will be recognized in that measure. But you, Sir, have asserted, that these commissioners possessed neither the right nor the power of giving any opinion on whatever may be transacted on this rock.

" The English ministry have caused the Emperor Napoleon to be transported to Saint Helena, two thousand leagues from Europe. This rock, situated under the tropic at the distance of five hundred leagues from any continent is, in that latitude, exposed to a devouring heat; it is, during three-fourths of the year, covered with clouds and mists; it is at once the driest and wettest country in the world. This is the most inimical climate to the Emperor's health. It is hatred which dictated the selection of this residence, as well as the instructions, given by the English ministry to the officers who command in this country; they have been ordered to call the Emperor Napoleon, General, being desirous of compelling him to acknowledge that he never reigned

7*

in France, which decided him not to take an incognito
title, as he had determined on quitting France. First
magistrate for life, under the title of first consul, he concluded the preliminaries of London and the treaty of
Amiens with the king of Great Britain. He received as
ambassadors, Lord Cornwallis, Mr. Merry, and Lord
Whitworth, who resided in that quality at his court.
He sent to the King of England, Count Otto and General
Andreossi, who resided as ambassadors at the Court of
Windsor. When, after the exchange of letters between
the ministers for foreign affairs belonging to the two
monarchies, Lord Lauderdale came to Paris, provided
with full powers from the King of England, he treated
with the plenipotentiaries provided with full powers from
the Emperor Napoleon, and resided several months at
the court of the Tuileries. When, afterwards, at Chatillon, Lord Castlereagh signed the ultimatum, which the
allied powers presented to the plenipotentiaries of the
Emperor Napoleon, he thereby recognized the fourth
dynasty. That ultimatum was more advantageous than
the treaty of Paris ; but France was required to renounce
Belgium and the left bank of the Rhine, which was contrary to the propositions of Frankfort and to the proclamations of the allied powers ; and was also contrary
to the oath by which, at his consecration, the Emperor
had sworn the integrity of the empire. The Emperor
then thought these national limits were necessary to the
security of France as well as to the equilibrium of
Europe ; he thought that the French nation, in the circumstances under which it found itself, ought rather to
risk every chance of war than to give them up. France
would have obtained that integrity, and with it preserved
her honour, had not treason contributed to the success
of the allies. The treaty of the 2d of August, and the
bill of the British parliament, style the Emperor, Napoleon Bonaparte, and give him only the title of General.
The title of *General Bonaparte* is, no doubt, eminently
glorious ; the Emperor bore it at Lodi, at Castiglione, a
Rivoli, at Arcole, at Leoben, at the Pyramids, at Aboukir : but for seventeen years he has borne that of First
Consul and of Emperor ; it would be an admission that

he has been neither first magistrate of the republic, nor sovereign of the fourth dynasty. Those, who think that nations are flocks, which, by divine right, belong to some families, are neither of the present age, nor of the spirit of the English legislature, which has several times changed the succession of its dynasties, because the great alterations occasioned by opinions, in which the reigning princes did not participate, had made them enemies to the happiness of the great majority of that nation. For kings are but hereditary magistrates, who exist but for the happiness of nations, and not nations for the satisfaction of kings. It is the same spirit of hatred, which directed that the Emperor Napoleon should not write or receive any letter, without its being opened and read by the English ministers and the officers of St. Helena. He has, by that regulation, been interdicted the possibility of receiving intelligence from his mother, his wife, his son, his brothers; and when, wishing to avoid the inconvenience of having his letters read by inferior officers, he wished to send sealed letters to the Prince Regent, he was told, that open letters only could be taken charge of and conveyed, and that such were the instructions of the ministry. That measure stands in need of no comment; it will suggest strange ideas of the spirit of the administration by which it was dictated; it would be disclaimed even at Algiers! Letters have been received for general officers in the Emperor's suite; they were opened and delivered to you; you have retained them, because they had not been transmitted through the medium of the English ministry; it was found necessary to make them travel four thousand leagues over again, and these officers had the misfortune to know, that their existed on this rock news from their wives, their mothers, and their children, and that they could not be put in possession of it, in less than six months!!!—The heart revolts.

Permission could not be obtained to subscribe to the Morning Chronicle, to the Morning Post, or to some French journals: some broken numbers of the Times have been occasionally sent to Longwood. In consequence of the demand made on board the Northumber-

land, some books have been sent, but all those which
relate to the transactions of late years have been carefully kept back. It was since intended to open a correspondence with a London bookseller for the purpose of
being directly supplied with books which might be
wanted, and with those relative to the events of the day;
that intention was frustrated. An English author, having
published at London an account of his travels in France,
took the trouble to send it as a present to the Emperor,
but you did not think yourself authorized to deliver it to
him, because it had not reached you through the channel
of your government. It is also said, that other books
sent by their authors, have not been delivered, because
the address of some was—To the Emperor Napoleon,
and of others—To Napoleon the Great. The English
ministry are not authorized to order any of these vexations. The law, however unjust, considers the Emperor
Napoleon as a prisoner of war; but prisoners of war
have never been prohibited from subscribing to the journals, or receiving books that are printed; such a prohibition is exercised only in the dungeons of the Inquisition.

"The island of St. Helena is ten leagues in circum-
ference; it is every where inaccessible; the coast is
guarded by brigs; posts within sight of each other are
placed on the shore; and all communication with the
sea is rendered impracticable. There is but one small
town, James Town, where the vessels anchor, and from
which they sail. In order to prevent the escape of an
individual, it is sufficient to guard the coast by land and
sea. By interdicting the interior of the island, one object only can be in view, that of preventing a ride of
eight or ten miles, which it would be possible to take on
horseback, and the privation of which, according to the
consultations of medical men, is abridging the Emperor's
days.

"The Emperor has been placed at Longwood, which
is exposed to every wind; a barren spot, uninhabited,
without water, and incapable of any kind of cultivation
The space contains about 1200 uncultivated fathoms. At
the distance of 11 or 1200 fathoms, a camp has been
formed on a small eminence; another has been since

placed nearly at the same distance in an opposite direc
tion, so that, in the intense heat of the tropic, whichever
way the eye turns nothing is seen but camps. Admiral
Malcolm, perceiving the utility of which a tent would be
to the Emperor in that situation, has had one pitched by
his seamen at the distance of twenty paces from the
house ; it is the only spot in which shade is to be found.
The Emperor, has, however, every reason to be satisfied
with the spirit which animates the officers and soldiers
of the gallant 53rd, as he had been with the crew of the
Northumberland. Longwood House was built for a
barn to the company's farm ; some apartments were
afterwards made in it by the Deputy-Governor of the island ; he used it for a country-house ; but it was, in no
respect, adapted for a residence. During the year that
it has been inhabited, people have always been at work
in it, and the Emperor has been constantly exposed to
the inconvenience and unwholesomeness of a house, in
which workmen are employed. His bedchamber is too
small to contain a bedstead of ordinary size ; but every
kind of building at Longwood would prolong the inconvenience arising from the workmen. There are, however,
in this wretched island, some beautiful situations, with
fine trees, gardens, and tolerably good houses, among
others Plantation House ; but you are prevented by the
positive instructions of the ministry from granting this
house, which would have saved a great deal of expense
laid out in building, at Longwood, huts covered with
pitched paper, which are no longer of any use. You
have prohibited every kind of intercourse between us and
the inhabitants of the island; you have, in fact, converted
Longwood House into a secret prison ; you have even
thrown difficulties in the way of our communication with
the officers of the garrison. The most anxious care
would seem to be taken to deprive us of the few resources
afforded by this miserable country, and we are no better
off here than we should be on Ascension Rock. During
the four months you have been at St. Helena, you have,
Sir, rendered the Emperor's condition worse. It was
observed to you by Count Bertrand, that you violated
the law of your legislature, that you trampled upon the

privileges of general officers, prisoners of war. You answered, that you knew nothing but the letter of your instructions, and that they were still worse than your conduct appeared to us.

I have the honour, &c.

(Signed)   COUNT DE MONTHOLON.

"P. S.—I had, Sir, signed this letter, when I received yours of the 17th, to which you annex the estimate of an annual sum of 20,000l. sterling, which you consider indispensable to meet the expenses of the establishment of Longwood, after having made all the reductions which you have thought possible. The consideration of this estimate can, in no respect, concern us; the Emperor's table is scarcely supplied with what is necessary; all the provisions are of bad quality and four times as dear as at Paris. You require a fund of twelve thousand pounds sterling from the Emperor, as your government allows you only eight thousand pounds for all these expenses. I have had the honour of telling you, that the Emperor had no funds; that no letter had been received or written for a year; and that he was altogether unacquainted with what is passing or what may have passed in Europe. Transported by violence to this rock, at the distance of two thousand leagues, without being able to receive or to write any letter, he now finds himself at the discretion of the English agents. The Emperor has uniformly desired and still desires to provide himself for all his expenses of every kind, and he will do so, as speedily as you shall give possibility to the means, by taking off the prohibition, laid upon the merchants of the island, of carrying on his correspondence, and releasing it from all kind of inquisition on your part or on that of any of your agents. The moment the Emperor's wants shall be known in Europe, the persons who interest themselves for him will transmit the necessary funds for his supplies.

"The letter of Lord Bathurst, which you have communicated to me, gives rise to strange ideas! Can your ministers then be so ignorant as not to know that the spectacle of a great man struggling with adversity is the most sublime of spectacles? Can they be ignorant, that Napoleon at St. Helena, amidst persecutions of every kind, against which his serenity is his only shield, is greater, more sacred, more venerable than on the first throne of the world, where he was, so long, the arbiter of Kings? Those, who, fail in respect to Napoleon, thus situated, merely degrade their own character and the nation which they represent!"

MY ENGLISH FAMILY.—JUST DEBT OF GRATITUDE TO THE ENGLISH ON THE PART OF THE EMIGRANTS, &c.—GENERAL JOUBERT.—PETERSBURG.—MOSCOW ; THE CONFLAGRATION.—PROJECTS OF NAPOLEON, HAD HE RETURNED VICTORIOUS.

24th.—I went, at two o'clock, to the Emperor, in his apartment. He had sent for my Atlas in the morning. I found him finishing his examination of the map of Russia and of that part of America adjoining the Russian establishments.

He had suffered, and coughed a great deal, during the night. The weather had, however, become milder. While he was dressing to go out, he often dwelt upon the happy idea of the Atlas, the merit of its execution, and the immensity of its contents. He concluded, as usual, with saying ; " What a collection! what details! How complete in all its parts!"

The Emperor went to the garden. I told him, that I had written, in the morning, to England, and answered the letter which I had read to him two or three days ago. " Your English family," he then observed, " seem to be very good kind of people; they are very fond of you, and you appear very much attached to them." I answered ; " Sire, I took care of them in France, during their ten years captivity, and they had taken care of me in England, during my ten years emigration. It is altogether the hospitality of the ancients which we exercise towards each other. I rely upon them, in every respect, and they are at liberty to dispose of all I possess."—" This," said he, is a very happy connexion. How did you obtain it? To what are you indebted for it?" I then told him how I became acquainted with this family.

"Never was the plank, by the assistance of which an unfortunate person, after shipwreck, preserved his life, dearer to him than this family is to me. There are, Sire, no favours, no treasures, which can compensate the kindnesses I have received from it, and the happiness it has conferred upon me.

" When the horrible excesses of our revolution compelled us to take refuge in England, our emigration produced the liveliest sensation in that country ; the arrival of so many illustrious exiles, their past fortunes, and their then forlorn condition, were impressed on every mind, and filled every heart. They became the subject of consideration in political assemblies, in places of divine worship, in fashionable circles, and in private families. That catastrophe agitated every class, and excited every sympathy.   We were surrounded by a generous and feeling multitude. We were the objects of the most delicate attentions, and of the most substantial favours. Such, it must be acknowledged, was the affecting sight held out by a vast portion of English society, even in spite of the difference of opinions. It is a testimony due from our gratitude to the truth of history.

" I was then in London, with a cousin of my name, whose situation at the court of Versailles had enabled her to be of some service to the most distinguished persons in Europe, where she was a lady of honour to the Princess Lamballe, who was herself sub-intendant of the Queen's household. That turned out a fortunate circumstance for our family. My cousin experienced proofs of the greatest benevolence ; a great number of persons were eager to make a tender of their services, and, among others, a certain young couple. The wife was charming, and distinguished for the elegance and dignity of her manners ; the husband was of an easy temper, of a mild and honourable character. Their house was almost instantly open to my cousin and to all her relations, who had every reason to find themselves as much at their ease there, as if they had been in their own families.

" This worthy couple took every occasion to oblige and to be of use to our refugees   Their house was frequented by the most distinguished emigrants. A great number of us there contracted a debt of gratitude which, notwithstanding all its extent, I should not despair of paying, were I alone left to discharge it. I shall leave it as a legacy to my children, who, if they resemble me, will look upon it as sacred, and deem themselves happy in redeeming the obligation.

" Elevation of soul, and the emotions of a French heart, characterized the conduct of Lady . . . When the Prince of Condé (arrived in London,) was looking for a country residence, she sent me to offer him the superb mansion which she possessed, in the county of Durham. The Prince, after hearing the particulars, having remarked that it would, no doubt, cost him a King's ransom, was agreeably surprised at learning that it was presented to him by a French woman, who would, she said, consider that she had received an inestimable price, should a Condé condescend to inhabit it. He went, instantly, to express his acknowledgments in person.

" This family visited Paris after the peace of Amiens, and it was in its bosom, and through its protection, that I was enabled, a few days sooner, to breathe the air of my country. I was exempted, through its means, from the tedious and painful formalities required from me by the act of amnesty on the frontier, and I felt it my duty to provide for their accommodation at Paris, with much more facility and less inconvenience than they could have done themselves. I had also the happiness, when the measure for detaining the English residents was carried into effect, and this family was placed among the number, of alleviating their condition in my turn, and becoming their security.

" We were, at length, separated by time and circumstances; but they have lost nothing in my recollection; and the needle is less constant to the pole, and less faithful in its guidance, than are my thoughts and my gratitude, with respect to those good and valuable friends. Such, Sire, is what your Majesty is pleased to call my English family."

We had, however, during my relation, walked to the stable, and called for the calash. The Emperor ordered

it to take us up at the bottom of the wood. We waited for
it a long time, because Madame de Montholon was seized
with a sudden indisposition. Her husband came to apolo-
gize for the delay, and the Emperor made him get in.

The conversation turned, during our ride, upon General
Joubert, whose brother-in-law and aid-de-camp M. de
Montholon had been.

" Joubert," said the Emperor, " entertained a high
veneration for me; he deplored my absence at every reverse experienced by the Republic, during the expedition
to Egypt. He was, at that time, at the head of the army
of Italy; he had taken me for his model, aspired to imitate my plans, and attempted to accomplish nothing less
than what I afterwards effected in Brumaire : he had,
however, the Jacobins to assist him. The measures and
intrigues of that party, to place the means of executing
that grand enterprise in his power, had raised him to
the command in Italy, after the disasters of Scherer; of
that Scherer who was an ignorant peculator, and deserv-
ing of every censure. But Joubert was killed at Novi, in
his first rencounter with Suwarrow; any attempt of his,
at Paris, would have failed; he had not yet acquired a
sufficient degree of glory, of consistency, and maturity.
He was, by nature, calculated for all these acquirements,
but, at that moment, he was not adequately formed; he
was still too young, and that enterprise was then beyond
his ability."

The Emperor could not take more than one round; he
found himself too much fatigued, and was far from being
well.

At half past eight o'clock, the Emperor ordered me to
be called. He told me that he had been obliged to take
a bath, and thought he was a little feverish. He felt
that he had suddenly caught cold, but he had ceased to
cough since he was in the bath. He continued for a
long time in the water. He dined in it, and a small
table was laid for me by the side. The Emperor reverted to the history of Russia. " Had Peter the Great,"
he asked, " acted with wisdom in founding a capital at
Petersburgh at so vast an expense? Would not the results have been greater, had he expended all his money
at Moscow? What was his object? Had he accom

plished it?" I replied: "If Peter had remained at Moscow, his nation would have continued Muscovite, a people altogether Asiatic; it was necessary that it should be displaced for its reform and alteration. He had, therefore, selected a position on the very frontiers, wrested from the enemy, and in founding his capital, and accumulating all his strength, he rendered it invulnerable; he connected himself with European society; he established his power in the Baltic sea, by which he could with ease prevent his natural enemies, the Poles and the Swedes, from forming alliances, upon occasion, with the nations situated in their rear.

The Emperor said that "he was not altogether satisfied with these reasons. Be it as it may," he observed, "Moscow has disappeared, and who can compute the wealth that has been swallowed up there? Let us contemplate Paris, with the accumulation of buildings and of industry, the work of centuries. Had its capital, for the 1400 years of its existence, increased but a million a year, what a sum! Let us connect with that the warehouses, the furniture, the union of sciences and the arts, the complete establishments of trade and commerce, &c., and this is the picture of Moscow; and all that vanished in an instant! What a catastrophe! Does not the bare idea of it make one shudder? . . . I do not think that it could be replaced at the expense of two thousand millions."

He expatiated at great length on all these events, and let a word escape him which was too characteristic not to be specially noted down by me. The name of Rostopchin having been pronounced, I presumed to remark that the colour at that time given to his patriotic action had very much surprised me, for he had interested me instead of exciting my indignation: nay, I had envied him! . . . . The Emperor replied with singular vivacity, and with a kind of contraction which betrayed vexation: "If many at Paris had been capable of reading and feeling it in that way, believe me, I should have applauded it! But I had no choice left me." Resuming the subject of Moscow, he said:—"Never, with all the powers of poetry, have the fictions of the burning of Troy

equalled the reality of that of Moscow. The city was of
wood, the wind was violent; all the pumps had been
taken away. It was literally an ocean of fire. Nothing
had been saved from it; our march was so rapid, our
entrance so sudden. We found even diamonds on the
women's toilets, they had fled so precipitately. They
wrote to us a short time afterwards that they had sought
to escape from the first excesses of a dangerous soldiery;
that they recommended their property to the generosity
of the conquerors, and would not fail to re-appear in the
course of a few days to solicit their kindness and testify
their gratitude.

"The population was far from having plotted that
atrocity. Even they themselves delivered up to us three
or four hundred criminals, who escaped from prison,
and had executed it."—"But, Sire, may I presume to
ask, if Moscow had not been burnt, did not your Majesty intend to establish your quarters there?"—"Certainly." answered the Emperor, "and I should then have
held up the singular spectacle of an army wintering in
the midst of a hostile nation, pressing upon it from all
points; it would have been the ship beset by the ice.
You would have been in France without any intelligence
from me for several months; but you would have remained quiet, you would have acted wisely. Cambacérés
would, as usual, have conducted affairs in my name, and
all would have been as orderly as if I had been present.
The winter, in Russia, would have weighed heavy on
every one; the torpor would have been general. The
spring also would have returned for all the world. All
would have been at once on their legs, and it is well
known that the French are as nimble as any others.

"On the first appearance of fine weather, I should
have marched against the enemy; I should have beaten
them; I should have been master of their empire. Alexander, be assured, would not have suffered me to proceed so far. He would have agreed to all the conditions
which I might have dictated, and France would then
have begun to enjoy all her advantages. And, truly, my
success depended upon a mere trifle. For I had undertaken the expedition to fight against armed men, not

BURNING OF MOSCOW.

of Russia, of the prosperity of which, he said, we had no idea. He dwelt, at great length, upon Moscow, which had, under every point of view, much surprised him, and might bear a comparison with any of the capitals of Europe, the greater number of which it surpassed. Here unfortunately I can find but bare outlines in my notes, which it is impossible for me to fill up now.

He was particularly struck with the gilded spires of Moscow, and it was that which induced him, on his return, to have the dome of the Invalids regilt; he intended to embellish many other edifices at Paris in the same manner.*

As the city of Moscow seems to have been so different from the idea which we have generally entertained of it in our Western world, I am inclined to think that a description of it in this place, supplied by an eye-witness, a distinguished person, attached to the expedition, will not prove disagreeable. It is by Baron Larrey, surgeon-in-chief to the grand army. I take it from a work of that celebrated character (Mémoires de la Chirurgie Militaire), in no great circulation, on account, perhaps, of its peculiarly scientific nature.

The relation begins at the moment when the French army was setting out for Moscow, after the battle of Mozaisk or of the Moskowa.

" We were hardly a few miles off from Mozaisk, when we were all surprised at finding ourselves, notwithstanding the vicinity of the spot to one of the greatest capitals in the world, on a sandy, arid, and completely desert plain. The mournful aspect of that solitude, which discouraged the soldiers, seemed an omen of the entire abandonment of Moscow, and of the misfortunes which awaited us in that city, from the opulence of which we had promised ourselves such advantages.

---

* Since the first appearance of this work it has been remarked to me that this is an anachronism ; as the gilding of the dome of the Invalids was begun before the campaign in Russia. It was the minarets of Cairo and not the steeples of Moscow which must have suggested the idea to Napoleon ; and this was no doubt what he meant to say : it is easy to imagine that a mistake of this kind might be made by him in a conversation without any special object : in fact every body is liable to such mistakes.

"The army marched, with difficulty, over that tract.
The horses were harassed, and exhausted with hunger
and thirst, for water was as rare as forage. The men
had also a great deal to suffer. They were, in fact, overwhelmed with fatigue, and in want of all subsistence.
The troops had not, for a long time, received any rations,
and the small quantity of provisions found at Mozaisk
was only sufficient for the young and old guard. A considerable number of the former corps fell victims to
their abuse of the spirits of the country. They were
observed to quit their comrades a few paces, to totter,
whirl round, and afterwards fall on their knees or sit
down involuntarily; they remained immoveable in that
attitude, and expired shortly afterwards, without uttering
a single complaint. These young men were pre-disposed
to the pernicious effects of that liquor by languor,
privations and excessive fatigue.

"We arrived, however, on the evening of the 14th of
September, in one of the suburbs of Moscow; we there
learnt that the Russian army had, in its passage through
the city, carried off all the citizens and public functionaries, some of the lower classes and servants alone were
left; so that, in going through the principal streets of
that great city, which we entered the following morning,
we scarcely met any one; all the houses were completely
abandoned. But what very much surprised us was to
see the fire break out in several remote quarters, where
none of our troops had yet been, and particularly in the
bazar of the Kremlin, an immense building, with porti-
coes which have some resemblance to those of the Palais
Royal at Paris.

"After what we had witnessed on our passage through
Little Russia, we were astonished at the vastness of
Moscow, at the great number of churches and palaces
which it contained, at the beautiful architecture of those
edifices, at the commodious disposition of the principal
houses, and all the objects of luxury which were found in
the greater part of them. The streets in general were
spacious, regular, and well laid out. Nothing had the
appearance of discordance throughout that city. Every
thing announced its wealth, and the immense trade it

carried on in the productions of the four quarters of the world.

"The variety displayed in the construction of the palaces, houses, and churches, was an infinite addition to the beauty of the city. There were places which, by the peculiar kind of architecture of the different edifices, indicated the nations that generally inhabited them; thus, the residence of the Franks, Chinese, Indians, and Germans, was easily distinguished. The Kremlin might be considered as the citadel of Moscow; it is in the centre of the town, situated on an eminence sufficiently elevated, surrounded by a wall with bastions, and flanked, at regular distances, by towers, mounted with cannon. The bazaar, which has been already noticed, usually filled with the merchandize of India, and valuable furs, had become the prey of the flames, and the only articles preserved were those which had been deposited in the vaults, where the soldiers penetrated, after the fire that consumed the whole of the exterior of that beautiful edifice. The palace of the Emperors, that of the senate, the archives, the arsenal, and two very ancient churches, occupy the rest of the Kremlin. These different buildings, of a rich style of architecture, form a magnificent appearance about the parade. One might imagine one's self transported to the public place of ancient Athens, where the Areopagus and the temple of Minerva on one side, and the academy and the arsenal on the other, were the objects of admiration. A cylindrical tower rises between the two churches, in the form of a column, known by the name of Yvan's tower; it is rather an Egyptian minaret, within which several bells, of different sizes, are hung. At the foot of this tower, is seen a bell of a prodigious magnitude, which has been noticed by all the historians. The whole of the city and its environs are seen from the top of the towers; it looks like a star, with four forked rays. The city has a most picturesque appearance, from the variegated colours of the roofs of the houses, and from the gold and silver which cover the domes and the tops of the steeples, of which there is a considerable number. Nothing can equal the richness of one of the

churches of the Kremlin (it was the burial-place of the
Emperors); its walls are covered with plates of silver
gilt, five or six lines thick, on which the history of the
Old and New Testament is represented in relievo; the
lustres and candelabra, of massy silver, were particularly
remarkable for their extraordinary size.

" The hospitals, to which my attention was peculiarly
directed, are worthy of the most civilized nation in the
world; I divide them into military and civil. The great
military hospital is divided into three parts, forming
altogether a parallelogram. The principal part was
constructed on the side of a great road, opposite to an
immense barrack, which may be compared to the military
school at Paris. Two lateral buildings, intersecting the
first at right angles, inclose the court, which communi-
cates with a fine and extensive garden appropriated to
the use of the sick. A portico, with columns of the
composite order, forms the front of this building, which
is two stories high. At the entrance is a spacious lobby,
with corresponding doors to the wards on the ground-
floor, and a large and magnificent staircase leading to
the upper stories. The wards occupy the entire length
of the building, and the windows on each side reach
from the ceiling to the floor; they are made with double
sashes, as is customary throughout Russia, and are completely closed in winter; stoves are placed in the inside at
suitable distances. The wards contain four rows of beds
of the same kind, separated by the requisite space for
wholesomeness: each row consists of fifty beds, and the
total number may be estimated at more than three
thousand; the hospital contains fourteen principal wards
of very nearly the same extent. The offices, dispensary,
kitchen, and other accessories, are very commodiously
situated, in separate places, at a convenient distance
from the wards.

" The civil hospitals are equally entitled to notice.
The four principal are those of Cheremetow, Galitzin,
Alexander, and the foundlings.

" The first, remarkable for its form, its structure, and
its internal arrangements, was used to receive the sick
and wounded belonging to the guard.

" This hospital, which is three stories high, is built in the form of a crescent; the requisite offices are situated in the rear. A beautiful portico, projecting from the centre of the half-moon, forms the entrance of a chapel which occupies the middle of the edifice; this chapel, surmounted by a dome, is the central point of all the wards, and contains the mausoleum of the Prince who founded the hospital: it is adorned with columns in stucco, statues, and beautiful pictures. The dispensary is one of the finest and best supplied that I know.

" The Foundling Hospital, situated on the banks of the Moscowa, and protected by the cannon of the Kremlin, is indisputably the largest and noblest establishment of the kind in Europe. It consists of two masses of building; the first, where the entrance is placed, is appropriated to the residence of the Governor, who is selected from the old generals of the army, of the board of management, of the medical officers, and of all those employed in the service of the hospital. The second forms a perfect square. In the centre of the court, which is very spacious, is a reservoir, that supplies the whole of the establisment with water from the river. Each of the sides consists of four stories, round which runs a regular corridor, not very broad, yet sufficiently spacious for the admission of air, and the accommodation of persons passing through it. The wards occupy the remainder of the breadth, and the whole length of each wing of the building. There are two rows of beds with curtains in each ward, their size corresponds with that of the children: the boys are kept separate from the girls, and the greatest cleanliness and regularity are observed.

" We had scarcely taken possession of the city, and succeeded in extinguishing the fire, kindled by the Russians in the most beautiful quarters, when, in consequence of two principal causes, the flames again broke out in the most violent manner, spread rapidly from one street to another, and involved the whole place in one common ruin. The first of these causes is justly reported to have been the desperate resolution of a certain class of Russians, who were said to have been confined

in the prisons, the doors of which were thrown open on
the departure of the army; these wretches, whether
incited by superior authority, or by their own feelings,
with the view, no doubt, of plunder, openly ran from
palace to palace, and from house to house, setting fire to
every thing that fell in their way. The French patroles,
although numerous and on the alert, were unable to
prevent them. I saw several of those miscreants taken
in the act; lighted matches and combustibles were found
in their possession. The pain of death inflicted upon
those caught in the actual commission of the atrocity
made no impression on the others, and the fire raged
three days and three nights without interruption; in
vain houses were pulled down by our soldiers, the flames
quickly overleaped the vacant space, and the buildings
thus insulated, were set on fire in the twinkling of an
eye. The second cause must be attributed to the
violence of the equinoctial winds, which are always very
powerful in those parts, and by means of which the
conflagration increased and extended its ravages with
extraordinary activity.

"It would be difficult, under any circumstances, to
imagine a picture more horrible than that with which
our eyes were afflicted. It was more particularly during
night, between the 18th and 19th of September, the
period when the fire was at the highest pitch, that its
effects presented a terrific spectacle : the weather was
fine and dry, the wind continuing to blow from East to
North, or from North to East. During that night, the
dreadful image of which will never be effaced from my
memory, the whole of the city was on fire. Large
columns of flames of various colours shot up from every
quarter, entirely covered the horizon, and diffused a
glaring light and a scorching heat to a considerable distance. These masses of fire, driven by the violence of
the winds in all directions, were accompanied in their
rise and rapid movement, by a dreadful whizzing and by
thundering explosions, the result of the combustion of
gunpowder, saltpetre, oil, resin, and brandy, with which
the greater part of the houses and shops had been filled.
The varnished iron plates, with which the buildings were

covered, were speedily loosened by the heat, and whirled
far away ; large pieces of burning beams and rafters of
fir were carried to a great distance, and contributed to
extend the conflagration to houses which were considered
in no danger, on account of their remoteness. Every
one was struck with terror and consternation. The
guard, with the head-quarters and the staff of the army,
left the Kremlin and the city, and formed a camp at
Petrowski, a mansion which belonged to Peter the Great,
on the road to Petersburg. I remained with a very
small number of my comrades, in a house built of stone,
which stood alone, and was situated on the top of the
quarter of the Franks, close to the Kremlin. I was
there enabled to observe all the phenomena of that tre-
mendous conflagration. We had sent our equipage to
the camp, and kept ourselves constantly on the look-out,
to be prepared for, or to prevent, danger.

" The lower classes, who had remained at Moscow,
driven from house to house by the fire, uttered the most
lamentable cries; extremely anxious to preserve what
was most valuable to them, they loaded themselves with
packages, which they could hardly sustain, and which
they frequently abandoned to escape from the flames.
The women, impelled by a very natural feeling of humanity, carried one or two children on their shoulders,
and dragged the others along by the hand ; and, in order
to avoid the death which threatened them on every side,
they ran, with their petticoats tucked up, to take shelter
in the corners of the streets and squares ; but they were
soon compelled, by the intenseness of the heat, to
abandon those spots, and to fly with precipitation by any
way that was open to them, sometimes without being
able to extricate themselves from that kind of labyrinth,
where many of them met with a miserable end. I saw
old men, whose long beards had been caught by the
flames, drawn on small carts by their own children, who
endeavoured to rescue them from that real Tartarus.

" As for our soldiers, tormented with hunger and
thirst, they exposed themselves to every danger, to
obtain, in the burning cellars and shops, eatables, wines,
liquors, or any other article more or less useful. They

were seen running through the streets, pell-mell with
the broken-hearted inhabitants, carrying away every
thing they could snatch from the ravages of this dreadful
conflagration.   At length, in the course of eight or ten
days, this immense and superb city was reduced to ashes,
with the exception of the Kremlin palace, some large
houses, and all the churches : these edifices are built of
stone.

"This calamity threw the army into great consternation, and was a presage to us of more serious misfortunes.
We all thought that we should no longer find either
subsistence, cloth, or any other necessary for equipping
the troops, and of which we were in the most urgent
want.   Could a more dismal idea suggest itself to our
imagination?   The head quarters were, however, after
the fire, again established at the Kremlin, and the guard
sent to some houses of the Franks, quarter, which had
been preserved.   Every one resumed the exercise of his
duties.

"Magazines of flour, meal, salt-fish, oil, wine and
liquors, were discovered by dint of perseverance.   Some
were served out to the troops, but there was too great a
wish to spare or hoard up these articles, and that excess
of precaution, which is sometimes a mere pretext, induced us to burn or leave behind us, in the end, provisions of every kind, from which we might have derived
the greatest benefit, and which would have even been
sufficient for the wants of the army for more than six
months, had we remained at Moscow.   The same conduct was pursued with regard to the stuffs and furs,
which ought to have been immediately worked up for
the purpose of supplying our troops with all the clothing
capable of preserving them, as much as possible, from
the inclemency of the cold that was at hand.   The
soldiers, who never think of the future, so far from
obviating, on their part and for their own advantage,
that want of precaution, were solely engaged in searching
for wines, liquors, and articles of gold and silver, and
despised every other consideration.

"This unexpected abundance, which was owing to the
indefatigable researches of the troops, was attended with

a bad effect on their discipline and on the health of those who were intemperate. That motive alone ought to have made us hasten our departure for Poland. Moscow became a new Capua to our army. The enemy's generals flattered ours with the hopes of peace; the preliminaries were to be signed from day to day. Meanwhile clouds of Cossacks covered our cantonments and carried off every day a great number of our foragers. General Kutusoff was collecting the wreck of his army and strengthening himself with the recruits who joined him from all parts. Imperceptibly, and under various pretences of pacification, his advanced posts drew near to ours. Finally, the period of negotiation had arrived, and it was at the moment in which the French ambassador was to obtain a first decision, that Prince Joachim's corps d'armée was surrounded. It was with difficulty that our general, the ambassador, surmounted the obstacles which were opposed to his return to Moscow. Several parties of our troops and some pieces of cannon had been already carried off. The different corps of this advanced guard, which were at first dispersed, were nevertheless rallied, broke the Russian column that hemmed them in, took up a favourable position, and charged successively the enemy's numerous cavalry, which they repulsed with vigour, retaking part of the artillery and some of the soldiers made prisoners in the first onset. At length, the arrival of General Lauriston, and of the wounded, was to us, at head quarters, a confirmation that hostilities would be resumed. Orders were immediately given for the sudden departure of the army; the drum beat to arms, and all the corps prepared to execute that precipitate movement. Some provisions were hastily collected and the march commenced on the 19th of October. "

ON THE CORONATION, &C. — DECREES OF BERLIN AND MILAN.—THE GRAND CAUSE OF THE HATRED OF THE ENGLISH.

25th.—The weather has become fine in every respect. The Emperor breakfasted in the tent and sent for us all. The conversation turned upon the ceremonies of the coronation. He asked for particulars from one of us, who had been present, but was unable to satisfy him. He made the same inquiries of another, but the latter had not seen it. " Where were you then at that time ?" asked the Emperor.—" At Paris, Sire."—" How then ! you did not see the coronation ! " — " No Sire. " The Emperor, then casting a side glance at him, and taking him by the ear, said; " Were you so absurd as to carry your aristocracy to that point ?" — " But, Sire, my hour was not come. " — " But at least you saw the retinue ? " — " Ah ! Sire, had my curiosity prevailed, I should have hastened to witness what was most worthy and most interesting to be seen. I had, however, a ticket of admission, and I preferred presenting it to the English lady whom I lately mentioned to your Majesty, and who, by way of parenthesis, caught a cold there, that nearly killed her. For my own part I remained quietly at home."—" Ah, that is too much for me to put up with," said the Emperor, " the villanous aristocrat ! How ! And you were really guilty of such an absurdity? — 'Alas ! I was," replied the accused, " and yet here I am near you, and at St. Helena." The Emperor smiled, and let go the ear.

After breakfast, a captain of the English artillery, who had been six years at the Isle of France, called upon me. He was to sail for Europe the next day. He entreated me in a thousand ways to procure him the happiness of seeing the Emperor. He would, he said, give all he had in the world for such a favour; his gratitude would be boundless, &c.

We conversed together for a long time; the Emperor was taking his round in the calash. On his return, I was fortunate enough to fulfil the English officer's wishes. The Emperor received him for upwards of a quarter of an hour; his joy was extreme, as he was aware that the favour became every day more rare. Every thing about the Emperor had struck him, he declared, in a most extraordinary manner; his features, his affability, the sound of his voice, his expressions, the questions he had asked; he was, he exclaimed, a hero, a god ! . . . . .

The weather was delightful. The Emperor continued

to walk in the garden in the midst of us. He discussed
the failure of a negotiation undertaken by one of us; a
business which the Emperor had judged very easy, but
which turned out to be of the most delicate nature for
the person entrusted with it. The object of it was to
prevail upon some English officers to publish a certain
paper in England.

The Emperor expressed his disapprobation of the
failure in his usual mode of reasoning, and with the intelligence and point that are familiar to him: he was,
however, very much disappointed at it: his observations
were rather strong; he pushed them to a degree of ill
humour of which the person he found fault with had
never, perhaps, before, received any proofs. At length,
he concluded with saying: "After all, Sir, would you
not have accepted yourself what you proposed to others,
had you been in their place?" — "No, Sire." — "Why
not? Well then," he added, in a tone of reproof, "you
should not be my Minister of Police." "And your
Majesty would be in the right," quickly replied the other,
who felt himself vexed in his turn; "I feel no inclination
whatever for such an office." The Emperor, seeing him
enter the saloon, a little before dinner, said: "Ah! there
is our little Officer of Police! Come, approach, my little
Officer of Police;" and he pinched his ear. Although
hours had passed since the warm conversation took
place, the Emperor recollected it; he knew that the person who had been the subject of it was full of sensibility,
and it was evident that he wished to efface the impression it had made upon him. These are characteristic
shades, and those which arise from the most trifling
causes are the most natural and the most marked.

After dinner, the Emperor was led, by the turn which
the conversation took, to review the special subject of his
maritime quarrel with England. "Her pretensions to
blockade on paper," he observed, "produced my famous
Berlin decree. The British council, in a fit of resentment,
issued its orders; it established a right of toll on the
seas. I instantly replied by the celebrated Milan decrees,
which denationalized every flag that submitted to the
English acts; and it was then that the war became, in

8*

England truly personal. Every one connected with trade was enraged against me. England was exasperated at a struggle and energy, of which she had no example. She had uniformly found those who had preceded me more complaisant."

The Emperor explained, on a later occasion, the means, by which he had forced the Americans to make war against the English. He had, he said, discovered the way of connecting their interests with their rights; for people, he remarked, fight much more readily for the former than for the latter.

At present, the Emperor expected, he said, some approaching attempt, on the part of the English, on the sovereignty of the seas, for the establishment of the right of universal toll, &c. "It is," said he, "one of the principal resources left them for discharging their debts, for extricating themselves from the abyss into which they are plunged; in a word, for getting rid of their embarrassments. If they have among them an enterprising genius, a man of a strong intellect, they will certainly undertake something of that kind. Nobody is powerful enough to oppose it, and they set up their claim with a sort of justice. They may plead, in its justification, that it was for the safety of Europe they involved themselves in difficulties; that they succeeded, and that they are entitled to some compensation. And then, the only ships of war in Europe are theirs. They reign, in fact, at present, over the seas. There is an end to existence of public rights when the ballance is the broken, &c., &c.

"The English may now be omnipotent, if they will but confine themselves to their navy. But they will endanger their superiority, complicate their affairs, and insensibly lose their importance, if they persevere in keeping soldiers on the continent."

ACCOUNT OF THE CAMPAIGN OF WATERLOO DICTATED BY NAPOLEON.

26th.—The Emperor went out early in the morning, before seven o'clock; he did not wish to disturb any of us. He began to work alone in the garden beneath the

tent, where he sent for us all to breakfast with him. He
continued there until two o'clock.

At dinner, he conversed a great deal about our situation in the island. He would not, he said, leave Longwood; he did not care for any visitors; but he was
desirous that we should take some diversion, and find out
some means of amusement. It would, he said, be a pleasure to him to see us move about and get abroad more.

The narrative of the battle of Waterloo, which the
Emperor had dictated to General Gourgaud, was read by
his desire. What a story! It is painful to think of it.
The destinies of France suspended by so slight a thread!

This production was published in Europe in 1820. The
measures contrived to transmit it clandestinely from
St. Helena proved successful, in spite of every kind of
vigilance. The instant this narrative appeared, every
body was agreed as to its author. An exclamation burst
from every quarter that Napoleon alone was capable of
describing in that manner, and it is confidently stated
that the Generalissimo, his antagonist, expressed himself
precisely in the same way. What noble chapters! It
would be impossible to attempt an analysis of them, or to
pretend to convey their excellence in terms adequate to
their merits. We literally transcribe, however, in this
place, the last pages, containing, in the shape of a summary, nine observations of Napoleon, on the faults with
which he has been reproached in that campaign.

They are points which will become classic, and we
are of opinion that our readers will not be displeased at
again finding here subjects which become, every time
the occasion presents itself, topics of earnest and important discussion.

We shall preface these observations with a description,
also from Napoleon's dictation, of the resources which
France still possessed after the loss of the battle.

" The situation of France was critical, but not desperate, after the battle of Waterloo. Every preparatory
measure had been taken, on the supposition of the failure
of the attack upon Belgium. Seventy thousand men were
rallied on the 27th, between Paris and Laon; from 25
to 30,000, including the depôts of the guard, were on

their march from Paris and the depots; General Rapp, with 25,000 men, chosen troops, was expected on the Marne, in the beginning of July; all the losses sustained 'n the *materiel* of the artillery had been repaired. Paris alone contained 500 pieces of field-artillery, and only 170 had been lost. Thus an army of 120,000 men, equal to that which had passed the Sambre on the 15th, with a train of artillery, consisting of 350 pieces of cannon, would cover Paris by the 1st of July. That capital possessed, independently of these means, for its defence, 36,000 men of the National Guard, 30,000 sharpshooters, 6000 gunners, 600 battering cannon, formidable en trenchments on the right bank of the Seine, and, in a few days, those of the left bank would have been entirely completed. The Anglo-Dutch and Prusso-Saxon armies, diminished, however, by more than 80,000 men, and no longer exceeding 140,000, could not cross the Somme with more than 90,000; they would have to wait there for the co-operation of the Austrian and Russian armies, which could not be on the Marne before the 15th of July. Paris had, consequently, twenty-five days to prepare for its defence, to complete the arming of its inhabitants, its fortifications, its supplies of provisions, and to draw troops from every point of France. Even by the 15th of July, not more than 30, or 40,000 men could have arrived on the Rhine. The mass of the Russian and Austrian armies could not take the field before a later period. Neither arms, nor ammunition, nor officers were wanting in the capital; the number of sharpshooters might be easily augmented to 80,000, and the field artillery could be increased to 600 pieces.

" Marshal Suchet, in conjunction with General Lécourbe, would have had, at the same time, upwards of 30,000 men before Lyons, independently of the garrison of that city, which would have been well armed, well supplied with provisions, and well protected by entrenchments. The defence of all the strong places was secured; they were commanded by chosen officers, and garrisoned by faithful troops. Every thing might be repaired, but decision, energy, and firmness, on the part of the officers, of the Government, of the Chambers, and of the whole

nation, were necessary. It was requisite that France
should be animated by the sentiment of honour, of glory,
of national independence ; that she should fix her eyes
upon Rome after the battle of Cannæ, and not upon
Carthage after that of Zama ! ! ! If France had raised
herself to that height, she would have been invincible.
Her people contained more of the military elements
than any other people in the world. The *materiel* of
war existed in abundance, and was adequate to every
want. .

" On the 21st of June, Marshal Blucher and the Duke
of Wellington entered the French territory at the head of
two columns. On the 22nd, the powder magazine at
Avesnes took fire, and the place surrendered. On the
24th, the Prussians entered Guise, and the Duke of Wellington was at Cambray. He was at Peronne on the
26th. During the whole of this time, the fortresses on
the first, second, and third line in Flanders were invested.
The two generals learned, however, on the 25th, the
Emperor's abdication, which had taken place on the 22d,
the insurrection of the Chambers, the discouragement
occasioned by these circumstances in the army, and the
hopes excited among our internal enemies. From that
moment, they thought only of marching upon the capital, under the walls of which they arrived at the latter
end of June, with fewer than 90,000 men ; an enterprise
that would have proved fatal to them, and drawn on their
total ruin, had they hazarded it in the presence of Napoleon : but that Prince had abdicated ! ! ! The troops of
the line at Paris, more than 6000 men of the depôts of
the guard, the sharpshooters of the National Guard,
chosen from among the people of that great capital, were
devoted to him ; they had it in their power to extermi-
nate the domestic enemy ! ! ! But in order to explain the
motives which regulated his conduct in that important
crisis, which was attended with such fatal results both
for him and for France, the narrative must go back to
an earlier period.

First Observation. — · " The Emperor has been reproached, 1st, With having resigned the dictatorship, at
the moment when France stood most in need of a dic-

tator , 2nd, With having altered the constitutions of the empire, at a moment when it was necessary to think only of preserving it from invasion , 3rd, With having permitted the Vendeans to be alarmed, who had, at first, refused to take arms against the imperial government; 4th, With having assembled the Chambers, when he ought to have assembled the army ; 5th, With having abdicated and left France at the mercy of a divided and inexperienced assembly; for, in fine, if it be true, that it was impossible for the Prince to save the country without the confidence of the nation, it is not less true that the nation could not, in these critical circumstances, preserve either its happiness or its independence without Napoleon.

Second Observation.—" The art, with which the movements of the different bodies of the army were concealed from the enemy's knowledge, on the opening of the campaign, cannot be too attentively remarked. Marshal Blucher and the Duke of Wellington were surprised ; they saw nothing, knew nothing, of the operations which were carrying on near their advanced posts.

" In order to attack the two hostile armies, the French might have out-flanked their right or left, or penetrated their centre. In the first case, they might have advanced by the way of Lisle, and fallen in with the Anglo-Dutch army; in the second, they might have moved forward by Givet and Charlemont, and have fallen in with the Prusso-Saxon army. These two armies would have remained united, since they must have been pressed the one upon the other, from the right to the left, and from the left to the right. The Emperor adopted the plan of covering his movements with the Sambre, and piercing the line of the two armies at Charleroi, their point of junction, executing his manœuvres with rapidity and skill. He thus discovered, in the secrets of the art, means to supply the place of 100,000 men, whom he needed. The plan was executed with boldness and prudence.

Third Observation.—" The character of several generals had been affected by the events of 1814 ; they had lost somewhat of that spirit, of that resolution, and that confidence, by which they had gained so much glory and so much contributed to the success of former campaigns.

"1st.—On the 15th of June, the third corps was to march at three o'clock in the morning, and arrive at Charleroi at ten; it did not arrive until three o'clock in the afternoon.

"2ndly,—The same day the attack on the woods in front of Fleurus, which had been ordered at four in the afternoon, did not take place until seven. Night came on before the troops could enter Fleurus, where the Commander in Chief had intended to establish his head-quarters the same day. The loss of seven hours was very vexatious on the opening of a campaign.

"3rdly,—Ney received orders to advance on the 16th with 43,000 men, who composed the left under his command, in front of Quatre-Bras, to take up a position there at day-break, and even to entrench himself; he hesitated, and lost eight hours. The Prince of Orange, with only 9000 men, retained, on the 16th until three o'clock in the afternoon, that important position. When at length, the Marshal received at twelve o'clock at noon the order dated from Fleurus, and saw that the Emperor was on the point of attacking the Prussians, he advanced against Quatre-Bras, but only with half his force, leaving the other half to cover his retreat at the distance of two leagues in the rear; he forgot it until six in the evening, when he felt the want of it for his own defence. In other campaigns, that General would have made himself master of the position in front of Quatre-Bras at six o'clock in the morning; he would have routed and captured the whole of the Belgic division, and either turned the Prussian army by sending a detachment on the Namur road to fall on the rear of their line of battle; or, by moving rapidly along the road to Gennapes, he would have surprised and destroyed the Brunswick division on its march, and the fifth English division as it advanced from Brussels. He would have afterwards marched to meet the third and fourth English divisions, which were advancing by way of Nivelles, and were both destitute of cavalry and artillery, and overwhelmed with fatigue. Ney, who was always first in the heat of battle, forgot the troops that were not directly engaged. The courage which a Commander in Chief should display is different from that of a general of division, as that of the latter ought to differ from the bravery of a captain of grenadiers.

"4thly.—The advanced guard of the French army did not arrive on the 16th, in front of Waterloo, until six o'clock in the evening; it would have arrived at three but for some vexatious hesitations. The Emperor was very much mortified at the delay, and, pointing at the sun, exclaimed, "What would I now give to have the power of Joshua, and to stop its progress for two hours!"

Fourth Observation.— "The French soldier never displayed more bravery, cheerfulness, and enthusiasm; he was animated with the sentiment of his superiority over all the soldiers of Europe. His confidence in the Emperor was altogether unabated; it had, perhaps, increased: but he was suspicious and distrustful of his other Commanders. The treasons of 1814 were always in his thoughts, and he was uneasy at every movement which he did not understand; he thought he was betrayed. At the moment when the first cannon-shots were firing near St. Amand, an old corporal approached the Emperor and said: "Sire, beware of General Soult; be assured that he is a traitor."—"Fear nothing," replied the Emperor, "I can answer for him as for myself." In the middle of the battle, an officer informed Marshal Soult that General Vandamme had gone over to the enemy, and that his soldiers demanded, with loud cries, that the Emperor should be made acquainted with it. At the close of the battle, a dragoon, with his sabre covered with blood, galloped up to him crying, "Sire, come instantly to the division, General Dhénin is persuading the dragoons to go over to the enemy."—"Did you hear him?"—"No, Sire, but an officer, who is looking for you, saw him and ordered me to tell your Majesty." During this time, the gallant General Dhenin received a cannon shot, which carried off one of his legs, after he had repulsed the enemy's charge.

"On the 14th, in the evening, Lieutenant-General

B . . . . , Colonel C . . . . , and V . . . . .   , an
officer of the staff, deserted and went over to the enemy.
Their names will be held in execration as long as the
French shall constitute a nation. The uneasy feelings
of the troops had been considerably aggravated by that
desertion.   It appears nearly certain that the cry of
Sauve qui peut was raised among the soldiers of the
fourth division of the first corps, on the evening of the
battle of Waterloo, when Marshal Blucher attacked the
village of La Haye.   That village was not defended as it
ought to have been.*   It is equally probable that several officers, charged with the communication of orders,
disappeared.   But, if some officers deserted, not a single
private was guilty of that crime.   Several killed themselves on the field of battle, where they lay wounded,
when they learned the defeat of the army.

Fifth Observation.—" In the battle of the 17th, the
French army was divided into three bodies ; 69,000 men
under the Emperor's command, marched against Brussels
by the way of Charleroi ; 34,000, under the command of
Marshal Grouchy, directed their operations against that
capital by way of Wavres, in pursuit of the Prussians ;
7 or 8000 men remained on the field of battle at Ligny,
of whom 3000, belonging to Girard's division, were employed in assisting the wounded, and in forming a reserve
for any unexpected casualty at Quatre-Bras ; and 4 or
5000 continued with the reserve at Fleurus and at
Charleroi.   The 34,000 men under the command of
Marshal Grouchy, with 108 pieces of cannon, were
sufficient to drive the Prussian rear-guard from any position it might take up, to press upon the retreat of the
conquered army, and to keep it in check.   It was a
glorious result of the victory of Ligny, to be thus enabled to oppose 34,000 men to an army which had consisted of 120,000.   The 69,000 men, under the Empe-

---

* General Durutte, who was mutilated on that disastrous day
and who commanded the fourth division here mentioned, declares
that there must be some mistake in regard to the number specified
in this dictation of Napoleon's ; or that there was some inaccuracy
or malice in the report that was made to him.

ror's command, were sufficient to bent the Anglo-Dutch
army, composed of 90,000. The disproportion which
existed on the 15th between the two belligerent masses
in the ratio of one to two, was materially changed, and
it no longer exceeded three to four. Had the Anglo-
Dutch army defeated the 69,000 men opposed to it,
Napoleon might have been reproached with having ill-
calculated his measures ; but it is undeniable, even from
the enemy's admission, that, unless General Blucher had
arrived, the Anglo-Dutch army would have been driven
from the field of battle between eight and nine o'clock at
night. If Marshal Blucher had not arrived at eight
with his first and second corps, the march on Brussels
with two columns, during the battle of the 17th, would
have been attended with several advantages. The left
would have pressed upon and kept in check the Anglo-
Dutch army ; the right, under the command of Marshal
Grouchy, would have pursued and restrained the operations of the Prusso-Saxon army ; and in the evening,
the whole of the French army would have effected its
junction on a line of less than five leagues from Mont
Saint Jean to Wavres, with its advanced posts on the edge
of the forest. But the fault committed by Marshal Grouchy, in stopping on the 17th at Gembloux, having marched scarcely two leagues in the course of the day, instead
of pushing on three leagues more in front of Wavres,
was aggravated and rendered irreparable by that which
he committed the following day, the 18th, in losing
twelve hours, and arriving at four o'clock in the afternoon in front of Wavres, when he should have been
there at six in the morning.

" 1st,—Grouchy, charged with the pursuit of Marshal
Blucher, lost sight of him for twenty-four hours, from
four o'clock in the afternoon of the 17th until a quarter
past twelve at noon on the 18th.

" 2dly,—The movement of the cavalry on the plain,
while General Bulow's attack was not yet repulsed,
proved a distressing accident. It was the intention of the
Commander in Chief to order that movement, but not
until an hour later, and then it was to have been sustained

by the sixteen battalions of infantry belonging to the guard, with one hundred pieces of cannon.

" 3dly.—The horse grenadiers and the dragoons of the guard, under the command of General Guyot, engaged without orders. Thus, at five in the afternoon, the army found itself without a reserve of cavalry. If, at half past eight, that reserve had existed, the storm which swept all before it on the field of battle would have been dispersed, the enemy's charges of cavalry driven back, and the two armies would have slept on the field, notwithstanding the successive arrivals of General Bulow and Marshal Blucher: the advantage would also have been in favour of the French army, as Marshal Grouchy's 34,000 men, with 108 pieces of cannon, were fresh troops and bivouacked on the field of battle. The enemy's two armies would have placed themselves in the night under cover of the forest of Soignes. The constant practice in every battle was for the horse-grenadiers and the dragoons of the guard never to lose sight of the Emperor, and never to make a charge but in consequence of an order verbally given by that Prince to the General who commanded them.

" Marshal Mortier, who was Commander in Chief of the guards, gave up the command on the 15th, at Beaumont, just as hostilities were on the point of commencing, and no one was appointed in his stead, which was attended with several inconvenient results.

Sixth Observation.—" 1st, The French army manœuvred on the right of the Sambre, on the 13th and 14th. It encamped, the night between the 14th and 15th, within half a league of the Prussian advanced posts; and yet Marshal Blucher had no knowledge of it, and when, on the morning of the 15th, he learned at his head-quarters at Namur that the Emperor had entered Charleroi, the Prusso-Saxon army was still cantoned over an extent of thirty leagues; two days were necessary for him to effect the junction of his troops. It was his duty, from the 15th of May, to advance his head-quarters to Fleurus, to concentrate the cantonments of his army within a radius of eight leagues, with his advanced posts on the Meuse and Sambre. His army might then have been assembled at Ligny on the 15th at noon, to await in that position the attack of the French army, or to march against it in the evening of the 15th, for the purpose of driving it into the Sambre.

"2dly.—Yet, notwithstanding this surprise of Marshal Blucher, he persisted in the project of collecting his troops on the heights of Ligny, behind Fleurus, exposing himself to the hazard of being attacked before the arrival of his army. On the morning of the 16th, he had collected but two corps, and the French army was already at Fleurus. The third corps joined in the course of the day, but the fourth, commanded by General Bulow, was unable to get up in time for the battle. Marshal Blucher, the instant he learned the arrival of the French at Charleroi, that is to say, on the evening of the 15th, ought to have assigned, as a point of junction for his troops, neither Fleurus nor Ligny, which were under the enemy's cannon, but Wavres, which the French could not have reached until the 17th. He would have also had the whole of the 16th, and the night between the 16th and 17th, to effect the total junction of his army.

"3dly.—After having lost the battle of Ligny, the Prussian General, instead of making his retreat on Wavres, ought to have effected it upon the army of the Duke of Wellington, whether at Quatre-Bras, where the latter had maintained himself, or at Waterloo. The whole of Marshal Blucher's retreat on the morning of the 17th was contrary to common sense, since the two armies, which were, on the evening of the 16th, little more than three miles from each other, and had a fine road for their point of communication, in consequence of which their junction might have been considered as effected, found themselves, on the evening of the 17th, separated by a distance of nearly twelve miles, and by defiles and impassable ways.

"The Prussian General violated the three grand rules of war; 1st, To keep his cantonments near each other; 2dly, To assign as a point of junction a place where his troops can all assemble before those of the enemy; 3dly To make his retreat upon his reinforcements.

Seventh Observation.—"1st, The Duke of Wellington

was surprised in his cantonments; he ought to have concentrated them on the 15th of May, at eight leagues about Brussels, and kept advanced guards on the roads from Flanders. The French army was for three days manœuvring close upon his advanced posts; it had commenced hostilities twenty four hours, and its head-quarters had been twelve hours at Charleroi, and yet the English General was at Brussels, ignorant of what was passing, and all the cantonments of his army were still in full security, extended over a space of more than twenty leagues.

"2dly.—The Prince of Saxe-Weimar, who belonged to the Anglo-Dutch army, was, on the 16th, at four o'clock in the afternoon in position before Frasne, and knew that the French army was at Charleroi. If he had immediately despatched an aide-de-camp to Brussels, he would have arrived there at six in the evening; and yet the Duke of Wellington was not informed that the French army was at Charleroi until eleven at night. He thus lost five hours, in a crisis, and against a man, that rendered the loss of a single hour highly important.

"3dly.—The infantry, cavalry, and artillery of that army were in cantonments, so remote from each other that the infantry was engaged at Waterloo without cavalry or artillery, which exposed it to considerable loss, since it was obliged to form in close columns to make head against the charges of the cuirassiers, under the fire of fifty pieces of cannon. These brave men were slaughtered without cavalry to protect or artillery to avenge them. As the three branches of an army cannot, for an instant, dispense with each other's assistance, they should be always cantoned and placed in such a way as to be able to assist each other.

"4th.—The English General, although surprised, assigned Quatre-Bras, which had been, for the last four and-twenty hours in possession of the French, as the rallying point of his army. He exposed his troops to partial defeats as they gradually arrived; the danger which they incurred was still more considerable, since they came without artillery and without cavalry; he delivered up his infantry to his enemy piece-meal, and

destitute of the assistance of the two other bran :hes.   He
should have fixed upon Waterloo for his point of junction :
he would then have had the day of the 16th, and the
night between the 16th and 17th, an interval quite
sufficient, to collect the whole of his army, infantry,
cavalry, and artillery.   The French could not have
arrived until the 17th, and would have found all his
troops in position.

Eighth Observation. — " 1st, The English General
gave battle at Waterloo on the 18th ; that measure was
contrary to the interests of his nation, to the general
system of war adopted by the Allies, and to all the rules
of war.   It was not the interest of England, who wants
so many men to recruit her armies in India, in her
American colonies, and in her vast establishments, to
expose herself, with a generous vivacity, to a sanguinary
contest in which she might lose the only army she had,
and expend, at the very least, her best blood.   The plan
of the Allies consisted in operating in a mass and in
avoiding all partial actions.   Nothing was more contrary
to their interests and their plan than to expose the success
of their cause in a doubtful battle with a nearly equal
force, in which all the probabilities were against them.
If the Anglo-Dutch army had been destroyed at Waterloo, of what use to the allies would have been the great
number of armies that were preparing to cross the Rhine,
the Alps, and the Pyrenees?

" 2ndly.—The English General, in accepting the battle
of Waterloo, placed his reliance on the co-operation of
the Prussians, but that co-operation could not be carried
into effect until the afternoon ; he therefore continued
exposed alone from four o'clock in the morning until
. five in the afternoon, that is to say, for thirteen hours ;
no battle lasts generally more than six hours ; that co-
operation was therefore an illusion.

" But, if he relied upon the co-operation of the
Prussians, he must have supposed that the whole of
the French army was opposed to him, and he must
consequently have undertaken to defend his field of
battle, during thirteen hours, with 90,000 men of different nations, against an army of 104,000 French.

That calculation was evidently false; he could not have maintained himself three hours; the battle would have been decided by eight o'clock in the morning, and the Prussians would have arrived only to be taken in flank. Both armies would have been destroyed in one battle. If he calculated that a part of the French army had, conformably to the rules of war, pursued the Prussian army, he ought, in that case, to have been convinced that he could receive no assistance from it, and that the Prussians, beaten at Ligny, having lost from 25 to 30,000 men on the field of battle, having 20,000 scattered and dispersed over the country, and pursued by from 35 to 40,000 victorious French, would not have risked any fresh operation, and would have considered themselves scarcely sufficient to maintain a defensive position. In that case, the Anglo-Dutch army alone would have had to sustain the shock of 69,000 French during the whole of the 18th, and there is no Englishman who will not admit that the result of that struggle could not have been doubtful, and that their army was not so constituted as to be capable of sustaining the attack of the imperial army for four hours.

" During the whole of the night between the 17th and 18th, the weather was horrible, and the roads were impassable until nine o'clock in the morning. This loss of six hours from day-break, was entirely in the enemy's favour; but could the English General stake the fate of such a struggle upon the weather which happened in the night between the 17th and 18th? Marshal Grouchy, with 34,000 men and 180 pieces of cannon, found out the secret, which one would suppose was not to be found out, of not being in the engagement of the 18th, either on the field of battle of Mont St Jean or of Wavres. But, had that Marshal pledged himself to the English General to be led astray in so strange a manner? The conduct of Marshal Grouchy was as unexpected as that his army should, on its march, be swallowed up by an earthquake. Let us recapitulate. If Marshal Grouchy had been on the field of battle of Mont St. Jean, as he was supposed to be by the English General and the Prussian General, during the whole night between the

17th and 18th, and all the morning of the 18th, and the weather had allowed the French army to be drawn up in order of battle at four o'clock in the morning, the Anglo-Dutch army would have been dispersed and cut in pieces before seven; its ruin would have been complete, and if the weather had not allowed the French army to range itself in order of battle until ten, the fate of the Anglo-Dutch army would have been decided before one o'clock; the remains of it would have been driven either beyond the forest or in the direction of Hal, and there would have been quite time enough in the afternoon to go and meet Marshal Blucher, and treat him in a similar manner. If Marshal Grouchy had encamped in front of Wavres in the night between the 17th and 18th. no detachment could have been sent by the Prussians to save the English army, which must have been completely beaten by the 69,000 French opposed to it.

"3dly.—The position of Mont St. Jean was ill chosen. The first requisite of a field of battle is to be without defiles in its rear. The English General derived no advantage, during the battle, from his numerous cavalry; he did not think that he ought to be and would be attacked on the left; he believed that the attack would be made on his right. Notwithstanding the diversion operated in his favour by General Bulow's 30,000 Prussians, he would have twice effected his retreat, during the battle, had that measure been possible. Thus, in reality, how strange and capricious are human events! the bad choice of his field of battle, which prevented all possibility of retreat, was the cause of his success!!!

Ninth Observation.—" It may be asked, what then should have been the conduct of the English General, after the battle of Ligny and the engagement of Quatre Bras? On this point posterity will not entertain two opinions: he ought, in the night between the 17th and 18th, to have crossed the forest of Soignes, by the road of Charleroi; the Prussian army ought also to have crossed it by the road of Wavres; the armies would have effected a junction by break of day in Brussels; left their rearguards for the defence of the forest, gained some days in order to give time to the Prussians, dispersed after the battle of Ligny, to join their army; reinforced themselves with fourteen English regiments, which were in garrison in the fortresses of Belgium, or had been just landed at Ostend, on their return from America, and let the Emperor of the French manœuvre as he pleased.

"Would he, with an army of 100,000 men have traversed the forest of Soignes to attack in an open country the two united armies, consisting of more than 200,000 men, and in position? It would have certainly been the most advantageous thing that could have happened to the allies. Would he have been content with taking up a position himself? He could not have long remained in an inactive state, since 300,000 Russians, Austrians, Bavarians, &c. were on their march to the Rhine; they would have been in a few weeks on the Marne, which would have compelled him to hasten to the assistance of his capital. It was then that the Anglo-Prussian army ought to have marched and effected its junction with the Allies, under the walls of Paris. It would have exposed itself to no risk, suffered no loss, and have acted conformably to the interests of the English nation, and the general plan of carrying on the war adopted by the Allies, and sanctioned by the rules of the military art. From the 15th to the 18th, the Duke of Wellington invariably manœuvred as his enemy wished; he executed nothing which the latter apprehended he would. The English infantry was firm and solid; the cavalry might have conducted itself better: the Anglo-Dutch army was twice saved, in the course of the day, by the Prussians—the first time before three o'clock, by the arrival of General Bulow with 30,000 men, and the second time by the arrival of Marshal Blucher with 31,000 men. In that battle, 69,000 French beat 120,000 men; the victory was wrested from them, between eight and nine, by 150,000 men.

"Let the feelings of the people of London be imagined, if they had been doomed to hear of the destruction of their army, and the prodigal waste of their best blood, in support of the cause of kings against that of

VOL. III.—9

nations, of privileges against equality, of the oligarchs against the liberals, and of the principles of the Holy Alliance against those of the sovereignty of the people ! ! ! "

PLAN FOR A POLITICAL DEFENCE OF NAPOLEON ; SKETCHED BY HIMSELF.

Tuesday, August 27th.—About four o'clock I joined the Emperor in the garden : he had been engaged in dictating during the whole of the morning. The wind was very rough, and the Emperor declined riding out in the calash : he therefore walked about for a considerable time in the great alley through the wood, attended by all the persons of his suite. He jokingly teased one of the party, by observing that he was sulky, and accusing him of being very often discontented and ill-humoured, &c.

The Emperor, on rising from the dinner table, adverted to his recent protest against the treaty of the 2d of August. He expatiated with warmth on the subject, and remarked, while he walked rapidly about the apartment, that he intended to draw up another protest, on a more extensive and important scale, against the Bill that had been passed in the British Parliament. He would prove, he said, that the Bill was not a law, but a violation of every existing law. Napoleon was proscribed, and not judged by it. The English Parliament had done, not what was just, but what was deemed to be expedient ; it had imitated Themistocles, without hearing Aristides. The Emperor then arraigned himself before all the nations in Europe, and proved that each would successively acquit him. He took a review of the different acts of his reign, and justified them all.

" The French and the Italians," said he, " lament my absence ; I carry with me the gratitude of the Poles, and even the late and bitter regrets of the Spaniards. Europe will soon deplore the loss of the equilibrium, to the maintenance of which my French empire was absolutely necessary. The Continent is now in the most perilous situation, being continually exposed to the risk of being overrun by Cossacks and Tartars. And

the English," said he in conclusion, "the English will
deplore their victory at Waterloo! Things will be
carried to such a length that posterity, together with
every well-informed and well-disposed person among
our contemporaries, will regret that I did not succeed in
all my enterprises."

In course of his remarks, the Emperor occasionally
rose to a pitch of sublimity. I shall not follow him
into all his details. He promised to dictate the observations he had made, and said that he had already
sketched out a plan for his political defence, in fourteen
paragraphs.

CATINAT; TURENNE; CONDÉ.—QUESTIONS RESPECTING
THE GREATEST BATTLE FOUGHT BY THE EMPEROR;
THE BEST TROOPS, &C.

28th.—The Emperor did not go out until four o'clock ;
he had spent three hours in the bath. The weather was
very unpleasant, and in consequence he merely took a
few turns in the garden. He had just written to inform
the Governor that henceforth he would receive no strangers, unless they were admitted to Longwood by passes
rrom the Grand Marshal as in the time of Admiral
Cockburn.

The Emperor proposed playing a game at chess ; but,
before he sat down to do so, he took up a volume of
Fenelon. It was *La Direction de Conscience d'un Roi.*
He read to us several articles, criticising them with considerable spirit and gaiety. At length he threw down
the volume, saying that the name of an author had never
influenced him in forming an opinion of his writings ;
that he always judged of works according to the sentiments with which they inspired him ; being always
equally willing to praise or to censure. He added that,
in spite of the name of Fenelon, he had no hesitation in
declaring that the work he had just looked through was
a mere string of rhapsodies ; and truly it would be difficult to refute this assertion.

After dinner, the Emperor conversed about the old
marine establishment, and alluded to M. de Grasse, and
his defeat on the 12th of April. He wished to learn

some particulars on this subject; and he asked for the Dictionary of Sieges and Battles. He looked over it, and it afforded him matter for a multitude of observations. Catinat came under his consideration, and the remarks ne made on that commander lowered him infinitely in our estimation. Napoleon said that he thought him very inferior to the reputation he enjoyed, after viewing the scenes of his operations in Italy, and reading his correspondence with Louvois. " Having risen from the *tiers-état*," said he, " and being educated for the law, distinguished for urbanity of manners and moral integrity, affecting the practice of equality, residing at St. Gratien, at the gates of Paris, Catinat became the favourite of the *literati* of the capital and the philosophers of the day, who exalted him beyond his real merits. He was in no way comparable to Vendôme."

The Emperor said, that he had endeavoured, in the same manner, to study the characters of Turenne and Condé, suspecting that they were also the objects of exaggerated eulogy; but that he was convinced those two men were fully entitled to all the commendation that has been bestowed on them. With regard to Turenne, he remarked that his intrepidity encreased in proportion as he acquired experience; as he grew old, he evinced greater courage than he seemed to possess in early life. The contrary was observable in Condé, who displayed so much dauntless valour at the commencement of his career.

Now that I am alluding to Turenne, Condé, and other distinguished men, I may mention, as a curious fact, that I never, by any chance, heard Napoleon utter the name of Frederick the Great. Yet many circumstances prove that Frederick held a high rank in Napoleon's regard. The large silver watch, a kind of alarum used by that Prince, which hangs by the fire-place in the Emperor's apartment at St. Helena; — the eagerness with which Napoleon, on his entrance into Potzdam, seized the sword of the Prussian hero, exclaiming, "Let those who will seek other spoil; I value this beyond millions!"—finally, his long and silent contemplation of the tomb of Frederick—sufficiently attest the deep interest which Napoleon attached to every thing connected with that sovereign.*

In the Dictionary of Sieges and Battles, which the Emperor was looking over to-day, he found his name mentioned in every page ; but connected with anecdotes either totally false, or at least misstated.   This led him to exclaim against the whole swarm of inferior writers, and their unworthy abuse of the pen.   " Literature," he said, " had become the food of the vulgar, while it ought to have been reserved exclusively for people of refined taste.

" For example," said the Emperor, " it is affirmed that, when at Arcole, I one night took the post of a sentinel who had fallen asleep.   This idea was doubtless conceived by a citizen, by a lawyer, perhaps, but certainly not by a soldier.   The author evidently wishes to represent me in a favourable point of view ; and he of course imagined that nothing could reflect greater credit on me than the story he has invented.   He certainly wrote it with the view of doing me honour ; but he knew not that I was totally incapable of the action he describes. I was much too fatigued for any such thing ; and it is very probable that I should myself have fallen asleep before the sentinel."

We then enumerated about fifty or sixty great battles that had been fought by the Emperor. Some one present having asked which was the greatest, the Emperor replied that it was difficult to answer that question, since it was first necessary to enquire what was meant by the greatest battle.   " Mine," continued he, " cannot be judged of separately.   They had no unity of place, action or design. They formed merely a portion of extensive plans.   They can therefore only be judged of by their results.   The battle of Marengo, which was so long undecided, procured for us the dominion of all Italy ; Ulm annihilated a whole army ; Jena threw the whole Prussian monarchy into our hands ; Friedland opened to us the Russian

---

* After my removal from Longwood, Napoleon undertook a special work on Frederick the Great, with notes and Commentaries on his Campaigns.

empire; and Eckmühl decided the fate of a war. The battle of Moscow was one in which the greatest talent was displayed, and in which the fewest results were obtained. Waterloo, where every thing failed, would, had every thing succeeded, have saved France and re-established Europe."

Madame de Montholon having asked what troops might be accounted the best, "Those who gain victories, Madam," replied the Emperor. "But," added he, "soldiers are capricious and inconstant, like you ladies. The best troops were the Carthagenians under Hannibal; the Romans under the Scipios; the Macedonians under Alexander; and the Prussians under Frederick." He thought, however, he might safely affirm that the French troops were, of all others, those who could most easily be rendered the best, and preserved so.

"With my complete guard of 40 or 50,000 men, I would have pledged myself to march through all Europe. It may, perhaps, be possible to produce troops as good as those who composed my army of Italy and Austerlitz; but certainly nothing can ever surpass them."

The Emperor, who had dwelt for a considerable time on this subject, which was so interesting to him, suddenly recollecting himself, asked what it was o'clock. He was informed that it was eleven.—"Well," said he, rising, "we at least have the merit of having got through our evening without the help of either tragedy or comedy."

MADAME DE COTTIN'S MATHILDE, &c.—ALL FRENCHMEN INTERESTED IN NAPOLEON. — DESAIX AND NAPOLEON AT MARENGO. — SIR SIDNEY SMITH.— CAUSE OF GENERAL BONAPARTE'S RETURN TO FRANCE. — ACCOUNT OF HIS VOYAGE. — INSTANCES OF THE CAPRICE OF FORTUNE.

29th. About two o'clock the Emperor desired me to attend him in his chamber, and he gave me some private orders. At four I rejoined him. I found him sitting under the tent, surrounded by all his suite; he was swinging backward and forward on his chair, laughing, talking, and making every effort to be cheerful, while, at

the same time, he continually repeated that he felt dull
and languid. He rose and took a drive in the calash.

After dinner, the conversation turned on romance
writing. Some one mentioned Madame Cottin's Mathilde, the scene of which is laid in Syria. The Emperor asked the person who had alluded to the work whether
he had ever seen Madame Cottin, whether she liked him
(Napoleon),whether her work was favourable to him,&c.,
but as he did not receive a ready answer he thus continued : "But every body has loved me and hated me :
every one has been for me and against me by turns. I
may truly say that there is not a single Frenchman in
whom I have not excited interest. All must have loved
me, from Collot d'Herbois (had he lived) to the Prince of
Condé; only not all at the same, time but at different
intervals and periods. I was like the sun which crosses
the equator to travel through the ecliptic. According
as my influence was felt in each different climate, all
hopes expanded, and I was blessed and adored; but when
I had departed, when I was no longer understood, unfavourable sentiments arose."

Egypt next became the subject of conversation ; and
the Emperor again sketched the characters of Kleber and
Desaix. The latter joined the First Consul on the eve
of the battle of Marengo. Napoleon asked him how he
could have thought of signing the capitulation of Egypt ;
since the army was sufficiently numerous to maintain
possession of it. "We ought not to have lost Egypt,"
he observed.—"That's very. true," replied Desaix, "and
the army was certainly numerous enough to enable us to
retain possession of the country. But the General-in-
chief left us ; and at that distance from home, the General-in-chief is not a single man in the army ; he is the
half, the three-fourths, the five-sixths of it. I had no
alternative but to resign the possession of the country.
I doubt whether I could have succeeded had I acted
otherwise ; besides, it would have been criminal to make
the attempt, for in such a case it is a soldier's duty to
obey, and I did so."

Desaix, immediately after his arrival at Marengo, obtained the command of the reserve. Towards the end of

the battle, and amidst the greatest apparent disorder,
Napoleon came up to him : — " Well," said Desaix,
" affairs are going on very badly, the battle is lost. I
can only secure the retreat. Is it not so ?"—" Quite
the contrary," said the First Consul ; " to me the result
of the battle was never for a moment doubtful. Those
masses, which you see in disorder on the right and left,
are marching to form in your rear. The battle is gained.
Order your column to advance : you have but to reap the
glory of the victory."

The Emperor afterwards spoke of Sir Sidney Smith.
He had, he said, just read in the Moniteur the documents relating to the convention of El-Arish, in which
he remarked that Sir Sidney had evinced a great share
of intelligence and integrity. The Emperor said he be-
wildered Kleber by the stories which he made him believe.
But when Sir Sidney received intelligence of the refusal
of the English Government to ratify the treaty, he was
very much dissatisfied, and behaved very honourably to
the French army. " After all," said the Emperor, " Sir
Sidney Smith is not a bad man. I now entertain a better
opinion of him than I did ; particularly after what I daily
witness in the conduct of his confederates."

It was Sir Sidney Smith who, by communicating the
European journals to Napoleon, brought about the departure of the General-in-chief, and consequently the
dénouement of Brumaire. The French, on their return
from St. Jean d'Acre, were totally ignorant of all that
had taken place in Europe for several months. Napoleon,
eager to obtain intelligence, sent a flag of truce on board
the Turkish admiral's ship, under the pretence of treating
for the ransom of the prisoners whom he had taken at
Aboukir, not doubting that the envoy would be stopped
by Sir Sidney Smith, who carefully prevented all direct
communication between the French and the Turks.
Accordingly, the French flag of truce received directions
from Sir Sidney to go on board his ship. He experienced
the handsomest treatment ; and the English commander,
having among other things ascertained that the disasters
of Italy were quite unknown to Napoleon, he indulged
in the malicious pleasure of sending him a file of newspapers.

cheerfulness and ease, and conversed on the most indifferent subjects.

General Menou was the last person to whom Napoleon
spoke on shore. He said to him, " My dear General,
you must take care of yourselves here. If I have the
happiness to reach France, the reign of ranting shall be
at an end. "

On a perusal of the papers furnished by Sir Sidney
Smith, Napoleon formed such an idea of the disasters of
France that he concluded the enemy had crossed the
Alps, and was already in possession of several of our
Southern Departments. When therefore the frigate approached the coast of Europe, Napoleon directed the
Admiral to make for Collioure and Port-Vendre, situated
at the extremity of the Gulf of Lyons. A gale of wind
drove them upon the coast of Corsica. They then entered Ajaccio, where they obtained intelligence of the
state of affairs in France.

Ganthaume informed me that he saw, at Ajaccio, the
house which was occupied by Napoleon's family, the
patrimonial abode. The arrival of their celebrated
countryman immediately set all the inhabitants of the
island in motion. A crowd of cousins came to welcome
him, and the streets were thronged with people.

Napoleon again set sail, and the frigate now steered
towards Marseilles and Toulon. However, just as they
were on the point of reaching the place of their destination,
a new source of alarm arose. At sunset, on the larboard of
the frigate, and precisely in the sun's rays, they observed
thirty sail making towards them with the wind aft.
Ganthaume proposed that the long boat of the frigate
should be manned with the best sailors, and that the
General should get on board, and under favour of the
night, endeavour to gain the shore. But Napoleon declined this proposition, observing that there would always
be time enough for that mode of escape; and he directed
the captain to continue his course as though nothing had
occurred. Meanwhile, night set in, and the enemy's
signal-guns were heard, at a distance, and right astern :
thus it appeared that the frigate had not been observed.
Next day they anchored at Frejus. The rest is well
known.

The Emperor concluded the evening's conversation, by relating to us three curious instances of the caprice of fortune, which took place in the same quarter of the world, and about the same period.

A corporal, who deserted from one of the regiments of the army of Egypt, joined the Mamelukes, and was made a Bey. After his elevation, he wrote a letter to his former General.

A fat sutler's wife who had followed the French army, became the favourite of the Pasha of Jerusalem. She could not write, but she sent a messenger with her compliments to her old friends, assuring them that she would never forget her country, but would always afford protection to the French and the Christians. " She was," said the Emperor, " the Zaire of the day."

A young peasant-girl of Cape Corso, being seized in a fishing-boat by corsairs, was conveyed to Barbary, and subsequently became the ruling favourite of the King of Morocco. The Emperor, after some diplomatic communications, caused the brother of this young girl to be brought from Corsica to Paris, and, after having him suitably fitted out, sent him to his sister; but he never heard of them afterwards.

It was late when the Emperor retired to rest; he had spent upwards of three hours in conversation.

30th.—I attended the Emperor at four o'clock. He had been engaged in dictating under the tent. The Governor had returned answers to the letters which M. de Montholon addressed to him by the Emperor's orders.

To the first communication, containing the protest against the treaty of the 2d of August, and various other complaints, no answer was returned, except that the Governor wished to be informed what letter he had kept back. This we could not tell him, since we had not seen the letters. We had asked *him* that question; and he was the only person capable of answering it.

To the second letter, which stated that the Emperor would not receive strangers at Longwood unless they were admitted by the Grand Marshal's passes, as was usual in the time of Admiral Cockburn, the Governor replied that he had been sorry to see General Bonaparte troubled by intrusive visitors at Longwood, and that he wished to prevent such importunity for the future. This was a most revolting piece of irony, considering the situation in which the Emperor was placed, and the tenor of M. de Montholon's letter.

After dinner the Emperor retired to the drawing-room, and desired us all to seat ourselves round the table, to form, as he said, an academic sitting. He began to dictate to us on some subjects; but when the parts that had been written were read over to him, he resolved to cancel them. Conversation was then resumed, and was kept up for a considerable time, partly in a serious and partly in a lively strain. It was near one o'clock when the Emperor retired. For some time past we have sat up later than we used to do. This is a good sign: the Emperor feels better, and he is more cheerful and talkative than he lately was.

HISTORICAL DOUBTS.—THE REGENCY OF THE DUKE OF ORLEANS.—MADAME DE MAINTENON.—HER MARRIAGE WITH LOUIS XIV.

31st.—The Emperor rose very early, and took a turn round the park alone. On his return, not wishing to have any one disturbed, he desired my son, who had risen, to sit down under the tent, and write from his dictation: in this manner he employed himself for two hours. We all breakfasted with him.

We took an airing in the calash. The conversation turned on the doubts that were attached to various points of history. The Emperor made some very curious remarks on this subject, and concluded with a circumstance relating to the Regent. "If," said he, "Louis XV. had died in his childhood, and nothing was more possible, who would have doubted that the Duke of Orleans had poisoned the whole royal family? Who would have ventured to defend him? Had not one child survived, that Prince would not have had justice done him." The Emperor then alluded to the character of the Duke of Orleans, and particularly to his errors in the affair of the legitimate princes. "There he degraded himself," said

Napoleon; " not to say, however, that their cause was
good. Louis XIV. usurped a right in nominating them
to the succession. On the extinction of the Royal House,
the choice of a Sovereign is unquestionably the prerogative of the nation. The act of Louis XIV. was doubtless
an error into which that Monarch was betrayed by his
own greatness. He conceived that every thing emanating from him must necessarily be great. Yet he seemed
to entertain a suspicion that the world might not be
exactly of his opinion ; for he took precautions to consolidate his work by giving his natural children in
marriage to the legitimate princes and princesses of the
royal family. As to the Regency, it is very certain that
it devolved by right on the Duke of Orleans. Louis
XIV.'s will was a downright absurdity : it was a violation of our fundamental laws. France was a monarchy,
and he gave us a republic for a Regency."

The Emperor then mentioned Madame de Maintenon,
whose career, he said, was most extraordinary. She
was, he observed, the Bianca Capello* of her age ; but
less romantic, and not quite so amusing. Pursuing his
historical doubts, he said a great deal on the subject of
Madame de Maintenon's marriage with Louis XIV. He
declared that he was sometimes inclined to regard the
circumstance as very problematical, in spite of all that
was said about it in the Memoirs of the time.

" The fact is," observed he, " that there does not, and
never did, exist any official and authentic proof of the
marriage. What could be Louis XIV.'s object in keeping the measure so strictly secret, both from his contemporaries and posterity? and how happened it that the
Noailles family, to whom Madame de Maintenon was

---

* A noble Venetian lady of great beauty, whose adventures
form a truly romantic and dramatic history. She eloped from
her father's house to follow a young Florentine pedlar, and was
reduced to the greatest wretchedness. She subsequently became
Grand Duchess of Tuscany, and she closed her career by coolly
poisoning herself at table, in a fit of vexation at seeing the Grand
Duke, her husband, partake of a poisoned dish, which she had
prepared for her brother-in-law, Cardinal de Medicis, who, on his
part, obstinately abstained from tasting it.

related, suffered nothing to transpire on the subject?
This was the more singular considering that Madame de
Maintenon survived Louis XIV."

The Emperor, feeling somewhat fatigued this evening,
retired to rest early. He seemed indisposed and low
spirited.

THE FRENCH MINISTERS, &c.—ANECDOTE OF M. DARU.— FADED FINERY AT ST. HELENA.

Sunday, September 1st.— The Emperor went out
about three o'clock : he said that he had felt feeble, languid, and dull the whole of the day. We all felt indisposed in the same way : it was the effect of the weather.
We strolled out to the great path in the wood, while the
calash was preparing; but no sooner had we reached
the extremity of the path than a shower of rain came
on. It was so heavy that the Emperor was obliged to
take refuge at the foot of a gum-tree, the scanty foliage
of which, however, afforded but little shelter. The
calash soon arrived to take us up; and we were returning home with all speed, when we perceived the Governor, at some distance, making towards us. The Emperor
immediately ordered the coachman to turn, observing,
that of two evils he would choose the least; and we took
a circuitous route homewards, in spite of the wind and
rain. We, however, escaped Sir Hudson Lowe: that
was an advantage.

Before dinner, the Emperor, in his chamber, took a
review of the individuals who had been attached to his
Household, the Council of State, and the different ministerial departments. Alluding to M. Daru, he observed
that he was a man distinguished for probity and for indefatigable application to business. At the retreat from
Moscow, M. Daru's firmness and presence of mind were
remarkable, and the Emperor often afterwards said that
he laboured like an ox, while he displayed the courage
of a lion.

Business seemed to be M. Daru's element; he was
incessantly occupied. Soon after he was appointed
Secretary of State, one of his friends was expressing a
fear that the immense business in which he would thence-

forth be absorbed might prove too much for him. "On the contrary," replied Daru, "I assure you that, since I have entered upon my new functions, I seem to have absolutely nothing to do." On one occasion only was his vigour ever known to relax. The Emperor called him up, after midnight, to write from his dictation: M. Daru was so completely overcome by fatigue that he scarcely knew what he was writing; at length he could hold out no longer, and he fell asleep over his paper. After enjoying a sound nap, he awoke, and, to his astonishment, perceived the Emperor by his side quietly engaged in writing. The shortness of the candles informed him that his slumber had been of considerable duration. While he sat for a few moments overwhelmed with confusion, his eyes met those of the Emperor, who said to him: "Well, Sir, you see I have been doing your work, since you would not do it yourself. I suppose you have eaten a hearty supper, and passed a pleasant evening; but business must not be neglected."—"I pass a pleasant evening, Sire!" said M. Daru. "I have been for several nights without sleep, and closely engaged. Of this your Majesty now sees the consequence, and I am exceedingly sorry for it."—"Why did you not inform me of this?" said the Emperor, "I do not want to kill you. Go to bed. Good night, M. Daru." This was certainly a characteristic trait, and one that was well calculated to remove the false notions which were generally entertained respecting Napoleon's harshness of temper. But I know not by what fatality facts of this kind were concealed from our knowledge, while any absurd inventions unfavourable to the Emperor were so actively circulated. Was it because the courtiers reserved their flattery for the interior of the palace, and sought to create a sort of counterpoise, by assuming elsewhere an air of opposition and independence? Be this as it may, had any individual related traits of the above kind in the saloons of Paris, he would probably have been told that he had invented them, or would have been looked upon as a fool for giving credit to them.

The Grand Marshal and his lady came to dine at Longwood, which they were accustomed to do every Sunday.

During dinner, the Emperor jokingly alluded to the
faded finery of the ladies. He said that their dresses
would soon resemble the gay trappings of those old
misers who purchase their wardrobes from the dealers
in second-hand clothes; they no longer displayed the
freshness and elegance that characterized the millinery
of Leroi, Despeaux, Herbault, &c. The ladies craved
indulgence for St. Helena; and their husbands reminded
the Emperor of his fastidiousness with regard to female
dress at the Tuileries, which, it was remarked, had
proved the ruin of some families. At this the Emperor
laughed, and said that the idea of his scrupulous taste in
dress was a mere invention of the ladies of the Court,
who made it a pretence, or an excuse, for their extravagance. The conversation then turned on our splendour
at St. Helena. The Emperor said that he had told
Marchand he would wear every day the hunting-coat
which he then had on, until it was completely worn out:
it was already very far gone.

Both before and after dinner the Emperor played a
few games at chess : he felt low-spirited and nervous,
and retired to bed early.

THE CAMPAIGN OF SAXONY IN 1813.—REFLECTIONS.—
ANALYSIS.—BATTLES OF LUTZEN AND WURTZEN.—
NEGOTIATIONS.—BATTLES OF DRESDEN, LEIPSIC, HA-
NAU, &c.

Sept. 2.—To-day there was some horse-racing at the
camp, at which one of the Emperor's suite was present.

The Emperor did not go out until late, and he walked
to the calash. The wind blew very hard, and he renounced his intention of taking a drive. He sat down
beneath the tent : but, finding it not very pleasant
without doors, he retired to his library, where he took up
the Letters of Madame de Chateauroux, looked through
the Expedition to Bohemia, and analysed the Life of
Marshal de Belle-Isle. He again went out to take a
walk in the garden ; but he returned almost immediately,
and directed me to follow him.

He took up a book relating to our last campaigns,
and, after perusing it for some time, he threw it down,

saying, "It is a downright rhapsody—a mere tissue of contradictions and absurdities." He conversed for a considerable time on the two celebrated campaigns of Saxony: his observations were principally moral, and few or none military; I noted down the following as the most remarkable: "That memorable campaign," said he, "will be regarded as the triumph of courage in the youth of France; of intrigue and cunning in English diplomacy; of intelligence on the part of the Russians; and of effrontery in the Austrian Cabinet. It will mark the period of the disorganization of political societies, the great separation of subjects from their Sovereigns, finally, the decay of the first military virtues—fidelity, loyalty, and honour. In vain people may write and comment, invent falsehoods and suppositions; to this odious and mortifying result we must all come at last: time will develop both its truth and its consequences.

"But it is a remarkable circumstance, in this case, that all discredit is equally removed from sovereigns, soldiers, and people. It was entirely the work of a few military intriguers and headlong politicians, who, under the specious pretext of shaking off the foreign yoke and recovering the national independence, purposely sold their own rulers to envious rival Cabinets. The results soon became manifest: the King of Saxony lost half his dominions, and the King of Bavaria was compelled to make valuable restitutions. What did the traitors care for that? They enjoyed their rewards and their wealth, and those who had proved themselves most upright and innocent were visited with the severest punishment. The King of Saxony, the most honest man who ever wielded a sceptre, was stripped of half his territories; and the King of Denmark, so faithful to all his engagements, was deprived of a crown! This, however, was affirmed to be the restoration and the triumph of morality! .... Such is the distributive justice of this world! ....

"To the honour of human nature, and even to the honour of Kings, I must once more declare that never was more virtue manifested than amidst the baseness which marked this period. I never for a moment had cause to complain individually of the Princes our allies.

The good King of Saxony continued faithful to the last; the King of Bavaria loyally avowed to me that he was no longer his own master ; the generosity of the King of Würtemburg was particularly remarkable; the Prince of Baden yielded only to force, and in the very last extremity. All, I must render them this justice, gave me due notice of the storm that was gathering, in order that I might take the necessary precautions. But, on the other hand, how odious was the conduct of subaltern agents! Military history will never obliterate the infamy of the Saxons, who returned to our ranks for the purpose of destroying us ! Their treachery became proverbial among the troops, who still use the term *Saxonner* to designate the act of a soldier who assassinates another. To crown all, it was a Frenchman, a man for whom French blood purchased a crown, a nursling of France, who gave the finishing stroke to our disasters! Gracious God !

" But in the situation in which I was placed, the circumstance which served to fill up the measure of my distress was that I beheld the decisive hour gradually approach. The star paled ; I felt the reins slip from my hands, and yet I could do nothing. Only a sudden turn of fortune could save us: to treat, to conclude any compact, would have been to yield like a fool to the enemy. I was convinced of this, and the event sufficiently proved that I was not mistaken. We had, therefore, no alternative but to fight; and every day, by some fatality or other, our chances diminished. Treason began to penetrate into our ranks. Great numbers of our troops sunk under the effects of fatigue and discouragement. My lieutenants became dispirited, and, consequently, unfortunate. They were no longer the same men who figured at the commencement of the Revolution, or who had distinguished themselves in the brilliant moments of my success. I have been informed that some presumed to allege, in their defence, that at first they fought for the Republic and for their country ; while afterwards they fought only for a single man, for his individual interests, and his ambition.

" Base subterfuge ! Ask the young and brave soldiers, and the officers of intermediate rank in the French army.

whether such a calculation ever entered their thoughts;
—whether they ever saw before them any thing but the
enemy, or behind them any thing save the honour,
glory, and triumph of France! These men never fought
better than at the period alluded to. Why dissemble?
Why not make a candid avowal? The truth is that,
generally speaking, the officers of high rank had gained
every object of their ambition. They were sated with
wealth and honours. They had drunk of the cup of
pleasure, and they henceforth wished for repose, which
they would have purchased at any price. The sacred
flame was extinguished; they were willing to sink to
the level of Louis XV.'s marshals."

If the words above quoted require any comment—if
the sense here, or in other similar passages of my
Journal, should be found to be incomplete, I must not
be held responsible. I have literally noted down what
Napoleon uttered, and I am accountable for nothing
more. I have already several times mentioned that,
when the Emperor spoke, I never ventured to interrupt
him by questions or remarks. On the subject of the
celebrated campaign of 1813, I may mention that, from
various detached conversations of Napoleon, which I
have not noted down at the time when they occurred,
he was far from being deceived as to the crisis which
threatened France, and he correctly estimated the full
extent of the risk by which he was surrounded in the
opening of the campaign. Ever since his return from
Moscow, he had seen the danger, he said, and endeavoured to avert it. From that moment he resolved on
making the greatest sacrifices; but the choice of the
proper moment for proclaiming these sacrifices was the
difficult point, and that which chiefly occupied his
consideration. If the influence of material power be
great, he said, the power of opinion is still greater;
it is magical in its effects. His object was to preserve
it; and a false step, a word inadvertently uttered, might
for ever have destroyed the illusion. He found it indispensable to exert the greatest circumspection, and
to manifest the utmost apparent confidence in his own
strength. It was, above all, necessary to look forward
to the future.

His great fault, his fundamental error, was in supposing that his adversaries always had as much judgment
and knowledge of their own interests, as he himself
possessed. From the first, he said, he suspected that
Austria would avail herself of the difficulties in which
he was placed, in order to secure great advantages to
herself; but he never could have believed that the
Monarch was so blind, or his advisers so treacherous as
to wish to bring about his (Napoleon's) downfall, and
thereby leave their own country henceforth at the mercy
of the uncontrolled power of Russia. The Emperor
pursued the same train of reasoning with regard to the
Confederation of the Rhine, which, he admitted, might,
perhaps, have cause to be dissatisfied with him; but
which, he concluded, must dread still more the idea of
falling under the power of Austria and Prussia. Napoleon conceived that the same arguments were not
inapplicable to Prussia; which, he presumed, could not
wish entirely to destroy a counterpoise, that was
necessary to her independence, and her very existence.
Napoleon made full allowance for the hatred of his enemies, and for the dissatisfaction and malevolence which,
perhaps, existed among his allies; but he could not
suppose that either wished for his destruction, since he
felt himself to be so necessary to all; and he acted accordingly. Such was Napoleon's ruling idea throughout
the whole of this important period. It was the key of
his whole conduct to the very last hour, and even to the
moment of his fall. It must be carefully borne in mind,
for it serves to explain many things, perhaps, all;—
his hostile attitude, his haughty language, his refusal to
treat, his determination to fight, &c.

If he should be successful, he thought he could then
make honourable sacrifices, and a glorious peace; while
the illusion of his superiority would remain undiminished.
If, on the contrary, he should experience reverses, it
would still be time enough to make concessions; and he
concluded that the interest of the Austrians and all true
Germans must secure him the support of their arms or
of their diplomacy; for he supposed they were convinced,
as he himself was, that his power had henceforth become
indispensable to the structure, repose, security, and ex-

istence of Europe. But that of which he had reason to doubt proved most prosperous : victory continued faithful to him; his first successes were admirable, and almost incredible. On the other hand, that which he believed to be infallible was precisely what failed him :— his natural allies betrayed him, and hastened his downfall.

In support of what I have just alleged, and with the view of throwing light on the Emperor's remarks above quoted, I shall here insert a brief recapitulation of the events of that fatal campaign. In France, at the time, we were made acquainted only with its results; the bulletins gave us but little information, and we received no foreign publications. Besides, the period is now distant, and so many important events have since occurred to occupy public attention, that these details may be partly forgotten by those who once knew them. They are here arranged in chronological order.

I extract this recapitulation from a work written by M. de Montveran, which was published in 1820. The author has bestowed great care on the collection of official and authentic documents; and he has availed himself of the information furnished by preceding writers. I am, therefore, of opinion, that this work is, unquestionably, the best that has been written on the subject. M. de Montveran is far from being favourable to Napoleon; however, it is but just to admit that he maintains a tone of impartiality which does credit to his character, while, at the same time, it enhances the merit of his work.

" On the 2nd of May, Napoleon opened the campaign of Saxony by the victory of Lützen, a most surprising event, and one which reflects immortal honour on the conquerors. A newly embodied army, without cavalry marched to face the veteran bands of Russia and Prussia; but the genius of the Chief, and the valour of the young troops whom he commanded, made amends for all. The French had no cavalry; but bodies of infantry advanced in squares, flanked by an immense mass of artillery, presenting the appearance of so many moving fortresses. Eighty-four thousand infantry, consisting of French troops, or troops of the Confederation, with only '

4,000 cavalry, beat 107,000 Russians or Prussians, with more than 20,000 cavalry. Alexander and the King of Prussia witnessed the conflict in person. Their celebrated guards could not maintain their ground against our young conscripts. The enemy lost 18,000 men; our loss amounted to 12,000, and our want of cavalry prevented us from reaping the usual fruit of our conquests. However, the moral result of the victory was immense. The enthusiasm of our troops resumed its ascendency, and the Emperor recovered the full influence of opinion. The Allies retreated before him without venturing the chances of another battle.*

" On the 9th, Napoleon entered Dresden as a conqueror, conducting back to his capital the King of Saxony, who, from the consciousness of his own interests, as well as the wish to remain faithful to his engagements, had retired on the approach of the Allies, whose proposals he had constantly rejected.

" On the 21st and 22d, Napoleon again triumphed at Würtzen and Bautzen. The Allies had chosen their ground, which the brilliant campaigns of Frederick had rendered classic. They had intrenched themselves, and they thought their position impregnable: but every thing yielded to the grand views and well-conducted plans of the French general who, at the very commencement of the conflict, declared himself to be certain of the victory.

" The Allies lost 18,000 or 20,000 men. They were unable to retain their position, and they retired in disorder. The Emperor pursued them. He had already passed through Lusatia, crossed Silesia, and reached the

---

* At the victory of Lützen the Emperor sustained a severe loss in the death of the brave and loyal Marshal Bessières, Duke of Istria, who was so sincerely devoted to Napoleon. The King of Saxony raised a monument to his memory on the very spot where he received his death-blow. By a glorious coincidence the monument is similar to that of Gustavus Adolphus, and is placed not far distant from it. It consists of a simple stone surrounded by poplars. This is not the only instance in which foreigners have rendered that homage to the memory of brave Frenchmen, which their own countrymen have neglected.

Oder, when the Allies demanded an armistice to treat
for peace; and Napoleon, thinking the favourable moment had arrived, granted it.

"On the 4th of June, the armistice of Pleissvitz was
concluded. This event had the most decisive influence
in producing our misfortunes; it was the fatal knot to
which were attached all the chances and destinies of
the campaign.

"Should the Emperor have granted this armistice, or
have followed up his advantages? This was, at the moment, a problem which time, and the events that have
proved so fatal to us, solved when too late. The Emperor, crowned with victory, halted before his fallen enemies, to whom he could now make concessions without
compromising his dignity; his sacrifices could be regarded only as moderation. Austria, hitherto uncertain
as to what course she should pursue, struck with our
success, rejoined us. Napoleon now reasonably hoped
to see the ratification of a peace which he wished for,
and he would not let slip so favourable an opportunity,
to run the risk of a check that might have lost all, and
which was the more likely to take place since his army
had marched forward in haste and in the utmost disorder,
and his rear was uncovered and harassed by the enemy.
He conceived that the armistice, at all events, afforded
him an opportunity of concentrating and organizing his
forces, and opening his communications with France, by
which means he should be enabled to receive immense
reinforcements, and to create a corps of cavalry."

Unfortunately, in spite of all the Emperor's calculations, this fatal armistice proved advantageous only to our
enemies: it was maintained for nearly three months, and
it served only to bring about their triumph and our destruction. Austria, who was still our ally, by a deception, which history will justly characterize, availed herself
of that title to oppose us with the greater advantage.
Requiring delay, she obtained it. The Russians, who
were waiting for reinforcements, received them; the
Prussians doubled their numbers; the English subsidies
arrived, and the Swedish army rejoined. Secret associa-
tions were set on foot; a general insurrection of the

whole German population was excited; while, at the same time, the defection of the Cabinets of the Rhenish Confederation, and the corruption of the Allied officers, were effected. Treason also began to creep into the superior ranks. General Jomini, the Chief of the Staff of one of our army corps, went over to the enemy with all the information he had been able to collect respecting the plans of the campaign, &c.*

The result sufficiently proved to the Emperor all the errors of the armistice, and convinced him that he would have done better had he persisted in pressing forward; for had he continued successful, the Allies, alarmed at finding themselves deprived of the aid of Austria, with whom they could no longer have maintained intelligence, cut off from the Prince of Sweden, who would have remained behind, seeing blockades of the fortresses of the Oder raised, and the war carried back to Poland, to the gates of Dantzick, amidst a people ready to rise in a mass—the Allies, I say, would infallibly have treated. If, on the other hand, we had sustained a reverse, the consequences could not have been more fatal than those which were actually experienced. The judicious calculations of the Emperor ruined him: that which seemed to be indiscretion and temerity would probably have saved him.

CONGRESS OF PRAGUE ON THE 29TH OF JULY.—

"After two months of difficulties and obstacles, the Congress opened under the mediation of Austria; if, indeed, the term Congress can be properly applied to an assembly in which no deliberations took place, and where one party had determined beforehand that none should be held.

"The mediator and the adversaries were equally our enemies: all concurred in their hostility to us, and they had already decided on war. Why then did they wait? Because Austria still possessed a shade of modesty, and

---

* A reference to Count Montholon's Memoirs of Napoleon will shew that the Emperor admits the falsehood of this charge against Jomini, who he says was not even acquainted with his plans.

she wished, in the debates, to gain a pretence for declaring war against us. Prussia and Russia, on their part, thought it necessary to preserve their credit in Europe by this false manifestation of their desire and their efforts to preserve peace. All were merely affixing the seal to their Machiavelian system.

" For them the real Congress was not the assembly at Prague ; it had already taken place two months before. Time has since thrown into our hands the authentic records of the intrigues, machinations, and even treaties, in which they were engaged during that interval. It is now evident that the armistice was resorted to by pretended friends and avowed enemies, only for the sake of artfully cementing the union that was to effect the overthrow of Napoleon, and creating the triumvirate destined to oppress Europe while it pretended to deliver her.

" Austria had, from interested motives, long delayed the opening of the Congress of Prague. Resolved to repair her losses at any price, she did not hesitate to sacrifice her honour, the better to ensure her success She masked her perfidy under the disguise of friendship. Declaring herself our ally, and eagerly complimenting us on every new triumph, she insisted, with an air of the warmest interest, on being our mediatrix when she had already entered into an agreement to make common cause with our enemies. Her propositions were accepted. But she wished to gain time for her preparations ; and thus every day fresh obstacles were started, while the utmost tardiness was evinced in settling them.

" Austria at first offered her services as a mediatrix ; but, changing her tone in proportion as her warlike preparations advanced, she soon signified her wish to become an arbitress, at the same time intimating that she expected great advantages in return for the services she might render. At length, after an armistice of two months, when Austria thought herself perfectly prepared, and when every thing was agreed upon among the coalesced powers, they opened the Congress, not to treat of peace and to establish amicable relations, but to develop their real sentiments, and to insult us unreservedly. The Russians, in particular, behaved with unusual ill

VOL. III.—10

grace. They were no longer the Russians who anxiously solicited an armistice after the routs of Lützen, Würtzen, and Bautzen. They now looked upon themselves as the dictators of Europe, which, indeed, they have since really become, by the spirit of their diplomacy, the blindness of their allies, their geographical situation, and finally by the force of things. But whom did Alexander select as his minister to this Congress? Precisely one who, by personal circumstances, was, according to the laws of France, unqualified for such a post;—one who was by birth a Frenchman. Certainly it would have been difficult to offer a more personal and direct insult. Napoleon felt it; but he concealed his resentment.

"Under such circumstances much could not be expected from the Congress : during the few days of its sitting, our enemies merely drew up a series of notes more or less acrimonious, while the conduct of Austria was marked by the most odious partiality.

"On the 10th of August, only two days after the first meeting of the negotiators, the Russians and Prussians haughtily withdrew; and on the 12th, Austria, that faithful ally, that obsequious and devoted friend, who had shewn herself so eager to become our mediatrix and arbitress, suddenly laid aside those titles to declare war against us, allowing no interval save that required for the signature of the manifesto, which she had been for two months secretly concerting with her new allies, and which will ever remain a record of her shame and degradation, since it acknowledges the sacrifice of an Archduchess to the necessity of crouching before a detested ally. History will decide on these acts. However, to the honour of the throne and of morality, there is reason to believe that most of these transactions, and in particular the real course of affairs, was unknown to the Emperor Francis, who is reputed to be the most gentle, upright, moral, and pious of princes. It has been affirmed that many of these acts were determined on without his knowledge. and that others were represented to him under a totally false colouring. The whole of these disgraceful proceedings must be attributed to British gold to the craftiness of Russian diplomacy, and to the passions of the Austrian aristocracy, excited by the English faction which at that time ruled Europe.

" The Congress broke up with mutual feelings of irritation. The Emperor then expressed his sentiments in official and public documents, in the most forcible language, and in a tone of the highest superiority. But this he did with the view of creating a favourable impression on the public mind; for he remained so far master of himself as that, though hastening to take up arms, he nevertheless demanded a renewal of the negotiations, which were resumed at Prague. He deemed it advisable not to lose the advantages of constant communications : Austria would be easily detached if we obtained advantages, and she would be easily convinced if we sustained reverses. Such was the Congress of Prague.

" It will perhaps be asked whether Napoleon was duped by this Congress and the circumstances arising out of it. The answer is that he was not, or at least not entirely. If he had not a knowledge of every fact, he was never for a moment mistaken as to the intentions and sentiments that were really entertained.

" Napoleon, from the moment of his first victory at Lutzen, had authentically proposed a general congress. This he conceived to be the only means of treating for a general peace, insuring the independance of France, and the guarantee of the modern system. Every other mode of negotiation appeared to him merely a lure; and if he seemed to depart from this principle, in accepting the mediation of Austria, and agreeing to the conferences at Prague, it was because, as time advanced, affairs became more complicated. The defeat of Vittoria, the evacuation of Spain, and the spirit of the French people, which was declining, had considerably diminished his prosperity. He anticipated the result of the negotiations : but he wished to gain time, in his turn, and to await the course of events. He was not deceived as to the part which Austria would act; and, without knowing precisely how far she would carry her deception, he could well discern, from her mysterious conduct and delays, what was likely to be her determination. At Dresden, he had even had personal conversations with the first negotiator of the

Austrian government, who had sufficiently .ndicated the
line of conduct he intended to pursue.   The Emperor
having remarked that he had, after all, eight hundred
thousand men to oppose the enemy, the negotiator
eagerly added, 'Your Majesty may say twelve hundred
thousand; for you may, if you please, join our force to
your own.'   But what was to be the price of this advantage ? Nothing less than the restitution of Illyria, the
cession of the Duchy of Warsaw, the frontier of the
Inn, &c. 'And after all,' said the Emperor, 'what should
I have gained by this ? Had we made all these concessions,
should we not have been humbling ourselves for nothing,
and furnishing Austria with the means of making farther
demands, and afterwards opposing us with greater advantage ?' He never relinquished the idea that the true
interests of Austria being closely connected with our
danger, we should be more certain of regaining her by
our misfortunes than of securing her by our concessions.
Napoleon was therefore deaf to every demand; but he
had so little doubt of the engagements which Austria
had already contracted with our enemies that he is
described as having said, half good-humouredly and half
indignantly, to the Austrian negotiator: 'Come now,
confess: tell me how much they have paid you for
this.'"

How severely did Napoleon suffer on this occasion !
What trials of patience did he not undergo ! And yet he
was accused at the time of not wishing for peace ! " How
was I perplexed," said he, " when conversing on this
subject, to find myself the only one to judge of the extent
of our danger and to adopt means to avert it.   I was
harassed on the one hand by the coalesced Powers, who
threatened our very existence, and on the other by the
spirit of my own subjects, who in their blindness, seemed
to make common cause with them; by our enemies, who
were labouring for my destruction, and by the importunities of my people and even my Ministers, who urged
me to throw myself on the mercy of foreigners.   And I
was obliged to keep up a bold look in this embarrassing
situation: to reply haughtily to some, and sharply to
rebuff others, who created difficulties in my rear, en-

couraged the mistaken course of public opinion, instead
of seeking to give it a proper direction, and suffered me
to be tormented by demands for peace, when they ought
to have proved that the only means of obtaining it was
to urge me ostensibly to war.

"However, my determination was fixed. I awaited
the result of events, firmly resolved to enter into no
concessions or treaties which could present only a tem-
porary reparation, and would inevitably have been attended
by fatal consequences. Any middle course must have
been dangerous; there was no safety except in victory,
which would have preserved my power, or in some
catastrophe, which would have brought back my allies."

I beg to call the reader's attention to this last idea,
which I have already noticed on a former occasion. It
will perhaps be thought I attach great importance to it;
but this is because I feel the necessity of rendering it
intelligible. Though 1 now enter into it completely, yet
it was long before I understood it, and it appeared to me
paradoxical and subtle.

"In what a situation was I placed!" continued the
Emperor. "I saw that France, her destinies, her
principles, depended on me alone!"—"Sire!" I ventured
to observe, "this was the opinion generally entertained;
and yet some parties reproached you for it, exclaiming,
with bitterness, Why would he connect every thing with
himself personally?"—"That was a vulgar accusation,"
resumed the Emperor warmly. "My situation was not
one of my own choosing, nor did it arise out of any
fault of mine; it was produced entirely by the nature and
force of circumstances—by the conflict of two opposite
orders of things. Would the individuals who held this
language, if indeed they were sincere, have preferred to
go back to the period preceding Brumaire, when our
internal dissolution was complete, foreign invasion
certain, and the destruction of France inevitable? From
the moment when we decided on the concentration of
power, which could alone save us; when we determined
on the unity of doctrines and resources which rendered
us a mighty nation, the destinies of France depended
solely on the character, the meas res, and the principles

of him whom she had invested with this accidental dictatorship: from that moment the public welfare, *the State,
was myself*. These words, which I addressed to men
who were capable of understanding them, were strongly
censured by the narrow-minded and ill-disposed; but
the enemy felt the full force of them, and, therefore, his
first object was to effect my overthrow. The same outcry was raised against other words which I uttered in
the sincerity of my heart: when I said that *France had
more need of me than I of her*. This profound truth
was declared to be merely excess of vanity. But, my
dear Las Cases, you now see that I can relinquish every
thing; and as to what I endure here, my sufferings
cannot be long. My life is limited; but the existence
of France . . . . ! " Then, resuming his former idea,
he said: " The circumstances in which we were placed
were extraordinary and unprecedented; it would be vain
to seek for any parallel to them. I was myself the key-
stone of an edifice totally new, and raised on a slight
foundation ! Its stability depended on each of my battles!
Had I been conquered at Marengo, France would have
encountered all the disasters of 1814 and 1815, without
those prodigies of glory which succeeded, and which
will be immortal. It was the same at Austerlitz and
Jena, and again at Eylau and elsewhere. The vulgar
failed not to blame my ambition as the cause of all these
wars. But they were not of my choosing; they were
produced by the nature and force of events; they arose
out of that conflict between the past and the future—
that constant and permanent coalition of our enemies,
which obliged us to subdue under pain of being subdued."

But to return to the negotiations of 1813. On a reference to the documents and manifestoes published at
the time by the two parties, whether because we can now
peruse them with more impartiality, or because our eyes
have been opened by the conduct of those who triumphed,
it is impossible to avoid feeling astonished at the two-
fold error which led the Germans to rise so furiously
against him from whose yoke they pretended to free
themselves, and in favour of those whom they expected
to become their regenerators !

Renewal of Hostilities—Battle of Dresden—26th and 27th of August.—" The hostile powers again presented themselves on the field of battle. The French, with a force of 300,000, of which 40,000 were cavalry, occupied the heart of Saxony, on the left bank of the Elbe; ar.d the Allies, with 500,000 men, of whom 100,000 were cavalry, threatened them in three different directions, from Berlin, Silesia, and Bohemia, on Dresden. This prodigious disproportion of numbers had no effect on Napoleon : he concentrated his forces, and boldly assumed the offensive. Having fortified the line of the Elbe, which had now become his *point d'appui*, and, protecting his extreme right by the mountains of Bohemia, he directed one of his masses on Berlin against Bernadotte, who commanded an army of Prussians and Swedes, while another marched upon Silesia, against Blucher, who commanded a corps composed of Prussians and Russians, and a third was stationed at Dresden, as the key of the position, to observe the great Austrian and Russian army in Bohemia. Finally, a fourth mass was placed as a reserve, at Zittau, with the threefold object :—1st, to penetrate into Bohemia, in case we should gain advantages over Blucher; 2d, to keep the great body of the allied force confined in Bohemia, through the fear of being attacked on their rear, should they attempt to debouch by the banks of the Elbe; 3d, to assist, if necessary, in assailing Blucher, or in the defence of Dresden; in case that city should be attacked.

" The Emperor, who had already made a rapid movement against Blucher, kept him in action before him, when he was suddenly called away for the defence of Dresden, where 65,000 French troops found themselves opposed to 180,000 of the allied forces. Prince Schwartzenberg, the General-in-chief, had on the 26th made a faint attack upon Dresden, instead of making a precipitate and decided assault; which, it was affirmed, was the intention of the deserter Jomini, who so well understood the real state of things. Napoleon came up with the rapidity of lightning and he combined a force of 100,000 French troops to oppose the 180,000 Allies. The affair was not for a moment doubtful; and to his sagacity and penetration the whole success must be attributed. The enemy was overwhelmed: he lost 40,000 men, and was for some time threatened with total destruction. The Emperor Alexander was present at the battle, and Moreau was killed by one of the first balls fired by our imperial guard, only a short time after he had spoken with the Russian Emperor.*

The happy chance, so anxiously looked for by Napoleon, which was expected to re-establish our affairs, to procure peace, and to save France, had at length arrived. Accordingly, on the ensuing day, Austria despatched an agent to the Emperor with amicable propositions. But such is the uncertainty of human destiny! From that moment, by an unexampled fatality, Napoleon had to encounter a chain of disasters. At every point, except that at which he was himself present, we sustained reverses. Our army in Silesia lost 25,000 men in opposing Blucher; the force which attacked Berlin was defeated by the Prince of Sweden with great loss; and finally, nearly the whole of Vandamme's corps, which, after the victory of Dresden, was sent into Bohemia with the view of assailing the enemy's rear and accomplishing his destruction, being abandoned to itself and to the temerity of its chief, was cut in pieces by that part of the Allied army which was precipitately falling back. This fatal disaster and the safety of the Austrians, were owing to a sudden indisposition of Napoleon's, who, at the moment, was supposed to have been poisoned. His presence no longer excited the ardour of the different corps in maintaining the pursuit; indecision and dejection ensued; Vandamme's force was destroyed, and all the fruit of the splendid victory of Dresden was lost!

After these repeated checks, the spell was broken; the spirit of the French troops became depressed, while that of the Allies was the more highly excited. The hostile forces were now to be estimated only by their numerical

---

* The death of the celebrated Moreau, while fighting under the Russian banner, and opposed to a French army, was and will ever continue to be a source of affliction to his sincerest friends and warmest partizans.

value; and a catastrophe seemed to be at hand. Napoleon, in despair, made vain efforts; he hastened to every threatened point, and was immediately called away by some new disaster. Wherever he appeared, the Allies retreated before him; and they advanced again as soon as his back was turned. Meanwhile, all the enemy's masses were constantly gaining ground; they had effected communications with each other, and they now formed a semicircle, which was gradually closing round the French, who were driven back upon the Elbe, and threatened completely to surround them. On the other hand, our rear, which was uncovered, was assailed by detached parties. The kingdom of Westphalia was in open insurrection; our convoys were intercepted, and we could no longer maintain free communications with France.

It was in this state of things that the negotiators of Prague submitted to the Emperor the result of their new conferences. In addition to numerous restitutions required from Napoleon and his allies, two propositions were made: 1st, the surrender of all the influence and acquisitions of France in Italy; 2nd, the resignation of the French influence and acquisitions in Germany. Napoleon was to take his choice of one of these two divisions of power; but the other was to be consigned to the Allies, to be entirely at their disposal, without any interference on his part. Neither friends nor enemies entertained a doubt that Napoleon would eagerly accept these proposals. "For," said those about him, "if you choose Italy, you remain at the gates of Vienna, and the Allies will soon dispute among themselves respecting the division of Germany. If, on the contrary, you prefer the surrender of Italy, you will thereby secure the friendship of Austria, to whose share it will fall, and you will remain in the heart of Germany. In either case you will soon re-appear in the character of a mediator, or a ruler." Napoleon, however, was not of this opinion: he rejected the propositions, and persisted in following up his own ideas.

Certainly, said he to himself, such proposals in themselves, and in the natural course of things, are most

10*

acceptable; but where is the guarantee of their sincerity? He saw plainly that the Allies were only endeavouring to lure him into the snare. They determined
thenceforth to abide neither by faith nor law. They did
not conceive themselves bound by any law of nations, or
any rule of integrity in their conduct towards us. In
opposition to the suggestions of his counsellors, Napoleon said; "If I relinquish Germany, Austria will but
contend the more perseveringly until she obtains Italy.
If, on the other hand, I surrender Italy to her, she will,
:n order to secure the possession of it, endeavour to expel
me from Germany. Thus, one concession granted will
only serve as an inducement for seeking or enforcing new
ones. The first stone of the edifice being removed, the
downfall of the whole will inevitably ensue. I shall be
urged on from one concession to another, until I am
driven back to the Tuileries, whence the French people,
enraged at my weakness, and blaming me for their
disasters will doubtless banish me, and perhaps justly,
though they may themselves immediately become the
prey of foreigners."

May not this be regarded as a literal prediction of the
events which succeeded the insidious declaration of
Frankfort, the propositions of Chatillon, &c. ?

" It would be a thousand times better to perish in
battle amidst the fury of the enemy's triumph," continued the Emperor; "for even defeats leave behind
them the respect due to adversity, when they are attended
by magnanimous perseverance. I therefore prefer to
give battle ; for, if I should be conquered, we still have
with us the true political interests of the majority of our
enemies. But, if I should be victorious, I may save all.
I have still chances in my favour—I am far from
despairing."

Intended movement on Berlin. — " In this state of
things, the King of Bavaria, the chief of the Confederation of the Rhine, wrote to the Emperor, assuring him,
confidentially, that he would continue his alliance for six
weeks longer. " This was long enough," said Napoleon,
" to render it very probable that he would no longer find
it necessary to abandon us." He determined imme-

diately to attempt a great movement, which he had long contemplated, and which plainly indicates the resources of his enterprising mind. Pressed upon the Elbe, the right bank of which was already lined by the great mass of the Allied force, and nearly turned on his rear, he conceived the bold idea of changing positions with the enemy, place for place; to penetrate the enemy's line, to form in his rear, and compel him to pass in his turn, with his whole force, to the left bank of the river. If, in this situation, he abandoned his communications with France, he would have in his rear the enemy's territory, a tract of country not yet ravaged by war, and which was capable of maintaining his troops, Berlin, Branden-burg, and Mecklenburg, he would recover his fortresses, with their immense garrisons, the separation and the loss of which would be a great fault after a reverse of fortune,. and would be regarded as resources of genius in case of triumph. Napoleon now looked forward to new combi-nations, and a new prospect of future success: he beheld before him only the errors, the astonishment, and the stupor of his enemies, and the brilliancy of his own enterprise and his hopes.

Battles of Leipsic, (16th, 18th, and 19th Oct.)—" At first fortune seemed to smile on the Emperor. But soon a letter from the King of Würtemberg informed him that the Bavarian army, seduced by the intrigues and the prevailing spirit of the moment, had joined the Austrians, against whom it was intended to be opposed; that it was marching on the Rhine to cut off the communication with France; and that the King of Würtemburg was himself under the necessity of yielding to circumstances. This unexpected event obliged Napoleon to suspend his preparations, and to fall back, in order to secure his retreat. This complication of false movements proved servicable to the Allies, who pressed and surrounded us: a great battle seemed inevitable. Napoleon assembled his forces in the plains of Leipsic. His army consisted of 157,000 men, and six hundred pieces of artillery; but the Allies possessed 1000 pieces of artillery, and 350,000 men. During the first day, the action was furiously maintained: The French remained triumphant and the

victory would have been decisive, if one of the corps
stationed at Dresden had taken part in the battle, as the
Emperor hoped it would.   General Merfeld was taken
prisoner, but liberated on parole, with an intimation that
the Emperor was at length willing to renounce Germany.
But the Allies, who were encouraged by the arrival of
an immense reinforcement, resumed the engagement on
the following day ; and they were now so numerous
that, when their troops were exhausted, they were regularly relieved by fresh corps, as on the parade.   The
most inconceivable fatality was now combined with in-
equality of numbers ; the most infamous treachery
unexpectedly broke out in our ranks ; the Saxons, our
allies, deserted us, went over to the enemy, and turned
their artillery against us.   Still, however, the presence
of mind, energy, and skill of the French general, together
with the courage of our troops, made amends for all, and
we again remained masters of the field.

" These two terrible engagements, which history will
rec rd as battles of giants, had cost the enemy 150,000
of his best troops, 50,000 of whom lay dead on the field
of battle.   Our loss amounted to 50,000 only.   Thus the
difference between our forces was considerably diminished : and a third engagement presented itself, with
changes much more favourable.   But our ammunition
was exhausted ; our parks contained no more than 16,000
charges ; we had fired 220,000 during the two preceding
days.   We were compelled to make arrangements for
our retreat, which commenced during the night, on
Leipsic.   At day-break the Allies assailed us ; they
entered Leipsic along with us, and an engagement commenced in the streets of the city.   Our rear-guard was
defending itself valiantly and without sustaining great
loss, when a fatal occurrence ruined all : the only bridge
across the Elster, by which our retreat could be effected,
was, by some accident or misunderstanding, blown up.
Thus all our forces on the Leipsic bank of the river were
lost, and all on the opposite bank marched in haste and
disorder upon Mentz.   At Hanau we were compelled to
force a passage through 50,000 Bavarian troops.   Only
the wrecks of our army returned to France ; and, to

render the misfortune complete, they brought contagion along with them."

Such was the fatal campaign of Saxony, our last national effort, the tomb of our gigantic power. Opposed to the united efforts of all the forces of Europe, and in spite of all the chances that were accumulated against us, the genius of a single man had, in the course of this campaign, been four times on the point of restoring our ascendancy, and cementing it by peace : after the victories of Lützen and Bautzen, after the battle of Dresden, at the time of the last movement on Berlin, and finally on the plains of Leipsic.

Napoleon failed only by a complication of fatalities and perfidies, of which history furnishes no example. I here note down only those which occur to me on a retrospective view of the events of this period.

FATALITIES.

(A.) Sudden indisposition of Napoleon.

(B.) Unexpected overflow of the Bober.

(C.) Confidential letter from the King of Bavaria.

(D.) Orders which did not reach the corps at Dresden.

(E.) Deficiency of ammunition after the two battles of Leipsic.

(F.) Blowing up of the bridge across the Elster.

PERFIDIES.

(G.) Machinations and bad faith of Austria, the first and true cause of our disasters.

(H.) Violation of the armistice of Pleisswitz, relative to our blockaded fortresses.

(I.) Desertion of the chief of the staff of the 3d corps.

(K.) Defection of the Bavarian government.

(L.) Treachery of the Saxons.

(M.) Violation of the capitulation of Dresden, &c.

The following are a few lines of explanation :—

(A.) After the victory of Dresden, some one complimented Napoleon on his great success. "Oh! this is nothing," observed he, while his countenance beamed with satisfaction; " Vandamme is in their rear, it is there that we must look for the great result." The Emperor was proceeding in person to assist in accomplishing this decisive operation, when, unfortunately, after one of his meals, he was seized with so violent a retching, that he was supposed to have been poisoned, and it was found necessary to convey him back to Dresden. Thus the operations were interrupted. The fatal consequences that ensued are well known. How trivial was the cause, and how calamitous were the results !

(B.) A sudden overflow of the Bober in Silesia was the principal cause of the disasters of Marshal Macdonald. His corps, while in full operation. were overtaken by the flood. which impeded their operations, and caused the terrible losses which have been above described.

(C.) About the end of September, the King of Bavaria addressed a confidential letter to Napoleon, stating that he would maintain his alliance with him for six weeks or two months longer; and that during that interval he would obstinately refuse every advantage that might be held out to him. The Emperor, who was placed in a most critical situation, and who, but for this circumstance, might, perhaps, have lent an ear to the propositions that were made to him, now no longer hesitated, but immediately determined on the bold movement which he had contemplated on Berlin. He conceived that six weeks would be sufficient to change the state of affairs, and to remove the fears of his allies. Unfortunately, military intrigues proved more powerful than the wishes of the King of Bavaria. Napoleon was forced to suspend his movement, and to give battle at Leipsic with disadvantage. The consequences have already been seen.

(D.) Napoleon, in making his arangements for the battles of Leipsic, had relied on a diversion of those corps of the army which he had left in Dresden. Their co-operation might have rendered the victory decisive, and have given a new turn to affairs. But, unfortunately the enemy's force was so numerous, and we were so completely surrounded, that the Emperor's orders could not be transmitted to Dresden

(F.) After the two terrible engagements at Leipsic, the
French were effecting their retreat across the Elster by a
single bridge. An officer who was stationed to guard it
was ordered to blow it up if the enemy should present
himself in pursuit of our rear-guard. Unluckily this
officer was, by some mistake or other, informed that the
Emperor wanted him. He immediately obeyed the sum-
mons, and in his absence a corporal of sappers, at the
first sight of some detached Russian corps, fired the train
and blew up the bridge, thus dooming to perdition that
portion of our force which still remained on the Leipsic
bank of the river. The whole of our rear-guard and
baggage, two hundred pieces of artillery, and thirty
thousand prisoners (stragglers, wounded and sick), fell
into the hands of the enemy.

On the publication of the bulletins containing this
intelligence, a general outcry was raised by the discontented party in Paris. It was asserted that the whole
was a fabrication, and that the Emperor himself had
ordered the blowing up of the bridge, with a view to
ensure his own safety at the expense of the rest of the
army. It was in vain to refer to the statement of the
officer, who confirmed the fact, while he attempted to
justify himself. This was declared to be another fabrication or a piece of complaisance on the part of the officer.
Such was the language of the time.*

---

* When I visited London in 1814, public attention was occupied
by the recent events of the Continent, and the battle of Leipsic was
the general topic of conversation. It was related that, at the
moment of the defeat, Napoleon's presence of mind completely forsook him. He wandered about the city, and lost his way in a
lonely street. Though on horseback, faintness obliged him to support himself against a wall, and in this situation he inquired his way
of an old woman, and asked her for a glass of water. The blowing up
of the bridge was not forgotten, and the story was related precisely as
at Paris. These details, which were echoed in the drawing-rooms,
and circulated about the streets, were credited among the higher
ranks, as well as by the vulgar. Prints, representing the different
events of the battle, were exhibited in the shop-windows. The subject of one of these engravings was the above described incident in
the street of Leipsic. Such a multitude of absurdities was circulated
that people of common sense had no resource but to shrug up their
shoulders and patiently endure all that they heard

(G.) The duplicity and bad faith of Austria, the numerous contradictions between her acts and her professions, have already been mentioned. Unmindful of the generosity of which she had been the object after the battles of Leoben, Austerlitz, and Wagram, she discharged her debt of gratitude according to the rules of policy, by eagerly seizing the opportunity of repairing her losses at any price.

She ruined us by making us consent to the armistice of Pleisswitz; and her conduct was the more odious, as she was determined to make war against us; and a few days afterwards, though still our friend and ally, and offering herself as a mediatrix, she entered into engagements hostile to us. Her participation in the conventions of Rechembach about the middle of June, and in the conferences of Trachenbergh, at the commencement of July, is now well known. The necessity of maintaining a certain appearance of decorum occasioned these matters to be kept a secret for about a month after the commencement of hostilities. They were at first proposed to Francis merely as eventual and precautionary measures; and he was induced to affix his signature to them only by the representations of his ministers, who described Napoleon as the scourge of mankind, and attributed to him the delays in the opening of the Congress, which in reality were occasioned by themselves. (*Montveran*, vol. vi. p. 262.)

But, in spite of the conduct of Austria, Napoleon still cherished the hope of seeing her resume her alliance with him; not that he could calculate on any misunderstanding between her and the other co lesced Powers, but because he supposed her to be sufficiently clear-sighted with respect to her own interests. This idea never forsook him until the moment of signing his abdication.*

---

* This supposition was not altogether ill-founded; for it still remains doubtfu whether the consent of Austria to the dethronement of the Emperor was compulsory or voluntary. By one of those fatalities which attended the close of Napoleon's career, a momentary success separated the Austrians and the Russians, and the order for marching upon Paris, as well as the famous declaration proscribing Napoleon and his family, proceeded solely from

(H.) The fortresses occupied by French troops in those places which were in the possession of the Allied forces, were to have a clear circuit of one league, and to receive supplies of provisions every five days; but this article was not honestly fulfilled.

When the Armistice was prolonged, the French commissaries demanded that officers of their army should be sent to the commanders of the fortresses; but the Russian General-in-chief objected to this, and circumstances were such that we were obliged to give up the point. (*Montveran*, vol. vi. p. 270.)

(I.) The chief of the staff of the 3d corps, a Swiss by birth, but educated in our ranks, went over to the enemy a few days before the renewal of hostilities, taking with him all the information he could collect. For this service the Emperor of Russia rewarded him with particular favour and made him one of his Aides-de-camp. It has been said that this officer, who was possessed of great talent, had reason to complain of some injustice; but can any thing palliate such an act, or remove the disgrace attending it?

(K.) Part of Napoleon's plan of Campaign was that the Bavarian army, stationed on the Danube, should act in concert with the army of Italy stationed in Illyria, and that their combined efforts should be directed upon Vienna. The important effect which these measures must have produced on the fate of the Campaign may be easily conceived. But the chief of the Bavarian army, under some pretence or other, but in reality because he had entered into an understanding with the enemy, remained constantly inactive, and thus paralyzed the efforts of the Viceroy, who had to oppose the great bulk of the Austrian force. It has already been stated that the open defection of the Bavarians, at the most critical moment of the campaign, mainly contributed to bring about our disasters.

(L.) But nothing equalled the infamous and disgraceful treachery of the Saxons, who, though they were then

_____

Alexander. When Francis presented himself, he had no alternative but to give his assent to measures which were already determined on; but many circumstances induce the belief that he did so with great repugnance and dissatisfaction.

serving in our ranks and were our companions in danger
and glory suddenly turned against us. Whatever might
be the fatal effects of their desertion, the disgrace
attached to themselves is greater than all the mischief
they occasioned to us.

The conduct of Napoleon during this period, when he
was described as a monster of deception and bad faith
presents, on the contrary, an example of singular magnanimity.

He had added a corps of Saxons to his Imperial
guard; but, on the desertion of their countrymen, he
ranged them round their Sovereign, whom he left at
Leipsic,* releasing him from all his engagements.   There
were also some Bavarians in his army, and he wrote to
their chief, informing him that, Bavaria having disloy-
ally declared war against him, this circumstance would
authorize him in disarming and detaining prisoners all
the Bavarians in his service; but that such a measure
would destroy the confidence which Napoleon wished
that the troops under his orders should repose in him.
He therefore ordered them to be supplied with provisions, and dismissed.†

(M.) I have before me the notes of a distinguished
officer relative to the capitulation of Dresden.   Estimat-
ing the number of troops which we had left behind us
in the fortresses from which we were separated, he
concludes that they must have amounted altogether to
177,000. The Emperor had but 157,000 men at Leipsic.   How different, therefore, might have been our

---

* The venerable and faithful King of Saxony followed his ally
Napoleon, at whose head-quarters he established himself.   The
coalesced powers, on their entrance into Leipsic, seized the person
of the King, and announced their design of disposing of his states.
His misfortunes are known throughout Europe; they excited a
deep interest in every generous heart

† Amidst the general disloyalty, the conduct of the King of
Würtemburg presents an honourable exception.   That prince,
though already at war with us, broke the brigade of cavalry, and
the corps of infantry, who went over to the enemy, and at
the same time withdrew the decoration of his Order from their
officers.

fate, had those masses, or even a portion of them, been at his disposal in this decisive event. But this unfortunate dispersion was occasioned by extraordinary circumstances, and was not the result of any regular system. The following particulars, relative to the violation of the capitulation of Dresden, are literally quoted from the notes above alluded to :—

" Above all, it is necessary to understand that it was determined in the plan of the coalition against France, of which Prince Schwartzenberg had the credit, that according as offers were made for the capitulation of each of our numerous garrisons, the conditions should be fairly and honourably granted, but without any intention of fulfilling them. This point being established, the reason of the refusal of the capitulation, signed at Dresden by Marshal St.-Cyr and Generals Tolstoy and Klenau, was, that Prince Schwartzenberg could not ratify it, because the Count de Lobau, Napoleon's aide-de-camp, who was shut up in Dresden with the Marshal, had protested against the capitulation. Some time after, the capitulation of Dantzick, with General Rapp, was declined, under the odiously false pretence that the garrison of Dresden, in spite of the conditions of its capitulation, had entered into service immediately on its arrival at Strasburg, and that, in consequence, the capitulation of Dantzick could not be approved without incurring the risk of similar inconveniences.

" The following is an additional proof of the bad faith of the Allies. The garrison of Dresden, which was composed of two *corps d'armée*, forming altogether 45,000 men, capitulated on the 11th of November.*

---

* The determination to surrender had been far from unanimous in the garrison. Opinions were divided on this point. Some were for returning to France by means of a capitulation, which course was adopted ; others were in favour of an enterprise of a much bolder nature. This was nothing less than to quit Dresden, with the chosen troops of the garrison, to descend the Elbe by successively raising the blockade of Torgau, where there were 28,000 men ; of Wittemberg, where there were 5000 ; of Magdeburg, where there were 20,000, and to proceed to Hamburg where there were 32,000. The army thus collected together, which would have amounted to 60 or 80,000 men, was

"According to the terms of the capitulation, the French were to evacuate the fortress in six columns and in six successive days, and to repair to Strasburgh.

"This capitulation was fulfilled, so far at least as regarded our evacuation of the fortress and its occupation by the enemy; but our sixth column had scarcely made a day's march from the town when it was announced that the capitulation was declined and rejected by the General-in-chief, Prince Schwartzenberg, by an order of the 19th of November.

"When Marshal Saint-Cyr remonstrated against this conduct, it was proposed, by way of compensation for the injustice, that he should be permitted to re-enter Dresden with his troops, and be again placed in possession of all the means of defence which he had before the capitulation : this was merely a piece of irony.

"In vain did the Marshal negotiate for the literal fulfilment of the articles agreed upon by Count Klenau, who had full powers for so doing; the unfortunate garrison, broken up and dispersed, was under the necessity of repairing to the different cantonments that were assigned to it in Bohemia, instead of pursuing its march towards the Rhine.

"The Marshal, indignant at this flagrant breach of

---

to repair to France, cutting a passage through the enemy's ranks, or compelling him to retrograde by manœuvring on his rear; while the levies in mass that might have advanced to assail our veteran bands would have been paralyzed. And even had this plan failed, the issue was not likely to be more fatal than the capitulation. This opinion was warmly advocated by the Count de Lobau, Generals Teste, Mouton-Duvernet, and others. The design was grand, worthy of our glory, and quite in harmony with our past acts. It was the Emperor's intention to carry it into effect, and for this purpose he issued orders, which, however, did not reach the place of their destination. The despair occasioned by the thought of surrendering was such that a portion of the troops urged the officer who was at the head of the opposing party to take the command upon himself. Respect for discipline at length prevailed over enthusiasm; but the officer above alluded to expressed himself in the most violent way in the council. It is said that, in his indignation, he exclaimed to the General-in-chief;—"The Emperor will tell me that, pistol in hand, I ought to have taken the command upon myself."

faith, despatched a superior officer to communicate the
circumstance to Napoleon; but the Allies retarded his
progress under various pretences, and he did not reach
Paris until the 18th of December. Subsequent events
had by this time rendered the evil past all remedy."

After the series of deceptions and perfidies which I
have here disclosed, and which the Allies had established
as a system, it is not surprising that Napoleon should
have placed no reliance on the famous declaration of
Frankfort, and that he should have felt indignant at the
blindness of our Legislative Body, the committee of
which, either from evil designs or mistaken views, completed the ruin of affairs. Napoleon assured me that he
was several times on the point of summoning the
members of this committee before him, in order to
consult with them confidentially and sincerely on the real
state of things, and the imminent danger with which we
were threatened. Sometimes he thought that he should
undoubtedly bring them back to a right sense of their
duty; sometimes, on the contrary, he feared that obstinacy of opinion, or mischievous intention, might have
involved the affair in controversy, which, considering
the spirit of the moment, would have weakened our
resources and hastened our dissolution.

The Emperor frequently adverted to this critical point
in the destinies of France; but I have hitherto refrained
from entering upon the detail of a subject which presents
nothing either agreeable or consolatory

BENEVOLENT ACTIONS PERFORMED BY THE EMPEROR.—
HIS VISIT TO AMSTERDAM.—OBSERVATIONS ON THE
DUTCH, &C.—THE MASSACRES OF THE THIRD OF
SEPTEMBER.—REMARKS ON REVOLUTIONS IN GENE-
RAL.—UNHAPPY FATE OF LOUIS XVI.

3rd. About three o'clock, the Emperor sent for me
to attend him in his chamber. He had just finished
dressing; and, as it was raining at the time, he went
into the drawing-room, where he communicated to me
some very curious particulars, which, as it may be supposed, concerned him, and in which I played a conspicuous part.

Some time afterwards the Emperor took a turn on the lawn contiguous to his library; but, finding the wind very violent, he soon returned to the house and played at billiards, a thing which he very seldom thought of doing.

In the course of the day, the Emperor related that, as he was once travelling with the Empress, he stopped to breakfast in one of the islands in the Rhine. There was a small farm house in the neighbourhood, and while he was at breakfast he sent for the peasant to whom it belonged, and desired him to ask boldly for whatever he thought would render him happy; and, in order to inspire him with the greater confidence, the Emperor made him drink several glasses of wine. The peasant, who was more prudent and less limited in his choice than the man described in the story of the three wishes, without hesitation specified the object which he was ambitious to possess. The Emperor commanded the prefect of the district immediately to provide him with what he had made choice of, and the expense attending the gratification of his wish did not exceed 6 or 7000 francs.

Napoleon added that, on another occasion, when he was sailing in a yacht in Holland, he entered into conversation with the steersman, and asked him how much his vessel was worth. "My vessel!" said the man, "it is not mine; I should be too happy if it were, it would make my fortune."—"Well, then," said the Emperor, "I make you a present of it;" a favour for which the man seemed not particularly grateful. His indifference was imputed to the phlegmatic temperament natural to his countrymen; but this was not the case. "What benefit has he conferred on me?" said he to one of his comrades who was congratulating him; "he has spoken to me, and that is all; he has given me what was not his own to give—a fine present truly!" In the mean time Duroc had purchased the vessel of the owner, and the receipt was put into the hands of the steersman, who, no longer doubting the reality of his good fortune, indulged in the most extravagant demonstrations of joy. The expense of this purchase was about the same as that attending the present made to the countryman. "Thus," said the Emperor, "it is evident that human wishes are not so

immoderate as they are generally supposed, and that it is
not so very difficult to render people happy! These two
men undoubtedly found themselves completely happy."

When the Emperor visited Amsterdam, the people, he
said, were very hostile to him; but he soon completely
ingratiated himself in the public favour. He declined
being attended by any other guard than the guard of
honour belonging to the city; and this mark of confidence
immediately gained him the esteem of the Dutch. He
constantly appeared among every class of citizens. On
one occasion he addressed a crowd of people in the following blunt manner:—" It is said that you are discontented—but why? France has not conquered, but adopted, you: you are excluded from no benefits which are
enjoyed by the French; you are a portion of the same
family, and participate in all its advantages. Consider
now: I have selected my Prefects, Chamberlains, and
Councillors of State from amongst you in a just proportion to the amount of your population, and I have augmented my guard with your Dutch guard. You complain
of distress; but, in this respect, France has still greater
reason to be dissatisfied. We all suffer, and we must
continue to do so until the common enemy, the tyrant of
the sea, the vampire of your trade, shall be brought to
reason. You complain of the sacrifices you have made;
but come to France and see all that you still possess
beyond what we do, and then, perhaps, you will deem
yourselves less unfortunate. Why not raher congratulate
yourselves on the circumstances that have brought about
your union with France. In the present state of Europe,
what would you be, if left to yourselves?—The slaves of
all the world. Instead of which, identified as you are
with France, you will one day possess the whole trade of
the great Empire." Then, assuming a tone of gaiety, he
said:—" I have done every thing in my power to please
you. Have I not sent you as a Governor precisely the
man who suits you—the good and pacific Lebrun. You
condole with him, he condoles with you: you bewail your
distresses together. What more could I do for you?"
At these words the assembly burst into a loud fit of
laughter. The Emperor had secured the good graces of

the multitude.—" However," said he, " let us hope that
the present state of things will not last long. Believe
me, I am as anxious for a change as you can be. Every
man of discernment among you must be aware that it is
neither my wish, nor for my interest, that matters should
remain as they now are."

The Emperor left the people of Amsterdam full of
enthusiasm for him ; and he, on his part, carried away
impressions decidedly in their favour. Previously to his
journey he had often complained that whosoever he sent
to Holland immediately became a Dutchman. After his
return, that circumstance occurred to his recollection in
the Council of State, and he said that he had himself
become a Dutchman. One day, when a member of the
Council spoke slightingly of the Dutch, the Emperor said,
" Gentlemen, you may be more agreeable than they; but
I can wish you nothing better than to be possessed of their
moral qualities."

After dinner, some one happened to mention the
date of the day, the 3rd of September ; upon which the
Emperor made some very remarkable observations ;
among which were the following :—"This," said he, " is
the anniversary of horrid and appalling executions, of a
repetition, in miniature, of Saint - Bartholomew's day :
less disgraceful, certainly, because fewer victims were
sacrificed, and because the atrocities were not committed
under the sanction of the Government, which, on the
contrary, used its endeavours to punish the crime. It
was committed by the mob of Paris ; an unbridled power,
which rivalled, and even controlled, the Legislature.

' The atrocities of the 3rd of September were the result of fanaticism rather than of absolute brutality : the
authors of the massacres put to death one of their own
party, for having committed theft during the executions.
This dreadful event," continued the Emperor, " arose
out of the force of circumstances and the spirit of the
moment. No political change ever takes place unattended by popular fury ; the people are never exposed
to danger, without committing disorders and sacrificing
victims. The Prussians entered the French territory ;
and the people, before they advanced to meet them, re-

solved to take revenge on their adherents in Paris.
Probably, this circumstance was not without its influence
on the safety of France. Who can doubt that if, during
recent events, the friends of the invaders had been the
victims of similar horrors, France would have fallen
under the yoke of foreigners? But this could not have
happened, for we had become legitimate. The duration
of authority, our victories, our treaties, the re-establishment of our old manners, had rendered our government
regular. We could not plunge into the same horrors
as had been committed by the multitude: for my part,
I neither could nor would be a King of the mob.

" No social revolution ever takes place unaccompanied
by violence. Every revolution of this kind is at first
merely a revolt. Time and success alone can exalt and
render it legitimate; but still it can never be brought
about without outrage. If people enjoying authority
and fortune are required to relinquish these advantages,
they of course resist: force is then resorted to; they are
compelled to yield. In France this point was gained
by the lantern and public executions. The reign of terror commenced on the 4th of August, with the abolition
of titles of nobility, tithes, and feudal rights, the wrecks
of which were scattered among the multitude, who then,
for the first time, understood and felt really interested in
the Revolution. Before this period there was so much
of dependence and religious spirit among the people that
many doubted whether the crops would ripen as usual
without the King and the tithes.

" A revolution," concluded the Emperor, " is one of
the greatest evils by which mankind can be visited. It
is the scourge of the generation by which it is brought
about; and all the advantages it procures cannot make
amends for the misery with which it embitters the lives
of those who participate in it. It enriches the poor, who
still remain dissatisfied; and it impoverishes the rich,
who cannot forget their downfal. It subverts every
thing; and, at its commencement, brings misery to all
and happiness to none.

" Beyond a doubt, true social happiness consists in the
harmony and the peaceful possession of the relative

VOL. III.—11

enjoyments of each class of people. In regular and tranquil times, every individual has his share of felicity : the
cobbler in his stall is as content as the King on his
throne; the soldier is not less happy than the general.
The best-founded revolutions, at the outset, bring universal destruction in their train; the advantages they may
produce are reserved for a future age. Ours seems to
have been an irresistible fatality : it was a moral eruption, which could no more be prevented than a physical
eruption. When the chemical combinations necessary
to produce the latter are complete, it bursts forth : in-
France the moral combinations which produce a revolution had arrived at maturity, and the explosion accordingly took place."

We asked the Emperor whether he thought it would
have been possible to suppress the Revolution in its
birth; and he replied that, if not impossible, the attempt
would at least have been difficult. "Perhaps," said he,
"the storm might have been laid or averted by some
great Machiavelian act; by striking with one hand the
great ringleaders, and with the other making concessions
to the nation, granting freely the reformation required
by the age, part of which had already been mentioned in
the famous royal sitting. And yet, after all," he observed, "this would only have been guiding and directing the Revolution." He thought that some other plan
of the same kind might perhaps have succeeded on the
10th of August, if the King had remained triumphant.
"These two periods," he said, were the only ones which
afforded any chance, however desperate; for, at the
affair of Versailles, the people had not yet entirely shaken
off their allegiance, and on the 10th of August they were
already beginning to be tired of disorder. But those
who were chiefly interested in quelling the revolutionary
spirit were not adequate to encounter the difficulties of
the moment."

The Emperor then rapidly ran over the series of errors
committed during this period. "The line of conduct
then pursued," said he, "was truly pitiable. Louis XVI.
should have had a prime minister, and M. Necker under
him in the finance department. Prime ministers seem to

have been invented for the last reigns of the French
monarchy; and yet the prevailing false notions and
vanity of the time caused them to be dispensed with."

A great deal was said respecting the equivocal conduct
of several great personages during this critical period,
and the Emperor said: "We condemn Louis XVI.;
but, independently of his weakness, he was placed in
peculiar circumstances. He was the first monarch on
whom the experiment of modern principles was tried.
His education, his innate ideas, led him to believe
sincerely that all that he defended, either openly or
secretly, belonged to him of right. There might be a
sort of honesty even in his want of faith, if I may so
express myself. At a subsequent period, the same
conduct would have been inexcusable, and even repre-
hensible. Add to all this that Louis XVI. had every
body against him, and one may form an idea of the
innumerable difficulties which Fate had accumulated on
that unhappy Prince. The misfortunes of the Stuarts,
which have excited such deep interest, were not more
severe."

THE BODY-GUARD OF THE KING OF FRANCE.—A DESERTER IN THE EMPEROR'S SUITE.

4th.—The Emperor sent for me after he had finished
his breakfast. He was stretched on a sofa, with several
books scattered about him. He wore his nightcap, and
looked pale. "Las Cases," said he, "I am unwell. I
have been looking over a great many books, but I can
find nothing to interest me. I feel wearied." He fixed
his eye on me; that eye, naturally so animated, was now
dim, and its expression told me more than his eye had
uttered. "Sit down," said he, pointing to a chair that
was beside him, loaded with books, "and let us chat."
He spoke of the Island of Elba, of the life he had led
there, of some visits which he had received, &c. He
then put some questions to me concerning Paris and the
French Court during the corresponding period. The
conversation having led to the mention of the King's
body-guard, some one present remarked, as a curious
circumstance, that there was a deserter from the guard

in Napoleon's suite at St. Helena. "How? explain
yourself," said the Emperor.—"Sire," continued the
person who had just spoken, "at the time of the restoration, one of the captains of the guard, for whom I entertained great friendship, and who, in spite of the difference
of our opinions, had always evinced a high regard for me,
proposed to enter my son in his company, assuring me
that he would treat him as though he were his own.
I replied that he was too young, and that the appointment might retard the progress of his education; but my
friend silenced all my objections. I however requested
some time to consider of the matter; and on my mentioning it to some persons of my acquaintance, they were
astonished that I should have declined so good an offer,
and assured me that in a short time my son might attain
great advancement, without any interruption of his
education. I then waited on the captain of the guard,
and acknowledged that I had not shewn myself sufficiently grateful for his offer; and he replied that he was
fully aware I had not understood the extent of the
advantage he proposed to me. However, by one circumstance or another, your Majesty returned before my
son had the honour of being presented to his colonel,
and as I took him from his Lyceum on our departure
for St. Helena, he is clearly and truly a deserter." The
Emperor laughed heartily and said; "This is another
effect of revolutions! What new interests, connexions,
and opinions do they create! It is fortunate when they
do not disunite families, and set the best friends at
variance with each other." He then began to question
me concerning my family, and concluded by saying, "I
saw in Alphonse de Beauchamp's work, your name mentioned among the individuals who, on the 30th of
March, endeavoured to excite demonstrations in favour
of the Royal Family in the Place Louis XV. I know it
was not you; I think you once explained the matter to
me, but I have forgotten the particulars."—"Sire," said
I, "it was a cousin of mine, of the same name. The
circumstance vexed me a good deal at the time; I
inserted contradictions in the journals; and it was rather

droll that my cousin, on his part, addressed letters to the public prints, desiring that he might be particularly specified as the individual alluded to. I believe that the general way in which the name was introduced, in Alphonse de Beauchamp's work, was kindly meant on the part of the author, who wished, by this means, to afford me an opportunity of ingratiating myself in the favour of the ruling party, if I had a mind to do so. I must do my cousin the justice to say that, when I obtained an appointment about your Majesty's person, I several times offered to solicit for him a post in your household or elsewhere; but this he constantly declined. I wish he may now enjoy the reward of his fidelity." The Emperor again repeated that all private interests were subverted by revolutions. "And it is these private wounds," said he, "which occasion the general ferment, and render the shocks so acute and violent."

The weather was so bad the whole of the day that it was impossible to go out. The Emperor dismissed me and sent for General Gourgaud, to whom he dictated in his library, from two to six o'clock, almost the whole of Moreau's campaign during the Consulate. After dinner, he read to us Madame de Maintenon's celebrated sumptuary letter to her brother, in which she fixes her household expenditure at six thousand francs a-year. The Emperor had several volumes of the *Grands Hommes* brought to him, and, after perusing some articles, he amused himself by looking at the outline portraits at the nd of each volume.

NAPOLEON'S REPROOFS, &C.—THE GOVERNOR BARGAINS FOR OUR EXISTENCE.

5th.—To-day, in the course of my morning conversation with the Emperor, I happened to mention some acts of oppression and injustice, which excited dissatisfaction in the public mind, and rendered him unpopular, because they were executed in his name, and were by many supposed to emanate from him. "But how?" said he, "was there no one among the multitude that surrounded me, none of my chamberlains, who had sufficient spirit and independence to complain and bring these matters to my

knowledge ? I would have rendered justice wherever it
had been withheld."—"Sire, few would have ventured
to call your attention to these things."—"Did you really
stand so much in awe of me ? I suppose you dreaded my
sharp rebuffs; but you ought to have known that I always
lent a ready ear to every one, and that I never refused to
administer justice. You should have balanced the reward
of the good action against the danger of the reprimand.
After all, I confess that my reproofs were in most instances the result of calculation. They were frequently the
only means I possessed of learning a man's temper, of
discovering by stealth the different shades of his character. I had little time for inquiry; and a reprimand was
one of my experiments. For example, I lately gave you
a repulse, and this enabled me to discover that you were
somewhat headstrong, extremely susceptible, sufficiently
candid, but sullen; and, I may say, too sensitive," he
added, pinching my ear. " I was," continued he, " obliged to surround myself, as it were, with a halo of fear;
otherwise, having risen as I did from amidst the multitude, many would have made free to eat out of my hand,
or to slap me on the shoulder. We are naturally inclined
to familiarity."

The weather continued very bad, and the Emperor
spent the chief part of the day in writing, as he did
yesterday.

The Governor has renewed his cavilling on the subject
of our supplies, descending into petty details about a few
bottles of wine, or a few pounds of meat. Instead of
eight thousand pounds, the sum fixed by Government, he
now applied for an allowance of twelve thousand, which
he himself declared to be indispensable; but he insisted
on having the surplus delivered into his own hands, or
subjecting us to great retrenchments. He bargained for
our existence. When this was mentioned to the Emperor
he replied that the Governor might do as he pleased; but
he desired, at all events, that he might not be troubled
about the business.

In the evening the conversation again turned on
Madame de Maintenon, and the Emperor made many
remarks on her letters, her character, her influence on the

affairs of her time, &c. He asked for the Historical
Dictionary to read the articles on the Noailles family;
and he retired to rest at eleven o'clock.

CONFIDENTIAL CONVERSATION.—THE LETTERS OF MADAME
DE MAINTENON AND SÉVIGNÉ.

6th.—The weather proved as bad as it had been on the
preceding day. After finishing his toilet, the Emperor
retired to his library, attended by one of his suite, with
whom he held a long confidential conversation on a topic
intimately concerning us.

"We have now," said he, "been at St. Helena more
than a year, and with regard to certain points we remain
just as we were on the first day of our arrival. I must
confess that I have hitherto come to no determination in
my own mind upon these subjects. This is very unlike
me; but how many mortifications have I to encounter!
A victim to the persecutions of Fate and man, I am
assailed every where and on all hands. Even you, my
faithful friends and consolers, help to lacerate the wound.
I am vexed and distressed by your jealousies and dissen-
sions."—"Sire," replied the individual to whom he
addressed himself, "these things should remain unnoticed by your Majesty. In all that concerns you, our
jealousy is merely emulation; and all our dissension ceases
on the expression of your slightest wish. We live only
for you, and will always be ready to obey you. To us
you are the *Old Man of the Mountain*; you may command us in all things, except crime."—"Well," said the
Emperor, "I will think seriously of the subject I have
just alluded to, and each shall have his own particular
task." He dictated a few notes, and afterwards went
down to the garden, where he walked about for a short
time alone, and then withdrew to his own apartment.

The Emperor did not quit his chamber until the moment dinner was announced. He resumed his remarks
on Madame de Maintenon, whose letters he had been
reading. "I am charmed," said he, "with her style, her
grace, and the purity of her language. If I am violently
offended by what is bad, I am at the same time exqui-
sitely sensible to what is good. I think I prefer Madame

de Maintenon's letters to those of Madame de Sevigne
they tell more. Madame de Sevigné will certainly always
remain the true model of the epistolary style; she has a
thousand charms and graces, but there is this defect in
her writings, that one may read a great deal of them
without retaining any impression of what one has read.
They are like trifles, which a man may eat till he is tired
without overloading his stomach."

The Emperor then made some observations on grammar. He asked for the grammar of Domairon, who had
been our professor at the military school at Paris. He
glanced through it with evident pleasure. "Such is the
influence of youthful impressions," said he; " I suspect
that Domairon's is not the best of grammars, yet to me
it will always be the most agreeable. I shall never open
it without experiencing a certain pleasure."

ERRORS OF THE ENGLISH MINISTERS.—MEANS OF WHICH
 ENGLAND MIGHT HAVE AVAILED HERSELF FOR THE
 LIQUIDATION OF HER DEBT.—THE GOVERNOR'S REDUC-
 TIONS.

7th.—The Emperor remained within doors the whole
of the day. The Governor appeared on the grounds
accompanied by a numerous party; but we fled at his
approach. Several vessels have been observed out at
sea.

I was summoned to attend the Emperor, and 1 found
him engaged in perusing a work on the state of England.
This became the subject of conversation; the Emperor
said a great deal respecting the enormous national debt
of England, the disadvantageous peace she had concluded,
and the different means by which she might have extricated herself from her difficulties.

Napoleon possesses in an eminent degree the instinct
of order and harmony. I once knew a man who, being
much engaged in arithmetical calculations, confessed
that he could not enter a drawing-room without being
led irresistibly to count the people who were in it; and
that, when he sat down to table, he could not help sum-
ming up the number of plates, glasses, &c. Napoleon,
though in a more elevated sphere, has also an irresistible

habit of his own, which is to develop the grand and the beautiful in every subject that comes under his attention. If he happens to converse about a city, he immediately suggests improvements and embellishments; if a nation be the object of his consideration, he expatiates on the means of promoting her glory, prosperity, useful institutions, &c. Many of his observations, that have already been noted down, must have rendered this fact obvious to the reader.

Either the contents of the journals and other publications of the day, or the nature of our situation here, occasioned the Emperor's attention to be constantly directed to the state of England. He frequently adverted to what she ought to have done, as well as to what she still had to do, and which might render her future condition more prosperous. I subjoin here a few of the observations, on this subject, which escaped him at various times :—

"The Colonial system," said he one day, " is now at an end for all; for England, who possesses every colony, and for the other powers, who possess none. The empire of the seas now belongs indisputably to England; and why should she, in a new situation, wish to continue the old routine? Why does she not adopt plans that would be more profitable to her? She must look forward to a sort of emancipation of her colonies. In the course of time, many will doubtless escape from her dominion, and she should therefore avail herself of the present moment to obtain new securities and more advantageous connexions. Why does she not propose that the majority of her colonies shall purchase their emancipation by taking upon themselves a portion of the general debt, which would thus become specially theirs. The mother-country would by this means relieve herself of her burthens, and would nevertheless preserve all her advantages. She would retain, as pledges, the faith of treaties, reciprocal interests, similarity of language, and the force of habit; she might moreover reserve, by way of guarantee, a single fortified point, a harbour for the ships, after the manner of the factories on

11*

the coast of Africa. What would she lose? Nothing;
and she would spare herself the trouble and expense of
an administration which, too often, serves only to render
her odious. Her ministers, it is true, would have fewer
places to give away; but the nation would certainly be
no loser.

"I doubt not," added he, " that, with a thorough
knowledge of the subject, some useful result might be
derived from the ideas which I have just thrown out,
however erroneous they may be in their first hasty conception. Even with regard to India, great advantages
might be obtained by the adoption of new systems. The
English who are here, assure me that England derives
nothing from India in the balance of her trade; the
expenses swallow up, or even exceed, the profits. It is
therefore merely a source of individual advantage, and
of a few private fortunes of colossal magnitude; but
these are so much food for ministerial patronage, and
therefore good care is taken not to meddle with them.
Those nabobs, as they are styled, on their return to England, are useful recruits to the aristocracy. It signifies
not that they bear the disgrace of having acquired fortunes by rapine and plunder, or that they exercise a
baneful influence on public morals by exciting in others
the wish to gain the same wealth by the same means;
the present ministers are not so scrupulous as to bestow
a thought on such matters. These men give them their
votes; and, the more corrupt they are, the more easily
are they controlled. In this state of things, where is the
hope of reform? Thus, on the least proposition of
amendment, what an outcry is raised! The English aristocracy is daily taking a stride in advance; but, as soon
as there is any proposal for retrograding, were it only
for the space of an inch, a general explosion takes place.
If the minutest details be touched, the whole edifice
begins to totter. This is very natural. If you attempt
to deprive a glutton of his mouthful he will defend
himself like a hero."

On another occasion the Emperor said :—" After a
twenty year's war, after the blood and treasures that

were lavished in the common cause, after a triumph beyond all hope, what sort of peace has England concluded? Lord Castlereagh had the whole Continent at his disposal, and yet what advantage, what indemnity, has he secured to his own country? He has signed just such a peace as he would have signed had he been conquered. I should not have required him to make greater sacrifices had I been victorious. But, perhaps, England thought herself sufficiently happy in having effected my overthrow; in that case, hatred has avenged me! During our contest, England was animated by two powerful sentiments—her national interest and her hatred of me. In the moment of triumph, the violence of the one caused her to lose sight of the other. She has paid dearly for that moment of passion!" He developed his idea, glancing at the different measures which demonstrated the blunders of Castlereagh, and the many advantages which he had neglected. "Thousands of years will roll away," said he, "before there occurs such another opportunity of securing the welfare and real glory of England. Was it ignorance, or corruption, on the part of Castlereagh? He distributed the spoil generously, as he seemed to think, among the Sovereigns of the Continent, and reserved nothing for his own country; but, in so doing, did he not fear the reproach of being considered as the agent rather than the partner of the Holy Allies? He gave away immense territories; Russia, Prussia, and Austria acquired millions of population. Where is the equivalent to England? She, who was the soul of all this success, and who paid so dearly for it, now reaps the fruit of the *gratitude* of the Continent, and of the errors or treachery of her negotiator. My continental system is continued; and the produce of her manufactures is excluded. Why not have bordered the Continent with free and independent maritime towns, such, for example, as Dantzick, Hamburg, Antwerp, Dunkirk, Genoa, &c., which would of necessity have become the staples of her manufactures, and would have scattered them over Europe, in spite of all the duties in the world. England possessed the right of doing this, and her circumstances required it: her decisions would have been just, and

who would have opposed them at the moment of the
iberation? Why did she create to herself a difficulty,
and, in course of time, a natural enemy, by uniting Belgium to Holland, instead of securing two immense resources for her trade, by keeping them separate? Holland, which has no manufactures of her own, would have
been the natural depôt for English goods; and Belgium,
which might have become an English colony, governed
by an English Prince, would have been the channel for
dispersing these goods over France and Germany.   Why
not have bound down Spain and Portugal by a commercial treaty of long duration, which would have repaid all
the expenses incurred for their deliverance, and which
might have been obtained under pain of the enfranchise-
ment of their colonies, the trade of which, in either case,
England would have commanded? Why not have stipulated for some advantages in the Baltic, and to balance
the States of Italy? These would have been but the
regular privileges attached to the dominion of the seas.
After so long a contest in support of this right, how happened its advantages to be neglected at the moment
when it was really secured?   Did England, while she
sanctioned usurpation in others, fear that opposition
would be offered to hers? and by whom could it have
been offered? Probably England repents now, when it
is too late; the opportunity cannot be recovered; she
suffered the favourable moment to escape her! . . .
How many *whys* and *wherefores* might I not multiply!
. . . . None but Lord Castlereagh would have acted
thus: he made himself the man of the Holy Alliance,
and in course of time he will be the object of execration.
The Lauderdales, the Grenvilles, and the Wellesleys,
would have pursued a very different course; they would
at least have acted like Englishmen."

At another time the Emperor said;—" The national
debt is the canker-worm that preys on England; it is
the chain of all her difficulties. It occasions the enor-
mity of taxation, and this in its turn raises the price of
provisions. Hence the distress of the people, the high
price of labour and of manufactured goods which are
not brought with equal advantage to the continental

markets. England then ought at all hazards to contend
against this devouring monster; she should assail it on
all sides, and at once subdue it *negatively* and *positively*,
that is to say, by the reduction of her expenditure and
the increase of her capital.

" Can she not reduce the interest of her debt, the
high salaries, the sinecures, and the various expenses
attending her army establishment, and renounce the latter, in order to confine herself to her navy ? In short,
many things might be done, which I cannot now enter
into. With regard to the increase of her capital, can
she not enrich herself with the ecclesiastical property
which is immense, and which she would acquire by a
salutary reform, and by the extinction of titular dignities which would give offence to no one ? But if a word
be uttered on this subject, the whole aristocracy is up in
arms, and succeeds in putting down the opposition ; for
in England it is the aristocracy that governs, and for
which the Government acts. They repeat the favourite
adage, that, if the least stone of the old foundation be
touched, the whole fabric will fall to the ground. This
is devoutly re-echoed by the multitude; consequently
reform is stopped, and abuses are suffered to increase
and multiply.

" It is but just to acknowledge that, in spite of a compound of odious, antiquated, and ignoble details, the
English constitution presents the singular phenomenon of
a happy and grand result ; and the advantages arising
out of it secure the attachment of the multitude, who
are fearful of losing any of the blessings they enjoy.
But is it to the objectionable nature of the details
that this result must be attribued ? On the contrary,
it would shine with increased lustre if the grand and
beautiful machine were freed from its mischievous
appendages.

" England," continued the Emperor, " presents an example of the dangerous effects of the borrowing system.
I would never listen to any hints for the adoption of that
system in France ; I was always a firm opposer of it. It
was said, at the time, that I contracted no loans for want
of credit, and because I could find no one willing to.
lend; but this was false. Those who know any thing

of mankind and the spirit of stock-jobbing, will be convinced that loans may always be raised by holding out the chance of gain and the attraction of speculation. But this was no part of my system, and, by a special law, I fixed the amount of the public debt at what had generally been supposed to be conducive to the general prosperity, namely, at eighty millions interest for my France in her utmost extent, and after the union with Holland, which of itself produced an augmentation of twenty millions. This sum was reasonable and proper; a greater one would have been attended by mischievous consequences. What was the result of this system? What resources have I left behind me? France, after so many gigantic efforts and terrible disasters, is now more prosperous than ever! Are not her finances the first in Europe? To whom and to what are these advantages to be attributed? So far was I from wishing to swallow up the future, that I had resolved to leave a treasure behind me. I had even formed one, the funds of which I lent to different banking-houses, embarrassed families, and persons who held offices about me.

" I should not only have carefully preserved the sinking fund, but I calculated on having, in course of time, funds which would have been constantly increasing, and which might have been actively applied for the furtherance of public works and improvements. I should have had the fund of the Empire for general works; the fund of the departments for local works; the fund of the communes for municipal works, &c."

In the course of another conversation, the Emperor observed :—"England is said to traffic in every thing : why, then, does she not sell liberty, for which she might get a high price, and without any fear of exhausting her own stock; for modern liberty is essentially moral, and does not betray its engagements. For example, what would not the poor Spaniards give her to free them from the yoke to which they have been again subjected? I am confident that they would willingly pay any price to recover their freedom. It was I who inspired them with this sentiment; and the error into which I fell might, at least, be turned to good account by another government

As to the Italians, I have planted in their hearts principles that never can be rooted out. What can England do better than to promote and assist the noble impulses of modern regeneration? Sooner or later, this regeneration must be accomplished. Sovereigns and old aristocratic institutions may exert their efforts to oppose it, but in vain. They are dooming themselves to the punishment of Sisyphus; but, sooner or later, some arms will tire of resistance, and, on the first failure, the whole will tumble about their ears. Would it not be better to yield with a good grace?—this was my intention. Why does England refuse to avail herself of the glory and advantage she might derive from this course of proceeding? Every thing passes away in England as well as elsewhere. Castlereagh's administration will pass away, and that which may succeed it, and which is doomed to inherit the fruit of so many errors, may become great by only discontinuing the system that has hitherto been pursued. He who may happen to be placed at the head of the English cabinet, has merely to allow things to take their course, and to obey the winds that blow. By becoming the leader of liberal principles, instead of leaguing with absolute power, like Castlereagh, he will render himself the object of universal benediction, and England will forget her wrongs. Fox was capable of so acting, but Pitt was not; the reason is, that, in Fox, the heart warmed the genius; while, in Pitt, the genius withered the heart. But it may be asked, why I, all-powerful as I was, did not pursue the course I have here traced out?—how, since I can speak so well, I could have acted so ill? I reply to those who make this inquiry with sincerity, that there is no comparison between my situation and that of the English government. England may work on a soil which extends to the very bowels of the earth; while I could labour only on a sandy surface. England reigns over an established order of things; while I had to take upon myself the great charge, the immense difficulty, of consolidating and establishing. I purified a revolution, in spite of hostile factions. I combined together all the scattered benefits that could be preserved; but I was obliged to protect

them with a nervous arm against the attacks of all par
ties; and in this situation it may truly be said that the
public interest, *the State, was myself.*

"Our principles were attacked from without; and, in
the name of these very principles, I was assailed in the
opposite sense at home. Had I relaxed ever so little, we
should soon have been brought back to the time of the
Directory; I should have been the object, and France
the infallible victim, of a *counter-Brumaire.* We are in
our nature so restless, so busy, so loquacious! If twenty
revolutions were to happen, we should have twenty constitutions. This is one of the subjects that are studied
most, and observed the least. We have much need to
grow older in this fair and glorious path; for here our
great men have all shewn themselves to be mere children.
May the present generation profit by the faults that have
hitherto been committed, and prove as wise as it is enthusiastic!"

To-day the Governor commenced his grand reductions, and it was thought proper to deprive us of eight
English domestics, who had formerly been granted to
us. To the servants this was a subject of deep regret,
and it was gratifying to ourselves to observe that we
won the regard of all who were permitted to approach us.
We are now absolutely in want of daily necessaries, to
supply which the Emperor proposes to dispose of his
plate; this is his only resource.

After dinner the Emperor read the *Cercle,* and retired
immediately, although it was very early in the evening.
He was indisposed, and could not sleep. He sent for me
about midnight. By chance I had not retired to rest,
and I remained in conversation with him for two hours.

THE EMPEROR'S COURT AT THE TUILERIES. — THE PRE-
SENTATION OF THE LADIES. — ON WOMEN'S AGES. —
MANUSCRIPT OF THE ISLAND OF ELBA.

8th.—The Emperor sent for me very early: he was
just finishing his toilet. He had had no sleep during the
night, and he seemed much fatigued. The weather had
become somewhat tolerable, and he desired to have his
breakfast under the tent. While it was preparing, he
took a few turns about the garden, and resumed the

conversation he had had with me on the preceding night.

He invited Madame de Montholon to breakfast, and afterwards we took a drive in the calash, of which the Emperor had made no use for a considerable time. He had scarcely breathed the fresh air for several days.

The conversation once more turned on the subject of the Emperor's Court at the Tuileries, the multitude of persons composing it, the spirit and address with which Napoleon went through the ceremony of the presentations, &c. I pass over many of the observations that were made, for the sake of avoiding repetition.

" It is more difficult than is generally supposed," said the Emperor, " to speak to every body in a crowded assemblage, and yet say nothing to any one; to seem to know a multitude of people, nine-tenths of whom are total strangers to one."

Again, when alluding to the period when he was in the plentitude of his power, he observed that it was at once easy and difficult to approach him, to communicate with him, and to be appreciated by him ; and that it depended on the merest chance in the world whether his courtiers made or missed their fortune. " Now that I am myself entirely out of the question," said he, " now that I am a mere private individual, and can reflect philosophically on the time when I was called to execute the designs of Providence, without, however, ceasing to be a man, I see how much the fate of those I governed really depended upon chance ; and how often favour and credit were purely accidental. Intrigue is so dexterous, and merit often so awkward, and these extremes approximate so closely to each other that, with the best intentions in the world, I find that my benefits were distributed like prizes in a lottery. And yet could I have done better ? Was I faulty in my intentions, or remiss in my exertions? Have other sovereigns done better than I did ? It is only thus that I can be judged. The fault was in the nature of my situation, and in the force of things."

We then spoke of the presentation of the ladies at Court, their embarrassment, and the plans, views, and hopes that were formed by some of them. Madame de Montholon revealed the secrets of several of her acquaintance, by which it appeared that if in the saloons of Paris some were heard to exclaim against the Emperor's coarseness of manners, harshness of expression, and ugliness of person, others, who were better disposed, better informed, and differently affected, extolled the sweetness of his voice, the grace of his manners, the delicacy of his smile, and above all, his famous hand, which was said to be ridiculously handsome.

These advantages, it was observed, combined with great power and still greater glory, were naturally calculated to excite and to give rise to certain romantic stories. Thus at the Tuileries how many endeavoured to render themselves pleasing to the sovereign! How many sought to inspire a sentiment which it is probable they themselves really felt!

The Emperor smiled at our remarks and conjectures; and he confessed that, notwithstanding the mass of business and the cloud of flattery in which he was enveloped, he had oftener than once observed the sentiments to which we alluded. A few of the least timid among his admirers had, he said, even solicited and obtained interviews. We now laughed in our turn, and said that, at the time, these stories had been the subject of a great deal of mirth. But the Emperor seriously protested that they were void of foundation. In a more private conversation at the Briars, during one of our walks by moonlight, the Emperor, as I have stated in a former part of my Journal, made the same assertion, and contradicted every report of this nature, except one.

Our next subject of conversation was the repugnance of women to let their age be known. The Emperor made some very lively and entertaining remarks. An instance was mentioned of a woman who preferred losing an important law-suit to confessing her age. The case would have been decided in her favour, had she produced the register of her baptism, but this she could not be prevailed on to do

Another anecdote of the same kind was mentioned. A certain lady was much attached to a gentleman, and was convinced that her union with him would render her happy; but she could not marry without proving the date of her birth, and she preferred remaining single.

The Emperor informed us that a distinguished lady, at the time of her marriage, had deceived her husband, and represented herself to be five or six years younger than she really was, by producing the baptismal register of her younger sister, who had been dead some time.

"However," said the Emperor, "in so doing, poor Josephine exposed herself to some risk. This might really have proved a case of nullity of marriage." These words furnished us with the key to certain dates, which, at the Tuileries, were the subject of jesting and ridicule, and which we then attributed wholly to the gallantry and extreme complaisance of the Imperial Almanack.

About four o'clock the Emperor took a short walk. I did not accompany him. On his return, he informed us that he had visited the Company's garden, where he had met several very pretty women. "But I had not my interpreter with me," he added pointing to me. "The rogue left me, and nothing could be more provoking, for I never felt more inclined to avail myself of his assistance." This little walk, however, did the Emperor no good, for he was presently seized with a severe tooth-ache.

A vessel, which had come from the Cape some time ago, sailed for Europe this day. Several English military officers, who were passengers in this ship, had not been permitted to wait on the Emperor, in spite of their repeated solicitations. This was a new instance of the Governor's spite. These officers were men of distinction, and their reports on their return home might have had some influence. The Governor, in defiance of all truth, informed them that Napoleon had determined to receive no one.

The Emperor some time ago analyzed to us a subject which he said he intended to dictate in fourteen chapters, and which had forcibly struck me by its truth, its force, its just reasoning, and its dignity. I frequently alluded to it when I happenend to be alone with him; and he laughed more than once at the perseverance I shewed, which, he said, was not usual with me. To-day he informed me that he had at length produced something, though not in fourteen chapters, nor on the promised subject; but that I must be content with it. I have read it, and it is certainly a very remarkable fragment. I do not believe that the Revolution has produced any thing more comprehensive and energetic on the governments of the last twenty-five years in France, namely, the Republic, the Consulate, and the Empire.

The exposition and development of the ten chapters which compose this work may be regarded as a perfect outline of the subject. The style is remarkably simple and nervous. Each chapter is full and forcible, and the whole, which consists of fifty pages, is struck off and finished with a masterly hand. I have understood that the substance of these ideas was to have formed the Emperor's manifesto at the time of his landing from Elba.

Since my return to Europe, this little work has been published, under the title of *Manuscrit de l' Ile d' Elbe*; though I have reason to believe that at first another title was intended for it. Be this as it may, since the work is but little known, and as those who have read it may be ignorant of its real origin, I here transcribe almost literally several chapters, which will serve to prove its source and its authenticity.

CHAP. I.—In the sixteenth century, the Pope, Spain, and the Sixteen, attempt in vain to raise a fourth dynasty to the throne of France. Henry IV. succeeds Henry III. without an inter-regnum: he conquers the League; but finds that the only way to secure himself on the throne is by sincerely joining the party which constitutes the majority of the nation.

"Henry IV. was proclaimed King at St. Cloud, on the day on which Henry III. died. His sovereignty was acknowledged by all the Protestant churches and by a part of the Catholic nobility. The Holy League which which had been formed against Henry III., in hatred of the Protestants, and to avenge the death of the Duke of Guise, was master of Paris, and commanded five-sixths of the kingdom. The Leaguers refused to acknowledge Henry IV., but they proclaimed no other sovereign.

The Duke of Mayenne, the chief of the League, exercised authority under the title of Lieutenant-general of the kingdom. The accession of Henry IV. produced no change in the forms adopted by the League for exercising its power; each town was governed as in disturbed and factious times, by local or military authorities. At no period, not even on the day succeeding his entrance into Paris, did Henry IV. acknowledge the acts of the League, and the latter never set up any pretensions that he should do so. No law, no regulation, emanated from the League. The Parliament of Paris was divided into two parties; one for the Leaguers, which sat at Paris, and the other for Henry IV., which assembled at Tours. But these parliaments drew up and registered none but judicial acts. The provinces retained their own organization and privileges, and were governed by their own common laws. It has already been observed that the League had not proclaimed any other sovereign; but it acknowledged for a moment as King, the Cardinal de Bourbon, Henry's uncle. The Cardinal, however, did not consent to second the designs of the enemies of his house. Besides, Henry had seized his person; no act emanated from him, and the League continued subject to the authority of the Lieutenant-general the Duke of Mayenne. There was therefore no interregnum between Hen. III. and Hen. IV.

"The League was split into several parties. The Sorbonne had decided that the rights of birth could confer no right to the crown on a Prince who was an enemy to the Church. The Pope had declared that Henry IV. having relapsed, had forfeited his rights for ever; and that he could not recover them, even though he should return to the bosom of the Church. Henry IV., King of Navarre, was born a Protestant; but on the massacre of St. Bartholomew, he was compelled to marry Margaret de Valois, and to abjure the reformed religion. However, as soon as he withdrew from the Court, and found himself amidst the Protestants on the left bank of the Loire, he declared that his abjuration had been wholly compulsory, and he again embraced the Protestant faith. This step caused him to be character-

ized as an obstinate renegado; but the majority of the
League were of opinion that it would be proper to
summon Henry to return to the bosom of the Catholic,
Apostolic, and Romish Church; and acknowledge him
as sovereign, as soon as he should abjure Protestantism and receive absolution from the Bishops.

" The leaguers convoked the States-general of the
kingdom at Paris. The Spanish ambassadors now un-
masked the designs of their sovereign, and urged the
States to establish a fourth dynasty on the throne of
France, on the ground that Henry and Condé, having,
by their apostacy, forfeited their rights to the crown,
the male line of the Capets was extinct. They accordingly set forth the claims of the Infanta of Spain, the
daughter of Henry II. of France, who was the first in
the female line. Even supposing that, by the extinction
of the male line of descent, the nation possessed the right
of disposing of the crown, they still insisted that its
choice ought to fall on the Infanta, for two reasons:
first, because it was impossible to select a princess of
more illustrious family; and secondly, because France
was indebted to Philip II. for his exertions in supporting
the cause of the League. The Infanta was to marry a
French Prince, and mention was even made of the Duke
of Guise, the son of the Duke who had been assassinated
at Blois. There was already a body of Spanish troops
in Paris, commanded by the Duke of Mayenne; and it
was proposed that an army of 50,000 Spaniards should
be maintained in Paris by the Court of Madrid, which
would devote its whole power and resources to ensure
the triumph of this fourth dynasty. The sixteen supported these propositions, which were sanctioned by the
Court of Rome, and seconded by the utmost efforts of
the Legate. But all was vain; public spirit was roused
at the idea of a foreign nation disposing of the throne
of France. That part of the Parliament which sat at
Paris addressed remonstrances to the Duke of Mayenne
the Lieutenant-general of the kingdom, and urged him
to enforce the observance of the fundamental laws of the
monarchy, and of the Salic law in particular. Had the
designs of the Spanish faction succeeded; had the States-

general declared the crown forfeited by the descendants of Hugues Capet; had a fourth dynasty been raised to the throne, accepted by the nation, and sanctioned by the religion acknowledged among the powers of Europe, the rights of the third dynasty would have been extinct.

" Henry conquered the League at Arques and on the plains of Ivry, and he then besieged Paris. However, he was convinced of the impossibility of reigning in France, unless he joined the national party. He had conquered with an army composed entirely of French troops: if he had under his command a small corps of English, the Leaguers had a still more considerable number of Spaniards and Italians. On both sides, therefore, the contest had been maintained by Frenchmen against Frenchmen ; the foreigners were merely auxiliaries ; the national honour and independence could not be compromised, whichever party might be declared victorious. *Ventre Saint-gris !* *Paris vaut bien une messe !* were the exclamations by which Henry used to sound the opinion of the Huguenots; and when, at the Council of Beauvais, he assembled the principal leaders of the Protestant party, to deliberate on the resolution which it was most expedient to adopt, the majority, and in particular the most intelligent persons among them, advised the King to abjure his faith and to join the national party. Henry pronounced his abjuration at Saint-Denis, and received absolution from the Bishops; the gates of Paris were thrown open to him, and his authority was acknowledged by the whole kingdom. He now frankly espoused the national party. Almost all the public posts were occupied by the Leaguers. The Protestants, those who had constantly served the King, and to whom he was indebted for his victories, frequently raised complaints against him, and taxed him with ingratitude. Still, however, in spite of all the discretion that was observed, the nation continued long to mistrust the secret intentions of Henry. It was remarked that *what is bred in the bone will never be out of the flesh.*

CHAP. II.—The republic sanctioned by the will of the people, by religion, by victory, and by all the Powers of Europe.

Hugues Capet ascended the throne by the choice of

the Parliament, consisting of Lords and Bishops which two classes then constituted the nation. The French monarchy was never absolute; the intervention of the States General has always been necessary for sanctioning the principal acts of the Legislature, and for levying new taxes. Subsequently, the French Parliaments, under the pretence of being States General on a small scale, and seconded by the Court, usurped the rights of the nation. In 1788, the Parliaments were the first to acknowledge them. Louis XVI. convoked the States General in 1789, and the nation exercised a portion of the sovereignty. The Constituent Assembly framed a new constitution for the state, which was sanctioned by the approval of the whole French people, and which Louis XVI. accepted and swore to maintain. The Legislative Assembly suspended the King. The convention, which consisted of the deputies of all the primary assemblies in the Kingdom, and which was invested with special powers, proclaimed the abolition of the monarchy and the establishment of the Republic. The adherents of the royal party fled from France, and solicited the aid of foreign arms. Austria and Prussia signed the convention of Pilnitz; and Austrian and Prussian armies, joined by the French royalist forces, commenced the war of the first coalition to subdue the French people. The whole nation took up arms ; and the Austrians and Prussians were conquered. The second coalition was afterwards formed by Austria, England, and Russia ; but this was destroyed like the first, and all the Powers in Europe acknowledged the French Republic.

1st.—The Republic of Genoa, by an extraordinary embassy, on the 15th of June, 1792.

2d. —The Porte, by a declaration, on the 27th of March, 1793.

3d. —Tuscany, by the treaty of the 9th of February, 1795.

4th. — Holland, by the treaty of 16th of May, 1795.

5th. — The Venetian Republic, by an extraordinary embassy, on the 30th of December, 1795.

6th.—The King of Prussia, by the treaty signed at Bâle, on the 5th of April, 1795.

7th. — The King of Spain, by the treaty signed at Bâle, on the 22nd of July, 1795.

8th. — Hesse-Cassel, by the treaty of the 28th of July, 1795.

9th.—Switzerland, by the treaty of the 19th of August, 1795.

10th. — Denmark, by a declaration, on the 18th of August, 1795.

11th. — Sweden, by an embassy, on the 23rd of April, 1795.

12th.—Sardinia, by the treaty of Paris, on the 28th of April, 1796.

13th.—America, by an extraordinary embassy, on the 30th of December, 1796.

14th.—Naples, by the treaty of the 10th of October, 1796.

15th.—Parma, by the treaty of the 5th of November, 1796.

16th.—Wurtemburgh, by the treaty of the 7th of August, 1796.

17th.—Baden, by the treaty of the 22d of August, 1796.

18th.—Bavaria, by the treaty of the 24th of July, 1797.

19th.—Portugal, by the treaty of the 19th of August, 1797.

20th.—The Pope, by the treaty signed at Tolentino on the 19th of February, 1797.

21st. — The Emperor of Germany, by the treaty of Campio-Formio, on the 7th of October, 1797.

22d.—The Emperor of Russia, by a treaty signed on the 8th of October, 1801.

23d.—The King of England, by the treaty signed at Amiens on the 27th of March 1802.

" The government of the Republic sent ambassadors to all the Powers of Europe, and received envoys from those powers in return. The tri-coloured flag was acknowledged in every sea, and throughout the world. At Tolentino, the Pope had treated with the Republic as a temporal sovereign; but he acknowledged and treated with it as head of the Catholic religion, by the Concordat which

was signed at Paris on the 18th of April, 1802. Most
of the Bishops, who had followed the Royalist party.
abroad, now submitted to the Republican government,
and those who refused forfeited their sees. In short,
the French Republic, which was sanctioned by the
citizens, and victorious by its armies, was acknowledged
by every sovereign, every power, and every religion, in
the world, and in particular by the Catholic Church.

"Not only was the Republic acknowledged by all
the powers in the world, after the death of Louis XVI.,
but none of these powers ever acknowledged a successor
to him. In the year 1800, therefore, the third dynasty
was ended as completely as the first and second. The
rights and titles of the Merovingians were extinguished
by the rights and titles of the Carlovingians; the rights
and titles of the Carlovingians were extinguished by the
rights and titles of the Capetians; and the rights of the
Capetians were, in like manner, extinguished by the
Republic. Every legitimate government supersedes the
rights and the legitimacy of the governments that have
preceded it. The Republic was a government, in fact
and in right, rendered legitimate by the will of the
nation, sanctioned by the Church, and by the adhesion
of all the world.

CHAP. III.—The Revolution rendered France a new nation:—it
    emancipated the Gauls from the tyranny of the Franks: it
    created new interests, and a new order of things conformable
    with the welfare and rights of the people, and the justice and
    knowledge of the age.

"The French Revolution was not produced by the
jarring interests of two families disputing the possession
of the throne; it was a general rising of the mass of
the nation against the privileged classes. The French
nobility, like that of every country in Europe, dates its
origin from the incursion of the barbarians, who divided the Roman Empire among them. In France,
nobles represented the Franks, and the Burgundians,
and the rest of the nation, the Gauls. The feudal system
which was introduced established the principle that all
land should have a lord. All political privileges were

exercised by the Priests and the Nobles; the peasants
were slaves, and in part attached to the glebe. The progress of civilization and knowledge emancipated the
people. This new state of things promoted industry and
trade. The chief portion of the land, wealth, and information, belonged to the people in the eighteenth
century. The nobles, however, still continued to be a
privileged class: they were empowered to administer
justice, and they possessed feudal rights under various
denominations and forms: they enjoyed the privilege of
being exempt from all the burdens of the state, and of
possessing exclusively the most honourable posts. These
abuses aroused the indignation of the citizens. The principal object of the Revolution was to destroy all privileges; to abolish signorial jurisdictions, justice being an
inseparable attribute of sovereign authority; to suppress
feudal rights as being a remnant of the old slavery of
the people; to subject alike all citizens and all property
to the burdens of the state. In short, the Revolution
proclaimed equality of rights. A citizen might attain
any public employment, according to his talent and the
chances of fortune. The kingdom was composed of provinces which had been united to the Crown at various
periods: they had no natural limits, and were differently
divided, unequal in extent and in population. They possessed many laws of their own, civil as well as criminal:
they were more or less privileged, and very unequally
taxed, both with respect to the amount and the nature
of the contributions, which rendered it necessary to de-
tach them from each other by lines of custom-houses.
France was not a state, but a combination of several
states, connected together without amalgamation. The
whole had been determined by chance and by the events
of past ages. The Revolution, guided by the principle
of equality, both with respect to the citizens and the
different portions of the territory, destroyed all these
small nations: there was no longer a Brittany, a Nor-
mandy, a Burgundy, a Champangne, a Provence, or a
Lorraine; but the whole formed a France. A division
of homogeneous territory, prescribed by local circumstances, confounded the limits of all the provinces. They

possessed the same judicial and administrative organization, the same civil and criminal laws, and the same
system of taxation. The dreams of the upright men of
all ages were realized. The opposition which the Court,
the Clergy, and the Nobility, raised against the Revolution and the war with foreign powers, produced the law
of emigration and the sequestration of emigrant property, which subsequently it was found necessary to
sell, in order to provide for the charges of the war. A
great portion of the French nobility enrolled themselves under the banner of the princes of the Bourbon
family, and formed an army which marched in conjunction with the Austrian, Prussian, and English forces.
Gentlemen who had been brought up in the enjoyment
of competency served as private soldiers: numbers were
cut off by fatigue and the sword; others perished of
want in foreign countries; and the wars of La Vendee
and of the Chouans, and the revolutionary tribunals,
swept away thousands. Three-fourths of the French
nobility were thus destroyed; and all posts, civil, judicial, or military, were filled by citizens who had risen
from the common mass of the people. The change produced in persons and property by the events of the
Revolution, was not less remarkable than that which
was effected by the principles of the Revolution. A
new church was created; the dioceses of Vienne, Narbonne, Frejus, Sisteron, Rheims, &c., were superseded
by sixty new dioceses, the boundaries of which were
circumscribed, in the Concordat, by new Bulls applicable to the present state of the French territory. The
suppression of religious orders, the sale of convents and
of all ecclesiastical property, were sanctioned, and the
clergy were pensioned by the State. Every thing that
was the result of the events which had occurred since the
time of Clovis, ceased to exist. All these changes were
so advantageous to the people that they were effected
with the utmost facility, and, in 1800, there no longer
remained any recollection of the old privileges and sovereigns of the provinces, the old parliaments and baili-
wicks, or the old dioceses; and to trace back the origin
of all that existed, it was sufficient to refer to the new

law by which it had been established.   One-half of the
land had changed its proprietors; the peasantry and the
citizens were enriched.   The advancement of agriculture
and manufactures exceeded the most sanguine hopes.
France presented the imposing spectacle of upwards of
thirty millions of inhabitants, circumscribed within their
natural limits, and composing only a single class of citizens, governed by one law, one rule, and one order.   All
these changes were conformable with the welfare and
rights of the nation, and with the justice and intelligence
of the age.

CHAP. IV.—The French people establish the Imperial throne, to
    consolidate the new interests of the nation.   The fourth dy-
    nasty did not immediately succeed the third; it succeeded the
    Republic.   Napoleon is crowned by the Pope, and acknowledged
    by the Powers of Europe.   He creates kings, and the armies of
    all the Continental Powers march under his command.

The five members of the Directory were divided.   Enemies to the Republic crept into the councils; and thus
men, hostile to the rights of the people, became connected with the government.   This state of things kept
the country in a ferment; and the great interests which
the French people had acquired by the Revolution were
incessantly compromised.   One unanimous voice, issuing
from the plains of France and from her cities and her
camps, demanded the preservation of all the principles
of the Republic, or the establishment of an hereditary
system of government, which would place the principles
and interests of the Revolution beyond the reach of factions and the influence of foreigners.   By the constitution of the year VIII. the First Consul of the Republic
became Consul for ten years, and the nation afterwards
prolonged his magistracy for life : the people subsequently
raised him to the throne, which it rendered hereditary in
his family.   The principles of the sovereignty of the
people, of liberty and equality, of the destruction of the
feudal system, of the irrevocability of the sale of national
domains, and the freedom of religious worship, were
now established.   The government of France, under the
fourth dynasty, was founded on the same principles as
the Republic.   It was a moderate and constitutional

monarchy. There was as much difference between the government of France under the fourth dynasty and the third, as between the latter and the Republic. The fourth dynasty succeeded the Republic, or, more properly speaking, it was merely a modification of it.

No Prince ever ascended a throne with rights more legitimate than those of Napoleon. The crown was not presented to him by a few Bishops and Nobles; but he was raised to the Imperial throne by the unanimous consent of the citizens, three times solemnly confirmed. Pope Pius VII. the head of the Catholic religion, the religion of the majority of the French people, crossed the Alps to anoint the Emperor with his own hands, in the presence of the Bishops of France, the Cardinals of the Romish Church, and the Deputies from all the districts of the Empire. The sovereigns of Europe eagerly acknowledged Napoleon : all beheld with pleasure the modification of the Republic, which placed France on a footing of harmony with the rest of Europe, and which at once confirmed the constitution and the happiness of that great nation. Ambassadors from Austria, Russia, Prussia, Spain, Portugal, Turkey, and America, in fine, from all the powers of Europe, came to congratulate the Emperor. England alone sent no ambassador : she had violated the treaty of Amiens, and had consequently again declared war against France; but even England approved the change. Lord Whitworth, in the secret negotiations which took place through the medium of Count Malouet, and which preceded the rupture of the peace of Amiens, proposed, on the part of the English government, to acknowledge Napoleon as King of France, on condition of his agreeing to the cession of Malta. The First Consul replied that, if ever the welfare of France required that he should ascend the throne, it would only be by the free and spontaneous will of the French people. In 1806, when Lord Lauderdale came to Paris to negotiate peace between the King of England and the Emperor, he exchanged his powers, as is proved by the protocol of the negotiations, and he treated with the Emperor's plenipotentiary. The death of Fox broke up the negotiations of Lord Lauderdale The English

Minister had it in his power to obviate the Prussian campaign,* to prevent the battle of Jena. When, in 1814, the Allies presented an *ultimatum* at Chaumont, Lord Castlereagh, in signing this *ultimatum*, again acknowledged the existence of the Empire in the person and the family of Napoleon. If the latter did not accept the propositions of the Congress of Chatillon, it was because he did not conceive himself at liberty to cede a portion of the Empire, the integrity of which he had, at his coronation, sworn to maintain.

The Electors of Bavaria, Wurtemberg, and Saxony, were created Kings by Napoleon.

The armies of Saxony, Bavaria, Wurtemberg, Baden, and Hesse, fought in conjunction with the French armies; and the Russian and French troops fought together in 1809, in the war against Austria. In 1812, the Emperor of Austria concluded at Paris an alliance with Napoleon, and Prince Schwartzenburg commanded, under his orders, the Austrian contingent in the Russian campaign, in which he attained the rank of Field Marshal, on the application of the French Emperor. A similar treaty of alliance was concluded at Berlin, and the Prussian army also fought with the French in the campaign in Russia.

---

* While Lord Lauderdale was in Paris, and negotiating with the Emperor's plenipotentiaries, Prussia took up arms and assumed a hostile attitude. Lord Lauderdale seemed to disapprove of this conduct, and to consider the contest very unequal. Being informed that Napoleon intended to march at the head of the army, he enquired whether the Emperor would consent to defer his departure, and to enter into arrangements with Prussia, if England would accept the basis of the negotiations, that is to say, the *uti possidetis* on both sides, including Hanover. The discussion was maintained on the subject of Hanover, which England wished to recover independently of this basis. By the reply of the Cabinet of St. James's, Lord Lauderdale was recalled. The Emperor set out, and the battle of Jena took place: Fox was then dead.

We were, at this period, eye-witnesses to the regret and repugnance which Napoleon evinced at the necessity of going to war with Prussia. He was disposed to leave Hanover in the possession of that power, and to recognise a Confederation of the North of Germany. He felt that Prussia, having never been beaten or humbled by France, and her power being still unimpaired, she could have no interests hostile to his; but that, if once she were subdued, she must be destroyed.

The Emperor healed the wounds which the Revolution had inflicted : the emigrants returned, and the list of proscription was obliterated. Napoleon enjoyed the glory most gratifying to a monarch, by recalling and re-establishing in their homes upwards of 20,000 families : their unsold property was restored to them; and, the veil of oblivion being thrown over the past, persons of every class, whatever line of conduct they might previously have pursued, were admitted to all public employments. Families who had distinguished themselves by the services they had rendered to the Bourbons, those who had shewn themselves most devoted to the Royal Family, filled places about the Court, and in the ministry, and held commissions in the army. All party denominations were forgotten : aristocrats and Jacobins were no longer spoken of; and the institution of the Legion of Honour, which was at once the reward of military, civil, and judicial services, placed on a footing of unity the soldier, the man of science, the artist, the prelate, and the magistrate; it became the badge of concord among all classes and all parties.

CHAP. V.—The blood of the Imperial dynasty mingled with that of all the monarchical Houses in Europe; with those of Russia, Prussia, England, and Austria.

The Imperial House of France contracted alliances with all the sovereign families of Europe. Prince Eugéne Napoleon, the adopted son of the Emperor, married the eldest daughter of the King of Bavaria, a princess distinguished for her beauty and her virtues. This alliance, which was contracted at Munich on the 14th of January, 1806, afforded the highest satisfaction to the Bavarian nation. The Hereditary Prince of Baden, the brother-in-law of the Emperor of Russia, solicited the hand of Princess Stephanie, the adopted daughter of the Emperor Napoleon : this marriage was celebrated at Paris on the 7th of April, 1806. On the 22d of August, 1807, Prince Jerome Napoleon married the eldest daughter of the King of Wurtemburg, cousin-german of the Emperor of Russia, the King of England, and the King of Prussia. Other alliances of this nature were contracted with sovereign

princes of Germany, of the House of Hohenzollern
These marriages have proved happy, and all have given
birth to princes and princesses, who will transmit to
future generations the recollection of the Imperial government of France.

" When the interests of France and the Empire induced
the Emperor and the Empress Josephine to break bonds
which were equally dear to them both, the greatest sovereigns in Europe courted the Alliance of Napoleon. Had
it not been for religious scruples, and the delays occasioned by distance, it is probable that a Russian princess
would have occupied the throne of France. The Archduchess Maria Louisa, who was married to the Emperor
by procuration granted to Prince Charles, at Vienna, on
the 11th of March, 1810, and at Paris on the 2d of April
following, ascended the throne of France. As soon as
the Emperor of Austria learned that Napoleon's marriage
was in agitation, he expressed his surprise that an alliance
with the House of Austria had not been thought of. The
choice was hitherto divided between a Russian and a
Saxon princess: Francis explained his sentiments on this
subject to the Count de Narbonne, the Governor of
Trieste, who was then at Vienna; and, in consequence,
instructions were forwarded to the Prince of Schwartzenberg, the Austrian ambassador at Paris. In February,
1810, a Privy Council was convoked at the Tuileries:
the Minister for Foreign Affairs submitted to the Council
the despatches of the Duke of Vicenza, the French ambassador at the Court of Russia. These communications
shewed that the Emperor Alexander was very much disposed to give his sister, the Grand-duchess Anne, in
marriage to Napoleon; but he seemed to make it a point
of importance that the Princess should be allowed the
public exercise of her religious worship, and a chapel
appropriated to the Greek rites. The despatches from
Vienna developed the insinuations and the wishes of the
Austrian Court. There was a division of opinions in the
French Council: the Russian, the Saxon, and the Austrian
alliance, all found supporters; but the majority voted for
the choice of an Archduchess of Austria. As Prince
Eugéne had been the first to propose the Austrian alliance,

12*

the Emperor, breaking up the sitting at two in the morning, authorized him to make overtures with Prince
Schwartzenberg. He at the same time authorized the
Minister for Foreign Affairs to sign, in the course of the
day, the contract of marriage with the Austrian ambassador; and, to obviate all difficulties with respect to the
details, he directed him to sign, word for word, the same
contract as that which had been drawn up for the marriage
of Louis XVI. and the Archduchess Marie-Antoinette.
In the morning, Prince Eugéne had an interview with
Prince Schwartzenberg : the contract was signed the same
day, and the courier who conveyed the intelligence to
Austria agreeably surprised the Emperor Francis. The
peculiar circumstances attending the signature of this
marriage contract led the Emperor Alexander to suspect
that he had been trifled with, and that the Court of the
Tuileries had been conducting two negotiations at once.
But this was a mistake : the negotiation with Vienna was
begun and concluded in one day.*

" Never did the birth of any Prince excite so much
enthusiasm in a people, or produce so powerful a sensation throughout Europe, as the birth of the King of Rome.
On the firing of the first gun, which announced the

---

* A report was pretty generally circulated that the marriage
of the Archduchess Maria-Louisa with the Emperor Napoleon was
a secret article of the treaty of Vienna: this idea is void of
foundation. The treaty of Vienna is dated Oct. 15, 1809, and
the marriage contract was signed at Paris on the 7th of Feb.
1810.
    Every individual who was present at the deliberations of the
Privy Council can attest that the circumstances of the marriage
were such as they have been above described; that no idea of the
Austrian alliance was entertained before the contents of the Count
de Narbonne's despatches were made known; and that the marriage
with the Archduchess Maria-Louisa was proposed, discussed, and
determined on in the Council, and signed within the space of twenty-
'our hours.
    The members of the Council were—the Emperor, the great Dig-
nitaries of the Empire, the high Officers of the Crown, all the
Ministers, the Presidents of the Senate and the Legislative Body,
and the Ministers of State, Presidents of the sections of the Council
of State; amounting, in all, to 25

delivery of the Empress, the whole population of Paris was in the most anxious suspense. In the streets, the promenades, at the places of public amusement, and in the interior of the houses, all were eagerly intent on counting the number of guns. The twenty-second excited universal transport: it had been usual to discharge twenty-one guns on the birth of a Princess, and a hundred and one on the birth of a Prince. All the European Powers deputed the most distinguished noblemen of their Courts to present their congratulations to the Emperor. The Emperor of Russia sent his Minister of the Interior; and the Emperor of Austria despatched Count Clary, one of his highest officers of the crown, who brought, as presents to the young King, the collars of all the Orders of the Austrian Monarchy set with diamonds. The baptism of the King of Rome was celebrated with the utmost pomp, in the presence of the French bishops, and deputies from all parts of the Empire. The Emperor of Austria was sponsor to the young king by proxy; he was represented by his brother, the Archduke Ferdinand, Grand-Duke of Tuscany.

CHAP. VI.—Containing some account of the campaign of Saxony,* and shewing that the league of 1813 was in its object foreign to the Restoration.

"The victories of Lützen and Würtzen, on the 2nd and 22nd of May, 1813, had re-established the reputation of the French arms. The King of Saxony was brought back in triumph to his capital; the enemy was driven from Hamburg; one of the corps of the grand army was at the gates of Berlin, and the imperial head-quarters were established at Breslau. The Russian and Prussian armies, disheartened by their defeats, had no alternative

---

* I did not choose to suppress this summary of the campaign in Saxony, although the same subject has already been particularly treated of at the commencement of this volume. If, however, some readers should consider it merely a repetition, others will find in it the means of comparing and verifying what has been before stated: one of the accounts is drawn up from documents published in Europe, whilst the other was dictated at St. Helena by Napoleon himself.

but to repass the Vistula, when Austria interfered and
advised France to sign an armistice.   Napoleon returned
to Dresden, the Emperor of Austria quitted Vienna and
repaired to Bohemia, and the Emperor of Russia and the
King of Prussia established themselves at Schweidnitz.
Communications took place between the different Powers.
Count Metternich proposed the Congress of Prague,
which was agreed on ; but it was merely the shadow of
a Congress.   The Court of Vienna had already entered
into engagements with Russia and Prussia, and intended
to declare itself in the month of May, when the unexpected success of the French army rendered greater circumspection necessary.   Notwithstanding all the efforts
which Austria had exerted, her army was still inconsider-
able in number, badly organized, and ill prepared to enter
upon a campaign.   Count Metternich demanded, on the
part of Austria, the surrender of the Illyrian Provinces,
one half of the kingdom of Italy, (that is to say, Venice,
as far as the Mincio,) and Poland.   It was moreover required that Napoleon should renounce the Protectorate
of Germany, and the departments of the thirty-second
military division.   These extravagant propositions were
advanced only that they might be rejected.   The Duke of
Vicenza proceeded to the Congress of Prague.   The
choice of Baron d'Anstetten, as the Russian plenipotentiary, shewed that Russia wished not for peace, but was
merely anxious to afford Austria time to complete her
military preparations.   The unfavourable augury, occasioned by the selection of Baron d'Anstetten as a negotiator, was confirmed : he declined entering upon any
conference.   Austria, who pretended to act as mediatrix,
declared, when her army was in readiness, that she ad-
hered to the coalition, though she did not even require
the opening of a single sitting, or the drawing up of a
single protocol.   This system of bad faith, and of perpetual contradictions between words and acts, was
unremittingly pursued, at this period, by the Court of
Vienna.   The war was resumed.   The brilliant victory
gained by the Emperor at Dresden, on the 27th of August, 1813, over the army commanded by the three
Sovereigns, was immediately followed by the disasters

which Macdonald, through his ill-concerted manœuvres, brought upon himself in Silesia, and by the destruction of Vandamme's force in Bohemia.   However, the superiority was still on the side of the French army, which supported itself on three points, viz: Torgau, Wittenberg, and Magdeburg.   Denmark had concluded a treaty of alliance, offensive and defensive, and her contingent augmented the army of Hamburg.

"In October, the Emperor quitted Dresden to proceed to Magdeburg, by the left bank of the Elbe, in order to deceive the enemy.   His intention was to recross the Elbe at Wittenburg and to march on Berlin.   Several corps of the army had already arrived at Wittenburg, and the enemy's bridges at Dessau had been destroyed, when a letter from the King of Wurtemburg informed the Emperor that the King of Bavaria had suddenly gone over to the enemy; and that, without any declaration of war or any previous intimation, the Austrian and Bavarian forces, cantoned on the banks of the Inn, had formed themselves into one camp; that these forces, amounting to 80,000, under the orders of General Wrede, were marching on the Rhine; that he (the King of Wurtemberg), seeing the impossibility of his opposing this united force, had been obliged to add his contingent to it.   The letter farther added that 100,000 men would soon surround Mentz, the Bavarians having made common cause with Austria.   Upon receiving this unexpected intelligence, the Emperor found himself compelled to change the plan of the campaign which he had projected two months previously, and for which he had prepared the fortresses and magazines.   This plan had for its object to drive the Allies between the Elbe and the Saale; and, under the protection of the fortresses and magazines of Torgau, Wittemberg, Magdeburg, and Hamburg, to establish the seat of war between the Elbe and the Oder (the French army being at that time in possession of the fortresses of Glogau, Cüstrin, and Stettin), and, according to circumstances, to raise the blockades of the fortresses of the Vistula, Dantzick, Thorn, and Modlin.   It was anticipated that the success of this vast plan would have been the means of breaking up the coalition, and

that, in consequence, all the German Princes would have
been confirmed in their allegiance and their alliance with
France. It was hoped that Bavaria would have delayed
for a fortnight to change sides, and then it was certain
that she would not have changed at all.

"The armies met on the plains of Leipsic, on the 16th
of October. The French were victorious; the Austrians
were beaten and driven from all their positions; and
Count Meerfeld, who commanded one of the Austrian
corps, was made prisoner. On the 18th, notwithstanding the check sustained by the Duke of Ragusa on the
16th, victory was still on the side of the French, when
the whole of the Saxon army, with a battery of sixty
guns, occupying one of the most important positions of
the line, passed over to the enemy, and turned its
artillery on the French ranks. Such unlooked-for
treachery could not but cause the destruction of the
French army, and transfer all the glory of the day to
the Allies. The Emperor galloped forward with half his
guard, repulsed the Swedes and Saxons, and drove them
from their positions. This day (the 18th) was now
ended: the enemy made a retrograde movement along
the whole of his line, and bivouacked in the rear of the
field of battle, which remained in the possession of the
French. In the night, the French army made a movement, in order to take its position behind the Elster,
and thus to be in direct communication with Erfurt,
whence were expected the convoys of ammunition that
were so much wanted. In the engagements of the 16th
and 18th, the French army had fired more than 150,000
discharges of cannon. The treachery of several of the
German corps of the Confederation, who were seduced
by the example of the Saxons on the preceding day, and
the destruction of the bridge of Leipsic, which was
blown up by mistake, occasioned the French army,
though victorious, to experience the losses which
usually result from the most disastrous engagements.
The French re-crossed the Saale by the bridge of Weissen-
feld: they intended to rally their forces, and await the
arrival of the ammunition from Erfurt, which had abundant supplies.

" Intelligence was now received of the Austro-Bavarian army, which, by forced marches, had reached the Maine. It was necessary therefore to repair thither, in order to come up with the Bavarians; and, on the 30th of October, the French fell in with them, drawn up in order of battle before Hanau and intercepting the Frankfort roads. The Bavarian force, though numerous, and occupying fine positions, was completely routed, and driven beyond Hanau, which was in the possession of Count Bertrand. General Wrede was wounded. The French forces continued their movement with the view of falling back behind the Rhine, and they re-crossed the river on the 2nd of November. A parley ensued: Baron de St. Aignan repaired to Frankfort, where he had conferences with Counts Metternich and Nesselrode and Lord Aberdeen, and he arrived at Paris with proposals for peace on the following bases:—That the Emperor Napoleon should renounce the Protectorship of the Confederation of the Rhine, Poland, and the departments of the Elbe; but that France should retain her boundaries of the Alps and the Rhine, together with the possession of Holland, and that a frontier line in Italy should be determined upon, for separating France from the States of the House of Austria The Emperor agreed to these bases; but the Congress of Frankfort, like that of Prague, was merely a stratagem employed in the hope that France would reject the terms which were proposed. It was wished to have a new subject for a manifesto to operate on the public mind; for at the moment when these conciliatory propositions were made, the Allied army was violating the neutrality of the cantons, and entering Switzerland. However, the Allies at last developed their real intentions; they named Chatillon-sur-Seine, in Burgundy, as the seat of the Congress. The battles of Champ-Aubert, Montmirail, and Montereau, destroyed the armies of Blucher and Witgenstein. No negotiations took place at Chatillon; but the coalesced Powers presented an *ultimatum*, the conditions of which were as follows:

" 1st, That France should surrender the whole of Italy, Belgium, Holland, and the departments of the Rhine;

2nd, that France should return to her limits as they existed previously to 1792. The Emperor rejected this *ultimatum.* He consented to sacrifice Holland and Italy to the circumstances in which France was then placed; but he refused to resign the limits of the Alps and the Rhine, or to surrender Belgium and particularly Antwerp. Treason secured the triumph of the Allies, notwithstanding the victories of Arcis and St. Dizier. Hitherto the Allies had intimated no design of interfering in the internal affairs of France; this is proved by the *ultimatum* of Chatillon, signed by England, Austria, Russia, and Prussia. At length, however, some of the returned emigrants, excited by the presence of the Austrian, Russian, and Prussian armies, in whose ranks they had long borne arms, imagined that the moment had arrived in which their dreams were to be realized: some mounted the white cockade, and others displayed the cross of St. Louis. This conduct was disapproved by the Allied Sovereigns; and it was even censured by Wellington at Bourdeaux, though in reality he secretly favoured all who endeavoured to raise the ensigns of the House of Bourbon. In the transactions which detached Prussia from her alliance with France, and bound her to Russia by the treaty of Kalisch; in the treaty which united Austria with the coalition; in the diplomatic proceedings, public and private, which took place down to the treaty of Chatillon; and even in that concluded in France, in 1814, the Allies never made any reference to the Bourbons.''

The VIIth, VIIIth, and IXth Chapters shew that the Bourbons after their return ought to have commenced a fifth dynasty, and not to have endeavoured to continue the third. The first course would have rendered all easy, the second has involved every thing in difficulty.

The Xth Chapter closes with a passage of a few lines which forcibly describe the magical effect of the Emperor's return on the 20th of March. These last chapters contain the most nervous and energetic writing, but the applications are direct, and indeed often personal. I have suppressed the details, because I wish not to afford

any ground for my being accused of bringing forward a
hostile statement. Time, which modifies all things, wil.
render this work merely an historical document, which is
the only light in which I wish it to be considered here,
as well, indeed, as all works of a similar nature that
I may think it necessary to quote. I have written in
France and other countries, under different laws and circumstances, and I have always found the liberty of the
press existing for me.

I hope to experience its influence on the present
occasion, although my subject is one of a most delicate
nature. I now look forward to the speedy termination
of my voyage; the port is within sight, and I hope to
reach it safely, in spite of all the shoals I may encounter.

MY DOMESTIC AFFAIRS.—THE EMPEROR'S VIEWS IN HIS MUNIFICENCE.

9th—10th. The Emperor passed a bad night. He
desired me to be called early in the morning. When I
went to him, he told me that he was half dead, that he
had had no rest, and was feverish. He has continued
very ill for these two days, and has reclined almost constantly on his couch, which in the evenings is drawn
near the fire. He has been unable to eat, and has drunk
nothing but warm lemonade. I have been in continual
attendance on him during these two days; he has enjoyed a little sleep at intervals, and the rest of the time
he has spent in conversing with me upon various subjects.
He spoke of the expense of giving parties in Paris; and,
passing from that subject to my domestic affairs, he
expressed a wish that I should make him acquainted
with the minutest details on that point.

I told him that my income had amounted only to
20,000 francs a year, 15,000 of which were derived
from my own property, and 5000 from my salary as a
Councillor of State. On hearing this he exclaimed:
" You must have been mad! How could you venture *c
approach the Tuileries with so straitened an income?
The expenses of attending the Court were enormous!"
—" Sire," I replied, " I contrived to keep up my dignity

as well as the rest: and yet I never solicited any thing from your Majesty." The Emperor observed, " I do not say you did; but you must have been ruined in less than four or five years."—" No, Sire," I rejoined, " I had been an emigrant during the greater part of my life : I had lived amidst privations, and, with a few exceptions, I still subjected myself to them. It is true that, in spite of all my economy, I ran through 7 or 8000 francs of my capital every year. But I calculated thus: it was well known that every person about you must, by dint of zeal and attention to their duties, sooner or later, attract your notice, and that he who once gained your favour might consider his fortune made. I had still four or five years left to try this chance; at the expiration of which, if fortune did not smile on me, I was determined to renounce the illusions of the world, and to retire from the capital with an income of ten or twelve thousand livres ; poor enough, to be sure, but, nevertheless, richer than ever I had been in Paris."—" Well," said the Emperor, " your scheme was not a bad one, and the moment had just arrived when you would have been indemnified for all your losses. I was just about to do something for you, and it was wholly your own fault that you did not make a more rapid and brilliant fortune. I believe I have told you before that you did not know how to avail yourself of favourable opportunities for securing your own advancement."

This conversation led us to speak of the enormous sums which the Emperor had lavished on the persons about him, and, gradually becoming animated, he said :—" It would be difficult to estimate all that I bestowed in this way. I might, on more than one occasion, have been accused of profusion, and I am grieved to see that it has been of little use in any respect. There must certainly have been some fatality on my part, or some essential fault in the persons whom I favoured. What a difficulty was I placed in ! It cannot be believed that my extravagance was caused by personal vanity. To act the part of an Asiatic monarch was not a thing to my taste. I was not actuated either by vanity or caprice· every thing was with me a matter of calculation.

Though certain persons might be favourites with me, yet I did not lavish my bounty on them merely because I liked them: I wished to found, through them, great families, who might form rallying-points in great national crises. The great Officers of my Household, as well as all my Ministers, independently of their enormous salaries, often received from me handsome gratuities,—sometimes complete services of plate, &c. What was my object in this profuseness? I required that they should maintain elegant establishments, give grand dinners and brilliant balls!—And why did I wish this? In order to amalgamate parties, to form new unions, to smooth down old asperities, and to give a character to French society and manners. If I conceived good ideas, they miscarried in the execution: for instance, none of my chief Courtiers ever kept up a suitable establishment. If they gave dinners, they invited only their party friends; and when I attended their expensive balls, whom did I find there? All the Court of the Tuileries: not a new face; not one of those who were offended at the new system—those sullen malcontents, whom a little honey would have brought back to the hive. They could not enter into my views, or did not wish to do so. In vain I expressed displeasure, intreated, and commanded: things still went on in the same way. I could not be every-where at once, and they knew that;—and yet it was affirmed that I ruled with a rod of iron. How, then, must things go under gentle sovereigns?"

REMOVAL OF THE EMPEROR'S BED.—ANECDOTE OF A GASCON SOLDIER.—THE GUARDS OF THE EAGLE.

11th.—The Emperor continued unwell. I found him very low-spirited. He had ordered the situation of his bed to be changed—that bed, so long the constant companion of his victories, was now a couch of sickness. He complained that it was too small for him, that he could hardly turn himself in it; but his chamber would not have afforded room for a longer one. He ordered the camp-bed to be carried into his cabinet, and placed beside a couch; so that the two combined formed a bed of tolerable size. To what an extremity is he reduced! The

Emperor stretched himself on his sofa, and entered into conversation, which revived him a little. Speaking of his accession to the Consulship, and of the dreadful disorders which he found existing in all the branches of the public service, he said that he had been compelled to adopt numerous measures of reform, which caused a great outcry, but which had not a little contributed to strengthen the bonds of society. These measures extended to the army, among the officers, and even among the generals, who, he said, had become such, Heaven knows how. Here I took the liberty to relate an anecdote which had at one time afforded great amusement to the circle in which I moved. One of my friends, (who was as dissatisfied with the then existing government as I was myself,) travelling in one of the small Versailles, diligences with a soldier of the guard, maliciously excited him to express his opinions. The man complained that every thing went wrong, because it was required that a soldier should know how to read and write before he could be advanced from the ranks. " So you see," he exclaimed, " the *tic has returned again*."* This phrase pleased us, and was often repeated among us. " Well," observed the Emperor, " what would your soldier have said when I created the Guards of the Eagle ? That measure would, doubtless, have re-established me in his good opinion. I appointed two sub-officers to be the special guards of the Eagle in every regiment, one of whom was placed on either side of the standard; and, lest their ardour in the midst of the conflict might cause them to lose sight of the only object which they ought to have in view, namely, the preservation of the Eagle, they were prohibited from using the sabre or the sword: their only arms were a few braces of pistols; their only duty was coolly to blow out the brains of the enemy who might attempt to lay hands on the Eagle. But, before a man could obtain this post, he was required to prove that he could neither read nor write, and of course you guess the reason why." " No, Sire." " Why, simpleton ! Every man who has received education is sure to rise in the army, but the soldier who has not these

---

* *Tic* is the French term for any bad habit.

advantages, never attains advancement except by dint of courage and extraordinary circumstances."

As I was in the humour for gossiping, I related another anecdote, which had also produced merriment in the saloons of Paris. It was said that, a regiment having lost its Eagle, Napoleon harangued the men on the subject, and expressed great indignation at the dishonour they had brought upon themselves by suffering their Eagle to be taken. "But we tricked the enemy," exclaimed a Gascon soldier, "they have only got the staff, for here is the *cuckoo* in my pocket;" and he produced the Eagle. The Emperor laughed and said, "Well, I could not venture to affirm that this circumstance, or something very like it, did not actually take place. My soldiers were very much at their ease and made very free with me; often addressing me familiarly by the pronoun *thou*."

I mentioned having heard that on the eve of the battle of Jena, or some other great engagement, as Napoleon was passing a particular station, accompanied by a very small escort, a soldier refused to let him pass, and, growing angry when the Emperor insisted on advancing, swore that he should not pass even though he were the *Little Corporal* himself. When the soldier ascertained that it was really the Little Corporal, he was not at all disconcerted. The Emperor observed, "That was because he felt the conviction of having done his duty; and indeed the fact is that I passed for a terrible tyrant in the saloons, and even among the officers of the army, but not among the soldiers: they possessed the instinct of truth and sympathy, they knew me to be their protector, and, in case of need, their avenger."

THE EMPEROR CONTINUES UNWELL.— HORRIBLE PROVISIONS, EXECRABLE WINE, &c.

12th.—To-day the Emperor, although no better than he had been for some days past, determined, as he said, to nurse himself no longer. He dressed and repaired to the drawing-room, where he dictated, for two or three hours, to one of his suite. He had eaten nothing for three days: he had not yet been relieved by the crisis which he expected, and which is usually produced by the singular regimen which he prescribes for himself. He

continued drinking warm lemonade. This circumstance
led him to inquire how long a person might live without
eating, and how far drink might supply the place of solid
food. He sent for the *Encyclopedia Britannica*, in which
he met with some very curious facts: for instance, he
found that a woman had existed for fifty days without
solid food, and drinking only twice. Another instance
was mentioned of a person who had lived twenty days
upon water alone.

Somebody observed, in reference to this subject, that
Charles XII., out of pure contradiction to the opinions of
those around him, had abstained from eating for the space
of five or six days, at the expiration of which, however,
he devoured a turkey and a leg of mutton, at the hazard
of bursting. Napoleon laughed at this anecdote, and
assured us that he felt no wish to run to such extremes,
however attractive the model might be in other respects.

The Emperor played a game at piquet with Madame
de Montholon. The Grand Marshal having entered, he
left off playing, and asked him how he thought he looked.
Bertrand replied, " Only rather sallow;" which was
indeed the case. The Emperor rose good-humouredly,
and pursued Bertrand into the saloon, in order to catch
him by the ear, exclaiming, " Rather sallow, indeed !
Do you intend to insult me, Grand Marshal ? Do you
mean to say that I am bilious, morose, atrabilarious,
passionate, unjust, tyrannical ! Let me catch hold of your
ear, and I will take my revenge."

The dinner-hour arrived, and the Emperor for some
time was undecided whether he would sit down to table
with us, or dine alone in his own room. He decided
upon the latter plan, lest, as he said, he should be tempted
to imitate Charles XII. if he sat at the great table: but
he would have found it difficult to do that. He returned
while we were at dinner, and, from the scanty way in
which our table was served, he said he really pitied us,
for in fact we had scarcely any thing to eat. This circumstance induced the Emperor to resort to a painful
extremity: he instantly gave orders that a portion of his
plate should be sold every month, to supply what was
necessary for our table. The worst thing connected with
our wretched dinner was the wine, which had for some

days been execrable, and had made us all unwell. We were obliged to send for some to the camp, in the hope that that which had been furnished to us would be changed, as we could not drink it.

In the course of a conversation which took place respecting the wine, the Emperor stated that he had received a great number of instructions and directions from chemists and physicians, all of whom had concurred in declaring that wine and coffee were the two things respecting which it was most necessary he should be on his guard. Every professional man had cautioned him to reject both wine and coffee if he found any unpleasant flavour in them. Wine, in particular, he was advised to abstain from, if he found any thing *uncommon* in the taste of it. He had always been in the habit of getting his wine from Chambertin, and had therefore, seldom occasion to find fault with it; but the case is different now, if he had refused wine whenever he found any thing *uncommon* in it, he must have abstained from it for a considerable time past.

CRITICISM ON PRINCE LUCIEN'S POEM OF CHARLEMAGNE :—HOMER.

13th.--The weather is very bad; and it has continued so for three weeks or a month. The Emperor sent for me before one o'clock: he was in his saloon; our Amphitryon had paid me a visit, and I took him to the Emperor, who spoke to him on matters of a private and personal nature.

Napoleon is much altered in his looks.—To-day he wished to set to work. I sent for my son, and he went over the chapters relating to the Pope and Tagliamento. He continued thus employed until five o'clock. He was very low-spirited, and appeared to be suffering much; he retired, saying he would try to eat a little.

Two ships came within sight, one was supposed to be the Eurydice, which was every moment expected to arrive from Europe, having touched at the Cape: they proved to be, however, one of the Company's ships and another vessel that was accidentally passing the island.

The Emperor came to us while we were at dinner; he

said he had eaten enough for four persons, and that this
had quite restored him.

He wanted something to read, and looked over his
brother Lucien's poem of Charlemagne. He analysed
the first canto, and afterwards glanced over a few others:
he then examined the subject and the plan of the work,
&c. "How much labour, ingenuity and time," he observed, "have been thrown away upon this book! what
a wreck of judgment and taste! Here are twenty thousand verses, some of which may be good, for aught I
know; but they are destitute of interest, design, or effect.
It might have been regarded as a compulsory task, had
it been written by a professed author. Why did not
Lucien, with all his good sense, consider that Voltaire,
master as he was of the French language and the art of
poetry, failed in a similar attempt, though that attempt
was made in Paris, in the midst of the sanctuary! How
could Lucien suppose it possible to write a French poem,
when living at a distance from the French capital? How
could he pretend to introduce a new metre? He has
written a history in verse, and not an epic poem. An
epic poem should not be the history of a man, but of a
passion or an event. And, then, what a subject has
Lucien chosen! What barbarous names has he introduced!
Does he think he has succeeded in raising the religion
which he conceived to be fallen? Is his poem intended
as a work of re-action? It certainly bears the stamp of
the soil on which it was written: it is full of prayers,
priests, the temporal authority of the Popes, &c. How
could he think of devoting twenty thousand lines to absurdities which do not belong to the present age, to prejudices which he could not enter into, and opinions which
he could not entertain! What a misapplication of talent!
He might undoubtedly have produced something more
creditable to himself; for he possesses judgment, facility,
and industry. He was in Rome amidst the richest materials, and with the means of satisfying the deepest
research. He understands the Italian language: and, as
we have no good history of Italy, he might have written
one. His talents, his situation, his knowledge of affairs,
his rank, might have enabled him to produce an excellent

classic work. It would have been a valuable acquisition to the literary world, and would have conferred honour on its author. But what is Charlemagne? What reputation will it gain? It will be buried in the dust of libraries, and its author will obtain at most a few scanty and perhaps ridiculous notices in biographical dictionaries. If Lucien could not resist the temptation of scribbling verses, he should have prepared a splendid manuscript, embellished with elegant designs and superb binding, with which he might now and then have gratified the eyes of the ladies, occasionally allowing a few quotations from it to creep into publicity; and finally he should have left it to his heirs, with a severe prohibition against committing it to the press. One might then have been able to understand his taste."

He laid the work aside, and said: "Let us turn to the Iliad." My son went to fetch it, and the Emperor read a few cantos, stopping at various passages, in order, as he said, to admire them at his ease. His observations were copious and remarkable. He was so deeply interested in what he read, that it was half-past twelve before he retired to rest.

SCARCITY OF PROVISIONS.—RIDICULOUS ALLOWANCE OF WINE.—NAPOLEON'S RETURN FROM ELBA.

14th.—The terrible state of the weather still continued, and confined us to our miserable huts. We are all indisposed.

The Emperor dictated during part of the day, and he felt himself much better.

At dinner we had literally scarcely any thing to eat. The Governor continued his successive reductions. The Emperor ordered some additional provisions to be purchased and paid for out of the produce of the sale of his plate.

The Governor intimated that the allowance of wine should continue fixed at one bottle for each person, the Emperor included. Will it be credited? *One bottle for a mother and her children!* these were the words used in the note.

The Emperor retired to his own apartment, and sent

for me to attend him. "I am not inclined to sleep,"
said he, "and I sent for you to help me to keep my
vigil; let us have a little chat together." The turn of
the conversation led us to speak of the Island of Elba, of
the Emperor's occupations, sensations, and opinions
while he continued there; finally, his return to France,
and the brilliant success which attended him, and which,
he said, he never for a moment doubted. Many observations were repeated, which I have already noted down
at different times. At one moment he said: "They
may explain this as they will: but I assure you, I never
entertained any direct or personal hatred of those whose
power I subverted. To me it was merely a political
contest: I was astonished myself to find my heart free
from animosity, and, I may add, animated by good will
towards my enemies. You saw how I released the Duke
d'Angoulême; and I would have done the same by the
King, and even have granted him an asylum of his own
choosing. The triumph of the cause in no way depended
on his person, and I respected his age and his misfortunes. Perhaps also I felt grateful for a certain degree
of consideration which he in particular had observed towards me. It is true that, at the moment to which I am
now alluding, he had, I believe, outlawed me and set a
price upon my head; but I looked upon all this as belonging to the *manifesto style*. The same kind of denunciations were also issued by the Austrian government, without, however, giving me much uneasiness; though I
must confess that my dear father-in-law was rather too
hard with the husband of his beloved daughter."

Since I have once more had occasion to mention the
Emperor's return from the Island of Elba, this is, perhaps,
the proper place to fulfil the promise I have made of
giving a narrative of the circumstances connected with
that extraordinary event. I here combine together the
statements that fell from him at different times.

Napoleon was residing at the Island of Elba, on the
faith of treaties, when he learned that at the Congress of
Vienna some idea was entertained of transporting him
from Europe. None of the articles of the treaty of Fontainebleau were fulfilled. The public papers informed him

of the state of feeling in France, and ！e accordingly formed his determination. He kept the secret until the last moment;* and, under one pretence or another, means were found for making the requisite preparations. It was not until they were all on board that the troops first conceived a suspicion of the Emperor's purpose : a thousand or twelve hundred men had set sail to regain possession of an empire containing a population of thirty millions !

There were nearly five or six hundred men on board the brig in which Napoleon embarked ; this was, he said, the crew of a seventy-four.   They fell in with a French brig of war, which they spoke.   It was asserted that the captain of the French brig recognised them, and at part .ng cried out three times, "A good voyage to you!" At all events, the officer who commanded the Emperor's vessel, proposed to pursue and capture the brig.   The Emperor rejected the idea as absurd ; such a proceeding could only have been excusable, had necessity demanded it.   "Why," said he, "should I introduce this new incident into my plan ? What advantage should I derive from its success ?   To what risks would its failure expose me !"

After the check they experienced on landing, by the capture of twenty men who had been sent to summon Antibes, a variety of opinions was advanced, and urged with some warmth.   Some proposed that they should make immediately an attack and carry Antibes, in order to obviate the evil consequences which might ensue

---

* I must take this opportunity of correcting an error which has occasioned considerable pain to an individual whom I greatly esteem. In a former part of this Journal it is mentioned that, *eight days* before the Emperor quitted Elba, General Drouot communicated his intentions to the Princess Borghese, &c.   General Drouot, however, affirms that he was not honoured with the Emperor's confidence until the *very last moment*, and that consequently he could not have divulged the secret at the time alluded to. General Drouot must of all others be the best informed, as well as most interested, with regard to these facts : for my own part I have only to observe, that, in this instance, I merely noted down a current report, which was repeated without any ill design, and which had never been contradicted.

from the resistance of that place and the imprisonment of
the twenty men.   The Emperor replied that the taking
of Antibes would be no step towards the conquest of
France; that, during the brief interval that would be
occupied in the execution of that project, a general alarm
would be raised throughout the country; and that obstacles would be opposed to them in the only course which
it was expedient they should pursue.   He added that
time was valuable; and that the ill consequences of the
affair of Antibes might be effectually obviated by marching forward with sufficient speed to anticipate the news.
An officer of the guard indirectly hinted that it was not
right thus to abandon the twenty men who had been
made prisoners; but the Emperor merely observed that
he had formed a poor idea of the magnitude of the enterprise; that, if half of his followers were in the same situation, he would not scruple to abandon them in the same
manner; and that if they were all made prisoners, he
would march forward alone.*

A few hours before nightfall he landed at the gulf of
Juan, where he bivouacked.   Soon after, a postilion in
splendid livery was conducted to him.   It turned out
that this man had formerly been in the Imperial household.   He had been a domestic of the Empress Josephine's, and was now in the service of the Prince of
Monaco, who himself had been equerry to the Empress.
The postilion, on being questioned by the Emperor, informed him, after expressing his great astonishment at
finding him there, that he had just come from Paris, and
that he was sure he would every where be joyfully greeted.
He affirmed that all along the road, as far as Avingnon,
he had heard nothing but regret for the Emperor's ab-
ence; that his name was publicly in every mouth, and
that, when once fairly through Provence, he would
find the whole population ready to rally round him.

---

* It must not, however, be supposed that he shewed any unfeel-
ing disregard of these men; for he directed the war commissioner,
Charles Vautier, who was with him, to repair with all haste to Antibes, and to release the prisoners by attempting to take the garrison.
When Vautier set out, he several times called after him."   " Take
care you do not get yourself made prisoner too "

The man added, that his splendid livery had frequently
rendered him the object of odium and insult.   This
was the testimony of one of the common class of society : it was very gratifying to the Emperor, and entirely
corresponded with his expectations.   The Prince of
Monaco himself, on being presented to Napoleon, was
less explicit.   Napoleon refrained from questioning him
on political matters : there were persons present, and he
did not wish to incur the risk of eliciting any detail which
might create unfavourable impressions on those about
him.   The conversation therefore assumed a lively character, and turned entirely on the ladies of the Imperial
court of the Tuileries, concerning whom Napoleon made
the minutest inquiries.

As soon as the moon had risen, which was about one
or two o'clock in the morning, the bivouack broke up,
and Napoleon gave orders for proceeding to Grasse.
There he expected to find a road which he had ordered
during the Empire.   However, the design had not been
executed, and he was reduced to the necessity of passing
through narrow defiles filled with snow. He therefore left
behind him, in the charge of the municipality of Grasse,
his carriage and two pieces of cannon, which had been
brought ashore : this was termed a capture in the bulletins of the time.

The municipality of Grasse was devoted to the royalist
party; but the sudden appearance of the Emperor afforded little time for hesitation, and they came to make
their submission to him.   The Emperor, having passed
through the town, halted on a little height at some distance beyond it, where he breakfasted,   He was soon
surrounded by the whole population of the town : and
went through this multitude as though he had been in the
midst of his Court circle at the Tuileries.   He heard the
same sentiments and the same prayers as before he quitted France.   One complained of not having received his
pension, another solicited an addition to his allowance,
a third represented that his cross of the legion of honour
had been withheld from him, a fourth prayed for pro-
motion, &c.   A number of petitions had already been
drawn up and were presented to him, just as though he

had come from Paris, and was making a tour through the departments.

Some enthusiastic patriots, who were well acquainted with the state of affairs, secretly informed Napoleon that the authorities of the place were very hostile, but that the mass of the people were devoted to him, and that they only waited until his back should be turned, in order to rid themselves of the miscreants. " Be not too hasty," said the Emperor. " Let them have the mortification of seeing our triumph, without having any thing to reproach us with. Be tranquil and prudent."

The Emperor advanced with the rapidity of lightning. " Victory," said he, depended on my speed, To me France was in Grenoble. This place was an hundred leagues distant, but I and my companions reached it in five days,* and by what roads and what weather ! I entered the city just as the Count d' Artois, warned by the telegraph, was quitting the Tuileries.

Napoleon himself was so perfectly convinced of the state of affairs, and of popular sentiment, that he knew

---

* March 1st. The Emperor landed at Cannes, at the Gulf of Juan.

2d. Entered Grasse.

3d. Slept at Barême.

4th. Dined at Digne, and slept at Maligeai.

5th. Slept at Gap.

6th. Slept at Corps, and a little beyond the town on the following day, the Emperor harangued and rallied the troops of the 5th. A few hours afterwards he was joined by Labédoyère, at the head of the 7th.

7th. Arrived at Grenoble and halted.

9th. Slept at Bourgouin.

10th. Reached Lyons, where he remained three days.

13th. Slept at Macon. Ney's famous proclamation issued.

14th. Slept at Chalons.

15th. Slept at Autun.

16th. At Avalon.

17th. At Auxeres, where he remained for a day, and was joined by the Prince of the Moskowa.

20th. Arrived at Fontainebleau, at four in the morning, and entered the Tuileries at nine in the evening.

his success in no way depended on the force which he might bring with him. A piquet of gendarmerie, he said, was all that was necessary. Every thing turned out as he had calculated : " Victory advanced *au pas de charge*, and the national Eagle flew from steeple to steeple, till at length it perched on the towers of Notre Dame." The Emperor, however, admitted that at first he was not without some degree of alarm and uncertainty. As he advanced, it is true, the whole population enthusiastically declared themselves in his favour; but he saw no soldiers : they were all carefully removed from the places through which he passed. It was not until he was between Mure and Vizille, within five or six leagues of Grenoble, and on the fifth day after his embarkation, that he met the first battalion. The commanding officer refused even to parley. The Emperor, without hesitation, advanced alone, and one hundred of his grenadiers marched at some distance from him, with their arms reversed. The sight of Napoleon, his costume, and in particular his grey military great coat, produced a magical effect on the soldiers, and they stood motionless. Napoleon went straight up to a veteran, whose arm was covered with *chevrons*, and very unceremoniously seizing him by the whisker, asked him whether he would have the heart to kill his Emperor. The soldier, his eyes moistened with tears, immediately thrust the ramrod into his musquet, to shew that it was not loaded, and exclaimed, "See, I could not have done thee any harm : all the others are the same. ' Cries of *Vive l' Empereur !* resounded on every side. Napoleon ordered the battalion to make half a turn to the right, and all marched on to Paris.

At a little distance from Grenoble, Colonel Labédoyère, at the head of his regiment, came to join the Emperor. The impulse was then confirmed, and the question was nearly decided.

The peasantry of Dauphiny lined the road-sides : they were transported and mad with joy. The first battalion, which has just been alluded to, still shewed some signs of hesitation; but thousands crowded on its rear, and by their shouts of *Vive l' Empereur !* endeavoured to

urge the troops to decision; while others, who were in
Napoleon's rear, excited his little troop to advance, declaring that no harm whatever would be done to it.

In a valley through which they passed, a very affecting
spectacle presented itself: many communes were assembled together, accompanied by their mayors and curates.
Amidst the multitude was observed a handsome young
man, a grenadier of the Guard, who had been missing
since the time of Napoleon's landing, and whose dis-
appearance had given rise to suspicion. He now advanced and threw himself at the Emperor's feet: the
tears glistened in his eyes, and he supported in his arms
an old man of ninety, whom he presented to the Emperor:—this was his father, in quest of whom he had
set off as soon as he landed in France. The Emperor,
after his arrival at the Tuileries, ordered a picture of this
circumstance to be painted.

It was night when Napoleon arrived before the walls
of Grenoble: his promptitude defeated all the measures
that were to have been taken to oppose him. There
was no time to cut down the bridges, nor even to put the
troops in motion. He found the gates of the city closed,
and the colonel commanding the fortress refused to open
them. " A peculiar circumstance attending this extraordinary revolution," said the Emperor, "was that the
soldiers were not deficient, to a certain degree, in discipline and obedience to their commanding officers: their
only resistance was by inert force, of which they availed
themselves as of a right." Thus the first battalion
performed all the movements that were ordered, retired
and refused to communicate; but the men did not load
their guns, and they would not have fired. When Napoleon arrived before Grenoble, the whole garrison,
assembled on the ramparts, shouted *Vive l' Empereur!*
They shook hands with Napoleon's followers, through
the wickets; but they would not open the gates, because
the commander had forbidden them to do so. The
Emperor found it necessary to force the gates; and this
was done under the mouths of ten pieces of artillery on
the ramparts, loaded with grape-shot. To complete this

union of singular circumstances, the commander of the first battalion and the colonel, who had so openly opposed the Emperor, when asked by him whether he could depend on them, replied that he could ;—that their troops had deserted them, but that they would never desert their troops; and that, since the men had declared themselves for Napoleon, they also would be faithful to him. The Emperor retained these officers in his service.

In none of his battles did Napoleon ever imagine himself to be in so much danger as at his entrance into Grenoble. The soldiers seemed to turn upon him with furious gestures; for a moment it might have been supposed that they were about to tear him in pieces. But these were merely transports of love and joy. The Emperor and his horse were both borne along by the multitude; and he had scarcely time to breathe in the inn where he alighted, when an increased tumult was heard in the streets: the inhabitants of Grenoble came to offer him the gates of the city, since they could not present him with the keys.

"Being once established in Grenoble," said the Emperor, "and having attained a positive power, I could have maintained hostilities had it been necessary to do so."

Napoleon, at this time, very much regretted not having got his proclamations printed at the Island of Elba; but of course this could not have been done without the risk of promulgating his secret designs. He dictated his proclamations on board the brig, where every man who could write was employed in copying them. It was found necessary to transcribe them over again during the Emperor's march to Paris, that they might be circulated on the road, so eager was the demand for them. They were then very scarce, often incorrect and even illegible; and yet the necessity of promulgating them was felt at every step, for wherever they were read they produced an immediate and powerful sensation. The events of the last twenty years have contributed in a high degree to enlighten the mass of the people, for, notwithstanding the joy they felt at the Emperor's re-

13*

turn, they eagerly enquired what was his object. All
were satisfied with the national sentiments contained in
the proclamations ; and the utmost joy was evinced when
it was understood that Napoleon had brought no foreign
troops with him. His advance had been so rapid and
his movements so unexpected, that a thousand reports
had been circulated respecting the amount and nature ·
of his forces. It was said that he was accompanied
by Neapolitans, Austrians, and even Turks.

From Grenoble to Paris, Napoleon may be said to have
made a triumphal march. During the four days of his
stay at Lyons, there were continually upwards of twenty
thousand persons assembled before his windows, and
their acclamations were incessant. It would never
have been supposed that the Emperor had for a moment
been separated from his subjects. He signed decrees,
issued orders, reviewed troops, &c. ; all military corps,
all public bodies, all classes ,of the citizens, eagerly
came forward to offer him their homage and demonstrate their attachment. Even the national horse
guards, a corps composed of men who had shewn themselves most ardent in the Royalist cause, solicited the
honour of forming his escort ; but these were the only
persons whom the Emperor treated with coldness. " Gentlemen," said he, " I thank you for this offer of your
services ; but your conduct towards the Count d' Artois
sufficiently proves how you would act by me, were fortune to forsake me. I will not subject you to this new
trial." On quitting Lyons, the Count d' Artois, it is
said, found only one of the guards willing to follow him
to Paris. The Emperor, whose heart was so keenly
alive to every generous sentiment, on hearing of the
fidelity of this volunteer, ordered the decoration of the
legion of honour to be presented to him.

At Lyons, Napoleon issued orders, through the medium of proclamations, with all that precision, firmness,
and confidence, which usually attend established and
uninterrupted power. His conduct indicated no trace of
the terrible reverses he had so lately sustained, or the
great risks he had yet to encounter. If it were possible
to mention every circumstance, that took place, I could

relate a very pleasant private anecdote indicative of the calmness of mind evinced by Napoleon, during the great crisis which was about to change the face of France and to rouse all Europe.

As soon as the Emperor quitted Lyons, he wrote to inform Ney, who, with his army, was at Lons-le-Saunier, that he must immediately march with his forces to join him. Ney, amidst the general confusion, abandoned by his troops, confounded by the Emperor's proclamations, the addresses of Dauphiny, and the defection of the garrison of Lyons, overpowered by the enthusiasm of the people of the surrounding provinces—Ney, the child of the Revolution, yielded to the general impulse, and issued his famous order of the day. But the recollection of the events of Fontainebleau induced him to write to the Emperor, informing him that, in his recent conduct he had been guided principally by a view to the interests of his country; and that, convinced he must have forfeited all claim to Napoleon's confidence, he solicited permission to retire from the service. The Emperor again wrote, desiring that he would immediately come and join him, and that he would receive him as he had done the day after the battle of the Moscowa. Ney, on presenting himself before the Emperor, was much embarrassed; and repeated that, if he had lost his confidence, he asked for nothing but to be reduced to the rank of one of his grenadiers. "Certainly," said the Emperor, "he had behaved very ill to me; but how could I forget his brilliant courage, and the many acts of heroism that had distinguished his past life ! I rushed forward to embrace him, calling him the ' *bravest of the brave*'—and from that moment we were reconciled."

The Emperor went nearly post haste all the way from Lyons to Paris. He no where experienced opposition, and no fighting took place. Literally his presence produced merely a theatrical change of scene. His advanced guard was composed of the troops which happened to be before him on the road, and to which couriers were sent forward. Thus Napoleon entered Paris, escorted by the very troops who in the morning had been sent out to oppose him. A regiment posted at Montereau spontaneously crossed the bridge, repaired to Melun, and charged a party of the body guards who were stationed at the latter place: this circumstance, it is said, occasioned the sudden departure of the Royal family.

The Emperor frequently told us that, if he had chosen, he might have brought with him to Paris two millions of peasants. On his approach the people every where rose in a mass; and he often repeats that there were no conspirators excepting opinion.

On the day after Napoleon's arrival at the Tuileries, some one having remarked to him that his life was a succession of prodigies, but that the last surpassed all the rest, I heard him say in reply, that his only merit, in this instance, consisted in having formed a just opinion of the state of affairs in France, and in having been able to penetrate into the hearts of Frenchmen. At another time he said to us, when conversing on this sub-ject: "If I except Labédoyère, who flew to me with enthusiasm and affection, and another individual who freely rendered me important services, nearly all the other generals whom I met on my route evinced hesitation and uncertainty: they yielded only to the impulse of their troops, if indeed they did not manifest a hostile feeling towards me.

"It is now clear to every one," said he, "that Ney quitted Paris quite devoted to the King, and that if he turned against him a few days afterwards, it was because he thought he could not do otherwise.

"I was so far from relying at all on Massena that, on my landing in France, I felt it necessary to get past him with all speed; and on my asking him some time after, at Paris, how he would have acted, had I not left Provence so precipitately as I did, he was frank enough to reply that he should feel some embarrassment in answering me; but that the course I had pursued was, at all events, the safest, and the best

"Saint-Cyr found himself in danger by attempting to restrain the soldiers under his command.

"Soult confessed to me that he had conceived a sin-cere regard for the King, so much did he admire his government; and he would not return to my service until after the *Champ de Mai.*

"Macdonald never made his appearance, and the Duke of Belluno followed the King to Ghent. Thus," said he, "if the Bourbons have reason to complain of the complete desertion of the soldiers and the people, they certainly have no right to reproach with infidelity the chiefs of the army, those pupils or even leaders of the Revolution, who, in spite of twenty-five years' experience, proved themselves, in this instance, mere children in politics. They could neither be looked upon as emigrants nor patriots!"

Napoleon seemed instinctively attached to his grand principle of acting only on masses and by masses. Both at the commencement of the enterprise, and after his landing in France, he was repeatedly urged to treat with some of the authorities, but he constantly returned the same excellent answer: "If I still hold a place in the hearts of the people, I need concern myself but little about persons in authority, and if I could only rely on the latter, what service could they render me in opposing the great mass?"

The following fact will shew how little communication Napoleon had maintained with the capital. On the morning of his entry into Paris, after his return from the Isle of Elba, a hundred and fifty half-pay officers quitted St. Denis, where they had been stationed by the Princes, and marched to the capital, bringing with them four pieces of artillery. They were met on the road by some generals, who placed themselves at their head; and the little troop thus proceeded to the palace of the Tuileries, where they assembled together the heads of the different departments of the ministry, who all agreed to act in the name of the Emperor. Thus Paris was tranquilly governed that day by the torrent of opinion and the transport of private affections. None of the great partisans of the Emperor, none of his former ministers, having received any communication from him, dared sign an order, or assume any responsibility. The public papers would not have appeared next day but for the zeal of private individuals, who, spontaneously and without authority, filled them with expressions of the feelings by which they were animated, and with the

statements of passing events. In the same manner
Lavalette took possession of the post-office. Paris was
that day without police and without government, and
yet never did greater tranquillity prevail in the capital.

The Emperor entered the Tuileries about nine o'clock
in the evening with an escort of a hundred horse, just
as if he had come from one of his country residences.
On alighting, he was almost squeezed to death by a
crowd of military officers and citizens, who thronged
around him, and fairly carried him in their arms into his
saloon. Here he found dinner ready, and he was just
sitting down to table, when the officer who had been
despatched in the morning to Vincennes to summon the
fortress, arrived. He brought intelligence of the capitulation of the commandant, whose only conditions were,
that he should receive a passport for himself and his
family.

It is a very singular circumstance that, on the morning
after the Emperor's arrival at the Tuileries, while a
messenger had gone out to procure a tri-coloured flag,
one was found at the pavilion Marsan, during the search
that was made, as a matter of prudence, through the
palace. This flag was immediately hoisted. It was
quite new, and larger than the usual size. No one could
guess how it had got into the Tuileries, and for what
purpose it had been intended.

In fact, the more light there is thrown on the subject,
the more evident it must be that there was no other
conspiracy than that of the nature of things. Party-
spirit alone can seek in the present age to raise a doubt
on this point; history will have none.

A few days after Napoleon's removal to Longwood,
his return from Elba became the subject of conversation
among the officers who were presented to him, when
one of them observed that that astonishing event
presented to the eyes of Europe the contrast of all that
was most feeble and most sublime, the Bourbons
abondoning a monarchy, and flying on the approach
of a single man, who by his own individual efforts boldly
undertook the conquest of an empire. "Sir," said the
Emperor, "you are mistaken, you have taken a wrong

THE RETURN FROM ELBA.

find little or no *impossibility*, But what do you complain of ? The want of a pestle, when the bar of any chair might answer your purpose ? The want of a mortar ? Any thing is a mortar that you choose to convert to that use ; this table is a mortar ; any pot or kettle is a mortar. Do you think you are still in the Rue Saint - Honoré, amidst all the shops in Paris ?"

The Grand Marshal here remarked that this circumstance reminded him of something that had occurred the first time he had the honour of being presented to Napoleon, and of the first words he had received from him. When Bertrand was about to leave the army of Italy, to proceed on a mission to Constantinople, the young General, perceiving that he was an officer of engineers, gave him a commission relative to that department. "On my return," said Bertrand, "I came up with you at a short distance from head quarters, and I informed you that I had found the thing impossible. On this your Majesty, whom I had addressed with great diffidence, said with the most familiar air—' But let us see how you set to work, Sir : that which you found impossible may not be so to me.' "Accordingly," continued Bertrand, "when I mentioned the means by which I had proposed to execute what your Majesty wished, you immediately substituted others. In a few moments I was perfectly convinced of the superiority of your Majesty's plans ; and this circumstance furnished me with sentiments and recollections which have since proved very useful to me."

The Emperor retired to rest early. We observed that he is very much altered in his looks, particularly since his last illness. He grows very weak, and feels fatigued after two turns round the garden.

STATISTICAL CALCULATION. — POPULATION OF THE ISRAELITES IN EGYPT.

17th—18th. The fine weather has now completely set in. The Emperor went into the garden, attended by all his suite. After walking about for a short time, he proceeded to the wood.

On his return from his walk, we all breakfasted together under the tent ; and, the weather being very favourable, the Emperor expressed his wish to take a drive in the calash.

About five o'clock, he desired me to attend him in his closet, to assist in searching for some documents on the interior of Africa, bordering upon Egypt. This is a point on which he has been engaged for some days past, as he intends to make it the subject of some chapters in his Campaign of Egypt.

He complained of being unwell, and desired me to order some tea for him. This was something extraordinary. The Grand Marshal soon after came to take my place in writing from his dictation.

After dinner, the Emperor was engaged with the pen in his hand, in investigating the comparative production of the soils of Egypt and France. He found the production of France to be greatly inferior to that of Egypt. This calculation was made from Peuchet's " Statistical Surveys of France." The Emperor was satisfied with the result at which he had arrived; it corresponded with the opinion he had previously formed. This naturally gave rise to the consideration of several other subjects; for instance, what was the probable and possible population of Egypt in ancient times ?—what might have been the population of the Israelites, if, during the short period that they remained in captivity, they had increased to the degree mentioned in Scripture? &c. The Emperor desired me to present to him next day something on this latter subject. A great deal was said on the probabilities of human life, the tables of which were also found in Peuchet's work; and on this subject the Emperor made some very ingenious, novel, and striking remarks.

I presented to the Emperor the calculation I had made on the problem which he had given to me the preceding day. The result surprised him not a little; and it furnished a subject for considerable discussion. The following is the substance of what I presented to him.

The Israelites remained two hundred years in Egypt during which time we may calculate ten generations they married early, and their marriages were very fruitful. I supposed the children of Jacob, the twelve chiefs

of tribes, to be all married; I also supposed each of them
to have had the same number of children, or six couples,
and so on in succession. The tenth generation would
then have amounted to 2,480,064,704 persons. But the
ninth generation and even the eighth was still in existence. Hence what an awful number of figures. At
any rate, let an ample deduction be made from the number of children, for the mortality occasioned by accidents,
disease, &c., and still it is very certain that no calculation
can be brought forward to contradict the account of
Moses. The Emperor amused himself for a considerable
time in detecting and shewing the errors of my
reasoning.

During dinner, he exercised himself. in English, by
asking my son questions in that language, in history
and geometry. After dinner the Emperor took up
the Odyssey, the reading of which afforded a treat
to us all.

THE EMPEROR ALTERS VISIBLY, AND LOSES HIS STRENGTH.—SALE OF HIS PLATE.

19th. — Napoleon spent the morning in collecting
information on the sources of the Nile, from the works
of several modern authors, Bruce, &c. . . . . I assisted
him in this labour. At three o'clock, he dressed and
went out. The weather was tolerably fine. He ordered
the calash, and then went into the wood on foot, and we
walked till we came within sight of the Signal Hill. He
conversed with me on our moral position, and the vexations which even circumstances arising from our intimacy
with him could not fail to cause him. The calash came
up with us, and Monsieur and Madame Montholon were
in it. The Emperor was very glad of this, as he said he
did not feel strong enough to walk back to the house.
He evidently grows feeble, his step becomes heavy and
lagging, and his features alter. His resemblance to his
brother Joseph is now striking; so much so, that, on
going to meet him the other day in the garden, I could
have sworn it was Joseph, until the very moment when
I came close to him. Others have remarked the likeness, as well as myself; and we have often said, that, if

we believed in the *second sight* of the Scotch High-
landers, we should be inclined to expect that something extraordinary would happen to Joseph or to the
Emperor.

On our return, the Emperor examined a large basket
full of broken plate, which was to be sent next day to
the town. This was to be for the future the indispensable complement for our monthly subsistence, in consequence of the late retrenchments of the Governor.

We knew that captains in the East India Company's
service had offered as much as a hundred guineas for a
single plate. This circumstance induced the Emperor to
order the arms to be erased and the pieces to be broken,
so as to leave no trace of the plate having belonged to
him. All the dish covers were topped with small massive
eagles; these were the only things he wished to save,
and he had them put by. These last fragments were the
objects of the wishes of every one of us; we looked upon
them as relics. There was something religious, and at
the same time mournful, in this feeling.

When the moment came for breaking up this plate, it
had produced a most painful emotion and real grief
amongst the servants. They could not without the
greatest reluctance, bring themselves to apply the
hammer to these objects of their veneration. This act
upset all their ideas; it was to them a sacrilege, a
desolation. Some of them shed tears on the occasion.
After dinner, the Emperor continued the Odyssey, and
afterwards read some passages of Esmenard's poem, "La
Navigation," which he was pleased with.

FRESH VEXATION FROM THE GOVERNOR.—TOPOGRAPHY OF ITALY.

20th.—The Emperor sent to wake me before eight
o'clock, desiring that I should join him with the calash
in the wood, where he was already walking with M. de
Montholon, conversing about the household expenses of
the establishment. The weather had at last become fine
once more, it was like a delightful spring morning. We
took two turns.

We have experienced to-day a fresh and inconceivable

vexation from the Governor. He has forbidden us to
sell our plate, when broken up, to any other person than
the one he should appoint. What can have been his
intention in committing this new act of injustice? To
make himself more obnoxious, and to give another
instance of the abuse of authority.

The Emperor breakfasted under the tent; immediately
afterwards, he dictated the account of the Battle of
Marengo to General Gourgaud. He bade me remain
with them and listen. About twelve o'clock he retired
to his apartment to endeavour to rest himself.

Towards three o'clock, the Emperor came into my
room again. He found my son and myself engaged in
comparing and looking over the account of the Battle of
Arcole. He knew that it was my favourite chapter, and
that I called it a canto of the Iliad. He wished to read
it again, and expressed himself also pleased with it.

The perusal of this account of Arcole awakened the
Emperor's ideas respecting what he called " that beautiful theatre, Italy." He ordered us to follow him into
the drawing-room, where he dictated to us for several
hours. He had caused his immense map of Italy, which
covered the greatest part of the drawing-room, to be
spread open on the floor, and having laid himself down
upon it, he went over it on his hands and his knees,
with a compass and a red pencil in his hand, comparing
and measuring the distance with a long piece of string,
of which one of us held one of the ends. " It is thus,"
said he to me, laughing at the posture in which I saw
him, " that a country should be measured in order to
form a correct idea of it, and lay down a good plan of a
campaign."

THE CELEBRATED BILLS OF ST. DOMINGO.—INSPECTORS
OF THE REVIEWS, &c.—PLANS OF ADMINISTRATION,
&c.—GAUDIN, MOLLIEN, DEFERMONT, LACUEE, &c.—
MINISTER OF THE TREASURY.—MINISTER SECRETARY
OF STATE.—IMPORTANCE OF THEIR FUNCTIONS.

21st.—Admiral Malcolm called upon me to-day. He
came to take leave of us all; he was to sail the next day
for the Cape, and would be two months absent.

We are sorry to lose the Admiral; his manners,
always polite, and a kind of tacit sympathy existing
between us, contrast him continually in our mind with
Sir Hudson Lowe, who is so unlike him.

The Admiral had seen the Emperor, who is also partial
to him. They had taken together some turns in the
garden, and the Admiral told me had collected some excellent information respecting the Scheldt and the
Nievendip, a maritime establishment in Holland which
was entirely unknown to him, and which was founded by
Napoleon.

After dinner, the conversation turned upon what the
Emperor termed the celebrated bills of St. Domingo.
It gave rise to the following curious details,—" The
administrator of St. Domingo," said the Emperor, " took
it into his head one day to draw from the Cape, without
authority, for the sum of sixty millions, in bills, on the
treasury in Paris, which bills were all payable on the same
day. France was not then, and had, perhaps, never
been, rich enough to meet such a demand. Besides,
where and by what means had the administration of St.
Domingo acquired such a credit? The First Consul
could not command any thing like it in Paris; it was as
much as M. Necker could have done at the time of his
greatest popularity. Be that as it may, when these bills
appeared in Paris, where they arrived before the letters
of advice, the First Consul was applied to from the
treasury, to point out what was to be done. ' Wait for
the letters of advice,' said he, ' in order to learn the
nature of the transaction. The treasury is like a capi-
talist; it possesses the same rights, and should follow
the same course. These bills are not accepted, they are,
consequently, not payable.' However, the necessary
information, and the vouchers, arrived. These bills
stated value received, but the receipts of the officers in
charge of the chest, into whose hands the money had
been paid, were for only one tenth, one fifth, one third
of the amount of the respective bills. The treasury,
therefore, would only acknowledge and refund the sum
really and *bona fide* paid; and the bills in their tenour
were declared to be false. This raised a great clamour,

and produced a terrible agitation amongst the merchants.
A deputation waited upon the First Consul, who, far
from endeavouring to avoid it, opened the business at
once, and asked ' whether they took him for a child,
whether they thought he would sport thus with the
purest blood of the people, or that he was so indifferent
a guardian of the public interest? What he refused to
give up,' he said, ' did not affect him personally, did not
trench upon his civil list, but it was public property, of
which he was the guardian, and which was the more
sacred in his eyes on that account.' Then, addressing
the two persons at the head of the deputation, he said:
' You, gentlemen, who are merchants, bankers, men of
business, give me a positive answer. If one of your
agents abroad were to draw upon you for very large
sums contrary to your expectations and to your interests,
would you accept, would you pay his bills?' They were
obliged to admit they would not. ' Then,' said the First
Consul, ' you, who are simple proprietors, and in the
right of your majority responsible for your own actions
only, you would wish to possess a right which you refuse
to allow to me, proprietor in the name of all, and who
am in that quality always a minor and subject to revision !
No, gentlemen, I shall enjoy your privileges in the name
and for the benefit of all; the actual amount received for
your bills shall be repaid you and no more. I do not
ask the merchants to take the bills of my agents: it is
an honour, a mark of credit, to which I do not aspire;
if the merchants do take them, it must be at their own
risk and peril; I only acknowledge and consider as
sacred the acceptance of my Minister of the Treasury.'
Upon this they again expostulated, and a great deal of
idle talk ensued. They should be obliged, they said, to
declare themselves bankrupts; they had received these
bills, for ready money; their agents abroad had committed the error of taking them, through respect for, and
confidence in, the government. ' Very well,' said the
First Consul, ' become bankrupts. But they did not,'
observed the Emperor, ' they had not received these bills
for ready money, and their agents had not committed
any error.'

"The members of the deputation left the First Consul, convinced in their own minds of the validity of his reasons; nevertheless, they filled Paris with their clamours and with falsehoods, misrepresenting the affair altogether.

"This transaction," said the Emperor, "and its details, explain many other transactions which have been much spoken of in Paris under the Imperial administration.

"The commercial world had particularly said, and repeated, that this proceeding was unexampled; that such a violation of credit was a thing hitherto unheard of; but to that the First Consul replied that he would set the question at rest by quoting precedents, and he recalled to their minds the Bills of Louis XIV., the liquidations of the Regent, the Mississippi Company the liquidations of the wars of 1763 and of 1782, &c.; and proved to them that what they contended to be a thing unexampled had been the constant practice of the monarchy."

From this affair the Emperor turned to different branches of the administration. He defended the institution of the post of Inspectors of Reviews. "It was only through them that the actual number of men present could be ascertained; through them alone had this advantage been obtained, and it was one of immense importance in the active operations of war. And these inspectors were not less useful in an administrative point of view; for, whatever trifling abuses might exist in the details, and however numerous these abuses might be, it is on a general principle that such things should be considered; and, in order to estimate fairly the utility of this institution, it should be asked what other abuses would have taken place if it had not existed? For myself," said Napoleon, "I must say that, checking the expenditure, by trying how much the total number of troops ought to have cost according to their fixed rates of pay, I have always found the sum paid by the treasury to fall short of my estimate. The army, therefore, cost less than it ought to have cost; what result more beneficial could be required?"

The Emperor quoted the administration of the navy as having been the most regular and the most honest; it had become a master-piece. "In that," said he, "consisted the great merit of Decrès." The Emperor considered that France was too large to have only one minister for the administration of the war department "It was," he said, "a task beyond the powers of one man. Paris had been made the centre of all decisions, contracts, supplies, and organizations; whilst the correspondents of the minister had been subdivided amongst a number of persons equal to the number of regiments and corps The contrary ought to have been the case; the correspondences should have been entered, and the resources subdivided, by raising them on the spot where they were required. I had long meditated a plan to establish in France twenty or twenty-five military districts, which would have composed so many armies. There would have been no more than that number of accountants; these would have been twenty under-ministers; it would have been necessary to find twenty honest men. The minister would have had only twenty correspondents; he would have centralised the whole and made the machine move with rapidity.

"Messieurs Gaudin and Mollien," said the Emperor, "were of opinion that it was necessary that the receivers-general, public financiers and contractors, should have very large fortunes, that they should have it in their power to make considerable profits, and openly avow them, in such a manner as to retain a degree of consideration which they might be careful not to endanger; and a character of honour, which they might be anxious not to compromise. This could not be otherwise," he said, "in order to obtain from them support, service, and credit, in case of need.

"Another set of men, Defermont, Lacuee, and Marbois, thought, on the contrary, that it was impossible to be too watchful, too economical, and too strict. For my own part, I was inclined to be of the opinion of the first, considering the views of the last to be narrow, and such as were applicable to a regiment, but not to an army; to the expenses of a private household; but not

to the expenditure of a great empire. I called them the
Puritans and the Jansenists of the profession."

The Emperor observed that the minister of the treasury,
and the minister secretary of state, were two or his institutions on which he most congratulated himself, and from
which he had derived the greatest assistance. " The
minister of the treasury concentrated all the resources,
and controlled all the expenses of the empire. From the
minister secretary of state all acts emanated. He was
the minister of ministers, imparting life to all intermediate acts; the grand notary of the empire, signing and
authenticating all documents. Through the first I knew,
at every moment, the state of my affairs; and through
the second I made known my decisions and my will in all
directions and every where. So that, with my minister
of the treasury and my minister secretary of state alone,
and half-a-dozen clerks, I would have undertaken to govern the empire from the remotest parts of Illyria, or
from the banks of the Niemen, with as much facility as
in my capital."

The Emperor could not conceive how affairs could go
on with the four or five secretaries of state of our kings.
" And, indeed, how did they go on?" said he. " Each
imagined, executed, and controlled his own operations.
They might act in direct opposition one to another; for
as the kings only affixed their sign on the margin of the
plans proposed, or authenticated only the rough draft of
their ordinances, the secretaries of state could fill them
up, or act as they pleased, without fear of any great responsibility. Add to this that the secretaries of state
had the *griffe**, a contrivance, which they wanted to
make me adopt, but which I rejected as a tool appropriated to the *Rois faineans*. Amongst these ministers,
some might have money for which they had no employment, and others might be unable to proceed for want of
a farthing. There was no common centre to combine
their movements, provide for their wants, and direct the
execution of their measures."

---

* A kind of seal on which a signature is engraved.

The Emperor said that a minister secretary of state was exactly suited for kings without talents, but vain, who would want the assistance of a prime minister and not like to own it. " Had my minister secretary of state been made president of the council of state," said he, " he would have been from that moment a real prime minister, in the fullest acceptation of the term; for he would have carried his plans to the council of state to have them digested into laws, and would have signed for the Prince. There can be no doubt that, with the manners and habits of the first race of our kings, or with princes like them, my minister secretary of state would have become in a very short time a Mayor of the Palace.

REVISION OF THE CHAPTERS ON THE ARMY OF ITALY.

22d.—The Emperor resumed his researches respecting Egypt. He gave me Strabo to look over; it was the edition which he had caused to be made. He commended the care and pains bestowed upon it, and said that it had been his intention to give us, in course of time, editions of all the works of the ancients, through the official medium of the Institute.—Before dinner the Emperor sent for me and my son, and spent at least six hours with us, reading over and recasting the chapters on the Tagliamento, Leoben, and Venice.

All is fine in these chapters on the Campaign of Italy. In that on the Tagliamento, we see how one single disposition, made on the banks of that river and hardly noticed, one of those movements which the Emperor calls *the thought of the battle*, must inevitably lead to the gates of Vienna.

The chapter on Venice is written after the manner of the ancients. However, the last chapter read always seems to be that which pleases most.

I was extremely unwell and very tired, not so much from fatigue occasioned by work, as from bodily indisposition. We amused ourselves this evening by reading the description of Ulysses' departure from the Island of Calypso, and his arrival amongst the Pheacians.

ON SENSIBILITY.—ON THE INHABITANTS OF THE EAST AND
WEST; DIFFERENCES OBSERVABLE BETWEEN THEM, &c.

23d.—This morning the Emperor, conversing in his
room, after touching on several subjects, spoke about
sentiment, feelings, and sensibility, and having alluded to
one of us who, as he observed, never pronounced the
name of his mother but with tears in his eyes, he said,
" But is this not peculiar to him? Is this a general feeling? Do you experience the same thing, or am I unnatural in that respect? I certainly love my mother with
all my heart; there is nothing that I would not do for
her, yet if I were to hear of her death, I do not think that
my grief would manifest itself by even a single tear; but
I would not affirm that this would be the case if I were
to lose a friend, or my wife, or my son. Is this distinction founded on nature? What can be the cause of it?
Is it that my reason has prepared me beforehand to expect the death of my mother, as being in the natural
course of events, whereas the loss of my wife, or of my
son, is an unexpected occurrence, a hardship inflicted by
fate, which I endeavour to struggle against? Perhaps
also this distinction merely proceeds from our natural
disposition to egotism. I belong to my mother, but my
wife and my son belong to me." And he went on mul-
tiplying the reasons in support of his opinion, with his
usual fertility of invention, in which there was always
something original and striking.

It is certain that he was tenderly attached to his wife
and his son. Those persons who have served in the interior of his household now inform us how fond he was of
indulging his feelings of affection towards his family; and
point out some shades in his disposition, the existence of
which we were far from suspecting at the time.

He would sometimes take his son in his arms, and embrace him with the most ardent demonstrations of paternal love. But most frequently his affection would manifest
itself by playful teazing or whimsical tricks. If he met
his son in the gardens, for instance, he would throw him
down or upset his toys. The child was brought to him
every morning at breakfast time, and he then seldom

failed to besmear him with every thing within his reach
on the table. With respect to his wife, not a day passed
here without his introducing her into his private conversations; if they lasted any length of time, she was sure to
come in for a share in them, or to become the exclusive
subject of them. There is no circumstance, no minute
particular relating to her, which he has not repeated to
me a hundred times. Penelope, after ten years' absence,
in order to convince herself that she is not deceived, puts
some questions to Ulysses which he alone could answer.
Well! I think that I should not find it difficult to present
my credentials to Maria-Louisa.

In the course of the conversation in the evening, the
Emperor, speaking of different nations, said he knew of
only two,—the Orientals and the people of the West.
" The English, the French, the Italians, &c." said he,
" compose one family, and form the western division;
they have the same laws, the same manners, the same
customs; and differ entirely from the Orientals, particularly with respect to their women and their servants.
The Orientals have slaves; our servants are free: the
Orientals shut up their women; our wives share in all
our rights: the Orientals keep a seraglio, but polygamy
has never been admitted in the West at any period.
There are several other distinctions," said the Emperor;
" it is said that as many as eighty have been reckoned.
The inhabitants of the East and of the West are therefore," observed the Emperor, " really two distinct nations:—with the Orientals every thing is calculated to
enable them to watch over their wives and make sure of
them; all our institutions in the West tend, on the contrary, to put it out of our power to watch over ours, and
to make it necessary for us to rely upon them alone.
With us, every man who does not wish to pass for an
idiot must have some occupation; and whilst he is attending to his business, or fulfilling the duties of his situation, who will watch for him? We must therefore, with
our manners, rely entirely on the honour of our women,
and place implicit confidence in them. For my part,"
added he good-humouredly, " I have had both wives and
mistresses; but it never came into my head to use any

particular precaution to watch over them, because I
thought that it was with these things as with the fear of
daggers and poison in certain situations of life; the torment of guarding against them is greater than the
danger we wish to avoid: it is better to trust to one's
fate.

"It is, however, a very knotty question to decide,
which is the best method, ours or that of the Orientals;
though, probably, not for you, ladies," said he, casting
an arch-look upon those who were present. "Yet it
is certain that it would be a very great error to suppose
that the Orientals have fewer enjoyments than we have,
and are less happy than we are in the West. In the
East, the husbands are very fond of their wives, and the
wives are very much attached to their husbands. They
have as many chances of happiness as we have, however
different they may seem; for every thing is conventional
amongst men, even in those feelings which, one would
suppose, ought to be dictated by Nature alone. Besides,
the women in the East have their rights and privileges,
as ours have theirs: it would be quite as impossible to
prevent them from going to the public bath, as it would
be to prevent our women from going to church; and
both abuse that liberty. You see, therefore, that the
imagination, feelings, virtues, and failings of human
nature, are circumscribed within a very narrow compass;
and that the same things, with few exceptions and
differences, are to be found everywhere."

He then proceeded to account for, or to justify, poly-
gamy among the Orientals in a very ingenious manner.
"It never existed," he said, "in the West: the Greeks, the
Romans, the Gauls, the Germans, the Spaniards, the
Britons, never had more than one wife. In the East, on
the other hand, polygamy has existed in all ages: the
Jews, the Assyrians, the Tartars, the Persians, the
Turcomans, had all of them several wives. Whence
could this universal and invariable difference have arisen?
Was it owing to accident and to mere caprice? Did it
depend on physical causes in individuals? No. Were
woman less numerous, in proportion, among us than in
Asia? No. Were they more numerous in the East than

the men ? No. Were the latter of superior stature, to
us, or differently constituted ? No. The fact 's that the
legislator, or that wisdom from on high which supplies
his place, must have been guided by the force of circumstances arising from the respective localities. All the
people of the West have the same form, the same colour;
they compose but one nation, one family: it has been
possible, as at the moment of the Creation, to assign to
them but one helpmate—happy, admirable, beneficent
law, which purifies the heart of the man, exalts the condition of the woman, and assures to both a multitude of
moral enjoyments !

The Orientals, on the other hand, differ from one
another as much as day and night, in their forms and
colours : they are white, black, copper-coloured, mixed,
&c. The first thing to be thought of was their conser-
vation, to establish a consanguineous fraternity among
them, without which they would have been everlastingly
persecuting, oppressing, exterminating one another : this
could only be accomplished by the institution of polygamy, and by enabling them to have at one and the same
time a white, black, mulatto, and copper-coloured wife.
The different colours now constituting part of one and
the same family, thus became blended in the affections
of the chief and in the opinions of each of the females
relatively to the others.

"Mahomet," he added, "seems to have been acquainted with the secret, and to have been guided by it :
otherwise how happened it that he, who treads so closely
in the steps of Christianity, and deviates from it so little,
did not suppress polygamy ? Do you reply that he retained it only because his religion was wholly sensual ?
In this case, he would have allowed the Mussulmans an
indefinite number of wives, whereas he limited it to four
only, which would seem to imply a black, a white, a
copper-coloured, and a mixed.

Besides, let it not be supposed that this favour of the
law was put in practice for the whole nation ; or there
would not have been wives for them all. In fact, eleven
twelfths of the population have but one, because they
cannot maintain more, but polygamy in the chiefs is

sufficient to attain the grand object : for, the confusion
of races and of colours existing, by means of polygamy,
in the higher class, it is enough to establish union and
perfect equality among all.   We must, therefore admit,"
he concluded, " that if polygamy was not the offspring
of a political combination, if it owed its origin to chance
alone, that chance has in this instance, produced as much
as consummate wisdom."

The Emperor said that he had seriously thought of
applying this principle to our colonies, in order to har-
monize the welfare of the Negroes with the necessity for
employing them.   He had even, he said, consulted
divines on this subject, to ascertain if there were not
means, considering local circumstances, of reconciling
our religious notions with this practice.

The Emperor continued conversing in this manner
until after midnight.

ON HOLLAND AND KING LOUIS.—COMPLAINTS OF THE
EMPEROR AGAINST THE MEMBERS OF HIS FAMILY.—
MATTERS OF HIGH POLICE, &C. — LETTER TO KING
LOUIS, THE EMPEROR'S BROTHER.

24th.—The Emperor sent for me at about half-past
twelve to his closet.   Our conversation turned upon the
succession of authors through which the light of history
has been transmitted to us from the remotest antiquity
down to the present time.   This led him to read that
part of the first table of the Historical Atlas which gives
a recapitulation of them, and presents the whole at one
view.

The conversation turned on the diversities of the human
species.   The Emperor sent for Buffon, to throw light
upon the question ; and continued for some time employed
in seeking information on the subject.

Having dressed, the Emperor sent for my son, and
we worked three or four hours at the chapters of the
Campaign of Italy.

When this was completed, the conversation, through
a variety of subjects, turned upon Holland and King
Louis, respecting whom he said some things worthy of
observation.

" Louis is not destitute of intelligence," said the Emperor, " and has a good heart; but even with these qualifications a man may commit many errors, and do a great deal of mischief. Louis is naturally inclined to be capricious and fantastical, and the works of Jean Jaques Rousseau have contributed to increase this disposition. Seeking to obtain a reputation for sensibility and beneficence, incapable by himself of enlarged views, and, at most, competent to local details, Louis acted like a Prefect rather than a king.

" No sooner had he arrived in Holland, than, fancying that nothing could be finer than to have it said that he was thenceforth a true Dutchman, he attached himself entirely to the party favourable to the English, promoted smuggling, and thus connived with our enemies. It became necessary from that moment to watch over him, and even to threaten to attack him. Louis, then, seeking a refuge against the weakness of his disposition in the most stubborn obstinacy, and mistaking a public scandal for an act of glory, fled from his throne, declaiming against me and against my insatiable ambition, my intolerable tyranny. What then remained for me to do ? Was I to abandon Holland to our enemies ? Ought I to have given it another King ? But in that case could I have expected more from him than from my own brother ? Did not all the kings that I created act nearly in the same manner ? I therefore united Holland to the empire; and this act produced a most unfavourable impression in Europe, and contributed not a little to pave the way to our misfortunes.

" Louis was delighted to take Lucien as his model: Lucien had acted nearly in the same manner; and if, at a later period, he has repented, and has even nobly made amends for his errors, this conduct did honour to his character, but could not produce any favourable change in our affairs.

On my return from Elba in 1815, Louis wrote a long letter to me from Rome, and sent an ambassador to me. It was his treaty, he said, the conditions upon which he would return to me. I answered that I would not make

14*

any treaty with him, that he was my brother, and that
if he came back he would be well received.

" Will it be believed that one of his conditions was
that he should be at liberty to divorce Hortense!   I
severely rebuked the negotiator for having dared to be
the bearer of so absurd a proposal, and for having believed
that such a measure could ever be made the subject of a
negotiation.   I reminded Louis that our family compact
positively forbade it, and represented to him that it was
not less forbidden by policy, morality, and public opinion.
I farther assured him that, actuated by all these motives,
if his children were to lose their state through his fault,
I should feel more interested for them than for him,
although he was my brother.

" Perhaps an excuse might be found for the caprice of
Louis's disposition in the deplorable state of his health,
the age at which it became deranged, and the horrible
circumstances which produced that derangement, and
which must have had a considerable influence upon his
mind ; he was on the point of death on the occasion, and
has, ever since, been subject to most cruel infirmities :
he is almost paralytic on one side.

" It is certain, however," added the Emperor, " that I
have derived little assistance from my own family, and
that they have severely injured me and the great cause.
The energy of my disposition has often been extolled ;
but I have been a mere milksop, particularly with my
family ; and well they knew it after the first moment of
anger was over, they always carried their point by perseverance and obstinacy.   I became tired of the contest,
and they did with me just as they pleased.   These are
great errors which I have committed.   If, instead of this,
each of them had given a common impulse to the different
bodies which I placed under their direction, we should
have marched on to the poles ; every thing would have
given way before us ; we should have changed the face
of the world ; Europe would now enjoy the advantages
of a new system, and we should have received the benedictions of mankind !   I have not been so fortunate as
Gengis Khan, with his four sons, each of whom rivalled
the other in zeal for his service.   No sooner had I made

a man a king, than he thought himself king *by the grace of God*, so contagious is the use of the expression. He was then no longer a lieutenant, on whom I could rely, but another enemy whom I was obliged to guard against. His efforts were not directed towards seconding me, but towards rendering himself independent. They all immediately imagined that they were adored and preferred to me. From that moment I was in their way, I endangered their existence! Legitimate monarchs would not have behaved differently; would not have thought themselves more firmly established. Weak-minded men! who, when I fell, had occasion to convince themselves that the enemy did not even do them the honour to demand the surrender of their dignities, or even to allude to it. If they are now put under personal restraint, if they are subject to vexation, it must proceed, on the part of the conqueror, from a wish to impose the weight of power, or from the base motive of gratifying his vengeance. If the members of my family excite a strong interest amongst mankind, it is because they belong to me and to the common cause; but assuredly there is not the least danger of any movement being produced by any of them. Notwithstanding the philosophy of several of them (for some of them had said, after the fashion of the chamberlains of the Faubourg St-Germain, that they were *forced* to reign,) their fall must have been sensibly felt by them, for they had soon accommodated themselves to the pleasures and comforts of their station; they were all really kings. Thanks to my labours, all have enjoyed the advantages of royalty; I alone have known its cares. I have all the time carried the world on my shoulders; and this occupation, after all, is rather fatiguing.

" It will perhaps be asked, why I persisted in erecting states and kingdoms? The manners and the situation of Europe required it. Every time that another country was annexed to France, the act added to the universal alarm which already prevailed, excited loud murmurs, and diminished the chances of peace. Then why, will it be farther said, did I indulge in the vanity of placing every member of my family on a throne? (for the generally of people must have thought me actuated by

vanity alone :) why did I not rather fix my choice upon
private individuals possessing greater abilities? To this
I reply that it is not with thrones as with the functions
of a prefect; talents and abilities are so common in the
present age, among the multitude, that one must be
cautious to avoid awakening the idea of competition.   In
the agitation in which we were involved, and with our
modern institutions, it was proper to think rather of
consolidating and concentrating the hereditary right of
succession, in order to avoid innumerable feuds, factions,
and misfortunes.   If there was any fault in my person
and my elevation, consistently with the plan of universal
harmony which I meditated for the repose and happiness
of all,'it was that I had risen at once from the multitude.
I felt that I stood insulated and alone, and I cast out
anchors on all sides into the sea around me.   Where
could I more naturally look for support than amongst
my own relations? Could I expect more from strangers?
And it must be admitted that if the members of my
family have had the folly to break through these sacred
ties, the morality of the people, superior to their blind
infatuation, fulfilled in part my object.   With them their
subjects thought themselves more quiet, more united as
in one family.

  " To resume : acts of that importance were not to be
considered lightly ; they were involved in considerations
of the highest order; they were connected with the
tranquillity of mankind, the possibility of ameliorating
its condition.   If, notwithstanding all these measures,
taken with the best intentions, it seems that no permanent good has been effected, we must admit the truth
of this great maxim, that to govern is very difficult for
those who wish to do it conscientiously."

  The following letter, of a very old date, will serve to
throw great light upon the words of Napoleon, mentioned a few pages back, respecting the conduct of his
brother in Holland.

  At a later period, King Louis published a sort of
account of his administration, addressed to the Dutch
nation; it is particularly interesting, after having read
the above paragraph and the accompanying letter, to

take up that document of King Louis, in order to be able
to form an opinion *on the subject founded on a due
knowledge of all the circumstances.

" Castle of Marach, 3d April, 1808.

" Sir and brother.—The auditor D——t delivered to
me an hour ago your despatch, dated 22d March. I
send a courier who will take this letter to you in
Holland.

" The use you have just made of the privilege of
mercy cannot but produce a very bad effect.   This
privilege is one of the finest and noblest attributes of the
sovereign power. In order not to bring it into discredit,
it must be used only in cases when the royal clemency is
not detrimental to the ends of justice, or when it is calculated to leave an impression of being the result of
generous feelings.   The present case is that of a number
of banditti, who attacked and murdered several custom-
house officers, with the intention of smuggling afterwards
without interruption.   These people are condemned to
death ; and your Majesty extends the royal mercy to
them . . . . to a set of murderers, to men whom nobody
can pity.   If they had been caught in the act of smuggling ; if, in defending themselves, they had killed some
of the officers, then you might perhaps have taken into
consideration the situation of their families, and their
own ; and have shewn an example of a kind of paternal
feeling, by modifying the severity of the law, by a com-
mutation of punishment.   It is in cases of condemnation
for offences against the revenue laws, it is more particularly in cases of condemnation for political offences, that
clemency is well applied.   In these matters the principle
is that, if it is the Sovereign who is attacked, there is a
certain magnanimity in pardoning the offender.   On the
first report of an affair of that kind, the sympathy of the
public is immediately excited in favour of the offender,
and not of him who is to inflict the punishment.   If the
Prince remits the sentence, the people consider him
superior to the offence, and the public clamour is directed
against those who have offended him.   If he follows the

opposite system, he is thought vindictive and tyrannical. If he pardons atrocious crimes, he is looked upon as weak, or actuated by bad intentions.

"Do not fancy that the privilege of mercy can always be used without danger, and that society will always commend the exercise of it in the Sovereign. The Sovereign is blamed when he applies it in favour of murderers or great malefactors, because it then becomes injurious to the interests of the community. You have too frequently, and on too many occasions, extended the royal mercy. The kindness of your heart must not be listened to when it can become prejudicial to your people. In the affair of the Jews, I should have done as you did; but in that of the smugglers of Middelburg, I should not have pardoned on any account. Many reasons ought to have induced you to let justice take its course, and give the example of an execution which would have produced the excellent effect of preventing many crimes by the terror which it would have inspired. Public officers are murdered in the middle of the night—the murderers are condemned. Your Majesty commutes the punishment of death into a few years' imprisonment! How much will this not tend to dishearten all the persons employed in the collection of your revenue! The political effect produced by it is also very bad, for the following reasons:— Holland was the channel through which England had, for many years, introduced her goods on the Continent. The Dutch merchants have made immense profits by this trade; and that is the reason why the Dutch nation is partial to England, and fond of smuggling, and why it hates France, who forbids smuggling and opposes England. The mercy which you have extended to these smugglers and murderers is a kind of compliment which you have paid to the taste of the Dutch for smuggling. You appear to make common cause with them,---and against whom? Against me.

"The Dutch love you: your disposition is amiable, your manners are unaffected, and you govern them according to their inclination; but you would make a beneficial use of the influence you possess if you shewed yourself positively determined to suppress smuggling, and if you

opened their eyes to their real interests : they would then
think that the system of prohibition is good, since it is
observed by the King. I cannot see what advantage your
Majesty can derive from a species of popularity which
you would acquire at my expense. Certainly Holland is
no longer what it was at the time of the treaty of
Ryswick ; and France is not in the situation in which it
was placed during the last years of the reign of Louis
XIV. If, therefore, Holland is unable to follow a system
of policy independent of that of France, it must fulfil
the conditions of the alliance.

" It is not to the present alone that sovereigns must
accommodate their policy ; the future must also be the
object of their consideration. What is at this moment
the situation of Europe ? On one side, England, who
possesses, by her sole exertions, a dominion to which the
whole world has been hitherto compelled to submit. On
the other side, the French Empire and the Continental
States, which, strengthened by the union of their powers,
cannot acquiesce in this supremacy exercised by England.
Those states had also their colonies and a maritime trade ;
they possess an extent of coast much greater than England ; but they have become disunited, and England has
attacked the naval power of each separately : England
has triumphed on every sea, and all navies have been
destroyed. Russia, Sweden, France, and Spain, which
possess such ample means for having ships and sailors,
dare not venture to send a squadron out of their ports. It
is, therefore, no longer from a confederation amongst the
maritime powers—a confederation which it would be besides impossible to maintain, on account of the distance,
and of the interference of the various interests of each
with those of the others—that Europe can expect its
maritime emancipation, and a system of peace, which can
be established only by the will of England.

" I wish for peace ; I wish to obtain it by every means
compatible with the dignity of the power of France ; at
the expense of every sacrifice which our national honour
can allow. Every day I feel more and more that peace
is necessary ; and the sovereigns of the Continent are as
anxious for peace as I am. I feel no passionate prejudice

against England; I bear her no insurmountable hatred: she has followed against me a system of repulsion; I have adopted against her the Continental system, not so much from a jealousy of ambition, as my enemies suppose, but in order to reduce England to the necessity of adjusting our differences. Let England be rich and prosperous; it is no concern of mine, provided France and her allies enjoy the same advantages.

" The Continental system has, therefore, no other object than to advance the moment when the public rights of Europe and of the French Empire will be definitively established. The sovereigns of the North observe and enforce strictly the system of prohibition, and their trade has been greatly benefited by it: the manufactures of Prussia may now compete with ours. You are aware that France, and the whole extent of coast which now forms part of the Empire, from the Gulf of Lyons to the extremity of the Adriatic, are strictly closed against the produce of foreign industry. I am about to adopt a measure with respect to the affairs of Spain, the result of which will be to wrest Portugal from England, and sub-ject all the coasts of Spain, on both seas, to the influence of the policy of France. The coasts of the whole of Europe will then be closed against England, with the exception of those of Turkey, which I do not care about, as the Turks do not trade with Europe.

" Do you not perceive, from this statement, the fatal consequences that would result from the facilities given by Holland to the English for the introduction of their goods on the continent? They would enable England to levy upon us the subsidies which she would afterwards offer to other powers to fight against us. Your Majesty is as much interested as I am to guard against the crafty policy of the English Cabinet. A few years more, and England will wish for peace as much as we do. Observe the situation of your kingdom, and you will see that the system I allude to is more useful to yourself than it is to me. Holland is a maritime and commercial power; she possesses fine sea-ports, fleets, sailors, skilful command-ers, and colonies, which do not cost any thing to the mother-country; and her inhabitants understand trade as well as the English.   Has not Holland, therefore, an interest in defending all those advantages? May not peace restore her to the station she formerly held? Granted that her situation may be painful for a few years; but is not this preferable to making the King of Holland a mere governor for England, and Holland and her colonies a vassal of Great Britain? Yet the protection which you would afford to English commerce would lead to that result. The examples of Sicily and Portugal are still before your eyes.

"Await the result of the progress of time. You want to sell your spirits, and England wants to buy them. Point out the place where the English smugglers may come and fetch them; but let them pay for them in money and never in goods, *positively never !* Peace must at last be made; and you will then conclude a treaty of commerce with England. I may perhaps also make one with her, but in which our mutual interests shall be reciprocally guaranteed. If we must allow England to exercise a kind of supremacy on the sea, a supremacy which she will have purchased at the expense of her treasure and her blood, and which is the natural consequence of her geographical position and of her possessions in the three other parts of the globe; at least our flags will be at liberty to appear on the ocean without being exposed to insult, and our maritime trade will cease to be ruinous.   For the present we must direct our efforts towards preventing England from interfering in the affairs of the Continent.

" I have been led on, from the consideration of the mercy which you have granted, to the above details, and I have entered into them because I feared that your Dutch Ministers may impress your Majesty's mind with false notions.

" I wish you to reflect seriously upon the contents of this letter, and to render the different subjects it treats upon objects of the deliberations of your councils, in order that your Ministers may give a proper direction and tendency to their measures.   Under no pretence whatever will France allow Holland to separate herself from the Continental system.

"With respect to these smugglers, since the fault has been committed, it cannot be undone. I advise you, however, not to leave them in the prison of Middelburg; it is too near the spot where the crime was perpetrated : send them to the remotest part of Holland. The present having no other object, &c.

(Signed)   "NAPOLEON."

During dinner the Emperor asked his groom how his horse was; the groom answered that it was well fed, in good spirits, and in excellent condition. "I hope he does not complain of me," said the Emperor, "if ever horse led the life of a canon, it is assuredly this." It is now two or three months since the Emperor was on horseback.

ZEAL FOR WORKING.—IDEAS AND PLANS OF NAPOLEON RESPECTING OUR HISTORY, &C.—ON THE WORKS PUB-LISHED, &C.—M. MÉNÉVAL; CURIOUS PARTICULARS.

25th—27th. The Emperor for some days past has been remarkably assiduous. All our mornings have been spent in making researches concerning Egypt, in the works of the ancient authors. We have looked over Herodotus, Pliny, Strabo, &c., together, without any other intermission than that which we required to eat our breakfast, which was served on his small table. The weather continued unfavourable, and the Emperor dictated every day and the whole day.

At dinner he told us that he found himself much better, and we then observed to him that for some time past, however, he had not been out of the house, and was occupied eight, ten, or twelve hours a day. "That is the very reason of my being better," said he : "occupation is my element; I was born and made for it. I have found the limits beyond which I could not use my legs; I have seen the extent to which I could use my eyes; but I have never known any bounds to my capability of application. I nearly killed poor Méneval; I was obliged to relieve him for a time from the duties of his situation, and place him for the recovery of his health near the person of Maria Louisa, where his post was a mere sinecure."

The Emperor added that, if he were in Europe and had leisure, his pleasure would be to write history. He complained of the very indifferent manner in which history was written every where. The researches in which he had lately been engaged had proved this fact to him to a degree beyond any thing he could ever have suspected.

"We have no good history," observed he, "and we could not have any; and the other nations of Europe are nearly in the same predicament as ourselves. Monks and privileged persons, that is to say, men friendly to abuses and inimical to information and learning, monopolized this branch of writing; they told us what they thought proper, or rather that which favoured their interests, gratified their passions, or agreed with their own views!—He had formed," he said, "a plan for remedying the evil as much as possible; he intended, for instance, to appoint commissions from the Institute, or learned men whom public opinion might have pointed out to him, to revise, criticize, and re-publish our annals. He wished also to add commentaries to the classic authors which are put in the hands of our youth, to explain them with reference to our modern institutions. With a good programme, competition, and rewards, this end would have been accomplished; every thing," he said, "can be obtained by such means."

He then repeated, what I believe I have mentioned before, that it had been his intention to cause the history of the last reigns of our kings to be written from the original documents in the archives of our Foreign Office. There were also several manuscripts, both ancient and modern, in the Imperial Library, which he intended to have printed, classifying and embodying them under their different heads, so as to form codes of doctrine on science, morality, literature, fine arts, &c.

He had, he said, several other plans of a similar nature. And could any other period be found equally favourable to the execution of such plans? When will there be again united in the same man the genius to conceive and the power to execute them?

In order to check the production of the immense number of inferior works with which the public was inundated, without however trenching upon the liberty of the press, he asked what objection there could have been to the formation of a tribunal of opinion, composed of members of the Institute, members of the University, and persons appointed by the government, who would have examined all works with reference to these three points of view, science, morality, and politics; who would have criticized them, and defined the degree of merit possessed by each. This tribunal would have been the light of the public; it would have operated as a warranty in favour of works of real merit, insured their success, and thus produced emulation; whilst, on the contrary, it would necessarily have discouraged the publication of inferior productions.

All our evenings were devoted to the Odyssey, with which we are delighted. Polyphemus, Tiresias, and the Syrens, have quite charmed us.

The following details relate to M. Méneval, to whom the Emperor alluded above: they will be considered invaluable, as they will serve to exhibit Napoleon in the sphere of his private life.

The Emperor, when First Consul, complained that he had no Secretary. He had just dismissed the one he had had during the campaigns of Italy and the expedition in Egypt; he was an old college acquaintance of the Emperor's, a man full of intelligence, and to whom he was very much attached; but he had been obliged to part with him. His brother Joseph then offered him his own secretary, whom he had only had for a short time: Napoleon accepted the offer, and acquired a treasure. This the Emperor has repeated several times since. It was Méneval, whom he has since made a baron, *Maître des Requêtes*, and *Secrétaire des Commandemens* to the Empress Maria Louisa.

Méneval's title, when attached to the First Consul, was Secretary of the Portfolio; a long regulation was even made expressly regarding him; the principal article of which was that he should never, under any pretence whatever, have a secretary, or employ an amanuensis, which condition was strictly observed.

M. Méneval was a man of gentle and reserved manners.

very discreet, working at all times and at all hours. The Senator never had reason to be dissatisfied or displeased with him, and was very much attached to him. The Secretary of the Portfolio had generally all the current business, all affairs that arose on a sudden emergency, or from a sudden thought. How many affairs, plans, and conceptions, have been discussed and transmitted through his medium! He opened and read all letters addressed to the Emperor; classed them for the Emperor's examination, and wrote under his dictation.

The Emperor dictated so fast that, most frequently, in order to save time, the Secretary was obliged to endeavour to recollect the words, rather than attempt to write them down at the moment they were pronounced. In this, Méneval particularly excelled. In the course of time, Méneval was authorized himself to return answers on many subjects. He might easily have acquired great influence; but it was not in his disposition to seek to obtain it.

The Emperor was almost always in his closet; it might be said that he spent the whole day and part of the night in it. He usually went to bed at ten or eleven o'clock, and rose again about twelve, to work for a few hours more. Sometimes he sent for M. Méneval, but most frequently he did not; and, aware of his zeal, he would sometimes say to him, " You must not kill yourself."

When the Emperor went into his closet in the morning, he found bundles of papers already arranged and prepared for him by Méneval, who had been there before him. If the Emperor sometimes allowed twenty-four hours, or two days, to elapse without going into it, his Secretary would remind him of it, and tell him that he would suffer himself to be overwhelmed with the mass of papers that were accumulating, and that the closet would soon be full of them. To this the Emperor usually answered good-humouredly: " Do not alarm yourself, it will soon be cleared;" and so indeed it was, for in a few hours the Emperor had despatched all the answers, and was even with the current business. It is true that he got through a great deal by not answering many things, and throwing away all that he considered useless, even when coming from his Ministers. To this they were accustomed; and when no answer appeared they knew what it meant. He himself read all letters that were addressed to him; to some he answered by writing a few words in the margin, and to others he dictated an answer. Those that were of great importance were always put by, read a second time, and not answered until some time had elapsed. When leaving his closet, he generally recapitulated those affairs that were of the greatest consequence, and fixed the hour at which they must be ready for him, which was always punctually attended to. If at that hour the Emperor did not come, M. Méneval followed him about from place to place through the palace to remind him of it. On some of these occasions the Emperor would go and settle the affair, at other times he would say, "To-morrow; night is a good adviser." This was his usual phrase; and he often said that he had indeed worked much harder at night than during the day; not that thoughts of business prevented him from sleeping, but because he slept at intervals, according as he wanted rest, and a little sufficed for him.

It often happened that the Emperor, in the course of his campaigns, was roused suddenly upon some emergency; he would then immediately get up, and it would have been impossible to guess from the appearance of his eyes that he had just been asleep. He then gave his decision, or dictated his answer, with as much clearness, and with his mind as free and unembarrassed, as at any other moment. This he called the *after-midnight presence of mind*; and he possessed it in a most extraordinary degree. It has sometimes happened that he has been perhaps called up as often as ten times in the same night, and each time he was always found to have fallen asleep again, not having as yet taken his quantum of rest.

Boasting one day to one of his ministers (General Clarke) of the faculty which he possessed of sleeping almost at pleasure and how little rest he required, Clarke answered in a jocular tone, " Yes, Sire, and that is a source of torment to us, for it is often at our expense; we come in for our share of it sometimes."

The Emperor did every thing himself and through the

medium of his Cabinet. He appointed to all vacant situations, and most frequently substituted new names to
those of the persons proposed to him. He read the plans
of his Ministers, adopted, rejected, or modified them. He
even indited the notes of his Minister for Foreign Affairs,
which he dictated to Méneval, from whom he kept no
secret.   It was through Méneval also that he wrote to
the different sovereigns; in addressing whom he observed
a formula which he had had drawn up from the reports
of former times, and to the strict observance of which he
attached great importance.   All the Ministers transacted
business with the Emperor together on one day of the
week, appointed for that purpose, unless something occurred to prevent it.   The business of each Minister was
transacted in the presence of all the others, who were
allowed to give their opinions respecting it, and each of
them thus emptied his portfolio.   A register was kept of
the deliberations, of which there must be many volumes.
Those documents that had been decided on were left to
have the signature affixed to them, which was done
through the medium of the Minister Secretary of State,
who countersigned them.   Sometimes some of these papers, after they had been thus decided on, were still sent
to the Emperor's cabinet to be revised and modified before the signature was put to them.   The Minister for
Foreign Affairs was the only one who, independently of
his share in the general business transacted by the other
Ministers, had besides, from the secret nature of his
functions, other business to despatch in private with the
Emperor.

One of the favourite aides-de-camp of the Emperor
was entrusted with all that related to the *personnel* of the
war-department.   For a long time Duroc occupied this
confidential post; afterwards Bertrand and Lauriston;
Count Lobau was the last who filled it.

M. Méneval, being in a very indifferent state of health,
worn down by fatigue from application, and requiring
some interval of repose, the Emperor gave him a situation in the household of the Empress Maria Louisa,
which was, he said, quite a sinecure.   However, the
Emperor only parted with him on condition that he should

come back to him as soon as he was well; and he never failed to remind him of it every time he saw him.

After Méneval's retirement, the business of the Emperor's cabinet ceased to be conducted by one person only; Méneval had a great many successors at the same moment, and the cabinet became a kind of office, in which several persons were employed. One of these persons, whom the Emperor had taken on the recommendation of others who had thought they could answer for him as for themselves, received an order, at the time of the disasters of 1814, to burn the documents that were in the closet; but, instead of obeying this order, he so far forgot his duty as to take them away with him: and, after the King's restoration, he wrote to one of his Ministers to offer them to him. The Emperor found the proof of his treachery amongst the papers left at the Tuileries at the period of the 20th of March; and one morning having gone into his closet before any body was come, he wrote several times on a piece of paper, as if he had been trying his pen, *Such a one (naming him) is a traitor—Such a one is a traitor;* and laid it on the table where sat one of those who had recommended him, and who was himself, said the Emperor, a man on whose zeal and fidelity every reliance could be placed. This was the only reproach he ever addressed to him, and the only revenge he ever exercised on the offender.

Several traces may therefore still be found, and several documents must exist, of the business transacted in the Emperor's cabinet. Some of these documents have been alluded to in the debates of the British Parliament; but Napoleon solemnly declared, on his return at the period of the 20th of March last, that these documents had been falsified. And they are not the only documents that are left of that ever-memorable administration.

There must be twenty or thirty folio volumes, and as many in quarto, containing the correspondence of the campaigns of Italy and of Egypt, collected and regularly classed.

There must be also about sixty or eighty folio volumes of the deliberations of the Council Ministers, collected by the Secretaries of State, the Duke of Bassano and Count

Daru; and lastly, the minutes of the sittings of the
the Council of State, written and arranged by M. Locré.

These are real and proud titles of glory for Napoleon.
Upon these immortal monuments, all subsequent governments have modelled and directed their administration ;
and from them all future governments, of every country,
will henceforth inevitably seek and derive information :
so sure and solid have been the foundations which he has
laid — so judiciously placed the landmarks—so deep are
the roots — so much, in one word, does the whole bear
the stamp of genius, and the character of rectitude and
of duration.

OBSERVATIONS OF THE EMPEROR CONCERNING MY WIFE. — DICTATION OF THE EMPEROR FOR ANOTHER PORTION OF HIS MEMOIRS.

28th. — The Emperor to-day availed himself of an interval of fine weather to take two turns in the calash :
he said he wanted a little jolting. His left cheek was
still swelled. About three o'clock he returned ; and, a
short time afterwards, having nothing to do, he sent for
me, and we walked round the garden for some time.
Having perceived the Doctor, he beckoned to him. The
Doctor came up to us, and from him Napoleon heard that
the Russian and Austrian Commissioners had come the
day before to the entrance to Longwood, from which they
had been turned away by the centry placed by the
Governor.

When we were alone, the Emperor, after having conversed upon a variety of subjects, spoke of my wife,
conjecturing what she might be doing, what had become
of her, &c.

"There is no doubt," said he, presently afterwards,
"that your situation at St. Helena inspires a lively interest, and must tend to cause your wife's company to be
sought after. Every thing relating to me is still dear to
many persons. From this rock I still bestow crowns !
. . . Yes, my dear friends, when you return to Europe,
you will find yourselves crowned !"

Then, speaking again of my wife, he said, with an expression of the utmost kindness, " The best thing she

could do would be to go and spend the time of her separation from you with Madame, or some other members of my family.   They would undoubtedly feel much pleasure in taking care of her," &c.

When we went back into the house, the Emperor sat down to work The Campaign of Italy was nearly finished but he provided me with a new subject.

" *Note, write :* " — These were the words which the Emperor uttered abruptly when a new idea occurred. What follows is literally what he dictated to me, in this instance : nothing has been altered in it, and he has never read it over.

" Note. — The Campaign of Italy being completed, Las Cases will, in the course of a week, undertake the period from the breaking of the treaty of Amiens to the battle of Jena.   In 1802 all Europe is at peace ; shortly afterwards all Europe begins war · the Republic is changed, and becomes the Empire ; the maritime question becomes the chief cause of the rupture of the peace of Amiens.

" Las Cases will begin by causing extracts to be made from the Moniteur of that time, by little Emanuel, under his directions : he must get through at least six or seven a· day, which will make one hundred and eighty, or a period of six months in one month.—There must be at least a period of six months extracted before we begin.

" The periods preceding and following that period will be prepared and arranged by the other gentlemen. In making the extracts, the plan already prescribed to M. Montholon must be followed ; that is, of extracting all that relates to one event, and referring to the page and month.

The following will be the great events of this period :—

" 1st, History of the flotilla.
" 2d, Declaration of Austria.
" 3d, Movements of the fleets.
" 4th, Battle of Trafalgar.
" 5th, Ulm—Austerlitz.
" 6th, Peace of Vienna.
" 7th, Negotiation of Lord Lauderdale at Paris.
" 8th, Battle of Jena.

"To be inserted in their respective places :—
" 1st, Conspiracy of Georges.
" 2d, Affair of the Duc d'Enghien.
" 3d, Coronation of the Emperor, by the Pope.
" 4th, Imperial organization.
" This will be one of the most glorious periods of the history of France; for it exhibits, in the space of one year, on one side a Pope coming to France to crown an Emperor,—an event which had not taken place for one thousand years before; and, on the other, the French flag waving over the capitals of Austria and Prussia, the Roman empire dissolved, and the Prussian monarchy destroyed."

I take pleasure in transcribing literally the above dictation of the Emperor's, with his first ideas and in his first words, in order to shew his style and manner.

It will be easily conceived with what zeal and ardour both my son and myself devoted ourselves to this our task, the importance of which we fully appreciated. We had not yet completed the analysis of our six months, when I was torn from Longwood.

ON A HOLE IN THE GARDEN.

29th. — During dinner somebody mentioned a pool which stands in our garden, not far from the house, and which is deep enough to admit of a lamb having once been drowned in it, in attempting to drink. The Emperor said on that occasion, to one of the inmates of the house: " Is it possible, Sir, that you have not yet had this pool filled up ? How guilty you would be, and what would not your grief be, if your son were to be drowned in it, as it might easily happen !" The person thus censured answered that he had often intended to have it done, but that it was impossible to get workmen. "That is not an excuse," said the Emperor sharply: " if my son were here, I should go and fill it up with my own hands."

The Emperor was already in bed when he sent for me: he wished, he said, to put some questions to me, and to inquire concerning some dates connected with matters which concerned us materially. . . . .
. . . .

30th.—Whenever the Emperor took up a subject, if
he was in the least animated, his language was fit to be
printed. He has often, when an idea struck him forcibly, dictated in an off-hand way to any one of us
who happened to be in his way, pages of the most
polished diction. The other gentlemen of his suite
must possess a great many of these dictations, which are
all most valuable. Unfortunately for me, the weak state
of my eyes, which prevented me from writing, most frequently deprived me of this advantage.

On one occasion, when the English ministerial newspapers adverted to the treasures which Napoleon must
possess, and which he, no doubt, concealed, the Emperor dictated as follows:

" You wish to know the treasures of Napoleon? They
are immense, it is true, but they are all exposed to light.
They are : The noble harbours of Antwerp and Flushing,
which are capable of containing the largest fleets, and of
protecting them against the ice from the sea,—the
hydraulic works at Dunkirk, Havre, and Nice,—the immense harbour of Cherbourg,—the maritime works at
Venice,—the beautiful roads from Antwerp to Amsterdam; from Mentz to Metz; from Bordeaux to Bay-
onne;—the passes of the Simplon, of Mont Cenis, of
Mont Genevre, of La Corniche, which open a communication through the Alps in four different directions; and
which exceed in grandeur, in boldness, and in skill of
execution, all the works of the Romans : in these alone
you will find eight hundred millions;—the roads from
the Pyrenees to the Alps, from Parma to Spezzia, from
Savona to Piedmont,—the bridges of Jena, Austerlitz,
the Arts, Sevres, Tours, Rouanne, Lyons, Turin, of the
Isere, of the Durance, of Bordeaux, of Rouen, &c.—the
canal which connects the Rhine with the Rhone by the
Doubs, and thus unites the North Sea with the Mediterranean; the canal which connects the Scheldt with the
Somme, and thus joins Paris and Amsterdam; the canal
which unites the Rance with the Vilaine; the canal of

Arles, that of Pavia, and the canal of the Rhine—the draining of the marshes of Burgoing, of the Cotentin, of Rochfort—the rebuilding of the greater number of the churches destroyed during the Revolution—the building of others—the institution of numerous establishments of industry for the suppression of mendicity—the works at the Louvre—the construction of public warehouses, of the Bank, of the canal of the Ourcq—the distribution of water in the city of Paris—the numerous sewers, the quays, the embellishments, and the monuments of that large capital—the works for the embellishment of Rome— the re-establishment of the manufactures of Lyons—the creation of many hundreds of cotton manufactories for spinning and for weaving, which employ several millions of hands — funds accumulated to establish upwards of 400 manufactories of sugar from beet-root, for the consumption of part of France, and which would have furnished sugar at the same price as the West Indies, if they had continued to receive encouragement for only four years longer—the substitution of woad for indigo, which would have been at last brought to equal in quality, and not to exceed in price, the indigo from the Colonies—numerous manufactories for all kinds of objects of art, &c.— fifty millions expended in repairing and beautifying the palaces belonging to the Crown— sixty millions in furniture for the palaces belonging to the Crown in France and in Holland, at Turin, and at Rome—sixty millions in diamonds for the Crown, all purchased with Napoleon's money—*the Regent* (the only diamond that was left belonging to the former diamonds of the Crown) withdrawn from the hands of the Jews at Berlin, with whom it had been pledged for three millions—the Napoleon Museum, valued at upwards of four hundred millions, filled with objects legitimately acquired either by money or treaties of peace known to the whole world, by virtue of which the master-pieces it contains were given in lieu of territory or of contributions—several millions amassed for the encouragement of agriculture, which is the paramount consideration for the interest of France—the introduction into France of Merino sheep, &c.——these form a treasure of several thousand

millions, which will endure for ages! these are the
monuments that will confute calumny!"

History will say that all these things were accomplished amidst perpetual wars, without having recourse
to any loan, and whilst the national debt was even
diminishing every day, and that nearly fifty millions of
taxes had been remitted. Very large sums still remained
in his private treasury; they were guaranteed to him by
the treaty of Fontainebleau, as the result of the savings
effected on his civil list and of his other private revenues.
These sums were divided and did not go entirely into the
public treasury, nor altogether into the treasury of
France!!

On another occasion, the Emperor reading in an
English newspaper that Lord Castlereagh had said, at a
meeting in Ireland, that Napoleon had declared at St.
Helena that he never would have made peace with
England but to deceive her, to take her by surprise, and
to destroy her; and that, if the French army was attached
to the Emperor, it was because he was in the habit of
giving the daughters of the richest families of his empire
in marriage to his soldiers: the Emperor, moved with
indignation, dictated as follows: "These calumnies
uttered against a man who is so barbarously oppressed,
and whose voice is not allowed to be heard in answer to
them, will be disbelieved by all persons well educated and
susceptible of feeling. When Napoleon was seated on
the first throne in the world, then no doubt his enemies
had a right to say whatever they pleased; his actions
were public, and were a sufficient answer to them; at
any rate, that conduct now belonged to public opinion,
and history; but to utter new and base calumnies against
him at the present moment is an act of the utmost mean-
ness and cowardice, and which will not answer the end
proposed. Millions of libels have been and are still published every day, but they are without effect. Sixty millions
of men, of the most polished nations in the world, raise
their voices to confute them, and fifty thousand English,
who are now travelling on the Continent, will, on their
return home, publish the truth to the inhabitants of the

three kingdoms of Great Britain, who will blush at
having been so grossly deceived.

"As for the Bill, by virtue of which Napoleon has been
dragged to this rock, it is an act of proscription similar to
those of Sylla, and still more atrocious. The Romans
unrelentingly pursued Hannibal to the utmost extremities
of Bithynia; and Flaminius persuaded King Prusias to
assent to the death of that great man; yet at Rome
Flaminius was accused of having acted thus in order to
satisfy his personal hatred. It was in vain that he urged
in his defence that Hannibal, yet in the vigour of life,
might still become a dangerous enemy, and that his death
was necessary; a thousand voices were raised, and
answered that acts of injustice and ungenerous actions
can never be useful to a great nation; and that, upon
such pretences as that now set forth, murder, poisoning,
and every species of crime might be justified ! Succeeding generations reproached their ancestors with this base
act. They would have paid a high price to efface the
stain from their history, and, since the revival of letters
among modern nations, there is not a generation that
has not added its imprecations to those pronounced by
Hannibal at the moment when he drank the fatal cup :
he cursed Rome, who, whilst her fleets and legions
covered Europe, Asia, and Africa, wreaked her vengeance
against a man alone and unprotected, because she feared,
or pretended to fear, him.

" The Romans, however, never violated the rights of
hospitality : Sylla found an asylum in the house of
Marius. Flaminius, before he proscribed Hannibal, did
not receive him on board his ship and declare that he
had orders to treat him favourably ; the Roman fleet did
not convey him to the Port of Ostia ; and Hannibal,
instead of placing himself under the protection of the
Romans, preferred trusting his person to a King of Asia.
When he was proscribed, he was not under the protection of the Roman flag ; he was under the banners of a
king who was an enemy of Rome.

" If ever, in the revolutions of ages, a King of
England should be brought before the awful tribunal of
his nation, his defenders will urge in his favour the

sacred character of a king, the respect due to the throne, to all crowned heads, to the anointed of the Lord! But his accusers will have a right to answer thus: 'One of the ancestors of this King, whom you defend, banished a man that was his guest, in time of peace; afraid to put him to death in the presence of a nation governed by positive laws and by regular and public forms, he caused his victim to be exposed on the most unhealthy point of a rock, situated in another hemisphere, in the midst of the ocean, where this guest perished, after a long agony, a prey to the climate, to want, to insults of every kind! Yet that guest was also a great Sovereign, raised to the throne on the shields of thirty-six millions of citizens. He had been master of almost every Capital of Europe; the greatest Kings composed his Court; he was generous towards all; he was during twenty years the arbiter of nations; his family was allied to every reigning family, even to that of England; he was twice the anointed of the Lord; twice consecrated by the august ceremonies of religion!!!'"

This passage is certainly very fine, for its truth, its diction, and above all, for its historical richness.

The Emperor always dictated without the least preparation. I never saw him, on any occasion, make any research respecting our history or that of any other nation; and yet no man ever quoted history more faithfully, more *apropos*, or more frequently. One might have supposed that he knew history by quotations only, and that these quotations occurred to him as by inspiration. And here I must be allowed to mention a fact which has often struck me, and which I never could satisfactorily account for to myself; but it is so very remarkable, and I have witnessed it so often, that I cannot pass it in silence. It is that Napoleon seems to possess a stock of information on several points, which remains within him, in reserve as it were, to burst forth with splendour on remarkable occasions, and which in his moments of carelessness appears to be not only slumbering, but almost unknown to him altogether. With respect to history, for instance, how often has it happened that he has asked me whether St. Louis reigned

before or after Philip the Fair, and other questions of the
same kind. But, when occasion offered, when his
moment came, then he would quote without hesitation,
and with the most minute details; and when I have
sometimes happened to be in doubt, and to go and
verify, I have always found him to be right and most
scrupulously exact: I have never been able to detect him
in error.

Another singular peculiarity in him of the same kind
is this :—In his common intercourse of life, and his
familiar conversation, the Emperor mutilated the names
most familiar to him, even ours; yet I do not think that
this would have happened to him on a public occasion.
I have heard him many times, during our walks, repeat
the celebrated speech of Augustus; and he has never
missed saying, "Take a seat, Sylla."* He would frequently create names of persons according to his fancy;
and, when he had once adopted them, they remained
fixed in his mind, although we pronounced them as they
should be, a hundred times in the day, within his hearing; but he would have been struck if we had used them
as he had altered them. It was the same with respect
to orthography: in general, he did not attend to it;
yet, if our copies had contained any faults of spelling, he
would have complained of it. One day the Emperor
said to me; "You do not write orthographically, do
you?" This question gave rise to a sarcastic smile from
a bystander, who thought that it was meant to convey
a reproach. The Emperor, who saw this, continued :—
"At least, I suppose you do not; for a man occupied
with public or other important business, a Minister, for
instance, cannot, and need not, attend to orthography.
His ideas must flow faster than his hand can trace; he
has only time for hieroglyphics; he must put letters for
words, and words for sentences; and leave the scribes to
make it out afterwards."—The Emperor left a great deal
for the copyists to do; he was their torment: his hand-
writing actually formed hieroglyphics; he often could

---

* Instead of Cinna, in Corneille's tragedy of *Cinna*, act v scene
1st.—*Eng. Ed.*

15*

not decipher it himself. My son was one day reading to
him a chapter of the Campaign of Italy : on a sudden he
stopped short, unable to make out the writing. " The
little blockhead," said the Emperor, " cannot read his
own writing !"—" It is not mine, Sire."—" And whose
then ?" " Your Majesty's."—" How, you little rogue !
do you mean to insult me ?" The Emperor took the
manuscript, tried a long while to read it, and at last
threw it down, saying, " He is right : I cannot tell
myself what is written."—He has often sent the copyists
to me, to try to read to them what he had himself been
unable to decipher.

The Emperor accounted for the clearness of his ideas,
and the faculty of extremely protracted application which
he possessed, by saying that the different affairs were
arranged in his head as in a closet. " When I wish to
turn from any business," said he, " I close the drawer
which contains it, and I open that which contains another.
They do not mix together, and do not fatigue me or inconvenience me." He had never been kept awake, he
said, by an involuntary pre-occupation of mind If I wish
to sleep, I shut up all the drawers, and I am soon asleep."
So that he had always, he added, slept when he wanted
rest, and almost at will.

MY ATLAS.—PREDESTINATION, &C.—THE GOVERNOR
MAKES FRUITLESS ATTEMPTS TO BE RECEIVED BY
THE EMPEROR.

Tuesday, 1st October. When I entered the Emperor's
room, he had my Atlas in his hands. He turned over
several of the genealogical maps, whose relation and
correspondence with each other he now understands
remarkably well. On closing the book, he said, " What
a concatenation ! how each part results from and corro-
borates what goes before it ! How every part unfolds
itself and remains fixed in the mind! Las Cases, if you
had done nothing more than point out the true method
for instruction, you would still have rendered a most
essential service. Every one may now clothe the
skeleton as they like; it will, no doubt, be improved
upon, but the first conception is yours," &c.

Amongst the numerous subjects of conversation which followed, predestination was mentioned. The Emperor made many remarkable observations on that subject; amongst others, " Pray," said he, "am I not said to be given to the belief in predestination?" "Yes, Sire, at least by many people." "Well, well! let them say on; one may sometimes be tempted to imitate, and it may occasionally be useful. . . . But what are men! . . . . How much easier it is to occupy their attention, and to strike their imaginations, by absurdities than by rational ideas! But can a man of sound sense listen for one moment to such a doctrine? Either predestination admits the existence of free will, or it rejects it. If it admits it, what kind of predetermined result is that which the mere will, a step, a word, may alter or modify, *ad infinitum?* If predestination, on the contrary, rejects the existence of free will, it is quite another question; in that case a child need only be thrown into its cradle as soon as it is born; there is no necessity for bestowing the least care upon it; for if it be irrevocably determined that it is to live, it will grow though no food should be given to it. You see that such a doctrine cannot be maintained: predestination is but a word without meaning. The Turks themselves, those patrons of fatalism, are not convinced of the doctrine, or medicine would not exist in Turkey; and a man residing in a third floor would not take the trouble to go down by the longer way of the stairs, he would immediately throw himself out of the window: you see to what a string of absurdities that will lead."

At about three o'clock, the Emperor was told that the Governor wished to communicate to him some instructions which he had just received from London. The Emperor replied that he was unwell, that the instructions might be sent to him, or communicated to some of his suite; but the Governor insisted on being admitted, saying, that he wished to communicate directly with the Emperor: he added that he had also a few words to say to us in private, after having spoken to *the General*. The Emperor again refused; upon which the Governor retired, saying that he begged he might be informed when

he *could* see *the General.* This period may be distant
indeed; the Emperor, with whom I was at that moment,
having said to me that he was determined never to
receive him again.

After dinner, the Emperor had Buffon and Valmont
de Bomare brought to him. He looked at what these
authors say respecting the diversities in the human
species, the difference between a negro and a white; but
he was not much satisfied with what he found in them on
the subject. He retired early to his apartment: he was
unwell.

2d. The Emperor having told me that he was determined to apply again to the study of English, and that I
must oblige him every morning to take his lesson, I
accordingly went to his apartment at about half-past
twelve. I was not fortunate in the choice of the moment,
for he was lying on his sofa asleep after his breakfast.
I must have vexed him, and was very much vexed
myself. However, he would not let me go away, and
read a little English for about half an hour. He was not
very well. He dressed. Having told him that we had
finished what he had given us to do, he at first proposed
to go to work on the chapters of the Campaign of Italy;
but he afterwards altered his mind, and was busy the
whole day on something else. At about five o'clock he
attempted to walk out, but found the weather too cold.
After dinner, he tried to read, but in vain; he could not
go on: he felt tired, drowsy, indisposed, and withdrew
almost immediately.

JURISPRUDENCE; THE CODE; MERLIN, &C.—MONUMENTS
IN EGYPT.—PLAN OF AN EGYPTIAN TEMPLE IN
PARIS.

3d. After breakfast, the Emperor took two or three
turns in the garden. We were all with him. He spoke
of the communications which the Governor had to make
to us, and took a review of the different conjectures—
some good, some bad—which each of us formed on the
subject. The weather was tolerable; he ordered the
calash, and we went round the wood. The heat and the
heaviness of the atmosphere, though the sun was ob-

scured, obliged him to go into the house again. He sat down and dictated to my son until five o'clock.

We again tried to take a few turns in the garden; but the air was cold and damp. He went in-doors again, and made me go to converse with him. He turned over an English book, and stopped at a part relating to juris-prudence, and the criminal codes of France and England, endeavouring to compare them. Every body knows how extremely well versed he is in our codes; but he has little knowledge of that of England, and, with the exception of some general points, I could not answer his questions. In the course of the conversation he said : Laws which in theory are a model of clearness become too often a chaos in their application; because men, with their passions, spoil every thing they touch, &c. . . Men can only avoid being exposed to the arbitrary acts of the judge, by submitting to the despotism of the law, &c. .
I had at first fancied it would be possible to reduce all laws to simple geometrical demonstrations; so that every man who could read, and connect two ideas toge-ther, would be able to decide for himself; but I became convinced, almost immediately that this idea was absurd. However," added he, "I should have wished to start from some fixed point, and follow one road known to all; to have no other laws but those inserted in the code; and to proclaim, once for all, that all laws which were not in the code were null and void. But it is not easy to obtain simplicity from practical lawyers: they first prove to you that simplicity is impossible, that it is a mere chimera; and endeavour next to demonstrate that it is incompatible with the stability and the existence of power. Power, they say, is exposed alone to the unforeseen machinations of all: it must therefore have, in the moment of need, arms kept in reserve for such cases: so that, with some old edicts of Chilperic or Pharamond, ferreted out for the occasion," said Napoleon, "nobody can say that he is secure from being hanged in due form and according to law.

"So long as the subjects of discussion in the Council of State," said the Emperor, " were referable to the code, I felt very strong; but when they diverged from it, I was

quite in the dark, and Merlin was then my resource —he
was my light. Without possessing much brilliancy, Merlin is very learned, wise, upright, and honest; one of
the veterans of the good old cause: he was very much
attached to me.

" No sooner had the code made its appearance, than it
was almost immediately followed by commentaries, explanations, elucidations, interpretations, and the Lord knows
what besides. I usually exclaimed, on seeing this : Gentlemen, we have cleaned the stable of Augeas ; for God's
sake do not let us fill it again !" &c.

During dinner, the Emperor made some very remarkable observations respecting Egypt, which will be found
in the chapters dictated to Bertrand.   He then reverted
to his expedition to Syria, and declared that the grand
object of the expedition to Egypt was to shake the
power of England in the four quarters of the world, by
effecting a revolution capable of changing the whole face
of the East, and giving a new destiny to India.   Egypt,
he said, was to stand us in stead of St. Domingo, and our
American Colonies, to reconcile the liberty of the blacks
with the prosperity of our commerce.   This new colony
would have ruined the English in America, in the Mediterranean, and even on the banks of the Ganges.

Then, answering the reproach preferred against him of
having deserted his army, he said : "I merely obeyed the
call of France, which summoned me to save her, and I
had a right to do so. I had received from the Directory a
carte blanche for all my operations in the basin of the
Mediterranean, in Africa, and in Asia. I had full powers
for treating with the Russians, the Turks, the Barbary
States, and the provinces of India. I was at liberty to appoint a successor, to bring back the army, or to return
myself, if I thought proper."

The Emperor thought that all he had seen in Egypt,
and, particularly, all those celebrated ruins so much
talked of, were not to be compared with Paris and the
Tuileries. The only difference between Egypt and us
was, in his opinion, that Egypt, thanks to the pureness
of its air and the nature of its materials, preserved her
ruins for ever ; whereas the nature of our European at-

mosphere would not admit of our having any for any length of time, every thing being soon corroded and gone.

Vestiges of a thousand years' date might be found on the banks of the Nile; but not one would subsist on the banks of the Seine in fifty years. He, however, regretted very much that he had not caused an Egyptian temple to be erected at Paris: he could have wished to adorn the capital with such a monument, &c.

RESOURCES DURING THE EMIGRATION: ANECDOTES, &C. —OFFICIAL COMMUNICATIONS.—NEW OFFENCES.

4th. At about twelve o'clock, I went to the Emperor's apartment. He took a good lesson of English in Telemachus: he resolved to take up my method again; he approves of it, he said, and derives great benefit from it. He observed that he thought I had excellent dispositions for being a very good schoolmaster; I told him it was the fruit of my experience. He then made me enter into a great many details respecting the time when I gave lessons in London, during my emigration, and he was very much amused by them. "However," said he, "you gentlemen, must have done credit to the profession, if not by your learning, at least, by your manners." I then told him that one of our Princes had taught mathematics during his emigration. "And this alone," said he, with animation, "would make a man of him, and shew him to have possessed some merit; that is assuredly one of the greatest triumphs of Madame de Genlis."

I then related to him the following curious anecdote, which I had heard on that subject. "The Prince was in Switzerland: and, being so circumstanced as to find it advisable to conceal his existence, he wished to take a name that might favour his disguise. One of our Bishops, from the South of France, fancied that nothing could be better than to give him the name of a young man from Languedoc then at Nismes, who was a very zealous Protestant; which was just as it ought to be, the Prince being in a Protestant canton. The Bishop added that there was no appearance that the young man would ever be in the way to falsify the Prince's assumption of his name. But it had so happened that the young man had gone into the army, and had become an aide-de-camp to M. de Montesquiou, and that shortly afterwards he had emigrated precisely into Switzerland with his general. What was his surprise to find himself at the *table d'hôte*, at dinner with a person of his own name, of the same religion, and who belonged to the same town! It was exactly like the scene of the two Sosias.* But the best of the joke was that the young man had also changed his name, and carefully concealed his own. Such incidents are only to be met with in novels; they are thought of impossible occurrence. Perhaps the present story has been rather embellished; yet, I think, I can affirm that I heard it from the young man himself."

"But," observed the Emperor afterwards, "those amongst you emigrants who had created for yourselves resources abroad must have felt quite lost when you returned to France, and ruined once more?"---"Certainly, Sire; for we found nothing of what we had formerly left in France, and we had just abandoned the little we had made ourselves. But we had not calculated: our impatience to revisit our native land had overbalanced every other consideration, and several amongst us soon found themselves in the greatest distress, in want of every thing, although acquainted and even intimate with many of the great personages of the day— with your Ministers, Sire, your Councillors of State, and others. This circumstance gave rise to a *bon mot* from one of our *wits*. Meeting one day, in the saloon of the Minister for Maritime Affairs, a friend who like himself hardly knew how to manage to subsist, he exclaimed, by way of consolation: "Well, my friend, if we die of hunger, we may still have two or three Ministers at our funeral." The Emperor laughed heartily at the jest, and admitted that it gave an exact description of the situation of affairs at the time.

After his lesson of English, and the conversation which followed, the Emperor went out for a walk. We walked to the end of the wood, where the calash drove up to us.

---

* In Moliere's Comedy of Amphitryon. *Eng. Ed.*

On the Emperor's return, the Doctor came to inform him that Colonel Reade, whom he had consented to receive instead of the Governor, wished to be presented to him.   Colonel Reade delivered to the Emperor a note of considerable length ; and I was sent for to translate it   It contained the communications which Sir Hudson Lowe had for three or four days past been vainly endeavouring to make in person.   The note was couched in the most offensive terms. and the Governor wished to have reserved to himself the satisfaction of communicating its contents to the Emperor.   This is a characteristic trait, and it requires no comment.   The harsh terms in which it was expressed, and in particular the repeated threat that we should be separated from the Emperor, vexed us exceedingly, and put us out of spirits for the remainder of the day.

THE EMPEROR READS MY JOURNAL, AND DICTATES TO ME.—CONFERENCE BETWEEN THE GRAND MARSHAL AND THE GOVERNOR.

5th.—At an early hour this morning, before I had risen, I heard some one softly open my chamber-door. My apartment is so encumbered with my own bed and that of my son, that it is no easy matter to enter it. I perceived a hand drawing aside my bed-curtain : it was the Emperor's.   I was reading a book of geometry, a circumstance which amused him very much, and, as he said, saved my reputation.   I instantly rose, and soon rejoined the Emperor, who was proceeding to the wood alone.   He conversed for a considerable time on the events of the preceding day.   He then returned to the house for the purpose of taking a bath : he was very ill, and had passed a bad night.

He sent for me at one o'clock.   He was in the drawing-room, and he expressed a wish to take his English lesson.   The weather was very hot and close.   The Emperor felt languid and dispirited : he could not bend his mind to study, and several times fell asleep.   At length he rose, saying he was determined to shake off his lethargy, and he proceeded to the billiard-room to breathe a little fresh air.

Conversing on the subject of the Campaigns of Italy, he enquired what I had done with the first rough draughts, observing that all the chapters had been several times re-copied. I told him that I had carefully preserved them. He desired to have all the manuscripts brought to him, and, laying aside two complete copies, he sent the rest into the kitchen to be burnt.

I have already several times mentioned that the Emperor knew I kept a Journal. This was a secret, and therefore he never spoke to me on the subject, except when we happened to be alone together. He often asked me whether I still continued my Journal, and what I could find to set down in it. "Sire," I replied, "all that your Majesty does and says, from morning to night." "Then," said he, "you must have a monstrous deal of repetition, and must tell many useless things! But no matter, go on, some day we will look it over together."

When he visited my chamber, he frequently found the faithful Aly engaged in re-copying my Journal; for he had kindly offered to employ himself in this way, during his leisure hours. The Emperor sometimes cast his eyes upon Aly's writing, and, after reading a few lines, that is to say, as soon as he ascertained what it was, he would turn away and speak about something else, without ever alluding to the subject. This is precisely what had occurred this morning; and the Emperor, recollecting the circumstance, said that he wished at length to have a sight of this famous *jumble of trifles*. My son brought a portion of the manuscript, and the Emperor spent upwards of two hours in perusing it. The introduction, which relates to myself personally, fixed his attention; he read it over twice, and then said: "Well, very well; this is a fine inheritance for little Emanuel." As to the Journal, he approved of its form and general plan. He made several corrections with his own hand, on those parts which related to his family and his childhood. He desired my son to take the pen, and he dictated to him some details respecting Brienne, Father Patrault, &c. When he had done, he desired me to continue my labours; as he was pleased with them; and he promised to furnish me with

many anecdotes, particularly concerning Alexander and
the other sovereigns.

He afterwards took a drive in the calash, in which I
accompanied him, and the Journal again became the topic
of conversation. The Emperor said a great deal on the
subject, and expressed himself very much pleased with
the idea. He gave me several hints respecting it, and
concluded by observing that, from the peculiar circumstances under which it was produced, it might become a
work truly unique in its character, and an invaluable
treasure to his son.

On our return to Longwood, we found the Grand Marshal, who had just returned from Plantation House, where
he had been to hold a conference on the subject of the
communications of yesterday. We anxiously awaited the
answer he might bring back. He informed us that a
proposition had been made, which was nothing less than
that four of us should be separated from the Emperor.
There were many other minor points of a very vexatious
nature ; but this one caused us to lose sight of all the rest.
The Governor had, however, finally agreed to remove
only the Pole and three of the domestics. According to
the report of the Grand Marshal, I was the individual
upon whom the storm had lowered, of whom the Governor most particularly complained, and whose removal, he
said, he should certainly have decided upon, had he not
thought me too useful to the Emperor. He complained
that I was constantly writing to Europe, declaiming
against the Government and the injustice and oppression
which I alleged were exercised towards us. His other
subjects of complaint were, that I spoke of the Emperor
to the strangers who visited Longwood in such a way as
to excite their interest ; that I was constantly endeavouring to establish communications with different individuals
on the island (and he mentioned the instance of Mrs.
Sturmer) ; that I had addressed, or endeavoured to transmit, various documents to Europe, &c. However, after
having spoken of me in the most angry terms, for some
reason or other, he endeavoured to soften down what he
had said by a few complimentary observations. He remarked that he could scarcely have expected such con-

duct in a man possessing so much information, and whose
good character was established throughout Europe.

After dinner, the Emperor amused himself by solving
some problems in geometry and algebra: this, he said,
reminded him of his youthful days; and it surprised us
all to find that the subjects were still so fresh in his recollection.

PECULIAR CIRCUMSTANCE CONNECTED WITH MY JOURNAL. —THE EMPIRE OF OPINION.—TALMA, CRESCENTINI, &C.

6th—7th. During these two days, a circumstance has
occurred, which is so nearly connected with the nature of
the present work, that I cannot omit noticing it. I have
just mentioned that the Emperor had expressed himself
well satisfied with my journal: he alluded to it several
times in the course of the day, assuring me that he should
feel great pleasure in perusing and correcting it. This
information, as it may be supposed, was highly gratifying to me. The moment which I had so long and ardently looked for had at length arrived. That which I
had hastily, and, perhaps, inaccurately, collected, was now
about to receive an inestimable correction and sanction.
Imperfect points would be developed, chasms filled up,
and obscurities explained. What a fund of historical
truths and political secrets was I about to receive! Ela-
ted by these expectations, I the first day presented myself
to the Emperor at the usual hour, having my journal
with me; but he began to dictate to me on a totally different subject, and I was obliged to put up with the disappointment. Next day, the same thing occurred again.
I now wished to call the Emperor's attention to my Journal; but he did not appear to understand me, and I took
the hint. I know Napoleon so well! He possesses in the
highest degree the art of not seeming to understand; he
resorts to it frequently, and always for some particular
object. In the present instance I understood him sufficiently, and I did not again attempt to draw his attention
to the subject. At first I was much puzzled to guess the
motive that had induced him to act thus; and I made
several conjectures, which have probably occurred to the
reader, as well as to myself. A few days afterwards I

was forced away from him, though I had not the least cause in the world to anticipate this fatal event.

I have dwelt on this circumstance with scrupulous exactness, because I conceive that it affords a new guarantee of my sincerity, and serves to explain precisely the nature of my Journal. Of the great bulk of its contents, and in particular the important events described in it, no doubt can be entertained. Some involuntary errors may, however, have crept into the details, from the hasty manner in which they were collected, and from my being deprived of the advantage of having the manuscript revised by the only individual who was capable of correcting its inaccuracies.

The Emperor, while he was dressing and waiting for the Grand Marshal to take his turn in writing, amused himself by conversing on different subjects.

He spoke of the influence of opinion, to which he so frequently alludes. He traced its secret progress, its uncertainty, and the caprice of its decisions. He then adverted to the natural delicacy of the French, which he said was exquisite in matters of decorum, the laudable susceptibility of our manners, and the graceful action and gentleness of touch which authority must employ, if an attempt is made to interfere with the national feeling.

" In conformity with my system," observed he, of amalgamating all kinds of merit, and of rendering one and the same reward universal, I had an idea of presenting the cross of the Legion of Honour to Talma; but I refrained from doing this, in consideration of our capricious manners and absurd prejudices. I wished to make a first experiment in an affair that was unimportant, and I accordingly gave the Iron Crown to Crescentini. The decoration was foreign, and so was the individual on whom it was conferred. This circumstance was less likely to attract public notice or to render my conduct the subject of discussion; at worst, it could only give rise to a few malicious jokes. Such," continued the Emperor, " is the influence of public opinion. I distributed sceptres at will, and thousands readily bowed beneath their sway; and yet I could not give

away a bit of ribbon without the chance of incurring
disapprobation; for I believe my experiment, with regard to Crescentini, proved unsuccessful." "It did,
Sire," observed some one present. "The circumstance
occasioned a great outcry in Paris; it drew forth a general anathema in all the drawing-rooms of the metropolis,
and afforded ample scope for the expression of malignant
feeling. However, at one of the evening parties of the
Faubourg Saint-Germain, a *bon - mot* had the effect of
completely stemming the torrent of indignation. A
pompous orator was holding forth, in an eloquent strain,
on the subject of the honour that had been conferred on
Crescentini. He declared it to be a disgrace, a horror,
a perfect profanation, and inquired what right Crescentini
could have to such a distinction? On hearing this, the
beautiful Madame G . . . . who was present, rose
majestically from her chair, and, with a truly theatrical
tone and gesture, exclaimed, ' *Et sa blessoure Monsieur!*
do you make no allowance for that ? ' This produced a
general burst of laughter and applause, and poor
Madame G . . . . was very much embarrassed by
her success."

The Emperor, who now heard this anecdote for the
first time, was highly amused by it. He often afterwards alluded to it, and occasionally related it himself.

At dinner, the Emperor informed us that he had
worked for twelve hours; and we observed that his
day was not yet ended. He seemed to be ill and
fatigued.

THE ODYSSEY.—COMBAT BETWEEN ULYSSES AND IRUS.

8th. When I entered the Emperor's apartment this
morning, I found him engaged in reading the files of the
Journal des Debats, which had lately arrived. At three
o'clock he began to dress. His first valet de chambre
was ill; and he observed that those who acted as his
substitutes were not equal to him in address.

The weather was tolerable, and we walked to the extremity of the wood, where the calash was to take us up.

I had a disposable sum of money in London, which I
had conveyed thither in 1814. The recollection of the

privations I had endured during my emigration, and the
chance of being exposed to future want, had prompted
me to this act of prudence, and I was now reaping the
fruits of it. Owing to this circumstance, I was more at
my ease, as to pecuniary affairs, than any other individual of the Emperor's suite at St. Helena; but what led
me to regard this sum as an inestimable treasure was
the happiness of being able to lay it at the feet of the
Emperor. I had already several times proposed that he
should accept it; and I now once more repeated the
offer, while I adverted to the renewed outrages which
we had just experienced from the Governor. At this
moment we were joined by Madame de Montholon, who
had set out after us. She observed that the Emperor
walked so fast that she should certainly have lost sight
of him, had not my gesticulations enabled her to keep
her eye upon us; and that she had been puzzled to guess
the cause of my vehemence of manner. "Madam," said
the Emperor with the most captivating grace, "he has
been trying to make me accept his bounty; he has been
offering to support us here."

We returned almost immediately to the house, as the
weather was very damp and the Emperor complained of
tooth-ache. For some time past he has been troubled
with a profuse secretion of saliva.

After dinner he resumed the reading of the Odyssey:
we had arrived at the passage describing the combat between Ulysses and Irus, on the threshold of the palace,
both in the garb of beggars. The Emperor very much
disapproved of this episode, which he pronounced to be
mean, incongruous, and beneath the dignity of the King.
"And yet," continued he, "independently of all the faults
which, in my opinion, this incident presents, I still find
in it something to interest me. I fancy myself in the
situation of Ulysses, and then I can well conceive his
dread of being overpowered by a wretched mendicant.
Every prince or general has not the broad shoulders of
his guards or grenadiers; every man has not the strength
of a porter. But Homer has remedied all this by representing his heroes as so many giants. We have no such
heroes now-a-days. What would become of us," he

added, glancing round at us all, "if we lived in those
good times when bodily vigour constituted real power ?
Why, Noverraz (his valet-de-chambre) would wield the
sceptre over us all. It must be confessed that civilization favours the mind entirely at the expense of the
body."

THE POLE ARRESTED BY THE GOVERNOR.—THE EMPEROR'S
REFLECTIONS ON HIS SON AND ON AUSTRIA.—NEW
VEXATIONS.—REMARKS ON LORD BATHURST.—OBSER-
VATIONS DICTATED BY NAPOLEON.

9th.—As we were walking to come up with the calash,
we received information that the Pole had just been put
under arrest by the Governor. This was, of course,
merely a first step—a warning of what we all had to expect. Intimidation seems to be the system to which the
Governor has resorted since the arrival of his last instructions, which he endeavours to fulfil to the utmost of his
ingenuity. We shall see how far he will go.

When I waited on the Emperor, before dinner, I found
him dull and apparently absent. The conversation led
him to mention Austria, and he alluded to the wrongs
which he had received from that Power, and the errors
of her policy. He described the weakness of the monarch, who, he said, had never evinced energy, except
when it tended to ruin him in the estimation of his subjects. He dwelt on the venality and want of principle
which distinguished the men who had advised and executed the measures of the Austrian cabinet. He spoke
of the blind policy of Austria, and described her dangerous situation. "She now stands," said he, "in the
most imminent peril, advancing to meet the embraces of
a colossus in her front, while she cannot recede a single
step, because an abyss is yawning on her flank and
rear."

This turn of the conversation naturally led the Emperor to speak of his son. "What education will they give
him?" said he. "What sort of principles will they incul-
cate in his youthful mind? On the other hand, if he
should prove weak in intellect—if they should inspire him
with hatred of his father! These thoughts fill me with

horror! and where is the antidote to all this? Henceforth there can be no certain medium of communication—uo faithful tradition between him and me! At best my Memoirs, or perhaps your Journal, may fall into his hands. But to subdue the false precepts imbibed in early life, to counteract the errors of a bad education, requires a certain capacity, a certain strength of mind and decision of judgment which fall not to the share of every one." He appeared deeply affected; and, after a pause of a few moments, he said, suddenly and with emphasis, "But let us talk of something else;" however, he still continued silent. I sat down to write, and after an hour or two the Grand Marshal came and took my place.

Just after I had quitted the Emperor's apartments, I was again sent for to translate to him a large packet of papers which had been received from the Governor. The state of my eyes, which are now altogether failing me, obliged me to avail myself of M. de Montholon's assistance in reading the papers.

Their contents were 1. Some of the new restrictions that have been imposed on us, in which the Emperor is treated in a way that may be termed curious; for indecency and indecorum are carried so far as to prescribe the nature and limits of the conversations which he is to be permitted to hold. This will scarcely be credited!

2. The form of the declaration which was presented for our signature. This was merely a series of arbitrary and useless vexations, heightened by every irritating circumstance that vengeance could suggest.

3. Finally a letter from the Governor to the Grand Marshal, founded on the note presented by Colonel Reade, which I translated to the Emperor, and which the colonel had refused to leave behind him; the reader will recollect my having already noticed it. However, in the letter now transmitted to the Emperor certain essential points were very ingeniously suppressed or modified: the Emperor frequently remarked that the Governor possesses a peculiar talent for business of this sort. I will here retrace this note from recollection. Though I read it only once, namely, at the time when I translated it to the Emperor, yet I think I can vouch for

the following being an accurate representation of its
contents.

"The Frenchmen who wished to remain with General
Bonaparte, were required to sign the formula which
should be presented to them, and by which they would
subject themselves to all the restrictions imposed on the
General.   This obligation was to be regarded as perpetual.   Those who should refuse to enter into this
agreement were to be sent to the Cape of Good Hope.
Four individuals were to be removed from the suite of
General Bonaparte.   Those who might remain were to
be considered as though they were Englishmen by birth,
and to be subject to the laws established for securing
the safe custody of General Bonaparte; that is to say,
they would incur the punishment of death by conniving
at his escape.   Any Frenchmen who might use insulting
language or reflections, or behave so as to give offence
to the Governor or the Government, would be immediately removed to the Cape of Good Hope, without being
provided with the means of returning to Europe: the
whole expense of the voyage devolving on himself."

During dinner, and the greater part of the evening
these documents became the subject of conversation.

We were much amused by that passage in the Governor's letter which transmitted the ministerial instructions, and informed us that those who might be wanting
in respect for the Governor, or render themselves obnoxious, would be removed to the Cape, and the expense
attending their return to Europe was to be defrayed by
themselves.   We thought this very droll, and the Emperor said, "Of course this threat appears to you very
extraordinary and ridiculous; but no doubt it was perfectly natural to Lord Bathurst.   I dare say he could
not imagine a more terrible punishment.   It is a true
shopkeeper idea!"

The Emperor concluded the evening by reading to us
Adelaide Duguesclin, which contains a fine rhodomontade
upon the Bourbons.

After reading it, the Emperor said, "During the time
of my power, an order was given for suppressing the performance of this drama, under the idea that it would be
offensive to me.   This circumstance accidentally came to

my knowledge, and I ordered the piece to be revived. Many things of the same kind took place; people often acted very unwisely under the idea that they were serving or pleasing me."

I transcribe here the restrictions to which I have just alluded. They are curious in themselves, and will serve better than volumes of description, to give a just idea of our situation; but what enhances the value of this document is that the observations which accompany each article were made by the Emperor himself.

Restrictions drawn up by Sir Hudson Lowe, and transmitted to Longwood on the 19th of October, 1816, but which he had already put into execution by different secret orders, since the preceding month of August, though he never communicated them to the English officers on duty, doubtless, because he was ashamed of them.

TEXT OF THE RESTRICTIONS.

"1st.—Longwood, with the road by Hut's Gate, along the hill, as far as the signal-post near Alarm-House, are to be fixed as boundaries."

Observation. Sir Hudson Lowe's predecessor had extended the boundary line to the summits of the hills; but in about a fortnight, he perceived that, by removing the sentinels to a little further distance, the house and garden of Secretary-general Brook would be included within the boundaries, and he immediately gave orders for the change.

At about forty fathoms from the road-side is Corbett's garden, which contains about eight or ten oak trees and a fountain; thus affording a cool and agreeable shade.* According to the new restrictions, which confined him to the high-road, a line is substituted for a surface, and the secretary's house and Corbett's garden are excluded from the boundaries.

"2d.—Sentinels will mark the boundary lines, which nobody must pass to approach the house or grounds of Longwood, without the Governor's permission."

---

* In the very spot here described by Napoleon is his grave.

OBSERVATION. By the regulations which were first laid down, respecting our establishment at St. Helena, and which were approved by the English Governor, persons were admitted to Longwood in the following manner: The Governor, the Admiral, the Colonel commanding the regiment and the camp, the two members of the East India Company's Council, and the Secretary-general, who were the persons highest in authority on the island, might pass the line of sentinels without any order or permission whatever. The inhabitants of the Island were required to have a pass from the Governor; naval men to be furnished with one from their Admiral, and military with one from their colonel; and finally, the inhabitants, sailors, and officers might all come to Longwood by the permission of Count Bertrand, when the Emperor wished to receive them. This arrangement, which continued for eight months, was attended by no inconvenience. By the present regulation (which has been in force since the month of August, though it was not formally communicated to us until we were furnished with the list of new restrictions,) we may be said to be kept in solitary confinement, and cut off from all intercourse with the inhabitants. The latter, the officers and seamen are all equally averse to the idea of being obliged to solicit the Governor's permission to visit Longwood, and to subject themselves to an interrogatory respecting the motive of their visit. Strangers, whether civil or military, officers, touching at St. Helena on their passage from India, and who might be desirous of seeing the Emperor, usually applied to Count Bertrand, who appointed the day and the hour when they would be received. During their stay in the island they were regarded as citizens, and with the permission of Count Bertrand, they might when they pleased visit Longwood; and it may once more be observed that this arrangement subsisted for eight months without being attended by any inconvenience. If any strangers touching at the island might excite the suspicion of the Governor, he could prevent them from landing, or passing the first post. Finally, the Governor, by the report of the sentinels, was daily made acquainted with the names of the persons who visited Longwood. But in the month of August, the Governor sought to impose on us the obligation of receiving strangers, to whom he wished to render himself agreeable, and also of receiving them at the time he might think proper to appoint. This was putting the finishing stroke to all his offensive conduct! To put a stop to all these insults, the Emperor found himself obliged to declare that he would in future receive no one.

"3d.—The road to the left of Hut's Gate, which turns off by Woodridge to Longwood, never having been frequented by General Bonaparte since the arrival of the Governor, the post by which it was observed, will be in a great measure withdrawn. But whenever the General may wish to ride on horseback in this direction, on giving timely notice to the officer he will experience no obstacle."

OBSERVATION.—In the first observation it was proved that the limits had been contracted in this quarter; and, by this third article, they are still more circumscribed. To say that the valley has not been frequented for six months is a strange reason for adopting this decision. It is certainly true that Napoleon has for several months declined going out, in consequence of the harassing conduct of the Governor; but it must also be observed that one part of the valley is not accessible in rainy weather, and that in the other part a camp has been formed. Yet Lord Bathurst stated, in his speech in Parliament, that "this road had been prohibited, when it was found that he (General Bonaparte) had abused the confidence which had been reposed in him, and had endeavoured to corrupt the inhabitants of the island." But here Lord Bathurst contradicts Sir Hudson Lowe. The offer of permission to ride in the valley, whenever it may be wished, is a mere pretence; the forms prescribed for the attainment of this permission render it impossible. This offer never has been, and never can be, fulfilled. The ride in the valley being thus prohibited, it has become impossible to visit Miss Mason's garden, in which there are some large trees which afford agreeable shade. Within the boundaries to which the captives are now

restricted, there is not a single spot in which they can
enjoy the sight of trees or water : sentinels are posted
at different distances throughout the boundaries; and,
under the pretence of misunderstanding in the orders,
&c., any individual may be arrested. This has frequently happened to the French officers.

 " 4th. If he (General Bonaparte) should wish to
prolong his ride in any other directions, an officer of
the Governor's staff (if he receives timely notice) will be
in readiness to attend him. If the notice should be
short, the officer on duty at Longwood may take the
place of the staff-officer.

 " The inspecting officer has orders not to approach
General Bonaparte, at least unless he be asked for; and
not to watch him in his rides, except so far as his duty
requires ; that is to say, he must observe that the established rules are not violated; and if they should be
transgressed, he must intimate the circumstance in a
respectful way."

 OBSERVATION. This regulation is useless. The Emperor will not go out so long as he sees there is a wish
to subject him to direct and public inspection. Besides,
the staff-officers have orders to report all that the French
may say when in conversation with them. This affords
opportunities for calumny. Several English officers
have refused to act this dishonourable part, declaring
that they would not degrade themselves to the level of
spies, and repeat the conversations that may take place
in the unguarded confidence of a ride or walk.

 " 5th. The rules already in force, for preventing
communications with any one whatever, without the
Governor's permission, must be strictly enforced. Consequently, it is requisite that General Bonaparte should
abstain from entering into any conversation (except such
as the interchange of customary salutations may demand)
with the persons whom he may happen to meet, unless
it be in the presence of an English officer."

 OBSERVATION.—Hitherto this extremity of insult had
been avoided. The Emperor does not acknowledge,
either in the Governor or his agents, the right of imposing any restrictions on him. But what is the object

of this article ? To insult and degrade the character of
the captives !—to give rise to disputes between them and
the sentinels. To prohibit them from speaking to any
one, or entering any house, is, in fact, a moral annulment
of the circuit allowed them. This is so extraordinary
that we are now actually induced to believe, what many
persons have already suspected, that Sir Hudson Lowe
is occasionally subject to fits of lunacy.

" 6th.—Those persons who, with the consent of General Bonaparte, may receive the Governor's permission to
visit him, must not communicate with any individual of
his suite, unless a permission to that effect be specially
expressed."

OBSERVATION.—This is useless ; for nobody has been
received since the present Governor abolished the regulations which were established by his predecessor. However, the consequence of this restriction is that, if Napoleon should receive a stranger, as none of his officers can
be present, and none of his servants in attendance, he
would be reduced to the necessity of opening the doors
himself. Besides, as the Emperor does not understand
English, it follows, if the individual admitted to him
should not speak French, that they must both remain
mute, and thus the interview would be reduced to a mere
exhibition.

" 7th.—At sunset, the garden round Longwood is to
be regarded as the extent of the boundaries. At that
time sentinels will be posted at the limits of the garden ;
but so as not to incommode General Bonaparte by observing his motions, should he wish to continue his
walks. During the night, sentinels will be stationed
close to the house, as they formerly were ; and all admission must be prohibited until the sentinels are withdrawn from the house and garden on the following
morning."

OBSERVATION.—During the excessively hot season,
the only time when it is possible to walk is after sun-set.
In order to avoid meeting the sentinels, the Emperor
finds it necessary to return to the house while it is still
broad day-light ; though the heat of the sun has rendered
it impossible for him to go out during the day, as the

grounds round Longwood are without shade, water, or
verdure. According to this new restriction, the Emperor cannot enjoy a walk in the evening; while he is
likewise deprived of the exercise of riding on horseback.
He is confined in a small house, in all respects insufficient
for his accommodation, badly built, unwholesomely
situated, and without a supply of water; and, in addition
to all this, every opportunity is taken to expose him to
insult and disrespect. His constitution, though naturally
robust, is very much enfeebled by the treatment he
experiences.

" 8th.—Every letter for Longwood will be enclosed
by the Governor in a sealed envelope, and forwarded to
the officer on duty, to be delivered, sealed, to the officer
of General Bonaparte's suite to whom it is addressed,
who by this means will be assured that nobody except
the Governor knows its contents.

" In like manner, letters from any of the residents of
Longwood must be delivered to the officer on duty, enclosed in a second sealed envelope and addressed to the
Governor, which will be a security that no individual
except the latter can peruse its contents.

" No letter can be written or sent, and no communication of any kind whatever can be made, except in the
manner above mentioned. No correspondence can be
maintained with any individual in the island, except for
the necessary communications to the purveyor. The
notes containing these communications must be delivered open to the officer on duty, who will forward
them to the proper quarter.

" The above-mentioned restrictions will be observed
from the date of the 10th inst.

" H. Lowe."

" *St. Helena, October 9th*, 1816."

Observation.—This last restriction has no reference
to the Emperor, who neither writes nor receives letters.
A simple explanation is, therefore, all that is required
Will the observations that may be contained in the confidential letters from the Emperor's officers to their
friends be regarded as offensive? When those who may

read these letters shall be convinced that they are in no way hostile to the safety or policy of the state, will they forget their contents, so that they may never become the subject of conversation or abuse? This explanation will decide whether all correspondence is, or is not, to be considered as prohibited. The seizure of the person of Count Las Cases completely justifies this observation.

The object of the 8th article of the restrictions, as the inquisitorial system established on the island sufficiently proves, is to prevent the European journals from giving publicity to the criminal conduct that is pursued here. A vast deal of trouble is taken to secure this object: it would have been far easier to have acted in such a way as to render concealment unnecessary. A letter addressed to Count Bertrand, dated the 1st of July, 1816, goes to still greater lengths; for it prohibits even verbal communications with the inhabitants of the island. This is the delirium of fury and hatred; or rather, it may be said to be a proof of downright madness. The regulation here alluded to is but a trifling example of the vexations to which we are exposed, and the invention of which seems to be the sole occupation of the present Governor. Can Lord Bathurst now affirm that Sir H. Lowe has imposed no restriction; that the instructions of the English ministry were of a nature advantageous to Napoleon and his suite, and had no other object than that of securing their safe custody? In consequence of this absurd and insulting treatment, the Emperor has not enjoyed exercise without doors for several months. His medical attendants foresee that this confinement will prove fatal to his constitution. It is a more certain, and far more inhuman, mode of assassination, than poison or the sword. [What a horrible prophecy!]

ANXIETY OCCASIONED BY THE NEW RESTRICTIONS.—ANECDOTES OF CAMPO-FORMIO.—MM. DE COBENTZEL, GALLO, AND CLARKE.—THE COUNT D'ANTRAIGUES.

20th.—This morning we had agreed to meet together at the Grand Marshal's, to deliberate on the restrictions which the Governor had recently transmitted to us, and to adopt a uniform resolution. I was unwell, and could

16*

not attend. I, however, wrote down my opinion: I
stated that in the delicate situation in which I was placed
I could do nothing; I could arrive at no positive conclusion; I always found 0—0.

The point in question was, indeed, of the most serious
and difficult nature. We were required to subject ourselves to new restrictions, to place ourselves under the
dependence of the Governor, who shamefully abused his
power, employed the most insulting language towards the
Emperor, and announced that we must submit to every
grievance, under pain of being immediately separated from
Napoleon, sent to the Cape, and thence to Europe.

On the other hand, the Emperor, indignant at the
mortifications to which we were exposed on his account,
insisted that we should no longer submit to them. He
urged us rather to quit him, and to return to Europe,
to bear witness that we had seen him absolutely buried
alive.

But how could we for a moment endure this thought!
Death was preferable to separation from him whom we
served, admired, and loved; to whom we daily became
more and more attached, through his personal qualities,
and the miseries which injustice and hatred had accumulated upon him. This was the real state of the question.
In these distressing circumstances, we knew not what
determination to adopt. I closed my letter by stating
that, if left to myself alone, I would sign, without scruple, any thing that the Governor might present to me;
and that, if a collective resolution were taken, I would
implicitly adopt it.

The Governor had now found out a method of attacking us in detail: he declared his intention of removing
any individual of Napoleon's suite according to his will
and caprice.

The Emperor was indisposed: the Doctor has observed
incipient scurvy. He desired me to attend him, and we
conversed on the subjects which chiefly occupied our attention at the moment. He wanted something to amuse
him, and he took up the chapter of Leoben, which happened to be beside him. When he had finished reading
it, the conversation turned on the conferences which

brought about the treaty of Campo-Formio. I refer to the chapters on that subject for the portrait and character of the first Austrian negotiator, M. de Cobentzel, whom Napoleon surnamed the "*great northern bear*," on account of the influence which, he said, his heavy paw had exercised on the green table of the conferences.

"M. de Cobentzel was at that time," said the Emperor, "the agent of the Austrian monarchy, the main spring of its plans, and the director of its diplomacy. He had been appointed on all the principal European embassies, and had been long at the Court of Catharine, whose peculiar favour he enjoyed. Proud of his rank and importance, he doubted not that his dignified and courtly manners would easily overawe a General who had just issued from the revolutionary camp. Thus," observed Napoleon, " he shewed a want of respect in addressing the French General: but the first words uttered by the latter sufficed to reduce him to his proper level, above which he never afterwards attempted to rise."

The conferences at first proceeded very slowly; for M. de Cobentzel, according to the custom of the Austrian Cabinet, proved himself very skilful in the art of retarding business. The French General, however, determined to bring matters to an issue: the conference, which he had declared should be the last, was maintained with great warmth. Napoleon came, resolved to have a decisive answer to his propositions; they were rejected. He then rose in a fit of passion, and exclaimed energetically: " You wish for war then?—You shall have it:" and laying his hands on a magnificent piece of porcelain (which M. de Cobentzel used with great complacency to boast of having received as a present from the great Catharine), he dashed it with all his force on the ground, where it was broken into a thousand pieces. " There," he exclaimed, " such, I promise you, will be the fate of your Austrian monarchy in less than three months: " and, so saying, he rushed out of the apartment. M. de Cobentzel stood petrified; but M. de Gallo, who was of a more conciliatory temper, followed the French General to his carriage, endeavouring to detain him. " He almost dragged me back by main force," said the Emperor, " and

with so pitiable an air, that, in spite of my apparent
anger, I could not refrain from laughing in my sleeve."

M. de Gallo was the ambassador from Naples to
Vienna, whither he had conducted the Neapolitan Princess, the second wife of the Emperor Francis. He
possessed the full confidence of the Princess, and she, in
her turn, ruled her husband : thus the ambassador enjoyed great influence at the Court of Vienná. When the
army of Italy, marching on Vienna, dictated the armistice of Leoben, the Empress, at this critical juncture,
cast her eyes on her confident, and charged him to avert
the danger. He was to gain an interview with the
French General, as if accidentally, and to endeavour to
prevail on him to accept his services as a negotiator.
Napoleon, who was well acquainted with every circumstance, determined to turn his knowledge to a good
account. Accordingly, on receiving M. de Gallo, he
inquired who he was. The favourite courtier, disconcerted to find himself under the necessity of telling his
name, replied that he was the Marquess de Gallo, and
that he had been charged by the Emperor of Austria to
make overtures to Napoleon. "But," said the latter,
"your name is not German." "True," replied M. de
Gallo, " I am the Neapolitan ambassador." "And how
happens it," said Napoleon drily, " that I have to treat
with Naples ? We are at peace. Has the Emperor of
Austria no negotiators of the old school ? Is the old
aristocracy of Vienna extinct ?" M. de Gallo, alarmed at
the idea of such observations being officially communicated to the Cabinet of Vienna, now became intent
on ingratiating himself into the favour of the young
General.

Napoleon enquired what news had been received from
Vienna, and spoke of the armies of the Rhine, the Sam
bre, and the Meuse. He obtained all the intelligence he
could ; and, when he was about to withdraw, M. de
Gallo, in the most suppliant tone, inquired whether he
might hope to be accepted as a negotiator, and whether
he should proceed to Vienna to obtain full powers. Napoleon had no wish to decline this proposal ; he had
gained an advantage which he was not willing to lose

M. de Gallo, who subsequently became ambassador from
Naples to the First Consul, and also ambassador from
Joseph to the Emperor Napoleon, frequently mentioned
this scene, and frankly avowed that he had never been so
frightened in the whole course of his life.

In the French negotiations, Clarke acted the same
kind of secondary part which M. de Gallo maintained
with regard to Austria. "Clarke," said the Emperor,
"had been sent to Italy by the Directory, which had
begun to consider me as dangerous. He was charged
with an ostensible and public mission ; but he had secret
orders to keep an eye upon me, and to ascertain if, in
case of necessity, it would be possible to arrest me. But
little reliance could have been placed on the officers of
my army, in an affair of this kind, and therefore the first
inquiries were addressed to the Cisalpine Directory. The
answer was that it would be as well to spare trouble on
this point, and to give up all idea of it. As soon as I
was made acquainted with Clarke's real instructions, I
frankly told him all I knew ; at the same time assuring
him that I should concern myself but very little about
any reports that might be made. He was soon convinced
of this. When, on his mission to Austria, he was dismissed, by that Power, I offered to find employment for
him, and he afterwards remained with me ; though
perhaps there was, in reality, but little sympathy between
us. I should undoubtedly have again taken him into
my service, after my return, if I had found him in the
ranks along with the rest. You know that I could not
easily rid myself of those to whom I had become accustomed : when people had once embarked with me, I
could never prevail on myself to throw them overboard.
Nothing but absolute necessity could force me to such a
course. Clarke's chief merit was that of being a good
man of business."

After Brumaire, Clarke naturally came in contact
with the First Consul as his aid-de-camp, &c. There
was then little etiquette observed at the palace ; the duties were not distinctly separated, and the whole presented a kind of family circle. The officers immediately
connected with the Consul dined at a general table.

Clarke, who was extremely susceptible and punctilious, got involved in quarrels with one of these persons. The circumstance having reached the ears of the First Consul, he appointed Clarke ambassador to Florence, to the court of the Queen of Etruria. This post was in itself highly agreeable; but Clarke had been appointed to it by way of disgrace. He urgently solicited his recal; and, at length, to his great satisfaction, he received an order to return to France. But his punishment was not yet at an end. The First Consul took but little notice of him: he sent him to the Tuileries, to St. Cloud, and to the camp of Boulogne, without explaining his intentions, or granting him any thing. Clarke, in despair, told one of his friends that he had no alternative but to throw himself into the Seine, as he could no longer endure the contempt to which he was exposed, added to the mortification of being deprived of his situation. Just at this time he was unexpectedly made Secretary of the Topographical Cabinet, Councillor of State, and appointed to some other posts, which altogether produced him a salary of 60 or 80,000 francs. This was Napoleon's way: his first favour was usually followed immediately by several others. In these cases his bounty was overwhelming. But it was necessary to take advantage of the interval of favour; it might be endless, or it might be instantly and irretrievably lost.

I knew General Clarke well; he had been my comrade at the Military School. He informed me that, some days before the battle of Jena, the Emperor, from whose dictation he had just written numerous orders and instructions, entering into a familiar conversation, while he walked up and down his chamber, said: "In three or four days I will fight a battle, which I shall gain: it will bring me at least as far as the Elbe, and perhaps to the Vistula. There I will fight a second battle, which I sha'' also gain. Then . . . . then . . . ," said he with a meditative air, and placing his hand on his forehead . . . . "but that is enough; it is useless to invent romances,— Clarke, in a month you will be Governor of Berlin; and history will record that, in the space of one year, and in two different wars, you were Governor of

Vienna and Berlin; that is to say, of the Austrian and Prussian monarchies. By the bye," continued he, smiling, "what did Francis give you for governing his capital?" —"Nothing at all, Sire." —" How, nothing at all?—That was hard indeed! Well, in that case, I must pay his debt." And he gave him, as far as I can recollect, a sum sufficient to purchase an hotel in Paris, or a country house in the vicinity of the capital.

The course of events exceeded even Napoleon's expectations. He fought but one battle, which brought him to Berlin, and enabled him to advance to the Vistula.

"Clarke," said Napoleon, " possessed a strong taste for family parchments. At Florence he spent a great portion of his time in investigating my genealogy. He also took great pains to trace out his own, and I believe he at length persuaded himself that he was related to the whole Faubourg Saint-Germain. Doubtless he has a much higher opinion of his own dignity, now that he is the Minister of a legitimate King then he had when he was merely the Minister of an upstart Emperor. It is said that he at present enjoys great favour; I wish it may last. It commenced a few days before my arrival at Paris, when the cause of the King was desperate. It certainly appeared useless to accept a ministry when all was lost; but I have nothing to say against that. This sort of conduct may have its fair side; yet it is necessary to observe some degree of decorum, and in that Clarke was wholly wanting. However, I willingly forgive him in all that concerns me . . . In 1813 and 1814 some persons endeavoured to inspire me with doubts of Clarke's fidelity; but I never would listen to any thing of the kind. I always believed him to be an honest man." The intimate friends of the Duke de Feltre can bear witness that Napoleon was correct in the opinion he had formed of the character of his minister.

The Duke de Feltre, on communicating to the Emperor the intelligence of the arrival of the Count d' Artois in Switzerland, advised him to make peace. Napoleon replied, under date of 22d of February, 1814 :—"As to your advice of making peace, it is too absurd : it is by cherish-

ing such notions as this that public spirit is destroyed.
Besides, it is supposing me either mad or stupid to
imagine that, if I could conclude peace, I would not
immediately do it.   To the prevailing notion that it has
been in my power to make peace for four months past,
but that I declined doing so, must be attributed all the
misfortunes of France.   I expected, at least, to have
been spared the pain of hearing such sentiments
expressed. ''

The Emperor, reverting to the events of Campo-Formio, alluded to the arrest of the Count d'Antraigues, the
papers that were found upon him, and the discoveries to
which they gave rise; he also mentioned the indulgence
which the Count experienced, and the treachery with
which that indulgence was repaid.

The Count d'Antraigues, who was a man of considerable talent, fond of intrigue, and endowed with personal
advantages, had acquired a certain degree of importance
at the commencement of our Revolution.   He was a
member of the right hand side of the Constituent Assembly, and he emigrated at the time of its dissolution.
At the period when the French were about to assail Venice, the Count d'Antraigues was residing there, where
he held a diplomatic appointment from the Russian
Government, and was the main spring and agent of all
the machinations that were plotting against France.   On
seeing the danger of the Venetian Republic, he attempted
to escape; but he fell in with one of our posts, and was
seized, with all his papers.   The General-in-chief appointed a special commission to examine these documents,
and the secrets which they unfolded were the subject of
great astonishment.   They contained, among other things,
full proof of the treason of Pichegru, who had sacrificed his
troops to faciliate the operations of the enemy.   " Pichegru," exclaimed the Emperor indignantly, " was guilty
of the most odious crime that can possibly be conceived,
that of coldly sacrificing the men whose lives had been
entrusted to his honour and discretion."

The Count D'Antraigues, finding that all his secrets
were discovered, conducted himself with so much address
and apparent candour, that Napoleon, conceiving he had

gained him over, or, to speak more properly suffering himself to be gained over by the Count, treated him with the utmost indulgence. He defended him against the proceedings of the Directory, which insisted on having him shot, and the Count was allowed to proceed to Milan on his parole. But what was Napoleon's surprise on learning that M. d'Antraigues had escaped to Switzerland, and had published an infamous libel against him, reproaching him with ill-treatment, and complaining of having been confined in chains? These falsehoods occasioned so much indignation that several foreign diplomatists, who knew how Napoleon had really acted towards the Count, spontaneously made a public declaration of what they had witnessed.

So late as the year 1814, the Count d'Antraigues died in England, in a horrible way, being assassinated by his valet-de-chambre in the presence of his wife, who was the celebrated singer Saint Huberti.

At the time of the seizure of the Count d'Antraigues' papers, Pichegru was at the head of the Legislative Body, and was almost at open war with the Directory. It may well be supposed that the members of the Directory were highly gratified by thus obtaining important and authentic documents against their adversaries. This discovery greatly influenced Napoleon in the course which he adopted in the events of Fructidor : it was one of the principal causes of his famous proclamation, which brought about the triumph of the Directory.

Desaix, who was serving under Moreau in the army of the Rhine, having taken advantage of the armistice to introduce himself to the General-in-chief of the army of Italy, for whom he had conceived the highest admiration, was with Napoleon at the time of the important discovery above mentioned. Napoleon having informed him of the treason of Pichegru, Desaix observed ; " But we knew all this on the Rhine three months ago. A waggon, belonging to General Klinglin's corps, which fell into our hands, furnished us with all Pichegru's correspondence with the enemies of the Republic."—" And did Moreau give no intimation of this to the Directory ?" " No."—" Then he is very blameable," exclaimed Napo-

leon; "when the safety of one's country is at stake
silence is guilt!" After Pichegru's fall, Moreau communicated to the Directory all he knew respecting the
conspiracy, at the same time pronouncing a severe reprobation on those who were concerned in it. "This was
but another instance of misconduct," said Napoleon; "by
not speaking earlier, he betrayed his country; and by
speaking so late, he merely struck a blow at one who
was already fallen."

THE EMPEROR'S DREAM.

11th—12th.   The produce of the sale of a portion of
plate, amounting to 6000 francs, was this day received.
This sum the Emperor considered indispensible to make
up our deficiencies at the expiration of every month,
and he ordered the sale to be repeated regularly.

The Emperor continues very ill, and is in very low
spirits.   To-day he did not leave his room until dinner-
time.   He conversed very little, and did not apply himself to any kind of occupation.   I remained with him the
greater part of the day,   He spoke frequently of the
situation in which we stood with respect to the Governor, and made some very remarkable observations on
that subject. .   .   .   .   .   , ...

.   .   .   .   .   .
      After dinner he mentioned a dream which he had had
during the night.   A lady with whom he had been but
little acquainted (Madame Clarke, Duchess de Feltre
appeared to him in his dream, and told him she was
dead. at the same time adding several observations which
were expressed in language perfectly connected and
intelligible.   "Every thing was so clear and distinct,"
said the Emperor, "that it has made a forcible impression
on me; so much so that if I were really to hear of the
death of the Duchess de Feltre, I must confess that my
established ideas would be shaken; and perhaps," said
he, smiling and looking at one of the company, "I
too should become a believer in dreams and ap-
paritions."

The Emperor ate little; his spirits were depressed,
and he was evidently very ill.   He retired almost im-

mediately, and his manner affected us greatly. We could not help remarking how much he was altered.

PRIVATIONS TO WHICH THE EMPEROR IS SUBJECTED.— HIS CLAIMS ON PRINCE EUGENE.

13th.—The Emperor came to me about ten o'clock. He looked in at my room-door, and blamed me for not having risen earlier. He found me using the foot-bath for I was not well. I soon joined him beneath the tent, where he wished to breakfast. He told me he had given orders for drawing up some notes relative to the new restrictions, to prevent condemnation being passed on us without a sort of responsibility being attached to those who passed the sentence. He then proceeded to calculate the lots of plate which remain to be sold, and the period during which they would serve to maintain us. I repeated the offers which I have already several times made, telling him that it was hard he should be reduced to the necessity of disposing of his plate ; but he replied, —" My dear Las Cases, under whatever circumstances I may be placed, those articles of luxury are never of any importance to me ; and as far as regards others, that is to say, as far as regards the public, simplicity will always be my best ornament." He added that he could, after all, claim the assistance of Prince Eugène ; and that he was even inclined to write to him for the loans which would be necessary for his subsistence when the plate should be exhausted. He also expressed his intention of commissioning Eugène to forward to him some important books which he wished to have sent from London, together with a small quantity of choice wine, which it was necessary he should take as a medicine. " This commission for wine," said he, will make our enemies in Europe say that we think of nothing here but eating and drinking." He said that he should feel no hesitation in addressing himself on this subject to Eugène, who owed to him every thing he possessed ; and that it would be insulting the character of the Prince to doubt his readiness to serve him, particularly as he had, besides, a legal claim upon him for about ten or twelve millions.

While we were at breakfast, the Emperor sent for the Pole, who is soon to leave us. After breakfast he wished to employ himself in reading or dictating; but he felt very drowsy, and fell asleep several times. He retired to his chamber, to lie down for a while, desiring me to attend him at one o'clock for his English lesson. But when the appointed hour arrived, he was still in the same state of drowsiness; and he only succeeded in rousing himself by taking a bath, in which, according to custom, he remained for a long time. It is surprising that this practice, joined to that of taking very hot baths, does not prove injurious to him.

The Emperor ate but little dinner, and he complained of not enjoying regular and sound rest. He conversed for some time on the subject of balloons, and laughed at those biographical notices which represent him as having forced himself, sword in hand, into the balloon of the military school. He mentioned, as a sort of prodigy, the circumstance of the balloon which ascended at his coronation having fallen, in the space of a few hours, in the neighbourhood of Rome, bearing intelligence of the ceremony to the inhabitants of that city.

The Emperor took up Don Quixote; but he closed the book in about half an hour: he cannot now apply himself to reading for a longer interval. His health visibly declines. He often observes to me that we are both growing very old, and that he is much the older of the two: these words tell a great deal.

THE REQUIRED DECLARATION IS SENT TO THE GOVERNOR. —THE EMPEROR REMARKS THAT MANY MODERN BOOKS ARE MERELY BOOKSELLERS' SPECULATIONS.—FALSE NOTIONS CREATED BY PARTY SPIRIT. — GENERAL MAISON.

14th.—To-day the Grand Marshal forwarded to the Governor the new declarations which he required us to make. They were all alike, and were as follows:

" I, the undersigned, hereby declare that I wish to remain at St. Helena, and to share the restrictions which are imposed on the Emperor Napoleon personally."

About one o'clock I went to attend the Emperor in his chamber. I gave him an account of some private commissions. He was reading a work on the government of France. He thought it very indifferent, and observed that, since he had been in the habit of perusing new publications, he had found them, for the most part, to be merely matters of speculation,—things got up for sale by booksellers. The world, he said, was now threatened with a deluge of bad books, and he saw no remedy that could effectually counteract so great an evil.

After having dressed, the Emperor repaired to the drawing-room, where he looked over a few English newspapers, and read some lines of Telemachus. But he felt fatigued and low-spirited, and suspended his reading. We discoursed on several subjects which intimately concerned the Emperor, who closed the conversation by several times repeating,—" *Poor human nature !*"

During another interval of conversation, Napoleon, taking a review of several well-known individuals, on whom he pronounced his opinion, alluded to one, whom he represented as being a most immoral and base character. I happened to be acquainted with this person, and I observed that I knew him to be quite the reverse of what I had just heard described. I was defending the individual in question with considerable warmth when the Emperor interrupted me, saying: " I give full credit to what you say; but I had heard a different account of him: and though I generally made it a rule to hear things of this kind with suspicion, yet you see I could not always avoid retaining some impression of what I heard. Was this my fault ? When I had no particular motive for inquiry, how could I arrive at the knowledge of facts ? This," continued he, " is the inevitable consequence of civil commotions : there are always two reputations between the two parties. What absurdities, what ridiculous stories, are related of the individuals who figured in our Revolution !* The saloons of Paris are

* I take this opportunity of correcting an error of the nature here alluded to. In a preceding part of this work, it is stated that Mr. Monge ascended the Jacobinical tribune, &c. The friends and

full of them. I have had my full share of this kind of
scandal. After me who can have any right to complain?
Yet I protest that nothing of this sort ever produced any
influence on my mind, or occasioned me in any instance
to alter my determinations, &c."

After alluding to several military officers, the Emperor mentioned General Maison. "His manœuvres," said
he, "round Lille, in the crisis of 1814, attracted my
attention, and fixed him in my recollection. He was
not with us in 1815. What became of him? Where
was he at that time?"—I could not answer these
questions, as I did not know the General.

DIFFICULTIES STARTED BY THE GOVERNOR RESPECTING
OUR DECLARATIONS. — THE EMPEROR'S SENTIMENTS
ON THAT SUBJECT. THE GOVERNOR'S CONVERSATION
WITH EACH INDIVIDUAL OF THE EMPEROR'S SUITE.—
NAPOLEON'S REMARK. — CONSUMMATION OF OUR
SLAVERY.

15th. For some time past I have found it impossible
to sleep; and I have passed whole nights without
closing my eyes. About eight o'clock this morning, as
I was endeavouring to compose myself to rest, the Grand
Marshal entered my chamber, to inform me that the
Governor had sent back our declarations, and was
coming himself to oblige us to sign that which he had
sent as a model, and which differed from ours only with
respect to the title which we gave to the Emperor. It
was wished that we should designate him merely by the
name *Bonaparte*.

The Grand Marshal proceeded to the Emperor's
apartments, whither I was almost immediately summoned. On entering, I found the Emperor walking
about and expressing himself with great warmth. All

---

relatives of that distinguished man have, however, assured me that
all who knew him at the time in question can bear witness that he
never appeared among them, and that he never spoke in any public
assembly. I feel pleasure in mentioning this circumstance; for
nothing affords me greater happiness than to be the means of
developing truth.

the individuals of the suite were assembled together.
"The insults," said he, "which are daily heaped upon
those who have devoted themselves to me, insults which,
it is very probable, will be multiplied to a still greater
extent, present a spectacle which I cannot and must not
longer endure. Gentlemen, you must leave me; I cannot see you submit to the restrictions which are about to
be imposed on you, and which will doubtless soon be
augmented. I will remain her alone. Return to Europe, and make known the horrible treatment to which
I am exposed; bear witness that you saw me sinking
into a premature grave. I will not allow any one of you
to sign this declaration in the form that is required. I
forbid it. It shall never be said that hands which I had
the power to command were employed in recording my
degradation. If obstacles are raised respecting a mere
foolish formality, others will be started to-morrow for an
equally trivial cause. It is determined to remove you in
detail ; but I would rather see you removed altogether
and at once. Perhaps this sacrifice may produce a result."
With these words he dismissed us, and we withdrew
overwhelmed with dismay.

In a few moments the Emperor again sent for me.
He was walking up and down, through the whole length
of his two little rooms. There was a peculiar tenderness
in the tone of his voice, and I never observed more easy
familiarity in his manner. "Well, my dear Las Cases,"
said he, "I am going to turn hermit," "Sire," said I,
"are you not one already? What resources does our
society present to you? We can only offer you prayers
and good wishes; which, though they can contribute but
little to your consolation, are every thing to us. Our
present situation is the most distressing that can possibly
be conceived; for, in the question under consideration,
we now perhaps, for the first time, find it difficult to obey
your Majesty. You hold the language of reason; while
we are guided only by sentiment. The arguments which
you just now addressed to us admit of no reply. Your
determination is in unison with your character; it will
astonish no one, but its execution is beyond our power.
The thought of leaving you here alone exceeds in horror

all that our imagination can picture."—"Such, howevei,
is my fate," replied the Emperor calmly, "and I must
prepare for the worst: my mind is strong enough to
meet it. They will cut short my life; that is certain."
—"Sire," I observed, "the step which you command is
not to be thought of.   To the last moment I will speak
out as your Majesty has done: on this point I will resist
to the utmost; but I shall find it impossible to act as I
speak."

The Emperor seated himself, and desired me to sit
down beside him.   He observed that he was much
fatigued; and he ordered breakfast, desiring me to stay
with him.   For a considerable time past, I had not been
in the habit of dining with him: he told me the reason
why I had been denied this happiness; and I considered
it as a favour that he should condescend to tell me.
When the coffee was brought in, there was no cup for
me.   Marchand was going to fetch one; but the Emperor called him back, saying: "Take that one from the
mantel-piece: he shall drink out of my handsome gold
cup."*

Just as breakfast was over, the Grand Marshal entered
and told us that the Governor had arrived, and had expressed a wish to see him at his (Bertrand's) new house,
which is a very short distance from our establishment,
and is at length on the point of being completed.   The
Emperor desired him to attend the Governor.   The
Grand Marshal, as he was about to withdraw, seemed
desirous to know whether the Emperor still persisted in

---

* This was the cup belonging to his dressing-table, which stood
on the chimney-piece as an ornament.
    I have now the happiness of possessing the saucer belonging to
this cup.   M. Marchand, that faithful servant, to whom Napoleon
declared himself so much attached, on his return from St. Helena,
came and presented this saucer to me, in a manner that forcibly
roused my gratitude and sensibility.   "The beautiful cup," said
he, "out of which you sometimes drank, belonged to the Emperor's
dressing-table, and was accordingly restored to its place.   The
saucer, however, among other articles, fell to my share; and I now
present it to you, being assured that you will feel as much pleasure
in receiving as I have in giving it."

the orders he had given us this morning, in case the Governor should not yield. The Emperor sharply observed : "I am not a child ; when I have once thoroughly considered a question, I no longer entertain two opinions upon it. I have directed battles which have decided the fate of empires, and the orders I issued were always the result of my mature deliberation. In this instance I am alone concerned. Go !"

The Grand Marshal soon returned with an account of the interview, which he had closed by his refusal. The Governor, he said, had desired to see the other three persons of the suite together ; but we thought that it would be more proper to present ourselves in succession.

I went to wait on the Governor. I found him, surrounded by several of his attendants, in the garden, near the path leading to the Grand Marshal's house. He withdrew on perceiving me ; but I joined him in the court before the house.

As he had expressed himself very much irritated against me, I went as well fortified as I possibly could. He, however, conducted me with great politeness into the house, leaving the officers of his suite on the outside, and, having told me that he awaited the arrival of Messrs. de Montholon and Gourgaud, to enter upon the business, I asked him whether he had any objection to treat immediately with me. He replied that he had not ; and, calling in his officers, he told me, in their presence, that I had no doubt learned from the Grand Marshal what he had to propose on the subject of my declaration. I replied in the affirmative, at the same time observing that I regarded the Grand Marshal as my model and guide, on account of his rank, as well as the respect and esteem I entertained for him, and therefore it was natural to expect that my answer should correspond with his. I added that I could not conceive why so much importance was attached to a mere matter of form, which was so painful to our feelings, while it could be of no service to those who insisted on it. "It is out of my power," said the Governor, "to make the alteration you wish. I am directed to present to you for signature the declaration written in my hand : now I, being an Englishman, can-

not write the title you wish."—"I was not aware of that"
replied I; "to that argument I have no reply to make.
You, as an Englishman, must write thus; but I, being a
Frenchman, must sign in my language; that is to say,
with the translation from yours. Allow me, therefore,
to add to my signature any phrase that you may think
proper to dictate to me, in which I can express myself
in my own language. You may now judge," added I,
"whether I deal candidly, and whether I seek to create
difficulties." This proposal seemed to claim his attention. "We are now," I continued, "merely disputing
about words, which may appear very silly, considering
the important circumstances in which we are placed; but,
Sir, who created these difficulties? Who will suffer from
them? Your refusal places us in a most distressing situation! You see me reduced to the utmost despair! To me
separation from the Emperor would be worse than death;
yet I would rather submit to it than suffer my hand to
be the instrument of his degradation. The Emperor
unites in himself all that constitutes an august character,
in the eyes of God and man: to deny this would be to
deny the light of the sun."

The Governor observed that he, as an Englishman,
could not acknowledge the Emperor; and I replied that I
could urge no objection to that. I added that however
much I might be hurt by his mode of designating the
Emperor, yet I did not mean to question his right of using
whatever terms he might think proper; and that, for the
same reason, he ought not to object to my opinions and
expressions, considering that I was a Frenchman, and
that he demanded my signature.

Here Sir Hudson Lowe angrily alluded to some past
circumstances relating to himself personally; and he observed that, after all, moral character was the only real
title to respect. "At that rate, Governor," replied I,
with some warmth, and turning to the Officers who were
in attendance, "the Emperor may divest himself of all
his titles, and he will but gain in the opinion of the
world, if his character be estimated by the scale to which
you allude." The Governor was silent: then, after a
pause of a few moments, he observed that we still treated

our General as though he were an Emperor. "And how can we treat him otherwise?"—"I mean to say, that you continue to look upon him as a Sovereign."— "Governor, you talk of revering him as our Sovereign; we do more—we worship him! We now consider the Emperor as removed from this world; we view him as though he were in Heaven! . . . . . When you leave us a choice that is in opposition to him, it is like the choice given to martyrs, when they are commanded to renounce their faith or die. "Death, therefore, must be our alternative." These words produced a visible impression on the officers who were present, and even on the Governor. Contrary to custom, his countenance assumed a mild expression, and the tone of his voice was softened.

"Our situation here," continued I, "is so horrible as to be almost beyond endurance. You know this;—but what we now suffer is nothing to the misery which is reserved for us. What I ask will be no sacrifice to you, and it will be every thing to us. I implore you to grant what I request; and this is something, for you know I am not in the habit of soliciting favours from you. Make but this one concession, and you will claim my eternal gratitude. Besides, consider that a responsibility rests with you; that there is a public opinion in Europe, which you may forfeit without gaining any advantage in return. You cannot be a stranger to the sentiments which animate me; they must, I am sure, go to the hearts of all who listen to me."

Here the Governor appeared somewhat moved; the officers were evidently affected. Sir Hudson Lowe, after a few moments' silence, bowed to me, and I took my leave.

Messrs. de Montholon and Gourgaud had each an interview in their turn; and we all four attended the Emperor during his toilet, without, however, being able to tell him whether any decision had been formed on the subject that so deeply interested us.

The Emperor expressed a wish to go out, though the wind was extremely boisterous: we all walked to the extremity of the wood. He took a review of the Gover-

nor's conduct, making remarks upon it in the rapid and
copious way peculiar to himself; and he concluded by
saying that if to-day we should agree to sign the declaration, in order to avoid being separated from him, to-
morrow another ground of expulsion would be brought
forward; and that he should wish our removal to be effected forcibly and at once, rather than tranquilly and in
detail. Then, suddenly assuming a tone of pleasantry,
he said that, after all, he could hardly believe the Governor wished to reduce his subjects to one only; and what
sort of subject would that one be! added he—an absolute porcupine, on which he would not dare to lay a
finger.

During our walk, two strangers approached pretty
near to us. The Emperor made some one enquire who
they were, and he was informed that they belonged to a
vessel which was about to sail to-morrow for Europe.
The Emperor asked whether they were likely to see any
of the Ministers on their arrival in London; and they
replied that they should see Lord Bathurst. "Tell him,"
said "Napoleon, that his instructions with respect to my
treatment here are most odious, and that his agent
executes them with scrupulous fidelity. If he wished to
get rid of me, he should have despatched me at a blow,
instead of thus killing me by inches. This conduct is
truly barbarous; there is nothing English in it; and I
can only attribute it to some personal hatred. I have
too much respect for the Prince Regent, the majority of
the Ministers, and the English nation, to suppose that
they are responsible for my treatment. Be this as it
may, their power extends only to the body; the soul is
beyond their reach: it will soar to Heaven even from
the dungeon."

The Emperor, on his return home, took a bath; he
was fatigued and harassed by the events of the day. He
fell asleep, and I watched beside him, meditating on our
new grievances.

At dinner he ate but a little. Some one made an
observation, and the Emperor, not having heard it
distinctly, asked what had been said—a thing which
frequently happens. The words were then repeated in a

louder tone, upon which he observed: "I am certainly
growing deaf, for I occasionally miss hearing what is
said, and I feel inclined to be angry when people speak
louder than usual." He concluded the evening by
reading a part of Don Quixote. He was much amused
at some comic passages; and, laying down the book, he
remarked that we certainly showed a great deal of courage, since we could laugh at such trifles under our present circumstances. He paused for some moments, and
seemed deeply wrapped in thought: then rising, he
withdrew, saying: "Adieu, my dear friends."

During dinner, a letter had been delivered to me from
the Grand Marshal; but I had kept it concealed, conceiving that it augured no good. I opened it as soon as
the Emperor withdrew. It enclosed a letter from the
Governor, announcing that if we still persisted in our
refusal to sign the declaration, he would immediately
give orders for our removal to Europe. We yielded to
the dictates of our hearts: to determine on leaving the
Emperor was beyond our power; while at the same time
it would have been going beyond his wishes, and perhaps
too beyond his orders. With unanimous sentiments, we
eagerly signed the declarations in the form in which they
were presented to us, and delivered them to the English
officer on duty at Longwood, together with a letter to
the Grand Marshal, acquainting him with what we had
done without his participation. We had been guided
solely by our feelings, and we trusted that those feelings
would afford us consolation, even though the Emperor
should disapprove of the step we had taken.

We have now reached the consummation of our absolute slavery and dependence on the will and caprice of
Sir Hudson Lowe; not merely by the signature we have
just given him, but because he now knows our secret,
and therefore it is in his power to compel us to submit to
any thing he pleases.

ANECDOTES OF SIEYES. — THE EMPEROR FREQUENTLY
ATTENDED POPULAR FESTIVITIES IN DISGUISE. — HIS
VISITS TO THE FAUBOURG SAINT-ANTOINE, AFTER HIS
RETURN FROM MOSCOW AND FROM THE ISLAND OF
ELBA. — MANNERS DURING THE TIME OF THE DIREC-
TORY. — REMARKABLE OFFICIAL NOTE.

16th.—The Emperor sent for me about noon. He
had been reading, and was just finishing his coffee. He
desired me to sit down, and he entered into conversation.
Not a word escaped him that could lead me to suppose
he knew the determination we had adopted yesterday
evening; he made no allusion to the subject, and it was
not mentioned throughout the whole of the day. After
breakfast, the Emperor walked about his apartments.
The turn of the conversation introduced some anecdotes
of former times, of which Sieyes was the subject. The
Emperor related that while Sieyes was chaplain to the
Princes of Orleans, being one day engaged in performing
mass, something unexpectedly occasioned the Princes to
withdraw during the service; upon which the Abbé,
looking up and seeing only the valets present, immediately closed his book, observing that he was not engaged
to perform mass to the rabble.

" Your Majesty," said I, " was the first who made me
acquainted with the name and person of Sieyes. A few
days after my presentation at Court, your Majesty, at one
of your audiences, having passed by me, stopped to speak
to the person who stood next to me, addressing him by
name. All my emigrant prejudices were yet in full force,
and I thought myself polluted by coming in contact with
one whom I regarded as an absolute monster, and whom
I had never heard mentioned except as an object of the
bitterest imprecation." " Doubtless," said the Emperor,
" you were thinking of the *mort sans phrase*. But I
have heard it affirmed that Sieyes denied that."

I now repeated an anecdote which used to be circulated in the Faubourg Saint-Germain, and on which, the
first time I related it, the Emperor made no observation.
Sieyes was described as having used the epithet *tyrant* in
speaking of Louis XVI., to which Napoleon was said to

have replied, "Monsieur l'Abbé, if he had been a tyrant
I should not be here, and you would still be performing
mass." "I might have thought so," said the Emperor,
on my relating this anecdote for the second time; "but
I should certainly not have been fool enough to say so.
This is one of the absurd stories invented in the drawing-
rooms of Paris. I never committed blunders of that
kind : my object was to extinguish, and not to feed, the
flame. The torrent of hostility was already too forcibly
directed against certain leaders of the Revolution. I
found it necessary to support and countenance them;
and I did so. Some one having procured—God knows
where—a bust of Sieyes in his ecclesiastical character, it
was publickly exhibited, and occasioned a universal up-
roar. Sieyes, in a furious passion, set out to make a
complaint to me; but I had already given the necessary
reprimand, and the bust was again consigned to obscu-
rity.

"My great principle was to guard against re-action,
and to bury the past in oblivion. I never condemned
any opinion, or proscribed any act. I was surrounded
by the men who had voted for the death of Louis XVI. :
they were in the Ministry, and in the Council of State.
I did not approve of their doctrines; but what had I
to do with them? what right had I to constitute myself
their judge? Some had been actuated by conviction,
others by weakness and terror, and all by the delirium
and fury of the moment. The fatality of the Greek
tragedy was exemplified in the life of Louis XVI."

I told the Emperor that it was reported in the Faubourg Saint-Germain that Sieyes had been detected in a
conspiracy against him, in the affair of M. Clement de
Ris ; and that he (Napoleon) had pardoned him, on
condition of his entirely withdrawing himself from any
participation in political affairs. "This is another idle
story, for which there is not the slightest foundation,"
said the Emperor. "Sieyes was always attached to me,
and I never had any cause to complain of him. He was
probably vexed to find that I opposed his metaphysical
ideas ; but he was at length convinced that it was necessary for France to have a ruler, and he preferred me to

any other. Sieyes was, after all, an honest and a very
clever man : he did much for the Revolution."

The Emperor mentioned that at one of the first public
festivals that took place during the Consulate, as he was
viewing the illuminations in company with Sieyes, he
asked him what he thought of the state of affairs. Sieyes
replied in a cold and even a disheartening tone. "And
yet," resumed Napoleon, " I had this morning very
satisfactory proofs of the spirit of the people."—"It is
seldom," replied Sieyes," that the people shew their real
spirit, when the man who is possessed of power presents
himself to their gaze. I can assure you they are far
from being satisfied."—"Then you do not think the
present government firmly established ?" — " No."—
" And when do you suppose we shall be settled ?"—
" When I see the Dukes and Marquises of the old court
in your ante-chamber."—"Sieyes," added the Emperor,
" little dreamed that this would so soon be the case. He
was short-sighted, and could not see very far before him.
I thought, as he did, that all could not end with the
Republic ; but I foresaw the establishment of the Empire.
Accordingly, two or three years afterwards, the circumstance I have just related being still fresh in my recollection, I said to Sieyes, at one of my grand audiences :
" Well, you are now pell-mell with all the old Dukes and
Marquises ; do you think all is settled now ?"—" Oh,
yes," replied Sieyes, bowing profoundly ; " you have
wrought miracles, which were never before equalled,
and which I never could have foreseen."

During the Consulate, Napoleon was once standing in
front of the Hotel de la Marine, viewing a public illumi-
nation. Beside him was a lady, who to all appearance,
had formerly moved in a distinguished sphere, accompanied by her daughter, a very pretty girl, to whom she
was pointing out all the persons of note, as they passed
to and fro in the apartments. Calling her daughter's
attention to a certain individual, she said : " Remind me
to go and pay my respects to him some day. We ought
to do so, for he has rendered us great service." " But,
mother," replied the young lady, " I did not know that
we were expected to shew gratitude to such people. I.

thought they were too happy in being able to oblige
persons of our quality." "Certainly," said the Emperor, "La Bruyere would have turned this incident to
good account."

Napoleon sometimes went out in disguise early in the
morning, traversing the streets of the capital alone, and
mingling with the labouring classes of the people, with
whose condition and sentiments he wished to make himself acquainted. In the Council of State I have often
heard him advise the Prefect of Police to adopt this plan.
He called it the *Caliph system of police,* and said he
esteemed it to be the best.

On his return from the disastrous campaigns of Moscow and Leipsic, Napoleon, in order to maintain the
appearance of confidence, frequently appeared amidst
the multitude with scarcely any attendants. He visited
the market-places, the faubourgs, and all the populous
districts of the capital, conversing familiarly with the
people; and he was every where received and treated
with respect.

One day, at La Halle, a woman with whom he had
been holding a little dialogue, bluntly told him he ought
to make peace. "Good woman," replied the Emperor,
"sell your greens, and leave me to settle my affairs.
Let every one attend to his own calling." The by-
standers laughed, and applauded him.

On another occasion, at the Faubourg Saint-Antoine,
when surrounded by an immense concourse of people,
whom he was treating very condescendingly, some one
asked whether affairs were really as bad as they were
represented to be? "Why, certainly," replied the Emperor, "I cannot say that things are going on very
well." "But what will be the end of this?" "Heaven
knows!" "Will the enemy enter France?" "Very
possibly; and he may even march to Paris if you do not
assist me. I have not a million of arms. I cannot do
all by my own individual efforts." "We will support
you," exclaimed a number of voices. "Then I shall
beat the enemy, and preserve the glory of France."
"But what must we do?" "You must enlist and
fight." "We will," said one of the crowd; "but we
17*

must make a few conditions!"   " What are they ?"
" We will not pass the frontier."   " You shall not be
required to do so."   " We wish to serve in the guards,"
said another.   " You shall do so."   The air instantly
resounded with acclamations.   Registers were immediately opened, and two thousand men enlisted in the
course of the day.   Napoleon returned to the Tuileries ;
and, as he entered the Place Carousel on horseback, surrounded by the multitude, whose acclamations rent the
air, it was supposed that an insurrection had broken out,
and the gates were about to be closed.

On his return from the Island of Elba, the Emperor
made another visit to the Faubourg Saint-Antoine, where
he was received with equal enthusiasm, and conducted
back to the palace in a similar manner.   As he passed
through the Faubourg Saint-Germain, the multitude who
escorted him halted before the principal hotels, and
manifested their disapprobation by angry words and gestures.   The Emperor observed that he had scarcely ever
been placed in so delicate a situation.   " How many
evils might have ensued," said he, " had a single stone
been thrown by the mob.   Had a single imprudent
word, or even an equivocal look, escaped me, the whole
Faubourg might have been destroyed ; and I am convinced that its preservation was to be attributed wholly
to my presence of mind, and the respect which the multitude entertained for me."

To-day I attended the Emperor at his toilet.   Santini
was cutting his hair, and a large tuft fell at my feet.   I
stooped to pick it up, and the Emperor, observing me,
asked what I was doing.   I replied that I had dropped
something, upon which he smiled and pinched my ear :
he guessed what I had picked up.

Speaking of the depravity and corruption of manners
which prevailed at the time when he commanded the
army of the interior in Paris, Napoleon mentioned that
a contractor came to solicit some signatures from him,
and to beg that he would give his support to certain appointments and supplies : this he promised to do without
hesitation, conceiving that there was nothing unfair in
the proposal.   Before he withdrew, the contractor dex-

trously took an opportunity of leaving on the chimney-piece two rouleaux containing a hundred Louis. This was an enormous sum in specie, for at that time paper money was chiefly in use. Fortunately, the General was the first to discover the circumstance, and the visitor was called back before he had gone far. He at first attempted to deny having left the money ; but he afterwards acknowledged it, observing that every one must live, and that the method he had adopted was, he believed, the general one. He, however, hoped that he might be forgiven if he had unintentionally done wrong, adding that it was very seldom necessary to ask pardon for such offences.

At the hour at which the Emperor generally takes his walk, he found himself very drowsy ; but he was determined to rouse himself, and he went out though the wind was blowing violently. After walking a short distance, he returned to the house, and we entered Madame de Montholon's apartment. The Emperor had no sooner seated himself on the sofa, than he felt inclined to fall asleep. He rose and proceeded to the drawing-room. He complained of great internal heat, and asked for a glass of toast and water. His drowsiness still continued, and he retired to his chamber to lie down.

About seven o'clock he sent for me, and gave me the following note, which he desired me to keep along with the rest of the official papers. It was the copy of a note which he had sent that morning to the Governor . . . .

Note.—" I recollect that in a conversation which took place between General Lowe and some of the gentlemen of my suite, (alluding to the conversation of the 15th,) some observations were made respecting my situation, which were not conformable with my ideas. I abdicated to the Representatives of the people and in favour of my son. I proceeded with confidence to England, with the intention of living either there or in America, in profound retirement, and under the name of a Colonel who was killed in battle by my side *I had resolved to have nothing to do with political affairs of any kind whatever.*

" When I went on board the Northumberland, I was informed that I was a prisoner of war, that I was to be

transported beyond the Line, and that I was to be called
General Bonaparte. This obliged me to retain ostensibly
the title of the Emperor Napoleon, in opposition to the
name of General Bonaparte, which was thus to be forced
upon me.

" About seven or eight months ago, Count Montholon
proposed to obviate the little difficulties that are continually arising, by my adopting an ordinary name. The
Admiral thought it necessary to write to London on this
subject, and there the matter rested.

" The name which is now applied to me has the advantage of not prejudging the past; but it is not in
unison with the forms of society. *I am still disposed to
assume a name that may be conformable with custom;* I
once more repeat that whenever I may be released from
my cruel captivity, *I am still willing to continue a stranger to all political affairs, whatever may take place in
the world.* Such is my determination; and no other
declaration, on this subject, has my sanction."

The Emperor ate but little dinner; there was something very extraordinary in the lethargy that had come
over him. He had been overpowered by drowsiness during the whole of the day; and yet when he withdrew he
said he was afraid he should not sleep, his sensations
were so extraordinary. He generally rests soundly when
he is inclined to sleep, but he had been dozing all day
long without being able to get any rest.

To-day a frigate sailed for Europe.

LOUIS XVI.—MARIE ANTOINETTE.—MADAME CAMPAN.
LEONARD.—THE PRINCESS DE LAMBALLE.

17th. About noon the Emperor sent for me; he had
just finished his breakfast. He was no better than he
had been yesterday. He endeavoured to converse a little,
and then read in English a few pages of the Vicar of
Wakefield. He still complained of drowsiness, and, after
several vain efforts to rouse himself, he retired to his
chamber to try to get a nap. He was the more astonished that this heaviness should continue, as he said he
had slept well during the night.

He did not leave his chamber until dinner was ready.

and after dinner he tried to read a little of Don Quixote; but he almost immediately laid down the book, and retired. As it was very early, he sent for me after he had gone to bed, and I remained with him nearly an hour conversing on different subjects.

We spoke of Louis XVI., the Queen, Madame Elizabeth, their martyrdom, &c. He asked me to tell him what I knew of the King and Queen, and what they had said to me on my presentation. The forms and ceremonies of the Court were, I informed him, the same as those which were adopted during the Empire. As to character, I observed, it was generally admitted that the Queen had disappointed public expectation. During the first moments of the revolutionary storm, there was every reason to suppose her to be a woman of great talent and energy; but subsequently these qualities seemed entirely to forsake her. With regard to the King, I mentioned the opinion formed of him by M. Bertrand de Molleville, with whom I had been well acquainted, and who was Minister of Marine to Louis XVI. at the height of the crisis. He pronounced the King to have possessed considerable information, sound judgment, and excellent intentions; but there it all ended. He lost himself by the multiplicity of advice which he solicited, and by his irresolute and wavering mode of following that advice.

The Emperor, in his turn, retraced the portrait of the Queen, by Madame Campan, who, he observed, having been her confidante, and having served her with zeal, affection and fidelity, might be expected to have known a great deal about her, and deserved to be considered as good authority. Madame Campan, he said, had communicated to him many details of the private life of the Queen; and he related some particulars which he had derived from that source.

The Queen, according to Madame Campan, was a fascinating woman, but destitute of talent: she was better calculated to be a votary of pleasure than a participator in affairs of State. She possessed an excellent heart, was parsimonious, rather than extravagant, and by no means possessed strength of character equal to the trying circumstances in which she was placed. She ob-

tained regular information of the schemes that were
carrying on abroad; and she never entertained a doubt
of her deliverance, even up to the fatal 10th of August,
the catastrophe of which was brought about solely by
the intrigues and hopes of the Court, which were developed to the world through the imprudence of the King
and those who surrounded him.

" On the terrible night of the 5th of October," said the
Emperor, " a person for whom the Queen entertained a
high regard, and whom I afterwards treated very ill at
Rastadt, hastened to join the Princess at Versailles:
whether he had been sent for, or whether he went of his
own accord to share her dangers, I know not. It is in these
trying moments," continued the Emperor, " that we feel
most in need of the advice and consolation of those who
are devoted to us. At the moment of the catastrophe,
when the palace was stormed, the Queen fled for refuge
to the King's apartments; but her confident was
exposed to the greatest dangers, and only escaped by
leaping out of a window."

I informed the Emperor that the Queen had greatly
fallen in the estimation of the emigrants, by her conduct
during the events of Varennes; she was reproached for
not having allowed the King to set out alone, and for
having betrayed a want of skill and energy during the
flight of the Royal family. Nothing indeed, could be
more ill managed and confused than the journey to Varennes. A curious circumstance connected with that
event was, that Leonard, the Queen's famous *coiffeur*,
found means to pass, in his cabriolet, through the midst
of the tumult; and he arrived at Coblentz, bringing with
him the Marshal's baton, which, it was said, the King
had carried away from the Tuileries, in order to deliver
it to M. de Bouillé, when he should join him.

" It was," said the Emperor, " an established rule
with the members of the House of Austria to observe
prıfound silence respecting the Queen of France. Whenever Marie Antoinette was mentioned, they cast down
their eyes, and dexterously changed the conversation, as
if to avoid a disagreeable and embarrassing subject. This
rule," continued the Emperor, " was adopted by all the

members of the family, and recommended to their agents abroad. The efforts lately made by the French Princes in Paris to revive the interest attached to the memory of the unfortunate Queen must certainly have been displeasing to the Court of Vienna."

The Emperor next asked me some questions concerning the Princess de Lamballe, of whom he said he knew nothing. I was enabled to answer his questions, as I had known the Princess well. One of my cousins had been her lady of honour; and, on my arrival at Aix-la-Chapelle, at the commencement of my emigration, I was received as one of her household, and treated with the utmost kindness.

At Aix-la-Chapelle the Princess de Lamballe had assembled round her many of the wrecks of Versailles: she was surrounded by nobles and persons of fashion, who had been connected with the old Court. She was also visited by many illustrious foreigners; and while I remained with her, I frequently saw Gustavus III., King of Sweden, who went by the name of the Count de Haga; Prince Ferdinand of Prussia, and his children, the eldest of whom (Prince Louis) was killed just before the battle of Jena; the duchess of Cumberland, widow of a brother of the King of England, &c.

When Louis XVI. solemnly accepted the Constitution, and thus recomposed the nation, the Princess received an official letter from the Queen, inviting her .to return to her situation. She consulted her old friends, who declared themselves of opinion that the Queen was not free, and, conceiving that there would be no safety in Paris, they advised her to take no notice of the Queen's letter, and to let it be supposed that it had never come to hand. The Princess, however, having asked some other individuals, how they would advise her to act, they unfortunately replied: "Madam, you shared the prosperity of the Queen, and you have now a noble opportunity of proving your fidelity, particularly since you are no longer her favourite." The Princess possessed lofty sentiments, warm affections, and was of a rather romantic turn of mind. She declared her intention of setting out next day for Paris. The unfortunate lady, therefore,

returned to the capital, with a full knowledge of the
danger to which she was exposed; and she fell the victim of generosity and noble sentiment.   When the Princess determined on proceeding to Paris, my friends proposed that I should accompany her as one of her suite.
My youth, together with the circumstance of my being
almost a stranger in Paris, would have enabled me to
pass unnoticed, and I might perhaps have been serviceable to her; but at the moment of her departure,
some difficulties arose which prevented me from accompanying her. However, I became her correspondent;
and every other day I transmitted to her the absurd stories of every kind, which served to feed our hopes, and
to which we failed not to give implicit credit.   I continued my correspondence while we remained in the
country; I even continued it after she had ceased to
exist !
   The extreme affliction in which I was plunged, on
hearing of her dreadful fate, was occasionally augmented
by the fear that my letters might perhaps have had some
share in producing it.   I happen to have now in my
possession some lines which she wrote a few days before
the horrible catastrophe that closed her existence. They
are dated *from my dungeon*; for so she called the
Pavilion of Flora, which she at that time occupied in
the Tuileries.

Lightning Source UK Ltd.
Milton Keynes UK
UKHW021904291222
414606UK00005B/79